Britain and the Baltic
Studies in Commercial, Political and Cultural Relations 1500-2000

Edited by

Patrick Salmon and Tony Barrow

**University of
Sunderland Press**

© University of Sunderland Press

ISBN 1873757 49 2

First published 2003

Published in Great Britain by
The University of Sunderland Press
in association with Business Education Publishers Limited
The Teleport
Doxford International
Sunderland
SR3 3XD

Tel: 0191 5252410
Fax: 0191 5201815

British Cataloguing-in-Publications Data
A catalogue record for this book is available from the British Library

Cover illustration: Stralsund c. 1615. Reproduced from Herbert Ewe (ed.), *Stralsunder Bilderhandschrift* (Rostock, 1979), with kind permission of the Stadtarchiv Hansestadt Stralsund.

Printed in Great Britain by Athenaeum Press, Gateshead.

Contents

List of Contributors

Martin Åberg is Research Fellow in History at University College of South Stockholm. His revious publications include *Baltic Cities. Perspectives on Urban and Regional Change in the Baltic Sea Area* (ed. with Martin Peterson, 1997) and *Era of Consent. Conflict, co-operation and networks in local politics* (1998: in Swedish). He is currently heading an inter-disciplinary research project on democratisation processes at the local level in Poland and Ukraine.

David Aldridge, PhD (London), lectured in history at the University of Newcastle upon Tyne from 1965 to 1993. He wrote his doctoral thesis on the Royal Navy in the Baltic during the reign of George I (1714-1727). He has published numerous articles on 17th and 18th-century naval history and other subjects, some under the auspices of the Association for the History of the Northern Seas of which he is a council member.

Tony Barrow, PhD (Newcastle Polytechnic), teaches at Newcastle College and is an associate lecturer of the Open University. His publications *include Tall Ships: Two Rivers. Six Centuries of Sail on the rivers Tyne and Wear* (with Adrian Osler) (1993); *Pressgangs* and *Privateers. Aspects of the Maritime History of North East England 1760-1815* (1993); *The Whaling Trade of North East England, 1750-1850* (2001). He is a Council Member of the British Commission for Maritime History.

Kaare Dahl Martinsen, PhD (Roskilde), completed his postgraduate studies at the Institute of Soviet and East European Studies at the University of Glasgow in 1988. Since then he has been working on Central and East European economic and political reforms. His PhD thesis was written on the privatisation of state-owned enterprises in the Czech Republic. Since 1999, he has been employed at the Norwegian Institute for Defence Studies. His research has focused on Central European security issues with a special emphasis on the consequences of Poland's NATO membership.

Lars Ericson wrote his PhD at Stockholm University on *Burghers and Bureaucrats. The reshaping of Stockholm's city administration 1599-1637*. Since 1983 he has been working at the Military Archives in Stockholm, since 1991 as Senior Archivist and Head of the Research Department. He is a member of the Swedish Academy for Military Sciences and Secretary General of the Swedish Commission for Military History. He has so far published nine books and number of articles, mainly dealing with Sweden's era of greatness (1560-1718) and the 20th century, with emphasis on military history. He has also written a number of works concerning Baltic history, especially the Baltic States and their relations to Sweden. His most recent books (in Swedish) are: *Lasse i Gatan. Privateering and the collapse of the Swedish Empire* (1997) and (as editor) *The Road to Westphalia. Sweden and the Thirty* Years *War* (1998).

Åsa Eklund is a doctoral student in the Department of Economic History at the University of Uppsala. She is working on a thesis on the export of Swedish iron to Britain in the eighteenth century, within the project 'Iron production, iron trade and iron markets: Swedish and Russian iron in the British market, 1700-1850'.

Chris Evans is a Principal Lecturer in History at the University of Glamorgan. He is the author of *The labyrinth of flames: work and social conflict in early industrial Merthyr Tydfil* (1993).

John D Fudge studied at McGill University and at the University of Edinburgh (PhD 1989). He lectures at the University of British Columbia, Vancouver, and at the University College of the Cariboo, Kamloops, Canada. He is author of *Cargoes, Embargoes, and Emissaries. The Commercial and Political Interaction of England and the German Hanse, 1450-1510* (1995).

Nicholas Hope is Reader in Modern History, Glasgow University. He is the author of *German and Scandinavian Protestantism 1700-1918* (1995; second paperback edition, 1999). Since September 2001 he has been Coordinator of the 'Churches and European Integration' project financed by the European Commission and comprising the universities of Helsinki, Tartu, Lund, Münster, and Glasgow.

David Kirby is Professor of Modern History at the School of Slavonic and East European Studies, University College London. He has written extensively on Finnish and Baltic history. Among his most recent works are *Northern Europe in the Early Modern Period: The Baltic World 1492-1772* (1990) and *The Baltic World 1772-1993: Europe's Northern Periphery in an Age of Change* (1995). He is joint author (with Merja-Liisa Hinkkanen) of *Seas in History: The Baltic and North Seas*, published in 2000.

Enn Küng, PhD, works at the History Archives of the Estonian National Archives in Tartu. He is mainly interested in Swedish economic policy and trade in the Baltic Sea area in the 16th and 17th centuries. His has published several articles about the trade in Narva in the 17th century. His publications include (with Dirk Erpenbeck), *Narvaer Bürger- und Einwohnerbuch 1581-1704* (2000) and *Rootsi majanduspoliitika Narva kaubanduse küsimuses 17. sajandi teisel poolel* (Swedish economic policy in the commercial aspect in Narva in the second half of the 17th century; includes summary in English) (2001).

Andrew Lambert is Laughton Professor of Naval History and director of the Laughton Naval History unit in the Department of War Studies, King's College,

University of London. He is also Secretary of the Navy Records Society, Vice President of the British Commission for Maritime History and a Fellow of the Royal Historical Society. His books include *The Crimean War: British Grand Strategy against Russia 1853-1856.* (1990); *The Last Sailing Battlefleet : Maintaining Naval Mastery 1815-1850* (1991); *The Foundations of Naval History: Sir John Laughton, the Royal Navy and the Historical Profession* (1998) *War at Sea in the Age of Sail* (2000).

Jerzy Litwin, PhD, has worked at the Polish Maritime Museum at Gdansk since 1972. He was appointed deputy director for research and education in 1991. Since 1996 he has been a member of the Council of the International Congress of Maritime Museums. Specialising in the history of boat-building (his 1990 PhD thesis was on the subject of traditional boat-building in Poland), he was responsible for experiments in reconstructing medieval Pomeranian ships and building models of them. Six of these became part of the Museum's permanent exhibition. He has published five books and some 150 articles, as well as being responsible for over 200 drawings of ships and boats and exhibitions in the Museum. Over thirty articles and one book have been published abroad.

Leos Müller is a Research Fellow in the Baltic and East European Graduate School, University College of South Stockholm. He studied history at Charles University, Prague, and at Uppsala University (PhD 1998). He is the author of *The Merchant Houses of Stockholm, c. 1640-1800. A Comparative Study of Early-Modern Entrepreneurial Behaviour* (1998). He has published a number of articles on history of Swedish commerce and shipping in the early modern time. His current research project is concerned with consular services and shipping in the 18th century. He is also the editor of *Forum Navale*, the journal of the Swedish Association for Maritime History.

Steven W. Murdoch completed his PhD thesis at the University of Aberdeen in 1998. It has subsequently been published by Tuckwell Press as *Britain, Denmark-Norway and the House of Stuart, 1603-1660: A Diplomatic and Military Analysis.* He has published extensively on Scottish relations with Scandinavia and northern Europe in the early modern period. He is currently engaged as a Research Fellow at the Institute for Irish and Scottish Studies, University of Aberdeen, where he directs one of the Migration and Mobility projects on the Scottish diaspora. His edited collection *Scotland and the Thirty Years' War 1618-1648* was published in 2001.

Dr Lutz Oberdörfer is a Privatdozent at the Ernst-Moritz-Arndt-University at Greifswald. He has published extensively on British policy towards Scandinavia and the Baltic region during the inter-war period and the Second World War.

Adrian Osler was formerly Curator of Maritime History with Tyne and Wear Museums (1976-1996). He is currently engaged in research for a PhD on late 19th-century trade between the north-east 'coal ports' and the southern Baltic. His publications include *Tall Ships: Two Rivers. Six Centuries of Sail on the rivers Tyne and Wear* (with Tony Barrow) (1993) and 'Newcastle's West Jutland Trade: the formative years, 1870-1940', *Fiskeri- og Søfartsmuseum studieserie* 11 (1995).

A. W. Purdue is Senior Lecturer in history at the Open University. He is the author of *The Second World War* (1999) and *Merchants and Gentry in North East England 1650-1830: the Carrs and the Ellisons* (1999). He is also the co-author of three books written with J.M.Golby: *The Civilisation of the Crowd: Popular Culture in England 1750-1900* (1984), *The Making of the Modern Christmas* (1986) and *The Monarchy and the British People 1760 – present* (1988).

Göran Rydén is a Research Fellow in the Department of Economic History at the University of Uppsala. He is the author of 'Iron production and the household as a production unit in nineteenth-century Sweden', *Continuity and Change* 10 (1995), and (with Chris Evans), 'Kinship and the transmission of skills: bar iron production in Britain and Sweden, 1500-1860', in Maxine Berg and Kristine Bruland (eds.), *Technological revolutions in Europe: historical perspectives* (1998).

Patrick Salmon is Professor of International History at the University of Newcastle upon Tyne and an associate director of the AHRB Centre for North-East England History (NEEHI). His publications include *Scandinavia and the Great Powers 1890-1940* (1997).

Jørgen Sevaldsen received his MA in History and English from the University of Copenhagen. Since 1976, he has been a lecturer in the Department of English of that university, teaching British history and politics to students of English. Published works include *Contemporary British Society* (5th ed., 2001) and articles in *Britain and Denmark: Political, economic and cultural relations in the 19th and 20th centuries* (2002), of which he is also a co-editor.

Natasha Vall is a research fellow at the AHRB Centre for North-East England History. She is based at Northumbria University and is researching twentieth-century comparative regional history. She also is one of the contributors to *Newcastle upon Tyne: A Modern History*, edited by Robert Colls and Bill Lancaster (2001), and is working on the publication of her thesis which compared Malmö and Newcastle during the twentieth century.

Antonijs Zunda (Dr. habil. hist.) is an associate professor of Modern and Contemporary History of Western Europe and America at the University of Latvia. Since 2000 he has been Advisor to the President of the Republic of Latvia on Issues of History. His publications include *Latvijas un Lielbritānijas attiecības 1930-1940. Realitāte un ilūzijas* (Relations between Latvia and Great Britain, 1930-1940. Reality and illusions) (1998*); Lielbritānija un Baltijas valstis 1933-1935* (Great Britain and the Baltic States, 1933-1935) (1989); 'Morāle un politiskais aprēķins Anglijas Baltijas politikā Otrā pasaules kara gados' (Morality and political calculation in the Baltic Policy of England during World War II), *Latvijas Vēsture* 1993, No. 4.

Introduction

For centuries the east coast ports of England and Scotland have been centres of shipping and commerce between Great Britain and the countries of Scandinavia and the Baltic. Merchants, missionaries, migrants, soldiers and sailors have passed through such ports as London, Hull, Newcastle and Aberdeen in both directions, and their contacts have helped to shape cultural and political identities on both sides of the North Sea. At national level, too, relations across the North Sea and the Baltic have been of vital importance, with Britain as a powerful neighbour, sometimes in a protective role, at other times as an aggressor, while Baltic powers such as Sweden, Russia and Germany have at various times challenged British security interests directly or indirectly. Yet, as David Kirby suggests in his preface to this volume, the Baltic Sea and the countries bordering on it have not been as well known, or as prominent in the British imagination, as some other regions of Europe. This may be partly to do with the cold war, which closed off much of the southern shore of the Baltic from contact with the West for nearly fifty years. The end of the cold war, however, has seen the prospects for the Baltic region transformed, with new opportunities for trade, investment and cultural contact, as well as new challenges in the fields of the environment, economic and political integration, and international security.

Scholarly study of Britain's relations with the Baltic region has also taken off in recent years. As the contributions to this volume make clear, there are rich archival resources to sustain it, some long available, others newly accessible. There are also new ways of analysing the data and new intellectual perspectives. Realising that such developments were taking place, but unsure about their nature or scale, a group of scholars under the auspices of the North East England History Institute (NEEHI) decided that an international conference would be the best way to bring Baltic specialists together and map out possible directions for future research. The response far exceeded their expectations. The conference *Britain and the Baltic: East Coast Connections*, held at the University of Durham in March 1999, brought together over seventy academics and interested members of the public. Thirty papers were delivered to the conference. The eighteen chapters of this volume represent a selection from those papers, together with others that were specially commissioned. They amply demonstrate the vitality of current research on British-Baltic relations and will, perhaps, form the basis for fruitful contact and collaboration among researchers in many countries.

In one respect, at least, this has already happened. In 2000 NEEHI became the AHRB Centre for North-East England History. Research in the new Centre is organized into five strands, each based at one of the region's universities (Durham, Newcastle upon Tyne, Northumbria, Sunderland and Teesside). One of the strands, 'External Relations' is based at Newcastle. With this strong institutional base, the North East of England will be well placed to collaborate with other organisations and networks in the UK and overseas.

The papers collected in this volume are arranged chronologically but have many themes in common. Of these trade is perhaps the most prominent. By the sixteenth century, when this volume begins, the Baltic and Scandinavian region had long been a source of timber, pitch, iron and other products vital to the economy of the British Isles. In return Britain exported a range of goods dominated first by textiles and later by coal. In addition, as several papers point out, British merchants increasingly acted as middlemen between the Baltic and the colonial economies of North America, the Caribbean and Africa. A consistent theme of many of the papers is the rise of British commercial and maritime supremacy, from the eclipse of the German Hanse in the early sixteenth century (John Fudge), through rivalry with the Dutch in the seventeenth century (Jerzy Litwin, Leos Müller, Enn Küng) and the vicissitudes of eighteenth-century warfare (Lars Ericson, David Aldridge, Åsa Eklund, Chris Evans and Göran Rydén, Bill Purdue) to the point, in the late nineteenth century, where Britain was poised on the verge of 'relative economic decline' (to use a contentious term) but where, as Adrian Osler shows, British shipping was still both numerically and technologically preponderant.

However, these papers also reveal the enormous risks attending Baltic trade until very recent times. Navigation was frequently hazardous, climatic conditions extreme, and the danger of shipwreck ever present. Of man-made dangers, war was by far the most prevalent though, as the examples cited by Kirby show, in medieval times war and trade could be practically indistinguishable. Of the wars discussed in these papers, the Great Northern War of 1710-21 was much the most disruptive to British trade, but much more could be said about the Napoleonic wars, not to mention the two world wars and the cold war of the twentieth century. Yet war also offered opportunities to enterprising traders. Müller describes the way in which the British supplanted the Dutch in the Swedish iron trade during the Dutch-Danish-Swedish wars of the mid-seventeenth century. Indeed both Müller and Küng trace a symbiotic relationship between Swedish and English mercantilism from the time of the Cromwell onwards.

The rise of the British presence in the seventeenth century coincided with the rise of Sweden as a Baltic and European power. It was marked by a shift away from Prussian ports such as Danzig/Gdansk (the focus of the papers by Fudge and Litwin) to Stockholm, Gothenburg and ports such as Narva under Swedish control in the eastern Baltic (discussed by Küng). Conversely, the collapse of Swedish power during Great Northern War also meant the exclusion of British trade – partly at hands of Swedes themselves. The papers by Ericson and Aldridge tell the story of Swedish privateering from both sides, focusing on the colourful figure of Lars Gathenhielm of Gothenburg and his even more resourceful wife. But, as Müller suggests, one commodity – iron – survived the pressures of commercial competition and warfare to become the staple of Swedish trade with the British Isles in the eighteenth century. Eklund, Evans and Rydén describe the process in detail, showing how the competition between Swedish and Russian iron paralleled the contest between the two powers for Baltic hegemony, and how the British market was instrumental in driving forward industrial development in both countries.

As large a constraint as these natural and man-made hazards was the sheer difficulty of conducting long-range commercial operations in the context of poor communications and an undeveloped or even non-existent banking infrastructure. In these circumstances personal relationships were all-important. Purdue's discussion of the eighteenth-century Newcastle merchant Ralph Carr places great emphasis on trust as the basis for successful economic endeavour in early modern times. Trust might be placed in family members but also in foreign merchants who shared similar social and religious values. In Carr's case this meant, above all, the merchant houses of Amsterdam. Thus the Anglo-Dutch rivalry of the seventeenth century gave way in the eighteenth century to Anglo-Dutch partnership. Eklund, Evans and Rydén demonstrate that a similarly close relationship developed in the iron trade between Graffin Prankard of Bristol and Francis Jennings (of Irish origin), one of the leading Stockholm merchants.

Mention of such individuals brings us to the second major theme of this volume: that of assimilation and identity – identity defined in several ways: national, regional, cultural and religious. Several of the papers, notably those by Steve Murdoch, Leos Müller, Enn Küng and Martin Åberg, describe the various ways in which trade and other forms of economic activity affected the lives of those engaged in them: above all, in deciding where to make their permanent home. While the merchants of Lynn might have conducted their trade with Danzig from their home port, others lived for a number of years, sometimes the rest of their lives, in foreign cities. Some became fully assimilated into their new societies. Murdoch shows how many Scots – but how few English – became burgesses of Scandinavian and Baltic towns in the first half of the seventeenth century. Müller reinforces the impression of Englishmen reluctant to put down roots, and using their years of residence in Stockholm merely as a stepping stone before returning to London, Hull or Newcastle to make their 'proper careers'. Yet Küng's account of the English in Narva tells another tale, with many becoming naturalised as citizens – a move encouraged by the Swedish authorities, but less welcome to their rivals among Narva's native tradesmen. Åberg's discussion of the migration of Scots and English to the ports of western Sweden tells a still more complex story. Whereas businessmen of British origin became increasingly integrated into Swedish society; on the other, that society itself became permeated by British cultural and political values. Several of these papers also discuss questions of freedom of worship and intermarriage which provide further clues to the multifaceted relationships between the British and the host communities in which they lived.

The extent to which, at different periods, people thought of themselves as British, Scottish or English, Swedish, Danish or German, is of course highly debatable. Presumably the merchants of Berwick cited by Kirby had some sense of their own identity, and its difference from that of their hosts, when they flung boiling water and hot ashes over the local dignitaries of Uddevalla. The papers in this volume throw out many hints about identity, of which only a few can be picked up here. The theme of Scottish versus English identity, for example, crops up repeatedly. One the one hand, Scots were for a long time not only numerically preponderant among those of British origin in Scandinavia and the Baltic, but also frequently rose to positions of wealth and authority. Murdoch's description of Scottish networks in the service of the Swedish king Gustav II Adolf in the early seventeenth century shows how kinship ties, combined with military prowess, could lead to advancement. In diplomacy and as military officers, as well as in trade, Scots were clearly pioneers, showing the way in which the English – or 'Britain' – later followed. On the other hand, then as now, foreigners sometimes had difficulty in distinguishing between Scots and English. Many traits identified as peculiarly English – or British – were in fact of Scottish origin. As Åberg remarks, 'Göteborg has become known as "Little London" whereas "Little Edinburgh" would perhaps have been more appropriate'. Nor does the distinction appear to have worried the 'British' congregation in Elbing to whom John Durie preached in the 1630s as an ordained minister of the Scottish Presbyterian Kirk.

Murdoch's paper introduces the theme of religion and religious conciliation. The efforts of John Durie in the seventeenth century link up interestingly with the twentieth-century ecumenism of Nicholas Hope's paper. Both John Durie and the Anglican churchmen discussed by Hope were living in an era of endemic warfare and ideological confrontation. Hope's conclusion that the value of dialogue 'lay really in the spirit and not so much in measurable benefit' may be relevant to both the seventeenth and the twentieth centuries. However, another participant in the conference, the Very Revd John Arnold, Dean of Durham, was able to show that the tentative contacts of the inter-war period did lead to solid ecumenical achievements in the last decades of the twentieth century. The question of religious freedom also crops up in other papers: several point to the establishment of churches serving the English, Scottish or 'British' communities in Baltic and Scandinavian cities – often reflecting the pragmatism of rulers keen to encourage trade irrespective of religious affiliation.

Perceptions of identity at national level are raised by Kirby at the beginning of the volume and by Jørgen Sevaldsen near the end. Kirby suggests that the image of 'Scandinavia' is more firmly fixed in British minds than that of 'the Baltic' – a development that may have been under way as early as the seventeenth century. Sevaldsen discusses British perceptions of Denmark and of Scandinavia more generally, through his analysis of a small but distinctive literary genre: books on Denmark by former British ambassadors to that country. The model is Robert Molesworth's celebrated dissection of the Danish absolute monarchy and Danish society published in 1694. His successor three centuries later, Sir Andrew Mellon, was far more charitable but nevertheless described Denmark as not a nation but a tribal society, and used this to explain many distinctive Danish qualities: the emphasis on welfare, consensus and so on. Denmark, even more than Sweden (the model of the Scandinavian 'middle way' from the 1930s to the 1960s), seems to have become the archetype of the 'bland Scandinavian society' to which – as some commentators sternly warned – Britain might be reduced if it lost its sense of 'mission'.

A third important theme is that of international security. As we have seen, warfare has been a recurrent reality in the Baltic. A rather different question is the role of the Baltic in the strategic calculations of the major powers. The papers addressing such questions in this volume focus mainly on the Baltic in British strategy and diplomacy over the last three centuries. Despite the density of contacts through shipping and trade, a British naval presence made itself felt only intermittently in the Baltic. Climate, distance, the lack of reliable allies, the threat from hostile Baltic powers, all combined to deter British politicians and sailors from sending naval contingents to the Baltic except under very unusual conditions. Exceptions discussed in these papers include the expedition led by Admiral Sir John Norris in 1715, the 'Crimean' war (in which the Baltic was a major theatre) and the anti-Bolshevik operations in the Gulf of Finland in 1919. Yet Andrew Lambert's paper on British naval strategy before 1914 suggests that such absence is deceptive. During the era of British naval supremacy in the nineteenth century, the Royal Navy did not need to be physically present in order to dominate the Baltic. Challenging orthodox interpretations, Lambert argues that the implicit threat to German security in the Baltic (occasionally made explicit) was a highly effective deterrent, thrown away needlessly by the Army's obsession with sending an expeditionary force to France.

The situation was transformed, however, at the end of the First World War when both Germany and Russia had been eclipsed by war and revolution.

Britain now found itself obliged to play an active role in the politics of the eastern Baltic, a region of which British officialdom – if not British sailors and merchants – knew little. Britain had to work with France, whose alleged hegemonic ambitions in the region were mistrusted, and had to confront recalcitrant and often aggressive new states, above all, France's ally Poland. Lutz Oberdörfer's paper explores the limits of British power in one case: that of the former German city of Memel, seized by Lithuania from the control of the League of Nations in 1923 – itself, in part, a reaction to the Polish seizure of Lithuania's historic capital, Vilnius, in 1920. The consciousness of British weakness and the need to avoid making commitments that could not be fulfilled, noted by Oberdörfer, were powerfully reinforced less than two decades later by the experience of World War II. Antonijs Zunda shows how the British government responded when the three Baltic States of Estonia, Latvia and Lithuania, which had gained their independence, in part, with the active support of British naval and military forces, came under Soviet pressure and were forcibly absorbed into the USSR in 1940. After the entry of the Soviet Union into the war in 1941, Great Britain came under strong pressure to give legal recognition to the Soviet occupation of the Baltic States, and many senior politicians and diplomats, Winston Churchill among them, found it hard to resist the temptation. In the end Britain followed the United States in refusing *de jure* recognition. Nevertheless, *de facto* recognition had been given in 1940 and, as Zunda points out, the British were deaf to Baltic appeals for their case to be heard at the Potsdam conference in 1945.

A further and far more positive transformation has taken place in the Baltic region since the end of the cold war. Kaare Dahl Martinsen's paper shows, however, that some of the underlying strategic and political realities remain unchanged. Here the focus is not on Britain directly, except as a member of the North Atlantic Alliance, but some of the themes are familiar: in particular Poland's effort to escape its historic role of buffer between east and west. Dahl Martinsen shows that NATO membership has reduced Poland's historic sense of vulnerability and that its position on NATO's eastern frontier has become not a liability but an asset.

What, finally, of North-East England itself? Three papers focus on Newcastle and the Tyne over the last three centuries: Purdue and Osler write about the eighteenth and nineteenth centuries respectively, while Natasha Vall compares cultural policies in Malmö and Newcastle in the late twentieth century. All, in their different ways, have some disturbing things to say about the vision and enterprise of the citizens of Newcastle. The restrictive practices of the Newcastle Merchant Adventurers in the time of Ralph Carr may come as no surprise. More significant is the failure, identified by Osler, of Tyneside shipowners to respond to the Baltic opportunities generated in their own port during the 1860s and 1870s, thus losing out to competitors from Hull and London. Vall, meanwhile, contrasts the enlightened cultural policies of post-industrial Malmö with Newcastle's preference for urban regeneration through a culture of night clubs and heavy drinking. She hints at the end, however, at the aura of cultural respectability that Newcastle has begun to acquire through its recent association with Gateshead, its traditionally less privileged neighbour on the other side of the Tyne. The new partnership builds on Gateshead's distinguished record of artistic patronage (the Angel of the North, the Baltic Centre for Contemporary Art) and is symbolised by the construction of the Gateshead Millennium Bridge, a source of pride on both sides of the river.

It remains to thank the many people and institutions who helped to make the 1999 Durham conference a success, and who have contributed to the publication of this book. The organizing committee comprised Tony Barrow, Sarah Davies, Susan Ketelaar, Adrian Osler, Bill Purdue, Patrick Salmon and Peter Waldron. Those who contributed financial or other support include the following: The British Academy, The Very Revd John Arnold, Dean of Durham, Professor Christopher Bailey, Dr Eric Cross, Mr John Dersley, Dr Alisoun Gardner-Medwin, Miss Anne Heywood, Emeritus Professor Norman McCord, Mrs Flora Mennie, Mr John Pescott, Royal Danish Consul, Professor Tony Pollard, Professor Michael Prestwich, The Hon Matt Ridley, Professor David Rollason, The Royal Historical Society, Scandinavian Seaways, Mr Christopher Souter, Royal Swedish Consul, The Vice-Chancellors of the Universities of Durham, Newcastle upon Tyne, Northumbria at Newcastle, Sunderland and Teesside, Mr John Walton, Finnish Consul. Secretarial and organizational support was provided by Scott Anthony, Sarah Badcock, Eleanor Cunningham, Richard Holmes, Mira Lüthje, Carole Parkin, Katie Salmon, Mick Sharp, Tracy Swaddle and Jenny Walker. We are grateful to Suzanne Robertson of Sunderland University Press for guiding this volume through to publication

We should like to record, finally, the presence at the 1999 conference of two people whose lives represent a link between the North East of England and the countries of Scandinavia and the Baltic. Dr Anne Orde, a retired member of the History Department at the University of Durham, spent part of her childhood in the Baltic States where her father, Sir Charles Orde, was the last British minister to Estonia, Latvia and Lithuania before their forcible incorporation into the Soviet Union in August 1940. Mrs Flora Mennie is the widow of Professor Duncan Mennie (1909-1998), Emeritus Professor of German and Scandinavian Languages at the University of Newcastle upon Tyne. By training a Germanist, Professor Mennie pioneered the teaching of Scandinavian Studies at Newcastle after the Second World War. Many distinguished scholars worked in the Department of German and Scandinavian Studies, which acted as a focal point in the development of Anglo-Scandinavian cultural relations before the untimely closure of Scandinavian Studies in the mid-1980s. We hope the present volume will help to mark a new beginning.

Preface

Locating the Baltic

David Kirby

Addressing an audience of specialists at the 1999 Durham conference on Britain and the Baltic was a great pleasure for me, not least because I could rest assured that the members of the audience would be familiar with the part of the world I was talking about, the Baltic. Regrettably, that is not the case with the wider public in Britain. The Baltic is not infrequently confused with the Balkans, often with embarrassing results in conversation. This low level of public awareness may of course reflect the relatively un-newsworthy status of the Baltic, which in these times of strife and trouble is undoubtedly a good thing; but it may also indicate how the Baltic has slipped out of the general ambit of British public life in the course of this century. The last time a ship from the Baltic sailed into English fiction, as far as I know, was in 1930, when *Lemmala* entered the Pool of London with its cargo of wood veneer and enticing concoction of strange smells, bottles and foreign languages that so entranced J.B.Priestley's romantically-inclined Miss Matfield. Few fictional Englishmen or women have spent time in a Baltic state since Anthony Powell's young man in *Venusberg* published around the same time.[1] If we exclude the relatively minor naval operations in 1919, at a time when the return to peace was probably uppermost in the minds of most people, the last time British forces were engaged in the Baltic was almost 150 years ago, during the Crimean War. The northern theatre of war was virtually eclipsed by actions elsewhere after May 1940; how many people, even those reasonably well-versed in the events of the Second World War, know of the Russian occupation of Bornholm, or of the war in Lapland in

---

[1] J.B. Priestley, *Angel Pavement* (London, 1930); A. Powell, *Venusberg* (London, 1932).

the winter of 1944-45? The post-war division of Europe served only to make the Baltic more obscure; as long ago as 1952, Clarence Manning, assistant professor of Slavic languages at Columbia University, was claiming that 'it is no exaggeration to say that the Baltic Sea and its surrounding countries have been in modern times the forgotten part of Europe.'[2]

The Baltic has always attracted far fewer visitors from western Europe than has the continent's other inland sea, the Mediterranean. Few were the knights who undertook a crusade against the heathen of Lithuania in comparison with the hundreds who ventured to the Holy Land – dare one say it, the rewards were greater, and the climate rather pleasanter, in the Near East than in the trackless wastes of north-eastern Europe. Even during that great age of travel and travel-writing of the eighteenth and nineteenth centuries, few ventured north, and those who did tended to convey an image of emptiness and desolation, where Mme de Stael imagined 'the vicinity of bears and wolves during the winter is so close, that all ideas are absorbed in the necessity of ensuring a tolerable physical existence'.[3] The best that could be said of such 'gloomy sterile solitudes', to quote an anonymous writer in the *Monthly Review* of 1802, was that 'Nature takes a bolder outline, and assumes those features of savage grandeur, which inspire emotions of the sublime'.[4]

It may also be significant that those who did visit and write about the region directed their steps northwards; it might be more correct to speak of a 'Scandinavian' rather than a 'Baltic' image percolating down to the British public during the course of the nineteenth and even twentieth centuries.[5] This may well have a good deal to do with the emergence of fairly clearly-defined national states on the northern shores, and the decline of the Hanseatic cities on the southern shores of the Baltic sea, although there were still a significant number of commercial connections between Britain and these cities, and it would be interesting to know more about what we might call the businessman's perception of the Baltic. However, I am going to speculate that the

---

[2] C. Manning, *The Forgotten Republics* (New York, 1952), p. v.

[3] Mme. de Stael, *Ten Years in Exile* (Fontwell, 1968), p.429.

[4] The writer was reviewing Guiseppe Acerbi's *Travels through Sweden, Finland and Lapland to the North Cape. Monthly Review*, vol. xxxix, 1802, p. 226.

[5] Travel-writing has recently become a fashionable topic for research, often of a rather tendentious kind, which seeks to apply the arguments advanced by Edward Said in his book *Orientalism* without really questioning their applicability. On travellers to Scandinavia, see H. Arnold Barton, *Northern Arcadia: Foreign Travelers in Scandinavia, 1765-1815* (Carbondale and Edwardsville, Ill., 1998) and M. Davies, *A Perambulating Paradox. British Travel Literature and the Image of Sweden c. 1770-1865* (Lund, 2000).

shift of emphasis, towards the 'northland' instead of the 'eastland', was already under way during the course of the seventeenth century.

The medieval connection was quite definitely with the eastland and the easterlings, who had a highly visible presence in the major trading cities of western Europe, 'the olde Haunce of the Sprusyners that owt of the cold contreys in the este porties, wher is frost and snow on eight monthis in the yere come but oons in the yere, bryngyng ther nedful comodites for England; pitche, tarre, bowstavis, wex, flesh and such other', according to the sixteenth-century writer, Clemens Armstrong.[6] But Armstrong's use of the word 'old' and his complaints about the aggressive trading of 'the Hansteddes in Almayn' are indicative of the declining presence of the easterlings in England. The English merchants who sought to break into the eastern European market during the seventeenth century through the medium of the Eastland Company were less than successful; that which ensured the real breakthrough in English trade with the Baltic was the rising demand for timber and naval stores from the time of the Commonwealth onwards, and an aggressive commercial policy, as embodied in the Navigation Acts. This also brought about a shift northwards, from the Prussian ports to those in Swedish possession. Sweden had of course come into the public gaze as a consequence of the Thirty Years' War, and the attempts of that country to wrest control of the Sound from Denmark had drawn in the maritime powers in the 1650s. The demands of the maritime powers for materials for shipbuilding and the potential for conflict between Sweden and its rivals conspired to draw the Baltic into the centre of European affairs. It was however the 'balance of the North' that British ministers hoped to maintain during the final phases of the Great Northern War; this was a northern European, not a Baltic or an eastland conflict, and it was a new 'Nordic' power, Russia, that eventually emerged victorious.

This vision of a 'Nordic' (*nordische*) Europe that stretched in an arc from the coasts of Norway to the Black Sea was especially strong in Germany. As late as 1846, J.G. Kohl could compare Bessarabia and Skåne as being on the 'northern' side of the European cultural frontier.[7] But northern Europe also had far more resonance in Britain than 'the Baltic'. Dr Johnson makes no mention of the word in his *Dictionary* (he does include 'easterling' but merely as 'a native of some country eastward to another'), and the Rev. John Boag's mid-Victorian *Imperial Lexicon* defines the Baltic

---

[6] Cited in L. Salzman, *English Trade in the Middle Ages* (Oxford, 1931), p.362.

[7] J.G. Kohl, *Resor i Danmarck jemte en utflygt til Södra Sverige* (Stockholm, 1847), vol.2, p.100.   Under Turkish rule, Kohl maintained, Bessarabia had followed southern customs of dress and dwelling, but under Russian rule, the people immediately became 'nordic', dressing in furs, building big tiled stoves and barricading their houses in winter.

as 'the sea which separates Norway and Sweden from Jutland, Holstein and Germany'.[8] The term as applied to a stretch of water has historically had a pronouncedly 'western' bias, and seems to have been mostly closely associated with the Danish Belts. In modern times, 'Baltic' has also acquired a narrower focus, applied to the territories between the Niemen and the Neva – the 'Baltic provinces', the twentieth-century 'Baltic states'.

It is 'northern', or 'Nordic', rather than 'Baltic', therefore, that has been more readily applied in modern times to embrace the area of which the 'East Sea' forms the watery core. I shall return to this a little later. What I would like to do now is correct or alter the picture I have so far presented of a general lack of knowledge or awareness of the Baltic in the British Isles. For, if we consider the relationship in historical perspective and accept the limitations of public awareness, it is pretty clear that there have been a wide variety of contacts, as the papers in this volume show. Here, I might say a few words about one period of history that is not so well represented in this volume, and that is the first millennium.

The *Ostsæ* is mentioned in King Alfred's translation of the fifth-century description of the world by the southern European monk Paulus Orosius. It is fairly clear that this is the passage of water known today as the Kattegat. It is also clear that the two travellers who gave the English king a first-hand account of their travels in these waters were thoroughly familiar with them, and were also frequent visitors to England. Other written sources are few, but there is enough archaeological evidence to persuade a number of experts in the Anglo-Saxon field to believe there were very strong links between the English kingdoms and the western Baltic. The most notable example is, of course, the Sutton Hoo ship burial, with its numerous connections with eastern Sweden. East Anglia is thought to have been ruled in the sixth century by kings hailing from present-day Sweden, and seems to have been an area of settlement from the Baltic and Scandinavian shores well before the Viking Age. Beowulf was, after all, a prince of the Geats, who made the short crossing to Denmark to do battle with the beast that had cruelly disturbed the just slumbers of the carousing Danes in their great hall. It was 'the ship with the curved prow', stuffed with treasures and weapons, that carried him 'into the possession of the ocean'. Beowulf was not simply a figment of the poet's imagination; men of his kind frequently ventured far afield by sea, attracted by the prospects of plunder and wealth. Sweden remained a rich recruiting-ground for the sea-kings and lords who mounted expeditions against the

---

[8]   S. Johnson, *A Dictionary of the English Language*, 12th. edition (London, 1787), vol.1, entry under 'Easterling'; J. Boag, *The Imperial Lexicon of the English Language*, (Edinburgh, s/d/), vol.1, p.111.

English and Frankish kingdoms in the tenth and eleventh centuries, as we know from runestone inscriptions.[9]

There has been some discussion about the extent of contacts across the North Sea. It has been pointed out that East Anglia, with its many long and sheltered inlets, was in all likelihood far more accessible by sea than overland; that in this respect, Jutland and even Angeln was nearer Ipswich than was Tamworth. It is possible that the direct crossing to the mouth of the Humber or the Wash was regularly used, though it is more likely that the 'inland' route was followed. This would allow the ship to sail in the lee of a string of islands through the shallow waters of the Wadden Sea from the coast of southern Jutland to Flanders, and across the Channel.[10] Furthermore, it was also possible for these vessels, with their shallow draught, to avoid the treacherous passage round Skagen at the northern tip of Jutland, which only came into common usage with the development of the sturdy medieval cog, with its improved steering gear, in the thirteenth century. Now, it would be idle to imagine a constant stream of boats threading their way through the rivers and creeks of Sjælland and Slesvig en route for England, and Peter Sawyer has taught us to be cautious in trying to estimate the numbers of settlers on English soil from Scandinavia; but it cannot be denied that transmarine migration completely changed the ethnic composition and character of the population of the British Isles during the post-Roman period, or that that migration came almost entirely from lands at the threshold of the Baltic. Furthermore, for several centuries, the political fate of the British Isles was largely determined by those from what I shall call the Skaggerak-Kattegat complex – the Danish rulers who could muster big fleets in the sheltered mouths of the fjards, the petty kings and jarls of Vestfold, who pushed into the North Atlantic and whose descendants were still able to lay claim to Scotland in the thirteenth century. That it was a descendant of an earlier wave of Northmen that settled in northern France, rather than a Danish or Norwegian king, who conquered England and thereby laid the foundation for a ruling dynasty whose ambitions lay to the south, is perhaps not quite as unexpected as N.A.M. Rodger seems to suggest; but he is right to point out that

> Nothing is pre-ordained in history, and there was no logical reason why England, the meeting place of the three cultures (Celtic, Norse and Anglo-Saxon), should not have been absorbed by any one of

---

[9] See J. Haywood, *Dark Age Naval Power: A reassessment of Frankish and Anglo-Saxon Activity* (London, 1991); P. Sawyer, *Kings and Vikings: Scandinavia and Europe 700 AD-1100 AD* (New York, 1994).

[10] See the contribution by M. Carver, 'Pre-Viking traffic in the North Sea', in S. McGrail (ed.), *Maritime Celts, Frisians, Saxons*, CBA Research Report 71 (London, 1990), pp.117-25.

them, or partitioned between them. In geographical terms, York is well placed to be a national capital of Britain, and if Æthelstan had lost the battle of Brunanburh, the Viking kingdom of York with its mixture of Norse, Celtic and English elements might have made a logical centre for a strong island kingdom. It would have been equally plausible at any period between the seventh century and the twelfth or even later to imagine a Norse-Celtic maritime empire, ruled from Dublin or Man and holding sway on both sides of the Irish Sea, perhaps with a land frontier in England with a Danish North Sea empire.[11]

If Anglo-Saxon England was transformed from an island kingdom into an Anglo-French empire, and if raids from across the North Sea dwindled in intensity and faded in their effectiveness, the maritime links with Scandinavia and the Baltic remained strong, especially for ports such as Boston, Lynn or Kingston-upon-Hull. One has to say, however, that judging from the records, they were far from harmonious. The historian L. Salzman described medieval Anglo-Scandinavian trade as 'full of robbery and violence'. At the height of the English-Scots wars of the reign of Edward II, there were numerous incidents, as when certain merchants of Berwick lying in the port of Wydahel [Uddevalla?] invited the provincial governor and ten local worthies to dine on board. These unsuspecting and unarmed men had as a second course boiling water and hot ashes flung upon them, and, blinded and scalded, were slain by the sailors.[12] There was further tension and conflict at the end of the fourteenth and in the early decades of the fifteenth century, between English and Hanseatic merchants. The most spectacular incident occurred in 1449, when Robert Wenyngton of Devon, cruising in search of the Breton squadron, 'mette with a flotte of a c. grate schyppys of Pruse, Lubycke, Campe, Rastocke, Holond, Salond, and Flandres betwyxte Garnsye and Portland; and then I cam abord the Admirall and bade them stryke in the Kyngys name of Englond, and they bade me skyte in the Kyngys name of Englond; and then I and my feleschyp sayd, but he wyll streke don the sayle, that I wyld over sayle hym by the grace of God and [if] God wyll send me wynd and wether, and dey bade me do my worst, by cause I had so fewe schyppys and so smale that they scornyd with me.' Favoured by the wind, Wenyngton captured the whole fleet, and threatened to kill the lot of them.[13]

---

[11] N Rodger, *The Safeguard of the Sea: A Naval History of Britain*, vol. 1, 660-1649 (London, 1997), p. 48.

[12] Salzman, *English Trade*, pp. 366-7.

[13] Ibid., pp. 274-5.

We know rather more about Robert Wenyngton, or John Tutbury, seven times mayor of Kingston-upon-Hull, merchant and pirate, because malefactors and those with a grievance find their way more often into the records than the usually anonymous persons whose commodities are taxed and recorded in port books and such like; but one has to admit that English or British maritime activities in the Baltic have all too often been tinged with aggression, and are certainly remembered as such by Finns or Danes, and probably those Russians ancient enough to recall British naval operations in the Gulf of Finland in 1919. The discourse of commerce also has an aggressive or complaining tone, from the York merchants bitching about the Easterlings not spending any of the money from their export earnings in the fifteenth century to the trade journalists of the early 1920s, moaning that the Germans were doing all the business in the Baltic; but perhaps that is the British way of coping with life when things are not going their way.

This is of course a one-sided and unbalanced picture of the British-Baltic relationship. It overlooks the many thousands who traded peaceably and profitably, who settled and set up businesses, and whose descendants were fully integrated into the life of their adopted homeland. The story of some of the English and Scottish merchants in the Baltic is told in other contributions to this volume, but one thinks also of settlers in Britain – artists such as Michael Sittow in the sixteenth century or the Kniller brothers in the reign of Queen Anne, the Norwegian timber merchants of the seventeenth century and the German merchants of the nineteenth, who settled in and around the port of London, or about distinguished visitors for whom the British experience was important – the Swedish historian Geijer, for example, or the Danish theologian and reformer N.F.S. Grundtvig. Since I have been pursuing a maritime theme, I will insert a snippet here which I hope will show that the British connection has had quite considerable repercussions at even the humblest level on occasion. The presence of Finnish sailors in British ports was considered of sufficient concern to merit not only the establishment of a Seamen's Mission in the late nineteenth century, but also a visit from the leader of the Finnish nationalist party, senator Yrjö-Koskinen in 1895. Reporting on his visit, the senator declared that the image of Finns and Finland abroad was largely that of drunken sailors. 'Englishmen had the lowest opinion of the Finnish people, whose representatives were composed of these roistering seamen. ... The Seamen's Mission has had to work against the Englishman's contempt for our people and the incorrect notion of our moral and material circumstances which was prevalent amongst the English, as well as the mistrust and hostility of their own countrymen.' Fortunately, 'I was glad to find during my stay in England that the Finnish Seamen's Mission has succeeded beyond all expectations in this task. In nearly all the families and circles which I visited, the work of the Finnish seamen's priests was known at least by reputation, and people talked of this and their work with obvious respect...'[14] It is not known to me whether luminaries such as Mr Disraeli or Lord Palmerston hastened to Danzig to see what was being done to deal with what the consul declared with regret to be 'a more troublesome and thoughtless set of men, to use the mildest term, to be met with than British merchant seamen', but I think it highly unlikely that they did, or even contemplated any such action.[15]

In modern times, as former centres of maritime activity have fallen redundant and been converted into leisure centres or housing developments, and as air travel has displaced the sea crossing, our direct experience of the sea has declined. This has perhaps tended to obscure the richness and variety of transmarine connections – the ideas, techniques, tricks and hints exchanged or picked up on the quays and in the boatyards, the words and phrases that have flitted into and out of the word-stores of the peoples of the northern European lands, the fashions that have flown and taken root, or fallen on stony ground. It is the historian's business to enquire into the nature of relationships, to ask, as does the Swedish poet Tomas Tranströmer of his passengers on a boat passing through the labyrinth of islands in northern Baltic waters, how much they got to know of one another.[16] As this book reveals, the peoples of the British Isles, particularly the north-easterly regions, have learnt to know a great deal about the peoples of the Baltic over the centuries – a connection weakened but never entirely obliterated by the Cold War division of Europe.

---

[14] T. Waltari, *Finska sjömansmission 1875-1925* (Helsingfors, 1925), p. 544.

[15] The consul is cited in R. Hope, *A New History of British Shipping* (London, 1990), p. 281.

[16] T. Tranströmer, *Östersjöar. En dikt* (Stockholm, 1974), cited in D. Kirby and M-L. Hinkkanen, *The Baltic and North Seas* (London, 2000), p.59.

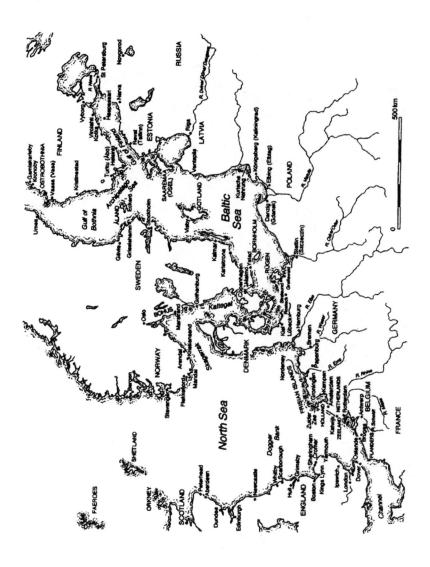

Map reproduced from David Kirby and Merja-Liisa Hinkkanen, *The Baltic and the North Seas* (Routledge, London, 2000), with kind permission of the publishers.

Part I: 1500-1700

Chapter 1

Maintaining a presence: Baltic enterprise and the merchants of Lynn during the reign of Henry VIII

John D. Fudge

Throughout the later Middle Ages the Baltic trade of merchants from England was concentrated at Danzig, the Prussian staple. Already the gateway to a vast resource hinterland, the port emerged in the fifteenth century as the principal conduit for commercial traffic between the eastern Baltic region and the Atlantic seaboard. Farther to the east, at Riga and Reval, protectionist ordinances discouraged foreign mercantile interests, and the same held true for Lübeck and neighbouring towns within the Wendish sector of the German Hanse. Although there were restrictions at Danzig as well, the English had long maintained a commercial presence there. Even so, for major cloth exporters from Hull, London, and southern England, the Baltic was a distant secondary market so long as a trade corridor through the Low Countries remained open. Ties with Prussia were sustained more consistently by Englishmen shipping to and from the East Anglian port of Lynn. In the aftermath of the Anglo-Hanseatic War of the early 1470s, they were instrumental in re-establishing English trade at Danzig. They were equally diligent in sustaining it, while exporters from other English ports were drawn increasingly to the international entrepôts of Antwerp and Bergen op Zoom.[1] Ahead lay the challenges and opportunities of the

---

[1] J.D. Fudge, *Cargoes, Embargoes, and Emissaries* (Toronto, 1995), pp. 98-101, 158-60.

sixteenth century, as commercial networks continued to adjust to the expansion of the northern seaborne economy.

The Hanseatic trade at Lynn, always the preserve of 'Easterlings' from Hamburg or the Baltic ports, was geared exclusively to northern markets. For Cologners and merchants from the lower Rhineland, so prominent at the Hanse's Steelyard enclave in the English capital, Lynn was of no importance. While German merchants in London sent vast quantities of woollen cloth to markets in Brabant, their counterparts at Lynn did not. Although the Hanse had received waterfront depots at Lynn and Boston, according to the terms of peace in 1474, the post-war period saw Hanseatic merchants concentrate much of their cloth export business in London and Hull. They had all but abandoned Boston by the end of the century. The fate of the Lynn *comptoir* depended entirely on its use by skippers from Danzig.

Shipping patterns relating to Lynn's overseas trade are discernible in extant particulars of Exchequer customs, which list the arrivals and departures of ships, their cargoes, and the values assigned to goods on which *ad* valorem customs and subsidies were paid. Duties on broadcloths were not *ad valorem*, so we must rely instead on comparably low estimated values, such as £3 sterling per cloth, suggested by T.H. Lloyd.[2] Estimated and assigned values do not, however, reflect substantially higher retail prices for woollens and other commodities. Complementing these records are the registers of the Danish toll collectors at Helsingør, who monitored traffic to and from the Baltic via the Sound and recorded the names of ships' masters and their provenances.[3]

There were two weekly markets in Lynn, and the town held fairs twice annually. The port also served a thriving waterborne trade to numerous inland centres, such as Ely and Cambridge. Barges and crayers plying the River Ouse and its tributaries carried commercial traffic to and from at least six counties. Of particular importance to Lynn's merchants was the annual Sturbridge Fair near Cambridge, to which they brought stockfish from Iceland and coal from northern England. There, too, they could buy cloth and deliver wares imported

---

[2] Public Record Office, London (hereafter PRO), E 122 Exchequer Customs Accounts. T.H. Lloyd, *England and the German Hanse 1157-1611* (Cambridge, 1991), p. 273. The pitfalls of relying on customs records for statistical data are discussed in N.J. Williams, *The Maritime Trade of the East Anglian Ports 1550-1590* (Oxford, 1988), pp. 1-49.

[3] Rigsarkivet, Copenhagen (*hereafter* RA), Øresunds toldregnskaber 1528, 1536-1547. An inventory of *English* skippers in these particular Sound Toll registers is appended to a commentary on the shipping patterns in J.D. Fudge, 'Home Ports and Destinations. English Shipping in the Baltic Trade, 1536-1547', *The Northern Mariner* 9 (1999), pp. 13-24.

from beyond the seas: Bordeaux wines, manufactured items from the Low Countries and heavy, bulky materials from the eastern Baltic.[4]

In the trade from Danzig cargoes of lumber, especially clapholts and waynscots, were augmented with bowstaves, pitch, and tar. Manufactured wares such as counters, tables and chests were also shipped, but the other mainstay of the Prussian export trade was grain. Shipments to England were not uncommon, although imports into Lynn were rare. Indeed, it was the export of grain produced locally, together with butter and cheese, that linked Lynn's economy to other English ports as well as Calais and the Low Countries.[5] Other imports to Lynn included sturgeon and eels, as well as wax, yarn, flax and iron, especially osmund. On the whole, then, Baltic cargoes consisted of fish, high-bulk raw materials and semi-finished items. Only occasionally were they supplemented with more exotic fare, such as hawks and gerfalcons.

England's export economy depended on woollen cloth but London dominated this sector, and cloth shipments ceased to be crucial to Lynn. By the mid 1530s Hanseatic merchants coming to the port had no serious interest in this trade and denizen shipments were modest at best. Nevertheless, of the cloth that was exported from Lynn, much was destined for Danzig. Consignments typically included worsteds and cheaper varieties converted to broadcloth equivalents for customs purposes. In addition to textiles, rabbit pelts (conies), lead and lambfells were exported to Prussia. So too was salt, including 'sallt de baye', which occasionally found its way from the Biscay coast to the Baltic via Lynn. These were the goods for which there was a demand at Danzig, but they were not all that Lynn could offer. Leather shoes, caps, horseshoes and 'cremery wares' were exported to Iceland and the Low Countries by many of the same merchants active in the Baltic sector. Moreover, the ships they dispatched to Iceland each year often carried quantities of osmund and lumber.[6]

[4] Williams, *East Anglian Ports*, pp. 58-60; D.M. Owen (ed.), *The Making of King's Lynn*, (1984) pp. 260-2; J.S. Brewer, J. Gairdner and R.H. Brodie (eds.), *Letters and Papers Foreign and Domestic of the Reign of Henry VIII* (hereafter LP) (1862-1932), XII/2 nr. 411(24).

[5] LP, V nr. 1706, VI nr. 480; H.J. Smit (ed.), *Bronnen tot de Geschiedenis van den Handel met England, Schotland en Ierland*, ('s-Gravenhage, 1928-50), II/1 nr. 547, 578.

[6] The butter, grain, osmund and waynscots carried by John Watson, John Peterson and John Manby in 1541 typify cargoes bound for Iceland. All three skippers returned to Lynn with stockfish. PRO, E 122/99/26.

Patterns of shipping and trade

The second decade of the sixteenth century was characterised by well-documented political attacks against Hanseatic interests in England, originating primarily with London mercers, and orchestrated by the chancellor, Thomas Wolsey.[7] They were aimed at ancient privileges that included preferential customs and subsidies. Principal targets were the men of the Steelyard and complaints were usually bound up with demands for reciprocal trading rights at Danzig. Relations between England and the Hanse were unsettled through the 1520s, perhaps contributing to the inconsistency of Hanseatic trade at Lynn. Affecting Anglo-Baltic trade just as profoundly were hostilities between Denmark and the Hanse's Wendish towns, which jeopardised passage through the Sound, beginning in 1510. Shipping in the Eastern Baltic was particularly vulnerable. In 1511 an English ship, freighted at Danzig for Lynn merchants Christofer Brodbank and Nicholas Bateman, fell victim to privateers from Stralsund. Indiscriminate attacks on neutral shipping were commonplace over the next three years – a situation exacerbated by the deployment of warships in the North Sea during England's naval conflict with France.[8] In 1513 English merchantmen did not bring large consignments of bulk goods to Lynn and the only Baltic freight was offloaded from a Danzig ship. It belonged to a single consignee, who, together with the ship's master and one other merchant, also owned the outbound cargo of lead, cloth, and conies. No substantial Baltic cargoes arrived in 1514, nor did any Hanseatic ships call at Lynn during that year. The malaise, reflected in annual cloth exports as well as correspondingly low *ad valorem* poundage and petty custom revenues, continued for half a decade.[9]

War between the Danes and Swedes hindered commercial traffic still further. Another English ship was plundered in Baltic waters and, in retaliation, a

---

[7] Lloyd, German Hanse, pp. 251-54; D. Schafer (ed), *Hanserecesse* (hereafter HR), series III, 1477-1530, (Leipzig, 1890-1913), series IV, 1531-1537, K. Friedland and G. Wentz (eds.), (Weimar, 1941 / Köln, 1970), III 7 nr. *188*, 203-11.

[8] HR, III 5 nr. 607; 6 nr. 9-20, 65-85, 185-88, 196#109, 203, 270, 468, 470; 7 nr. 39#112-16, 43, 110#7,15, 455#7,8, 457#13; IV 2 nr. 86#479, 95#7,8,23; *Regesta Diplomatica Historiae Danicae*, series II, 1448-1536, (Copenhagen, 1885-92), nr. 9750, 9776; *Diplomatarium Islandicum*, (Reykjavik, 1915-25), *XI* nr. 65#16, 73.

[9] PRO, E 122/99/2-4; E 356/25; E.M. Carus-Wilson and O. Coleman (eds.), *England's Export Trade 1275-1547*, (Oxford, 1967), p.114.

Hanseatic vessel was arrested at Hull.[10] At Lynn, meanwhile, Hanseatic traders continued to keep a markedly low profile, as the claims of Bateman and Broadbank remained unsettled. In the summer of 1519, preparatory to an upcoming Anglo-Hanseatic summit, the issue was used to intimidate the German merchant community in London. Wolsey ridiculed the Hanse men as being worse than Scots and ordered them to pay damages. However, when Brodbank and Bateman turned up at the Steelyard brandishing the chancellor's decree, they refused to do so, preferring instead a return to the Star Chamber, where they insisted it be recorded that they gave the money under duress. Only then was it handed over – all £500 of it in a sealed leather bag.[11]

The recorded trade at Lynn in 1518 and 1519 points to a pattern that became the norm a decade later, as East Anglian merchants displaced their German counterparts. Hanseatic merchandise offloaded from two Danzig ships in 1518 was customed only to their captains. Denizens investing in the Baltic trade used an English vessel, the *Clement* of Lynn. Again in 1519 denizen and Hanseatic traders placed goods in English and Prussian vessels. The English consignees were part of a coterie of denizens preponderant in Lynn's Baltic trade for the next two decades.[12]

The summer of 1520 saw the first round of discussions between English and Hanseatic delegates at Bruges. Making the voyage to the Baltic that year was the *Margaret* of Lynn, freighted in April with the goods of William Kenette, William Blowfeld, and Steven Bateman. The same men owned the flax, wood, sturgeon, and eels that the ship brought home in August. No Hanseatic craft came to Lynn in 1520. Instead, in a rare instance of English merchants using a carrier from the Low Countries for the return leg of a Baltic venture, more bulk cargo arrived in the *Berre* of Zierikzee.[13] Reluctance to use Prussian carriers may have been due to Danzig's strained relations with Denmark. This, rather than the stalled Anglo-Hanseatic negotiations, stifled Anglo-Baltic commerce the following year. Returning from his bloody foray into Sweden, Christian II punished Danzig for assisting his Swedish enemies. The Sound was closed and a hundred salt-laden ships bound for the eastern Baltic were forced to turn back. Ten Danzig merchantmen, several of them returning from England with lead

[10] *Regesta Diplomatica*, II nr. 10255, 10302, 10376; *HR*, III 7 nr. 204-10; PRO, C 1/853/25-27.

[11] HR, III 7 nr. 39#112-116, 45#59, 110#7, 203-11; *LP*, III/1 nr. 347#6.

[12] PRO, E 122/99/5, 6, 8, 9.

[13] PRO, E 122/99/11. The Anglo-Hanseatic talks: *HR*, III 7 nr. 332; LP, III/1 nr. 974, 978-9.

and cloth, were confiscated.[14] Lübeck and the Wendish towns were soon drawn into the fray and, along with Danzig, contributed to Christian's overthrow and the installation of his uncle, Frederick I, in late 1523. Throughout this period direct commercial traffic between the Baltic and the Atlantic seaboard was disrupted. Shipping between Danzig and Lynn does not appear to have normalised until the later 1520s.[15]

Even so, by the end of the decade Lynn's Baltic trade was firmly in English hands. Up to sixteen denizens participated directly, occasionally employing Prussian carriers and also sending two or more of their own vessels to Danzig each year.[16] Of the two dozen English captains who freighted their vessels there in 1530, four came from Lynn. They brought cloth and rabbit pelts belonging to Kenette and his associates and returned home with over £250 worth of goods for the same merchants. The following summer this same group of merchants dispatched three ships to Prussia.[17]

Lynn's merchants also routinely sent several ships to Iceland each year and some Lynn men may have been part of a fracas there in 1532 that involved Danish authorities and men from Bremen and Hamburg. There were several English casualties[18] but the affray did not precipitate a suspension of England's Icelandic fishery, nor were there discernible consequences for the traffic to and from Prussia. The same can also be said of the succession war of the mid 1530s, following the death of Frederick I. It played havoc with international shipping,[19] yet does not seem to have had a long-term, detrimental impact on England's Baltic trade although English merchants were certainly inconvenienced by it. Danzig assisted the successful claimant, Christian III, and in 1535 several Prussian hulks, some carrying goods for Englishmen, were detained by rival Lübeckers. English merchantmen, delayed and stripped of ordnance at Copenhagen, sailed on to Danzig. They spent the rest of the summer there

---

[14] T. Hirsch et al (ed), *Scriptores Rerum Prussicarum*, (Leipzig, 1861-74), V *522*.

[15] PRO, E 122/99/15, 16, 17; E 122/205/2, 3.

[16] RA, Øresunds toldregnskaber 1528, 6, 17; PRO, E 122/99/16, 17.

[17] Three Lynn ships went to Danzig in 1530: the *Barnaby*, the *Thomas*, and the *Martin*, commanded by Robert Bray, John Hatfeld, and John Makmayd. They were joined by John Mowell's *Mary James* of Brightlingsea. PRO, E 122/99/18; *Archiwum Panstwowe w Gdansku* 300.19/11. 95v, 130, 233, 245. In 1531 Baltic cargoes were brought back in the *Barnaby*, now captained by Raff Hardyng, John Moller's *James* of 'Saynte Tollous', and Robert Glass's *Mary Michell* of Lynn. PRO, E 122/99/19.

[18] G. Schanz, *Englische Handelspolitik gegen Ende des Mittelalters*, (Leipzig, 1881), II nr. 106; *Diplomatarium Islandicum*, XI nr. 104; *LP*, V nr. 1417, 1633, *HR*, IV 2 nr. 86#481.

[19] *HR*, IV 2 nr. 74, 101, 102, 121, 124#10, 144.

because civic authorities would not permit them to be freighted without assurances from Denmark regarding their return passage. When a dozen of them did reach the Sound in late August they were detained again, this time by captains acting on Christian III's behalf. Blaming their misfortune on the delay in Prussia, English merchants clamoured for the arrest of Danzigers' property in England. The Crown obliged, and there was retaliation in kind. Although nine of the ships returned home by late November with their cargoes intact, goods in Danzig and London remained impounded until early in the New Year.[20] Related correspondence indicates that the vessels were from London and Newcastle. In any case the incident, like the one in Iceland, did not deter ventures in the later 1530s. Denizens trading from Lynn to Prussia consistently used English carriers: four in 1536, two the following summer, and three more in 1538.[21] The summer of 1539 saw the *Christofer* of Newcastle and the *Peter* of Lynn make the return voyage from Lynn to Danzig.[22]

The 1530s may have marked a strengthening of England's Baltic trade, as Lloyd has suggested, due in part to a reduction in the trade of Danzigers at Hull and Lynn.[23] Certainly, in contrast to East Anglian merchants shipping to and from Prussia, Hanseatic activity at Lynn was marginal and intermittent. Merchants of the Hanse frequently complained that they were made to pay exorbitant duties on lead shipments from east coast ports, including Lynn. Few of them now did business there. Lumber delivered from two Danzig hulks in 1530 was customed to the ships' captains. There was no recorded trade the

---

[20] P. Simson (ed), *Danziger Inventar 1531-1591* (hereafter DI), (Leipzig, 1913), nr. 641, 649, 751, 783, 794-6, 819, 829, 867; G. Schanz, Englische Handelspolitik, II nr. 107-8; HR, IV 2 nr. 187, 337; LP, VIII nr. 1170, IX nr. 246, 285-6, 290-1, 323, 417, 594, 732, 776, 831, 861, X nr. 283; *Regesta Diplomatica*, II nr. 14368; K. Hohlbaum(ed.), *Kölner Inventar*, (Leipzig, 1896), nr. 65, 67, 70.

[21] The Danish records list four skippers from Lynn in 1536 and two in 1537, including Robert Bray. It is not certain that they left from or returned to Lynn, though in Bray's case it seems likely. The customs ledger for 1538 confirms the Danish tally of three ships: John Harryson's *Robert* of Newcastle, Robert Wrenche's *Trinity* of Burnham and Nicholas Foster's *Anne* of Lynn. RA, Øresunds toldregnskaber 1536, 11-12, 19; 1537, 12, 32; 1538, 27-29, 37, 40, 43; PRO, E122/99/23; N.E. Bang (ed), *Tabeller over Skibsfart og Varetransport gennem Øresund 1497-1660*, (Copenhagen, 1906-32), I 5-7.

[22] *Tabeller*, I 8; RA, Øresunds toldregnskaber 1539, 35, 37, 56, 58; PRO, E 122/99/24. Only a dozen English ships sailed to Danzig in 1539.

[23] Lloyd, *German Hanse*, p. 288.

following summer and very little in the mid 1530s.[24] Three Danzig ships did bring Baltic freight in 1538 but all of it belonged to Englishmen. In subsequent years the trade of the Easterlings was sporadic.[25]

For Lynn's own Baltic traders the 1540s began well enough, but the middle of the decade brought a series of setbacks. Six of more than thirty English vessels clearing the Sound in 1540 were from Lynn.[26] Among the many Englishmen in Prussia that summer was London merchant and Crown agent William Watson, armed with a letter from Henry VIII requesting fair treatment for his English subjects. Evidently they presumed to assert trading privileges comparable to those of Hanseatic merchants in England and by mid June some of them, having worn out their welcome, were under arrest. Indignant pleas soon reached London, where the Privy Council required the Steelyard aldermen to answer complaints that Englishmen in Prussia were prohibited from trading with foreigners. Indeed, this was still true, but Danzig offered no concessions. The following summer Watson and his colleagues persisted in defying their Prussian hosts, whose frustration paralleled the consternation of a Steelyard fellowship always vulnerable to retaliation by the English government. Watson himself admitted to bargaining with a Polish merchant and then balked at paying a hefty fine for doing so, insolence that earned him a brief stay in a 'vyle and stynkyng prison'. Accusing the Danzig authorities of extortion, he urged that compensation be wrung from the Danzigers in London.[27] He also claimed to speak for his fellow countrymen, though it is open to question whether Lynn's merchants were at all well served when he vexed Danzig's civic oligarchy. The king's man was a Londoner, who, as well as buying supplies for the navy, dealt in large quantities of English cloth. His attempt to bypass Prussian middlemen might have appealed to entrepreneurs from southern England and Yorkshire hopeful of expanding overseas markets for woollens. For Norfolk men, whose modest business at Danzig was not dominated by cloth shipments, the controversy was unnecessary, if not counter-productive. They had managed to

---

[24] HR, III 5 nr. 115#11; 7 nr. 110#4, 340#13; IV 2 nr. 95#16. Goods to the value of £56 were customed to Hanseatic merchants in 1535. In 1534 Hanseatic goods amounted to twelve cloths and £33 worth of other merchandise. PRO, E 122/99/21; E 356/26.

[25] RA, Øresunds toldregnskaber 1541, 35, 48; PRO, E 122/99/24, 26; E 356/26.

[26] RA, Øresunds toldregnskaber 1540, 20, 22, 26, 28.

[27] DI, nr. 1317, 1375, 1378, 1404-5, 1414, 1463, 1514, 1547, 1554. Thereto: DI, nr. 1614, 1617, 1621, 1624, 1633, 1649-50, 1655, 1664-6, 1674, 1683-4, 1686, 1696; Sir Harry Nicholas (ed), *Proceedings and Ordinances of the Privy Council*, (London, 1837), VII 252, 301, 308-9, 318. *Watson's* lament: PRO, STAC 2/30/2.

turn a profit there for many decades, despite the protectionist policies, and without the help of William Watson.

Lynn's denizen cloth trade declined steadily after 1500 and by the early 1540s the Prussian market helped to sustain what was left of it but the volume was insignificant. However, cloth exports were augmented with other merchandise that, prior to 1530, added between £20 and £40 annually to the value of trade to Danzig. As their cloth exports dwindled during the next two decades, denizens continued to ship a range of other goods: conies, lambfells, lead, salt and a variety of cheap textiles. Between 1538 and 1542 English merchants consistently sent £40 to £80 worth of hides and lead to Danzig each summer. Even so, their outbound shipments, including cloth exports, seldom equalled the value of their imports from Prussia. For a three-year period beginning in 1529, denizens brought in about £200 worth of Baltic freight annually, only slightly less than the average a decade later. Hanseatic woollen exports usually left Lynn with Danzig carriers, although shipments seldom exceeded two or three dozen units in most years, except between 1527 and 1530.[28] After that the Hanseatic presence at Lynn was intermittent. In years when there were Hanseatic cloth exports, it was unusual for their value to exceed or even equal that of the goods imported by Hanse men.

Lynn's merchants sent a pair of ships to Prussia in 1541 and three the following year.[29] Thereafter the acrimony in Danzig coincided with more uncertainty regarding freedom of the seas. When Christian III closed the Sound to ships from the Habsburg Low Countries in 1543, Henry VIII's alliance with Emperor Charles raised doubts about other vessels as well. So serious were the misgivings in England that as late as April ships readied for the Iceland voyage still had not departed. William Watson, attempting to transship woollens to Danzig via Hamburg and Lübeck with German carriers, held them in Lübeck rather than chance the onward voyage. It was late August before Henry received word from Denmark that Englishmen would be allowed through the Sound and by then the shipping season was lost. Only one vessel from England paid the toll at Helsingør[30] and fewer than usual Prussian carriers. For them and others from

---

[28] Carus-Wilson and Coleman, *England's Export Trade*, pp.113-19.

[29] Robert Lyell and Lawrence Dowffe in the *James* of Newcastle and the *Trenyte* of London made the voyage in 1541. PRO, E 122/99/26; *RA*, Øresunds toldregnskaber 1541, 21, 35, 37. In 1542 John Lawrence, Nicholas Foster, and Edmund Cumerforthe took three Lynn ships, the *Anthony*, the *Mary James* and the *Gregory*. PRO, E 122/99/27; *RA*, Øresunds toldregnskaber 1542, *22*, 31, 32, 39.

[30] LP, XVIII/1 nr. 416, 781, 878; XVIII/2 nr. 152; *RA*, Øresunds toldregnskaber 1543, 3.

the Low Countries, the interruption lasted only until Denmark made peace with the Emperor the following spring. Hanseatic traffic quickly normalised[31] but few English vessels returned to eastern waters, for Henry now waged war on France and Scotland. Once again, commercial traffic was at risk. Moreover, numerous merchant ships and their crews were pressed into royal service and in December 1544 a royal proclamation authorised all English subjects to equip vessels and take to the sea against the Scots and French.[32]

A great part of England's merchant marine was co-opted into the war effort. Dozens of English and foreign merchantmen, including several from Danzig and other German ports, were requisitioned by the Crown.[33] English warships and individuals empowered by the royal decree attacked neutral shipping, thus contributing to a serious deterioration of Anglo-Habsburg relations. Fewer carriers were available for commercial ventures, and local skippers no longer made the annual trip to Danzig. For the time being Lynn had no semblance of an Iceland fleet either and the Easterlings, whose trade at Lynn was irregular anyway, avoided the port almost completely. Even when the war ended in 1546 and Anglo-Baltic traffic showed signs of reviving, Lynn's merchants were slow to respond. Although a half dozen English ships sailed through the Sound that summer, none brought Baltic cargoes back to Lynn.[34]

Little overseas trade was recorded at Lynn in the mid 1540s although the situation was not entirely bleak. When the siege of Boulogne ended in September 1544, grain and provisions could be shipped there free from export duties. Lynn merchant Thomas Water, who already supplied Calais and Berwick, took advantage of the opportunity; he was unlikely to have been the only one to do so. Such conventional trade was supplemented by potentially lucrative privateering expeditions. Several Lynn merchants were implicated in the seizures of ships, not all of which belonged to the king's enemies. Among the

---

[31] LP, XIX/1 nr. 536, 567; DI, nr. 1825; *Tabeller*, I 12-15; *PRO*, E 122/99/31.

[32] LP, XIX/1 nr. 84, 147, 269, 353, 550, 996; DI, nr. 1816, 1819; E. Jones, 'Merchant Shipping in Peace and War: the Bristol Marine of the 1540s', *Northern Seas Yearbook*, (1996), pp.36-40; P.L. Hughes and J.F. Larkin (eds.), *Tudor Royal Proclamations*, (New Haven, 1964), I nr. 243.

[33] DI, nr. 1886-7, 1897, 2006; PRO, E 122/64/18-19; E 122/109/12; LP, XVIII/1 nr. 59, 68, 75, 434; XVIII/2 nr. 115, 194, 224(2), 355, 502, 600, 617; XX/1 nr. 1295, 1324; XX/2 nr. 12, 27(2), 38, 39, 49, 72.

[34] RA, Øresunds toldregnskaber *1546*, 1547; *Tabeller*, I 15-16; PRO, E 122/99/34, 35.

most successful of these new privateers was William Overende, a future mayor, who had been trading to Danzig only two years before.[35]

Merchants, masters and their ships

Although some of Lynn's merchants concentrated on the Baltic sector, for several the Danzig market was but one facet of a trade that integrated a variety of commercial interests. Two sample years demonstrate both the diversity and the specialisation. Well over forty denizens had cargoes customed either for import or export in 1530, including sixteen Baltic traders.[36] Of these, eleven were also involved in other overseas ventures, such as the fishing/trading expeditions to Iceland. A number of them imported Bay salt, wood, wine, herring and glass, indicative of trade to Biscay or the Low Countries. But the Baltic sector, like the Iceland trade, also attracted specialists. Five of those who did business in Prussia had no other recorded trade, and the value of their cargoes reflects various levels of capital investment. With £8 worth of exported conies and little over twice that much in imported goods, William Blowfeld was a relatively minor player. Another merchant who shipped £8 worth of rabbit skins to Danzig was William Kenette. He sent eight cloths as well, and his return cargo was valued at almost £60.

Turning to 1541, we find about thirty merchants trading overseas, including eleven to the Baltic.[37] The value of Kenette's goods in that sphere was considerably lower than it had been a decade earlier, but this year he invested in the Iceland venture as well. Of the four merchants who focused exclusively on the Prussian market, Richard Osse was the leader, exporting £14 10s worth of goods and importing merchandise valued in excess of £53. An even more valuable consignment of Baltic freight should be considered an anomaly, since it belonged to William Watson who normally shipped his timber and cables to Hull and London. He used Lynn only occasionally. However, given the difficulties he claimed to be encountering in 1541, he may well have been anxious to get his goods safely out of Danzig aboard any ships bound for an

---

[35] J. Roche Dasent (ed.), *Acts of the Privy Council of England*, new series, (London, 1890), I 79, 163, 199, 246, 263, 378; *LP*, XVIII/1 nr. 90; XX/1 nr. 139, 294, 483, 518, 557, 630, 755, 841, 997; XX/2 nr. 175, 397; Hughes and Larkin, *Tudor Royal Proclamations*, I nr. 239; PRO, E 122/99/27; *Calendar of the Freemen of Lynn 1292 -1836*, (Norwich, 1913), p.94.

[36] PRO, E 122/99/18 (the *Exchequer* year from Michaelmas 1529 to Michaelmas 1530).

[37] PRO, E 122/99/26 (the Exchequer year from Michaelmas 1540 to Michaelmas 1541).

English port. One of the available carriers was Christian Telskow, who regularly went to Lynn each summer.

Some denizens who imported substantial quantities of Baltic freight but had no recorded trade in other sectors were undoubtedly employed as factors, transacting business on behalf of various merchants and then having entire cargoes delivered and customed at Lynn in their own names. Richard Osse, for instance, worked in the Baltic trade throughout the 1530s, and on at least one occasion was Blowfeld's agent at Danzig. With him there was William Hall, also prominent in the trade for many years. In the late 1530s and again in 1541, Baltic freight delivered at Lynn was customed jointly to Hall and Osse.[38]

At some point prior to this a dispute arose with ship-owner Cecily Some over a flax cargo Osse had placed in her ship at Danzig.[39] It belonged to Blowfeld. Both Osse and Hall were aboard when, nearing Lynn on the homeward voyage, the ship began to take on water, resulting in spoilage of some of the cargo. Subsequent distribution of the merchantable portion was overseen by three members of the civic council: Kenette, Sybram Paulson, and Edward Baker. Blowfeld got only half of what Osse had purchased for him, but the widow, Cecily Some, sought full payment for the freight charges. All of the individuals involved in the dispute had long-term connections with the Baltic trade. William Blowfeld had been carrying on a modest but consistent trade to Danzig for the better part of two decades. The involvement of Baker, Kenette, Paulson, Osse, and Hall can be traced to the 1520s, and all of them except Paulson were part of the core group of denizens trading to Prussia throughout the 1530s. Cecily Some, too, was acquainted with the Danzig market, having shipped cloth and lead there in 1518 in exchange for wax, eels, flax and pitch. Some's overseas investments typify the diversity that characterised the maritime trade of many of her compatriots. In the 1520s there were grain and lead exports to the Low Countries and return cargoes of soap, glass, salt, woad, herring and 'orthen potts'. In 1527, a year when no Lynn skippers sailed to Danzig, Some had grain, osmund and horseshoes aboard one of the ships bound for Iceland and owned a share of the stockfish that it brought home in July. In the autumn of 1529 she had kerseys customed for export, probably to Brabant. As was customary for successful members of the merchant community, Cecily Some also sponsored worthy individuals who sought the liberty of Lynn and the right to trade there. At least three gained 'freeman' status as her apprentices. Whether she owned

---

[38] PRO, E 122/99/23, 24, 26.

[39] PRO, C 1/736/64-67. The relevant petitions date to the chancellorship of Thomas Audley, 1533-38.

more than one ship is uncertain but at the time of her quarrel with Blowfeld she was not Lynn's only matron entrepreneur in the shipping business. The *Trinity*, part of Lynn's Iceland fleet in 1533, was owned jointly by William Hall and Katherine Crampe.[40]

Of course, not all denizen merchants trading from Lynn to Danzig were burgesses of Lynn; some came from Norwich and perhaps some from Cambridge as well. They did not always use the port of Lynn, nor was their foreign trade necessarily concentrated in the Baltic sector. Substantial business interests in France, the Low Countries and/or the coastal traffic were not uncommon. John Paris, for instance, was a Norwich merchant involved in Baltic ventures in the 1520s and 1530s, whose circle of Norwich associates included other Baltic traders Gregory Cansse and Reynold Lytylprow. At Danzig they were served by Thomas Lappage of Ipswich, who arranged for the shipment of Baltic goods to Yarmouth, Norwich's outport. There, John Paris could also be found chartering ships for France, buying and selling imported wine cargoes and sending grain consignments across the Narrow Seas to Veere and Middelburg. In the Low Countries he was represented by yet another Norwich merchant, William Waller.[41]

Most denizens within Lynn's maritime trading community had interests in the grain trade.[42] Surplus grain from the Norfolk hinterland reached Ireland, Scotland, Calais, London and the border garrison at Berwick from Lynn and Yarmouth. Among the principal exporters in the 1520s were Thomas Miller and John Brown who invested in the trade to Prussia as well. Cereals and consignments of mixed cargo were also sent to Iceland in return for fish. Some of the fish, such as the 1,500 ling sold by John Water to London tallow chandler James Quyk in 1528, were delivered to Sturbridge.[43] Merchants such as Sybram Paulson, Thomas and John Water and others, owned the ships they used in this trade and they probably used them in the Baltic trade too. Thomas Water was part owner of at least two ships in Lynn's Iceland fleet in the 1530s, as well as

---

[40] PRO, SP 1/80/61-72; E 122/99/5, 6, 18; E 122/205/2, 3; *Calendar of the Freemen of Lynn*, 83, 87, 89.

[41] PRO, E 122/99/18; E 122/205/2-4; C 1/552/9, C 1/557/17, C 1/771/46, C 1/866/13-14, C 1/867/13-15, C 1/871/10-11, C 1/872/24-5, C 1/874/22, C 1/1051/30; *LP*, V nr. 356, VI nr. 171, 189; *Bronnen*, II/1 nr. 403, 423, 592; *DI*, nr. 19. Thomas Lappage had many business interests, including the Iceland fishery. *PRO*, C 1/842/13-16; HCA 24/1a/12.

[42] *LP*, V nr. 413, 766(22, 23), 884, 1706, VI nr. 185-6, 385, 480, 1129; V. Parker, *The Making of King's Lynn*, (London, 1971), p.118.

[43] PRO, C 1/667/40.

the *Barke* of Lynn, used for voyages to Iceland and Bordeaux. In 1543 he was provisioning the king's northern garrisons and also furnishing ships of war.[44]

Restrictions on grain exports were not uncommon however, and East Anglian merchants frequently paid fines for shipping contrary to proclamation.[45] An Admiralty Court investigation into shipments to the Low Countries in 1541 required depositions from several Lynn merchants who were, or had been, part of the Baltic trade as well.[46] They included Thomas Miller and Richard Permeter: the latter had claimed the liberty of the town in 1523 as Miller's apprentice. The focus of the enquiry was Edward Baker a merchant who continued to export grain and import stockfish from Iceland although he no longer invested directly in Baltic ventures. Richard Permeter and Thomas Nesse were the only Lynn merchants who traded to Danzig in the early 1540s.

Amongst the ships' masters employed by these merchants was Robert Bray, a freeman of Lynn,who sailed the *Barnaby* to Prussia and back in 1530. He also made a voyage to Iceland the following year at the helm of one of John Water's ships, the *Barbara.*[47] As well as numerous voyages to Prussia and Iceland, Bray also sailed to the Low Countries. Lynn, however, was not the provenance of all the skippers or ships chartered for Baltic enterprises. Newcastle men – Robert Lyell, John Rossell, John Lawrence, and others – appear repeatedly in the Danish toll registers. The rubric, 'aff Nykastell', with which so many are identified, did not imply that direct traffic between the Tyne and Danzig was the cornerstone of Anglo-Baltic commerce. In fact Rossell's port of lading in 1539 was Lynn, as it was for Lyell two years later. In 1541 Lawrence's Baltic voyage originated in Hull, but in 1542 he departed from and returned to Lynn.[48] Just as the Newcastle captains served any number of other east coast ports, Lynn skippers could often be found elsewhere. Nicholas Foster, for instance, operated

---

[44] PRO, SP 1/80/61-*72*; HCA 13/2/247v; *Acts of the Privy Council of England*, I 79, 93.

[45] LP, V nr. 356, 413, 451, 1707; Hughes and Larkin, *Tudor Royal Proclamations*, I nr. 94, 134, 225, 258-9, 262-3, 269; *PRO*, STAC 2/22/17, 2/23/183, 2/27/80, 2/27/93, 2/29/96.

[46] PRO, STAC 2/29/*175.*

[47] PRO, SP 1/80/61-72; E 122/99/18, 19; *Archiwum Panstwowe w Gdansku*: 300.19/11. 233.

[48] PRO, E 122/99/24, 26, 27; E 122/64/15; *RA*, Øresunds toldregnskaber 1539, 35, 58; 1541, 21, 23, 37, 39; 1542, 31, 39; Fudge, 'Home Ports and Destinations.'

primarily on the Lynn/Danzig run but in 1541 he undertook a round voyage from Yarmouth.[49]

Unlike the wool-laden ships bound for Calais from Hull, Boston and London, those sailing to Prussia departed independently or in small groups, rather than in large fleets. While it was not unusual for London mercers to raise 'conduit money' and hire armed escort vessels to escort shipments to and from Brabant, skippers plying northern waters fended for themselves.[50] However, consecutive entries in both the English and Danish records suggest that for the Baltic leg of the voyage – from the Sound to Danzig – and perhaps for most of the return trip to England, they may have sailed in close formation.

English merchant ships chartered for Danzig usually made one voyage a year. Clearing from Lynn in April or early May, they were normally home again before mid August, in plenty of time to offload cargoes destined for the September fair at Sturbridge. The Iceland ships had a similar voyage pattern. During the winter ships were used in the coastal trade or employed in voyages to the Low Countries. For example, John Werell, who sailed the *Peter* of Lynn to Danzig in the summer of 1539, had left Lynn the previous October with a substantial grain cargo returning in January 1539 with Bay salt, herring, wine, wood and iron.[51] The timing of the voyages, together with the cargo descriptions, suggests that he had carried goods to be sold at the autumn and winter fairs at Antwerp and Bergen op Zoom. Robert Lyell provides another example. In December 1540 he was in Zealand with the *James* of Newcastle and by mid May was on his way to Danzig with that ship, having weighed anchor at Lynn.[52] Vessels serving Lynn's Baltic traders between April and August were not sent to Iceland in the same year. An Iceland voyage was a seasonal enterprise that employed ships between February and August. Hanseatic ships sometimes came to Lynn as early as May but usually came in July or August either in company with, or within days of the arrival of English vessels returning from the Baltic.

---

[49] Foster often sailed from Lynn. PRO, E 122/99/23, 27; *RA*, Øresunds toldregnskaber 1538, 28, 43; 1540, 22, 51; 1542, 31, 39. The 1541 toll register lists John Wolter 'aff Jarmoe' [Yarmouth], and Yarmouth customs particulars indicate John Walters was the principal owner of outbound cargo in the ship commanded by Foster. He also owned £75 worth of bulk freight and hawks that Foster returned with in August. He may have owned the ship and/or made the voyage to Danzig. PRO, E 122/210/5; RA, Øresunds toldregnskaber 1541, 21, 34.

[50] LP, VI nr. 653; L. Lyell and F.D. Watney (eds.), *Acts of Court of the Mercers' Company 1453-1527*, (*Cambridge*, 1936), 419, 535, 542-3, 548-9, 633-4.

[51] PRO, E 122/99/24.

[52] PRO, E 122/99/26; *Bronnen*, II/1 nr. 673(II).

Although it was feasible to make a return voyage twice in one season, the modest volume of Hanseatic trade and the increased use of English carriers meant that Prussian captains seldom did so.

A presence maintained

In his study of East Anglian ports in the later sixteenth century N.J. Williams suggested that as late as 1567 the greater part of trade between Lynn and Danzig was carried in foreign craft.[53] If this was so, then a profound transition must have occurred after the mid-1540s, because up until then precisely the opposite was true. English merchantmen rather than Hanseatic or Dutch vessels accounted for most of the shipping employed in the Danzig trade. Lynn was by no means the provenance of all the English ships employed in the traffic, but it clearly was for many of them. Hanseatic skippers certainly brought cargoes to Lynn but no more frequently than their English counterparts. Even by the 1530s the trade of the Easterlings was intermittent and seldom comparable to that of denizens.

If, as Williams contends, the early sixteenth century saw much of England's Baltic trade controlled by Dutch or Hanseatic interests, it was not true of Lynn. The Dutch did not play a significant role in direct trade between Lynn and Danzig, either as merchants or shippers. Moreover, in many years there was no recorded Hanseatic trade and even when there was, few Germans had goods customed. Foreigners may have been preponderant in ports such as Hull, where many more merchants of the Hanse had goods customed than at Lynn. Some of them also did business at the Steelyard which points to a consolidation of commercial interests at Hull and London coincidental with the Easterlings' increasingly sporadic use of Lynn as a point of entry for imports.

Lynn was of middling importance in terms of England's wide-ranging seaborne economy. While the development of a reasonably diverse export base lessened dependency on cloth exports, there were limits on the port's ability to accommodate a significantly larger share of Anglo-Baltic commerce. Its rich agricultural hinterland meant that there was no dependence on imported Baltic grain. Maintenance of the trading and fishing fleets required a steady supply of timber, tar and cordage from the Baltic, but not on a scale comparable to some of the larger ports or the royal dockyards. Given the somewhat limited capacity for expansion of their modest trade, Lynn's merchants were unlikely to take the lead in challenging the Danzig authorities over protectionist restrictions. That was the agenda of men like William Watson and others from London and Hull.

---

[53] Williams, *East Anglian Ports*, p.103.

Disputes that clouded relations between England and the German Hanse often centred on the high-volume and extremely lucrative traffic between London and the Low Countries or on English 'rights' in Prussia. For the denizens of Lynn the Danzig trade was a matter of sufficient carriers and unhindered passage. Only prolonged obstruction of the shipping lanes and/or a severe reduction in available tonnage shut it down, which was indeed the situation in the mid 1540s, as Henry VIII's reign drew to a close.

The war ran its course, only to be followed by renewed tensions at Danzig. At the end of the decade Lynn's merchants had to ride out yet another storm of controversy there. Taking the construction of new storage facilities as a measure of mercantile prosperity, Vanessa Parker suggested the mid sixteenth century marked an era of commercial expansion for Lynn. Warehouses were built to accommodate a greater volume of heavy, high-bulk goods.[54] Extant customs for the 1550s do much to confirm this impression. Departing England with substantial denizen cloth cargoes in 1552 and 1554, Lynn ships returned home with large consignments of bulk freight and of the three ships sent there in 1556, one apparently made a second trip.[55] Further evidence of a vibrant trade comes from particulars for the following year, which include rare details of destinations. One ship sailed to Hamburg and another to Reval, while six more departed 'versus Danske'. They carried the equivalent of two hundred and sixty broadcloths, returning with flax, iron, timber and tar. All were Lynn vessels and all of the consignees were Englishmen[56]. But these and later years are beyond the scope of this study. For now, the final word rests with Williams, who ascribed to Lynn's merchants a leading role in the organisation of the Eastland Company. Immediately before its incorporation in 1579 at least sixteen merchants from Lynn still carried on a regular Baltic trade.

---

[54] Parker, *Making of Kings Lynn*, pp. 118-19.

[55] PRO, E 122/100/8, 13; E 122/205/6.

[56] PRO, E 122/100/18.

Chapter 2

Kith and Kin: John Durie and the Scottish community in Scandinavia and the Baltic, 1624-34

Steve Murdoch

From the sixteenth century onwards, large trading communities drawn from all the nations of the British Isles existed throughout Scandinavia and the Baltic States. The region also witnessed a massive influx of British and Irish soldiers in the first half of the seventeenth century, mostly serving the Scandinavian monarchs during the Thirty Years' War. Added to these men came a significant number of students, theologians and academics, mostly from Scotland.[1] In a bid to help researchers interpret these migrations, the Scottish-Scandinavian Project at the University of Aberdeen has developed the *SSNE* online database.[2] It contains biographical details of individuals from Scotland, England and Ireland

---

[1] See for example Th. Fischer, *The Scots in Germany* (Edinburgh, 1902), *The Scots in Eastern and Western Prussia* (Edinburgh, 1903) and *The Scots in Sweden* (Edinburgh, 1907); A.F. Steuart, *Scottish Influences in Russian History: From the end of the 16th to the beginning of the 19th Century* (Glasgow, 1913); T. Riis, *Should Auld Acquaintance Be Forgot .... Scottish-Danish Relations c. 1450 -1707* (Odense, 1988); D Fedosov, *The Caledonian Connection: Scotland-Russia Ties, Middle Ages to Early Twentieth Century. A concise biographical list* (Aberdeen, 1996).

[2] S. Murdoch and A. Grosjean, *Scotland, Scandinavia and Northern Europe, 1580-1707* (Aberdeen, 1998 & 1999). The database can be found at www.abdn.ac.uk/history/datasets/ssne. A methodology for the database has been published. See S. Murdoch, 'The Database in Early Modern Scottish History: Scandinavia and Northern Europe, 1580-1707' in *Northern Studies* 32 (1997), pp. 83-103.

who migrated to or worked in Denmark-Norway, Sweden, Russia and the Baltic region between 1580 and 1707. Specifically, the *SSNE* houses information on military and naval officers, diplomats and members of the intellectual elite who worked in the aforementioned countries. Without such comparative information, we might be left with a skewed view of history which over-emphasises the contribution of one nationality over another.[3]

There is no room in this chapter to interpret the results from the database in anything other than sketch form. This paper does not, therefore, propose to explain or describe every Scottish migratory grouping in Scandinavia or the Baltic States during the seventeenth century. Rather it focuses on one case study which neatly knits together the Scottish mercantile, military and diplomatic communities during a snapshot of the period. In doing so it tackles a problem which continues to confuse historians, and that is to account for the 'rise from obscurity' of the Scottish clergyman, John Durie. This man famously spent his life in pursuit of a reconciliation of the Christian denominations. What has remained an enigma is his life before he came to the attention of the European theological community. Indeed, Howard Hotson has contended that John Durie, stepped 'from the central European Reformed world into the pages of English intellectual history as if from a void'.[4]

This chapter challenges the assumption that there is anything mystical in John Durie's rise to prominence. Hotson appealed for a greater understanding of the world that John Durie came from adding that 'we are singularly ill prepared to make use of the knowledge we have'.[5] Perhaps that has been because interpretations of John Durie's Irenicist career tend to focus on his later

---

[3] For example, Dr. Dimitry Fedosov published details of the Scotsman, Robert Carr, who ventured into Russia in 1618 bearing testimonials from King James VI & I. This information suggests that Carr was a man of some importance. When the wider context of his journey is looked at, however, we find that he was a relatively junior figure in a Stuart embassy led by Sir Dudley Digges and largely composed of Englishmen. That information is vital to understanding the context of Carr's journey and the wider Scottish-Russian relationship in general. See Fedosov, *The Caledonian Connection*, p. 19.

[4] Howard Hotson, 'Philosophical pedagogy in reformed central Europe between Ramus and Comenius; a survey of the continental background of the "Three Foreigners"', in Mark Greengrass, Michael Leslie and Timothy Raylor (eds.), *Samuel Hartlib and the Universal Reformation: Studies in intellectual communication* (Cambridge, 1994), p. 30.

[5] Ibid., p. 30.

theological contacts and overlook the individuals who facilitated them.[6] This is, of course, with the exception of Sir Thomas Roe who, though much dwelt upon, was of only minor significance to Durie in the 1628-31 period.[7] Thus the major biographical sources leave us with an unsatisfactory explanation of the world John Durie came from.[8]

By quarrying the information collected in the *SSNE* database it has been possible to map out a previously unidentified patronage network which sponsored Durie's theological agenda. Drawn from all strands of Scottish society, this group allowed Durie to infiltrate the most intimate circle of the Swedish king, Gustav II Adolf, by 1631 and the Danish Court between 1633-34. This has been made possible by adopting a different approach to the topic and simply running a database query to find prominent individuals who cropped up in the same vicinity as Durie throughout the chosen period. An assessment of the various strands of the Scottish community in Scandinavia and the Baltic reveals that the world from which John Durie emerged to prominence was anything but a 'void'.

Scottish communities in Scandinavia and the Baltic

The Baltic region and hinterland provided the raw materials required to guarantee the future of Scotland and England as sea-borne trading nations in the seventeenth century.[9] In particular, the English conducted a significant trade with Russia through the establishment of the English Muscovy Company in the

---

[6] The person who did most in this direction was undoubtedly Gunnar Westin. See G. Westin, *Negotiations about church unity 1628-1634: John Durie, Gustavus Adolphus, Axel Oxenstierna* (Uppsala, 1934-6).

[7] *DNB*, VI, p.261; B. Hildebrand (ed.), *Svenskt Biografiskt Lexicon* [hereafter *SBL*], XI, p.582; Fischer, *The Scots in Germany*, p. 176; Karl Brauer, *Die Unionstätigkeit John Duries unter dem Protektorat Cromwells* (Marburg, 1907), p. 2; Scott Mandelbrote, 'John Dury and the Practice of Irenicism' in Nigel Aston (ed.), *Religious Change in Europe 1650-1914: Essays for John McManners* (Oxford, 1997), p. 44.

[8] *SBL*, XI, p. 582; *DNB*, VI, p. 261; Anthony Milton, 'The Unchanged Peacemaker'? John Dury and the politics of Irenicism in England, 1628-1643' in Greengrass, Leslie and Raylor, *Samuel Hartlib*, p. 95.

[9] Scottish trade with the Baltic is discussed in an unpublished MLitt thesis by D. MacNiven, 'Merchant and Trader in Early Seventeenth Century Aberdeen' (University of Aberdeen, 1977). Also S.G.E. Lythe, 'Scottish trade with the Baltic, 1550-1650' in J.K. Eastham (ed.), *Economic Essays in Commemoration of the Dundee School of Economics 1931-1955* (Dundee, 1955). Scottish trade with Denmark in the seventeenth century is discussed by Riis in *Should Auld Acquaintance*, I, pp. 39-80. For more on general 'British' trade see J. Lisk, *The Struggle for Supremacy in the Baltic* (London, 1967).

mid-sixteenth century.[10] This trade was conducted via handling ports in the eastern Baltic, or directly with Russia via Archangel. After James VI & I became the monarch of Great Britain and Ireland in 1603, new opportunities presented themselves for Scottish merchants to expand their trade with Russia which had been developing since the previous century.[11] In the main, however, Scottish trade continued to centre on Denmark-Norway, Sweden, Poland and Danzig rather than Russia. Denmark sustained numerous Scottish communities engaged in the 'carrier trade' in the Baltic Sea and by the timber trade around Stavanger, Bergen and Trondheim in Norway.[12] So important was the timber trade that in Norway it is still called the 'Scottish Trade' while the sixteenth and seventeenth centuries are known as 'the Scottish period' of Norwegian history.[13] Indeed, one of the richest men and largest landowners in seventeenth-century Norway was Axel Mowatt, son of the Scottish admiral, Andrew Mowatt.[14] The importance of Norway to Scottish trade becomes apparent when one considers that 180 Scots became burgesses in Bergen alone between 1600 and 1660. During the same time period there were only ten Englishmen who attained similar status.[15] The

---

[10] For more on the Muscovy Company see T.S. Willan, *The Early History of the Muscovy Company 1553-1603* (Manchester, 1968).

[11] There must have been Scottish-Russian trade in the sixteenth century as the Swedes wrote to Scotland seeking support against Russia and asking that Scottish shipping and trade there be stopped. See *Calendar of Scottish Papers*, II, 1563-1569, p. 683, Randolphe to Cecil, February 6, 1562-3; *RPCS*, 14, p. 183.

[12] See in particular Riis, *Should Auld Acquaintance*, I, pp.39-80 and II, pp.148-277; A. Espelland, *Skottene i Hordaland og Rogaland fra aar 1500-1800* (Norheimsund, 1921), p. 31; A.M. Wiesener, 'Axel Movat og hans slegt' in *Bergens Historiske Forening Skrifter*, no. 36 (Bergen, 1930), p. 98; F. Tennfjord, *Stamhuset Rosendal* (Oslo, 1949), pp. 7-8; E. Vaage, *Kvinnherad* (Bergen, 1972), pp. 206-213; A. Lillehammer, 'The Scottish-Norwegian Timber Trade in the Stavanger Area in the Sixteenth and the Seventeenth Centuries' in T.C. Smout (ed.), *Scotland and Europe 1200-1850* (Edinburgh, 1986), pp. 97-111. The Scottish community in Trondheim was specifically mentioned in two letters written by Christian IV in 1638 and 1639. See *Norske Rigs-Registranter*, pp. 467 and 502. Christian IV to Eiler Urne, 22 November 1638 and Christian IV to Oluf Parsberg, 3 February 1639.

[13] Lillehammer, 'The Scottish-Norwegian Timber Trade', p. 97.

[14] Espelland, *Skottene i Hordaland og Rogaland*, p. 31; Vaage, *Kvinnherad*, pp. 2-3; Wiesener, 'Axel Movat', p. 98; Tennfjord, Stamhuset *Rosendal*, pp. 7-8.

[15] See N. Nicolaysen, *Bergens Borgerbog 1550-1751* (Kristiana, 1878), pp. 16-87.

other six most important trading centres combined produced only one hundred and thirty Scottish burgesses.[16]

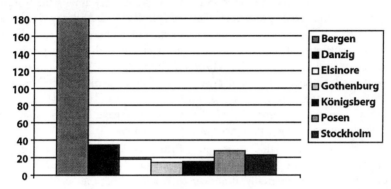

Number of Scotsmen who became burgesses in Scandinavian and Baltic towns 1600-1660

Legend:
- Bergen
- Danzig
- Elsinore
- Gothenburg
- Königsberg
- Posen
- Stockholm

Fig. 1: **Trading Centres**

(Source: *SSNE* database)

The Bergen statistic reflects the regal alliance between Scotland and Denmark-Norway of 1589 which accorded the Scots privileged trading status and rights of citizenship.[17] In the post-1603 period, this treaty also tenuously covered England and Ireland, but not officially until 1621, and then only under the auspices of the Crown of Great Britain and Ireland.[18] In Sweden, the Scots also held a dominant position in the fledgling city of Gothenburg. Throughout the seventeenth century 22 Britons became burgesses in the city; 21 of these

---

[16] The other trading centres in question being Danzig, Elsinore, Gothenburg, Königsberg, Posen and Stockholm.

[17] For detail of the various embassies between Scotland and Denmark-Norway during the marriage negotiations, and their various remits see *RPCS*, 5, 1585-1592, passim, and 6, 1592-1599, passim; G. Donaldson (ed.), *The Memoirs of Sir James Melville of Halhill*, (London, 1969), pp. 129-146; D. Stevenson, *Scotland's Last Royal Wedding: The Marriage of James VI and Anne of Denmark* (Edinburgh, 1997), pp. 1-16.

[18] PRO SP75/5, f. 262. Confirmation of the treaty with Denmark-Norway, 11 November 1621; PRO SP75/7, f. 66. Ratification of the treaty with Denmark-Norway, 9 December 1625; *Danmark-Norges Traktater 1523-1750*, pp. 620-37. Alliance between Great Britain, Denmark-Norway and the United Provinces signed in The Hague, 29 November/9 December 1625.

were Scots and only one was an Englishman, Anthony Knipe.[19] Scotsmen frequently acted in senior positions in the Gothenburg trade council and counted among their number one Hans Macklier (John Maclean). A contemporary of Axel Mowatt in Norway, Macklier became one of the two richest men in Sweden and personal financier to the Swedish Crown.[20]

Englishmen too could be found in positions of authority among the British-Scandinavian mercantile community. For example, in 1621, Anthony Knipe was to be found serving as one of 15 members of the Gothenburg trade council. He chose to leave the city in 1643 after a disagreement with Hans Spalding, a Scottish member of the council.[21] However, Knipe did not give up his trading interests and he later reappeared as a favourite of Frederik III of Denmark-Norway. No longer merely a burgess, Knipe found himself in charge of all the customs collected in Norway by 1652.[22] Knipe must have been an influential individual indeed, and a man in need of further research.

On the southern Baltic coast more British communities flourished. An integrated Scottish and English trading company had been established in Elbing as early as 1578.[23] Numerically, if not commercially as well, the Scots dominated the British and Irish presence in the region. They emigrated there at a phenomenal rate. Two separate contemporary documents allege that there were some 30,000 Scots in Poland alone in the year 1620.[24] These migrants spread out across Poland and the East Prussian coastal cities. They often served as important links between the Baltic ports and Scandinavia. Scottish merchants, particularly those in Elbing and Danzig, have even been singled out by Scandinavian historians as having played an important role in Sweden's

---

[19] *SSNE* no. 4676.

[20] *SSNE* no. 1631.

[21] *SSNE* no. 4677.

[22] C. Rise Hansen (ed.), *Aktstykker og Oplysninger til Rigsraadets og Stændermødernes Historie i Frederik III's Tid*, (2 vols., Copenhagen, 1959 & 1974), II, p. 337. Risgsraad minute, May 1652.

[23] Fischer, *The Scots in Germany*, pp.18n, 52-53; A. Tønnesen, 'Skotterne og englænderne' in *Helsingørs udenlandske borgere og indbyggere ca.1550-1600* (Ringe, 1985), p. 21; Most English sources say that it was to the English Merchant Company. The Swedes more accurately call it 'brittiska köpmansförsamlingen i Elbing'. See *SBL*, XI, p. 581.

[24] There are at least two contemporary sources for this piece of information. See *Calendar of State Papers Domestic*, (hereafter *CSPD*) 1619-1623, p. 237, Chamberlain to Carleton, March 24, 1621; William Lithgow, *The Totall Discourse of the Rare Adventures and Painefull Peregrinations of long Nineteene Yeares Travayles from Scotland to the most famous Kingdomes in Europe, Asia and Affrica* (Glasgow, 1906) p. 368.

mercantile growth.[25] Many of the Baltic Scots formed themselves into brotherhoods and societies which had seats in Danzig and throughout Poland.[26] These societies ensured the Scottish community upheld a solidarity with members of their own nation. They also frequently concealed numbers of illegal Scottish migrants who traded in the towns. This bolstered the size of the Scottish communities and enlarged the population of the cities.[27] The sheer quantity of illegal immigrants placed tensions on the relations between the Scots and the host communities, eventually leading to action by the Polish authorities designed to curb the influx.[28] The Stuart ambassador to Danzig and Poland, Patrick Gordon, drew up a strict code in 1616 to alleviate the problem.[29] However, this measure failed, compelling the Scottish community in Danzig to seek the intervention of James VI & I to prevent any more of the 'exorbitant numberis of zoung boyis and maidis vnable for any seruice, transported hier zierlie'.[30]

King James sent another agent, Hugh Mowatt, to try to resolve the problem, though the success of his mission is hard to determine.[31] What is evident is that the strength of the Scottish community gave them a distinct advantage over their English and Irish colleagues in terms of influence in the region. James VI & I compounded this Scottish mercantile and cultural advantage after 1603 by ensuring that his English and Irish subjects were represented in Scandinavia and the Baltic by Scottish diplomats.

---

[25] Tønnesen, 'Skotterne og englænderne', p. 22.

[26] Stanisław Seliga and Leon Koczy, *Scotland and Poland: A Chapter of Forgotten History* (Scotland, 1969), p. 6.

[27] Anna Biegańska, 'A note on the Scots in Poland, 1550-1800' in T.C. Smout (ed.), *Scotland and Europe 1200-1850* (Edinburgh, 1986), p. 159.

[28] *Edict against the Scots issued by Sigismund III*, 12 September 1594, reprinted in Fischer, *The Scots in Eastern and Western Prussia*, p. 158; Biegańska, 'A note on the Scots in Poland', p. 158; Seliga and Koczy, *Scotland and Poland*, pp. 6-7.

[29] The eighty Articles drawn up by Patrick Gordon for the Scots in Prussia (Königsberg, 1616), reproduced in Fischer, The Scots in Eastern and Western Prussia, pp. 159-70. Seliga and Koczy, Scotland and Poland, pp. 6-7; SSNE no. 4317.

[30] See 'Scottish subjects at Dantzic to King James VI, Dantzic, this penult August 1624' reprinted in the Abbotsford Club, Letters and State Papers during the Reign of King James the Sixth, chiefly from the manuscript collections of Sir James Balfour of Denmyln (Edinburgh, 1837).

[31] *SSNE* no. 800.

Diplomatic networks

King James undertook a rationalisation of resources which effectively meant the removal of many English diplomats from northern Europe.[32] Richard Lee's four-year Swedish residency also terminated in 1604 leaving Stuart-Swedish diplomacy to be conducted in an ad hoc manner by soldiers and merchants until the Stuarts established formal political relations with Karl IX in 1609.[33] For the next 23 years Sir James Spens of Wormiston represented the Stuart monarchy in Sweden.[34] Direct English representation in Denmark-Norway terminated after the withdrawal of the English diplomats Roger Manners and Robert Naughton in August 1603. Scotsmen already resident in the country, especially Sir Andrew Sinclair and Sir Robert Anstruther, filled the diplomatic vacuum.[35]

The Scottish diplomatic monopoly in Scandinavia was reinforced by the fact that Scottish ambassadors representing the Stuart interest also formed an integral part of the diplomatic institutions of the countries to which they were accredited. During James's reign, Andrew Sinclair conducted at least seven diplomatic missions to the Stuart Court on behalf of Denmark-Norway and Robert Anstruther several more. Anstruther also acted as Danish ambassador to other countries. In 1624, Christian IV chose him to represent Denmark-Norway to Frederick V of the Palatinate at The Hague and in 1625 he was accredited as the Danish ambassador both to and from John George of Saxony.[36] The Vasa monarchy in Sweden also employed Stuart subjects as their ambassadors. Andrew and John Stewart served as Swedish envoys to Russia during the

---

[32] Two recent doctoral theses survey Scottish, English and British diplomacy in Scandinavia and Northern Europe: Steve Murdoch, 'Scotland, Denmark-Norway and the House of Stuart; A Diplomatic and Military Analysis 1603-1660', unpublished PhD thesis, Aberdeen 1998; Alexia Grosjean, 'Scots and the Swedish State: Diplomacy, Military service and Ennoblement 1611-1660', unpublished PhD thesis, Aberdeen 1998. See also S. Murdoch, 'Robert Anstruther: A Stuart Diplomat in Norlan Europe 1603-1625' in *Cairn*, vol. I, pp. 46-55.

[33] *SSNE* no. 1259.

[34] PRO, SP95/1, ff. 158-158v, James VI to Karl IX, 22 September 1609; *SSNE* no. 1642.

[35] *Dansk Biografisk Lexicon*, (Copenhagen, 1933-44), XIII, pp. 399-400; Riis, *Should Auld Acquaintance Be Forgot*, II, pp. 111-2; Sinclair, *SSNE* no. 1578; Anstruther, *SSNE* no. 1472.

[36] E. Marquard, *Danske Gesandter og Gesandtskabs Personale indtil 1914* (Copenhagen, 1952), p. 27.

Swedish-Russian treaty negotiations of 1611.[37] More importantly for Scottish interests, Sir James Spens also acted as the senior ambassador to London from the Swedish Court until his death in 1632.[38]

In northern Europe, it was only in Muscovite Russia that Englishmen continued as the majority diplomatic representatives from the Court of King James. This was due largely to the enormous influence of the English Muscovy Company. The main envoy during the Jacobean period was Sir John Merrick who had been raised for many years in Russia and eventually became the governor of the Muscovy Company.[39] He returned to England in 1619 as part of a Russian embassy. By 1620 he was fully accredited as the Stuart ambassador to Russia, in the main to sort out the diplomatic debris left after the aborted embassy of Sir Dudley Digges in 1618.[40] Englishmen continued to dominate Stuart-Russian diplomacy leaving Scandinavia as the domain of the Scots.

The most important point about the Scottish diplomats in Denmark-Norway and Sweden is that they had an extraordinary amount of credibility with the Scandinavian monarchs. After the death of his father, Charles I continued to employ Sir Robert Anstruther and Sir James Spens as the main Stuart ambassadors for Denmark-Norway and Sweden. Their work was essential in the diplomatic quagmire enveloping Europe as the Thirty Years' War convulsed through its various phases.[41] The Scottish diplomatic presence in Scandinavia spilled over into the Baltic ports as Gustav II Adolf of Sweden took possession of

---

[37] There are references to both Anders and Hans Stewart going to Russia as legates in 1611. See E. Elgenstierna (ed.), *Den Introducerade Svenska Adelns Ättartavlor, med tillägg och rättesler,* [hereafter *SAÄ*] 9 vols. (Stockholm, 1925-36), VII, p. 782; J. Berg and B. Lagercrantz, *Scots in Sweden* (Stockholm, 1962), p. 21; Andrew, *SSNE* no. 1646; John, *SSNE* no. 1645.

[38] *DNB*, XVIII, pp. 789-790; *SAÄ*, VII, pp. 428-9; James Spens proved to be an instrumental character is Scottish and British relations. His diplomatic correspondence can be found in the Swedish National Archives [Riksarkivet, hereafter Sv. Ra.] in the Anglica collection. An English translation of these can be found in Uppsala University Library: A. Duncan, 'The Diplomatic Correspondence of Sir James Spens of Wormiston' unpublished manuscript.

[39] *SSNE* no. 1940.

[40] I. Lubimenko, 'A Project for the acquisition of Russia by James I', *English Historical Review* XXIX (1914), pp. 246-56; Konovalov, *Oxford Slavonic Papers,* 1 (1950), pp. 64-103; *SSNE* no. 3958.

[41] For more on the Thirty Years' War see J.V. Polisensky, *The Thirty Years' War* (London, 1971); G. Parker, *The Thirty Years' War* (London, 1984); S.J. Lee, *The Thirty Years' War,* (London, 1991). Reference to Scottish and English participation can be found in S. Murdoch, 'The House of Stuart and the Scottish Professional Soldier 1618-1648: A Conflict of Nationality and Identities' in B. Taithe and T. Thornton (eds.), *War: Identities in Conflict 1300-2000,* (Thrupp, Stroud, Gloucestershire, 1998), pp. 37-56.

territories in the region. After the Swedes occupied Elbing, Sir James Spens moved his diplomatic base to the city which had also been garrisoned by Scottish troops.[42]

Military networks

The arrival of a Scottish regiment in Elbing in 1628 proved symptomatic of a far greater British military participation in Germany since the outbreak of the Thirty Years' War in 1618. James sent many troops to the Palatinate in 1620 to help his son-in-law, the Elector Palatine in his dispute with the Holy Roman Empire.[43] British volunteers, mostly Scots, under Colonels Andrew Gray and James Seton took a leading part in the war, including the battle of White Mountain.[44] The outcome of the battle is well recorded, the Imperialists won, but Seton's regiment fought on in Bohemia until February 1622, long after Frederick V and Sir Horace Vere had fled the field.[45] Indeed by the end of 1622 the Scots had probably contributed about 5,000 of the 8,000 soldiers who had left the British Isles for the war to defend Elizabeth Stuart.[46] These were only the first of many men who would see service in the war, particularly in Danish and Swedish service.

Charles I continued his father's policy of appearing aloof from the German wars by sanctioning a minimal military response from his kingdom of England while actually allowing the Scots to enlist abroad in droves. This has led to many misconceptions as to the degree of military support Charles I lent the Scandinavian monarchs. Ernest Beller erroneously declared that Sir Charles

---

[42] Fischer, The Scots in Germany, p. 53.

[43] G.M.D. Howatt, *Stuart and Cromwellian Foreign Policy* (London, 1974) p. 28.

[44] RPCS, vol. 12, 1619-1622, pp. 255-261, 412, 431, 453; CSPV, vol. 16, 1619-1621, pp. 204-7. Girolamo Lando to Doge and Senate, 19 March 1621. Information about Gray's levy in letters no. 266, 288, 295, 373, 411, and 427; Anon., *A most true relation of the late proceedings in Bohemia, Germany, and Hungaria [...] As also of the happie arriual of Sir Andrew Gray into Lusatia* (London, 1620), p. 10; J. Taylor, *Taylor his trauells From the Citty of London in England, to the Citty of Prague in Bohemia* (London, 1620), p. 12; Polisensky, *The Thirty Years' War*, pp. 125-6, 159; SSNE no. 378.

[45] Polisensky, *The Thirty Years' War*, p. 159.

[46] For motivation such as the defence of Elizabeth Stuart see Murdoch, 'The House of Stuart and the Scottish Professional Soldier', pp. 43-8. For estimates of numbers see CSPV Vol. 16, 1619-1621, pp. 326-7. Girolamo Lando to Doge and Senate, 9 July 1620. Lando estimated at that point that, including the ongoing levy of Sir Horace Vere, there were about 8,000 'British' troops engaged in the war. See also pp. 617-20, Girolamo Lando to Doge and Senate, 26 March 1621.

Morgan's unsuccessful expedition to Germany in 1627-1629 was 'the only military assistance given to Christian by his nephew Charles I [and] the King of Denmark's military situation demanded more than the army of under 5,000 men which Morgan commanded'.[47] Such a view ignores the contribution of some 13,400 Scots soldiers who entered the Danish-Norwegian army during the same period.[48] Nonetheless it remains a common belief among many historians of Charles I that he sanctioned only minimal support for the conflict. Kevin Sharpe stated that in 1630 Charles I only allowed the levy of 6,000 troops for Swedish service and 'contributed no more to the Swedish campaigns'.[49] The Sharpe figure falls well below that cited by Scottish and Scandinavian historians of the period, who usually conclude that the number of Scots in the Swedish army exceeded 20,000.[50] The sheer numbers of Scots who took part in the conflict, some 40,000, added yet another dimension to the Scottish presence in the Baltic region. More important than the numeric contribution were the positions of authority many Scots reached within the Scandinavian armies and the territories under their control.

No single country provided such a large proportion of the military elite to Denmark-Norway as Scotland did between 1625 and 1629. During those four years, 303 Scottish officers were taken into service by Christian IV.[51] This meant that Scotsmen outnumbered Danish and Norwegian officers by a staggering 3:1 in their own army.[52] They also had 20 times as many officers as the English who fielded only 16 officers throughout the same period. These officers were given senior positions and included the two generals, Robert Maxwell Earl of

---

[47] E. Beller, 'Recent Studies on the Thirty Years' War', *Journal of Modern History* 3 (1931), p.74; SSNE no. 89.

[48] It is also a view that has been challenged in doctoral research: see J. Fallon, 'Scottish Soldiers in the service of Denmark and Sweden, 1626-1632' (unpublished PhD thesis, University of Glasgow, 1972). Grant, *Memoirs of Sir John Hepburn*, p. 3. Colonels Mackay, Leslie and Seaton commanded some 4,400 men between them by the end of 1625. The following year Charles I paid £8,000 to Lords Nithsdale, Spynie and Sir James Sinclair of Murkle for the three regiments of 3,000 men (9,000 total) for Denmark's service.

[49] Sharpe, *The Personal Rule*, p. 79. The Sharpe figure appears to ignore the issuing of royal warrants between 1624 and 1637 allowing for the levying of 41,400 for continental service. See RPCS second series, passim and E. Furgol, *A Regimental History of the Covenanting Armies*, (Edinburgh, 1990), p. 2.

[50] See W. S. Brockington jnr., 'Scottish mercenaries in the Thirty Years' War' in *Proceedings of the South Carolina Historical Association* (1986), p.41.

[51] Murdoch, 'Scotland, Denmark-Norway and the House of Stuart', p. 259.

[52] Ibid., p. 258.

Nithsdale and Sir Robert Scott.[53] Twenty-five other Scots held the rank of Major or above.[54] One of these, Alexander Seaton, commanded the Scottish-Danish garrison stationed in Stralsund where he remained until he was relieved as governor by Alexander Leslie, the future Earl of Leven, then serving in the army of Sweden.[55] The Scots were also highly represented in the Danish-Norwegian navy. Christian IV appointed 23 Scottish officers before 1629, four of whom became admirals including John Cunningham and Axel Mowatt.[56] Only two English naval officers were contracted by Christian IV during the same period, Captains James Hall and Marcus White.[57] The dominant position of Scots within the Danish-Norwegian armed forces was mirrored in Sweden.

The number of Scottish troops in Swedish service reached about 12,000 men, or 17% of the total army, by 1630.[58] Of these, 7,000 arrived between 1628-1630 while the rest were veterans of previous conflicts.[59] Sir James Spens observed that in the mid- 1620s about 500 Scots served as officers in the Swedish army.[60] Once Gustav II Adolf launched his German campaign proper in 1630, the Scottish officer corps within his army expanded. High rates of attrition meant that the actual number of Scots remained similar to pre-war statistics despite the influx of new men. Of the 3,262 officers at his disposal in 1632, 413 were Scots, 36 were English, two were Irish and 22 others were of unspecified 'British' origin. In all, the Scots made up 13% of Sweden's officer corps.[61] The contribution of these men to the Swedish army was huge and even noted by

---

[53] For Nithsdale's appointment see PRO SP75/8, f. 42. Anstruther to Buckingham, 9 March 1627; PRO SP75/8, f. 45. Anstruther to Charles I, 9 March 1627; PRO SP75/8, f. 61. The State of the King of Denmark's Army, March 1627; SSNE no. 531. For Scott see Riis, *Should Auld Acquaintance*, II, p.116; O. Blom, 'Smaa Bidrag til Artilleriets Historie under Kristian d. 4de; I. Robert Scott og Læderkanonerne', *Historisk Tidsskrift* III (1900-2), pp.322-44; SSNE no. 409.

[54] Murdoch, 'Scotland, Denmark-Norway and the House of Stuart', p. 262.

[55] Grosjean, 'Scots and the Swedish State', p. 79; Seaton, SSNE no. 91; Leslie, SSNE no. 1.

[56] Murdoch, 'Scotland, Denmark-Norway and the House of Stuart', pp. 223-4; Cunningham, SSNE no. 1479; Mowatt, SSNE no. 1817.

[57] Murdoch, 'Scotland, Denmark-Norway and the House of Stuart', p. 227; Hall, SSNE no. 1316; White, SSNE no. 4190.

[58] Brockington, 'Scottish mercenaries in the Thirty Years' War', p. 41.

[59] Grosjean, 'Scots and the Swedish State', p. 87.

[60] Westin, Negotiations about church unity 1628-1634, p. 67.

[61] Grosjean, 'Scots and the Swedish State', p. 94.

contemporary Englishmen.[62] They would eventually include amongst their number eight field marshals and generals, 69 colonels, 49 lieutenant colonels and 57 majors, providing a military pedigree the Swedes themselves found hard to match.[63] The Scots were also well represented within the Swedish navy providing no fewer than six admirals in the first half of the seventeenth century alone. There were a further 21 Scottish naval officers compared to only one Englishman.[64]

The officers in Danish-Norwegian and Swedish service provided another layer to the fabric of the Scottish community in Scandinavia and the Baltic. They were frequently rewarded for service by grants of land, especially in the Swedish-occupied Baltic. Thus they were in a strong position to meet and interact with the Scottish mercantile community and act as go-betweens for them and the Swedish State.[65] For example, Alexander, Master of Forbes served as an officer in the Swedish army. While returning to Sweden from a protracted leave in 1636, he travelled to Denmark and Sweden with a brief to establish trading staples in each country. These objectives were not achieved, probably due to the increased unrest in Scotland toward the end of the 1630s. Nonetheless, he was one of many such men bridging the gap between the Scottish mercantile and military communities. Other strands of the Scottish diaspora were also involved in knitting the various networks together, especially the many scholars in the region.

Theologians and intellectuals

The north German and Scandinavian universities attracted large numbers of Scottish students, academics and theologians. The matriculation records of Åbo, Uppsala, Lund, Copenhagen, Sorø, Kiel, Rostock and Königsberg, show four Irish students, 15 Englishmen and some 221 Scots between 1580-1707. Many of these students were travelling an established circuit before returning to their home countries. Others were the sons of migrants who had no intention of returning home. Even the sons of Scottish soldiers found places within these establishments. In one particular case, and in recognition of his military service, Christian IV arranged for the sons of Colonel Donald Mackay to attend the

---

[62] PRO SP75/16, f. 270 & f. 303. Letters between Joseph Averie and Secretary Coke.

[63] Grosjean, 'Scots and the Swedish State', p. 98.

[64] Grosjean, 'Scots and the Swedish State', pp.101-6.

[65] Dk. Ra. TKUA England 14, 1636, Documents relating to the service of Alexander Forbes; A. and H. Tayler (eds.), *The House of Forbes* (Bruceton Mills, 1987), p. 178.

Academy of Sorø in 1628 at the Danish king's expense.[66] Added to the academic presence were a significant number of clergymen and theologians attracted to the region.

In Elbing, as elsewhere in the Baltic, the Scottish merchants endeavoured to have one of their countrymen acting as the preacher for their community.[67] By 1624, John Durie, had been called to minister the Scottish and English Presbyterian congregation in Elbing.[68] Another important figure, Adrian Stoddart, became the Dean of the Lutheran church in Danzig in the same year.[69] Indeed in Poland alone the names of over 40 Scottish Catholic and Protestant clergy have been recorded.[70] The numbers of Scots clergy in the Baltic were swollen as military chaplains arrived with Scottish regiments. Individual clergymen in exile such as the Episcopal Archbishop Archibald Hamilton also added to these numbers.[71] Scandinavia and the Baltic region were therefore replete with Scottish clergy from all the major denominations, some simply ministering to their flocks and others with higher objectives.

While the war in Germany progressed, an intellectual circle of theologians and academics determined to unify the Protestant states of Europe. Scotland produced a number of such men. Dr John Forbes, sometime Professor of Divinity at Kings College Aberdeen, had studied divinity at Heidelberg and

---

[66] HMC *Sixth Report* (London, 1877), p. 685. John Mackay to Sir Robert Farquhar, 6 October 1628. John Mackay wrote that 'hauing at last obtained of the King of Denmarks Majestie to giue us frie intertinament, hes Majestie hes dereckted us to an Universitie called Soare, quhilk is eight Dutch myle laying from this toune [Copenhagen], and there we three geat frie meat and chamer, our father furnishing the rest off our necessaries'.

[67] Anna Biegańska, 'In Search of Tolerance: Scottish Catholics and Presbyterians in Poland' in *Scottish Slavonic Review* XVII (1991), p.43.

[68] Fischer, *The Scots in Germany*, p. 175; *DNB*, VI, p. 261; *SBL*, XI, p. 582; Mandelbrote 'John Dury', p. 44.

[69] *SSNE* no. 1166.

[70] Biegańska, 'In Search of Tolerance', p. 43.

[71] Archbishop Archibald Hamilton fled to Sweden after the 1641 rebellion and died there in 1659 as a Swedish nobleman. He is usually referred to as an Irishman due to his position as Episcopal Archbishop of Cashel in Ireland. In fact he was the son of Sir Claud Hamilton of Cochno, Dumbartonshire who settled in Co. Tyrone in 1610. After Archibald fled Ireland he was recommended to Durie by Sir David Ramsay, Durie's uncle. See S. Murdoch, 'Northern Exposure: Irishmen and Scandinavia in the seventeenth century' in *History Ireland*, Autumn 1998, p. 5; Grosjean, 'Scots and the Swedish State', pp.111-12; Hartlib Papers, CD ROM edition [hereafter HP], 3/1/16A-16B; *SSNE* no. 1345.

Sedan partially under David Pareus author of the famous *Irenicum* in 1615.[72] Forbes had been deeply influenced by his mentor and his earliest published work, also entitled *Irenicum*, reached print in Aberdeen in 1629. It was dedicated to both Pareus and the lovers of truth and peace in the Scottish Kirk. Gunnar Westin has established that John Forbes and John Durie were friends but does not develop any theory as to the influence of Forbes on Durie's theology.[73]

Another Aberdonian, Bishop William Forbes, also sought ecclesiastical reconciliation, but he went further than most of his colleagues by repeatedly preaching, between 1624-1634, to bring the Protestant and Catholic churches together.[74] Just at the same period that William and John Forbes embarked on their campaigns in search of religious tolerance, John Durie, preached to the British congregation in Elbing as an ordained minister of the Scottish Presbyterian Kirk.[75] He must surely have been aware of the work of these men before 1628, albeit that William Forbes operated on the Episcopalian fringes of the church they all worked for.

Born in Edinburgh in 1596, John Durie came from a renowned family of outspoken Scottish Presbyterian theologians. Durie's grandfather, also called John Durie, had been a convert from Catholicism to the reformed faith and a staunch devotee of John Knox.[76] Following in their father's footsteps, John Durie the elder's children Joshua, Robert (father of John 'the Irenicist') and Simon all entered into the Presbyterian ministry. Robert eventually had to seek exile in the Netherlands after being banished from Scotland for taking part in a General Assembly of the Kirk in 1605 since it had been had been prohibited by James VI.[77] Durie's uncle, James Melville, another Presbyterian minister, also fell foul of the authorities due to his extreme views that ultimately led to his exile

---

[72] Rev. R. Lippe (ed.), *Spalding Club. Selections from Wodrow's Biographical Collections. Divines of the North-East of Scotland*, (Aberdeen, 1890), p. 331.

[73] Westin, *Negotiations about church unity 1628-1634*, p. 65. He also seems to confuse John Forbes and William Forbes giving the latter's date of death as that of the former, 1634. See ibid., note 17. John Forbes actually died on 29 April 1648.

[74] Lippe, *Wodrow's Biographical Collections'*, pp. lxxii-lxxvi and 245-69.

[75] *SBL*, XI, p. 581.

[76] Andrew Melville was so taken by the elder John Durie that he composed eight Latin epitaphs to him. See Lippe, *Wodrow's Biographical Collections'*, pp. 124-64; *DNB*, VI, p. 261.

[77] For information on Robert Durie see the *DNB*, VI, p. 263.

from Scotland.[78] It is little wonder that John Durie (the Irenicist) held a deep-rooted interest in theology in his early youth, particularly Scottish Presbyterianism. This curiosity became reinforced when Durie studied in Sedan under his great uncle Andrew Melville.[79]

No doubt while studying at this college, Durie either met Dr John Forbes, or at least became familiar with the work of his father's friend. One printed pamphlet from 1657 noted the University of Aberdeen as one of the places with which Durie maintained contact during the early phase of his Irenicist career, 1628-1641, thus linking John Forbes directly to John Durie.[80] Whatever the actual nature of the relationship, the release of Forbes's *Irenicum* in 1629 occurred at a time when John Durie had become well placed to further the ideal of ecclesiastical pacification through his Scottish patronage network.

The Scottish network of John Durie

Sir James Spens undertook a diplomatic mission to the Swedish Court in 1627. His primary motive was to take part in the Swedish-Polish peace negotiations, but he also delivered the Order of the Garter to Gustav II Adolf in Dirschau.[81] He thereafter spent some time in the city of Elbing which had fallen to Swedish control the previous year. During his time there, Spens employed John Durie as his secretary.[82] One historian noted that, coincidentally, Spens' wife happened to be called Agnes Durie but believed there to be no evidence of a relationship between Lady Spens and the cleric.[83] But the two men certainly were related. Sir James Spens had a quite distinguished son-in-law in Swedish service, Sir James

---

[78] *DNB*, XIII, pp. 241-4.

[79] John Durie's entry in the *DNB* states that John Dury and Andrew Melville were cousins. My suspicion is this cannot have been the case and that Andrew Melville was his great uncle. The *DNB*, VI, pp.261 and 263 states that James Melville was the son-in-law of John Durie the elder, making him the irenicist's uncle. Andrew Melville's *DNB* entry states that during his confinement in the Tower of London in 1608, Melville 'was indulged with the company of a young nephew and great nephew'. See *DNB*, XIII, pp. 230 and 235; *DNB*, XIII, p. 241.

[80] HP, 14/2/1/1A-6B. The effect of Master Dury's negotiation for the uniting of Protestants (1657).

[81] *SAÄ*, VII, pp. 428-9; *DNB*, XVIII, pp. 789-90; Westin, *Negotiations about church unity 1628-1634*, pp. 65-6.

[82] Westin, *Negotiations about church unity 1628-1634*, p. 65.

[83] Turnbull, *Hartlib, Dury and Comenius*, p. 130.

Ramsay (the Black), one of the many Scottish officers mentioned above.[84] Ramsay and Durie were first cousins, thus linking Durie to Spens through marriage.[85] Indeed given this relationship it is probable that Ramsay ensured that Durie got the job with Spens in the first place. It is also certain that it was the contact with Spens that facilitated the initial contact with the Swedish king in 1628. This challenges the received wisdom which tells us that Durie's contact with the Swedish Court occurred due to his meeting with Sir Thomas Roe which did not take place until the following year.[86] Very interestingly, John Durie confirmed this when he reminded Roe that Sir James Ramsay had to reconcile a serious 'mistake' which Roe had made with Gustav II Adolf at their first meeting in Prussia in 1629.[87]

John Durie submitted his 'Humble Petition' to Gustav II Adolf in 1628 while working for Sir James Spens.[88] Through this document Durie requested aid from the Swedish King in his bid to re-establish ecclesiastical peace among the Protestant churches of Europe. Given the evidence of his later statements, we can be sure that it was Sir James Spens who ensured that the petition got through to Gustav II Adolf.[89]

Dr Jacob Godemann served as one of the king's councillors employed in Prussia in the Swedish-operated High Court of Justice.[90] As a result of Durie's

---

[84] The relationship is mentioned in PRO, SP95/II/f.197, Sir James Spens to Sir John Coke, Pillau, 30 October 1627. For more on Ramsay see the *DNB*, XVI, pp. 682-3. Ramsay's present *DNB* article makes no mention of this relationship. This has been updated by Dr Alexia Grosjean and will appear in the *New DNB*. More on his career can be found in *SSNE* no. 3315.

[85] For Durie's mention of this relationship see HP, 20/11/15a-28b, Memo on Durie & Ecclesiastical Peace, 1631-1633, n.d.; HP, 60/5/1a-8b, Durie to Hartlib, Narrative of his German travels, c.1632. Westin observed that Durie stayed 'with his "Cosen Coronell Ramsay at Wirtzburg" about the middle of January 1632', Westin, *Negotiations about church unity 1628-1634*, p. 125. He did not know the relationship between Spens and Ramsay or the significance of Ramsay's part in Durie's relations with Axel Oxenstierna or Gustav II Adolf.

[86] *SBL*, XI, p.582. 'Sen sommaren 1629 kom den engelske legaten sir Thomas Roe till Elbing för underhandlinger, och han ivrade för en "protestantisk politik" från Englands sida'; Fischer, *The Scots in Germany*, p. 176; Brauer, *Die Unionstätigkeit John Duries*, p. 2; Mandelbrote, 'John Dury and the practice of Irenicism', p. 44.

[87] John Durie to Sir Thomas Roe, 28 January 1633, reprinted in Westin, *Negotiations about church unity 1628-1634*, pp. 230-3. This piece of text appears to have been ignored by Westin himself while relating Roe's diplomatic duties. See pp.84-5.

[88] HP, 19/9/1a-6b, John Durie's Petition to Gustav II Adolf, 1628.

[89] HP, 20/11/15a-28b, Memo on Durie & Ecclesiastical Peace, 1631-1633, n.d.

[90] Fischer, *The Scots in Germany*, pp. 175-6; Turnbull, *Hartlib, Dury and Comenius*, pp.129-30.

petition Gustav II Adolf is reported to have encouraged discussions between Dr Godemann and John Durie in 1628.[91] Jacob Godemann died in 1629 but Durie maintained a correspondence with his son, Caspar, who held several positions as a Swedish diplomat, including one to the Stuart Court in 1630-31.[92] Once resolved to pursue his agenda at the highest level possible, John Durie left Elbing and travelled to England in 1630. He was well aware that he had some influential support at the Court of Charles I. Sir Thomas Roe had promised to vouch for him during their meeting of 1629 and, apparently, invited him to England.[93] But far more importantly for Durie, Sir James Spens had arrived in London in March 1629, as an ambassador from Gustav II Adolf.[94] The presence of this family member at Court can only have helped to boost Durie's confidence. Indeed he found himself in quite a secure environment since another of his Scottish uncles, Sir David Ramsay, attended Charles I as a Gentleman of his Bedchamber.[95] Ramsay provided Durie with recommendations at Court and lodgings in his own home during his nephew's many visits to England.[96] The positions of influence of both these relatives of John Durie are missing from all modern accounts of his visit to England of 1629-1630.[97]

---

[91] Turnbull, *Hartlib, Dury and Comenius*, pp.129-31; Westin, *Negotiations about church unity 1628-1634*, pp.79-80. Karl Brauer believed that Durie first became aware of the topic of ecclesiastical pacification from Caspar Godemann, Jacob's son, in 1628. Howard Hotson has observed that Durie described Johannes Mylius, rector of the gymnasium in Elbing, as his mentor – presumably in the field of ecclesiastical peace. Yet given Durie's education he would surely have been aware of the work of David Pareus, and/or either of the Forbes' first. Perhaps they all had an equal influence; Brauer, *Die Unionstätigkeit John Duries*, p. 2; Hotson, 'Philosophical pedagogy', pp. 38 and 45.

[92] Turnbull, *Hartlib, Dury and Comenius*, pp. 129 and 142.

[93] Westin, Negotiations about church unity 1628-1634, p. 87.

[94] The first of Spens's dispatches to the Swedish Court from London can be found in Sv. Ra. Anglica 3, James Spens to Gustav II Adolf, 15 April 1629; See also *DNB*, XVIII, p. 790; Westin, *Negotiations about church unity 1628-1634*, p. 82.

[95] Durie makes reference to 'my Oncle Dauid Ramsay' in HP, 3/2/125A-B, 24 May 1645. See also *DNB*, XVI, pp.682-6 for more on Ramsay.

[96] HP, 7/16/1A-2B. Hartlib to John Dury, 20 September 1630 at 'Mr David Ramsayes house, Master of the King's Clockes, & one of his Bedchamber; Hartlib Papers 14/4/17A-18B, 24 March 1634 to 'Mr Iohn Durye Minister at Mr Ramsay his house in Fynes Alley in Channell Rowe Westminster'.

[97] See most recently T.H.H. Rae, 'John Dury and the Royal Road to Piety' *Studia irenica* 37 (1998), pp. 59-60.

Theological support for Durie's ideas came initially from Archbishop Abbot, the Bishops Bedell and Hall and about 20 other English and Scottish theologians.[98] He also linked up in London with Casper Godemann who had arrived in the city on official Swedish business. Godemann left London bearing two letters from John Durie. One of these was addressed to Gustav II Adolf and the other to Axel Oxenstierna, the Swedish Chancellor. Godemann wrote to Durie in March to say that the letters had been delivered and that the king had responded positively to them.[99] Heartened by this Durie resolved to visit the Swedish king to move matters forward.

In July 1631, and secure in the knowledge that his patron Sir James Spens was again in the entourage of the Swedish king, Durie set out to find Gustav II Adolf in Germany.[100] En route he suffered several setbacks including foul seas and delays which left him in Stettin with little money and no lodgings. Fortunately for Durie, he heard that an old acquaintance and fellow Scot, Colonel David Drummond, had command of some Swedish forces in the area.[101] On hearing of Durie's plight, Drummond arranged lodgings for him. Here Durie met with another Scotsman, Eleazer Borthwick, an old friend and chaplain to Sir James Spens.[102] Borthwick confirmed that Gustav II Adolf had already been primed by Spens in relation to Durie's theological ambitions.[103] Durie later mentioned this point to Samuel Hartlib when he wrote that 'knowing my Lord Spence was with the King and had giuen him information of myne intentions, which his Majesty testified to like very well, I resolved to follow the king'.[104]

Lady Ramsay, Durie's cousin's wife, also happened to be in Stettin during this period. She had known Durie for two years in Elbing and she interceded with Drummond to arrange a small guard to move Durie to the king's camp at Wittenburg.[105] Despite their protection, some Finnish soldiers robbed Durie as

---

[98] Fischer, *The Scots in Germany*, p. 176; *DNB*, VI, p. 261.

[99] Turnbull, Hartlib, Dury and Comenius, p. 142.

[100] Westin, Negotiations about church unity 1628-1634, p. 88.

[101] Krigsarkivet Stockholm Muster-rolls 1621/3-1638/24; *SSNE*, no. 2396.

[102] HP, 60/5/1a-8b, Durie to Hartlib, Narrative of his German travels, c.1632; Turnbull, *Hartlib, Dury and Comenius*, p. 151; *SSNE* no. 1064.

[103] HP, 60/5/1a-8b, Durie to Hartlib, Narrative of his German travels, c.1632; Turnbull, *Hartlib, Dury and Comenius*, p. 144.

[104] HP, 20/11/15a-28b, Memo on Durie & Ecclesiastical Peace, 1631-1633, n.d.

[105] HP, 60/5/1a-8b, Durie to Hartlib, Narrative of his German travels, c.1632; *SBL*, XI, p. 582.

he settled into his lodgings in one of the military camps. Their choice of victim proved rather unfortunate since their commanding officer transpired to be none other than Durie's cousin, Colonel James Ramsay. Durie remained with Ramsay for about ten days and gleaned from him, and others in the camp (undoubtedly Spens included), how best to approach the Swedish king.[106] He must have been well briefed to get so close to the king for in his own words he

> Stood in the King his way when he went from his chamber to supper; who seeing me to be a stranger looked very earnestly upon me ... he asked of me what I was; I told him a preacher who had lived at Elbing heretofore. Then he enquired if I was hee, that hadde sent some theses to him by my Lord Spence, concerning Ecclesiastical peace; to which I answered that I was the same.[107]

It should be noted here that by Durie's own recollection of Gustav II Adolf's words it was Sir James Spens who brought the Swedish king's attention to Durie's work and not, as we are so often told, Sir Thomas Roe. Two days later the cleric and the king met once more whereupon Gustav II Adolf submitted Durie to a 'stern examination'. Apparently satisfied by the Scotsman's answers he agreed to support Durie's ecclesiastical ambitions. So encouraged was Durie that he chose to remain near the Swedish king, stating that 'I stayed with my Coazen Coronell Ramsay at Wirtzberg, & while the King remained their I conversed with his two Chaplaines Dr Fabricus & Mr Mathey whome I found ready to second all my desires'.[108] During this period, Durie also kept the company of William Forbes, a staunch supporter of Archbishop Laud and the future Bishop of Edinburgh mentioned previously.[109] Thus, through yet another Scottish connection, Durie can be shown to have links with a different strand of ecclesiastical reconciliation from that of the Protestant hard-liners. In addition

---

[106] HP, 60/5/1a-8b, Durie to Hartlib, Narrative of his German travels, c.1632; HP, 20/11/15a-28b, Memo on Durie & Ecclesiastical Peace, 1631-1633, n.d.

[107] HP, 60/5/1a-8b, Durie to Hartlib, Narrative of his German travels, c.1632; HP, 20/11/15a-28b, Memo on Durie & Ecclesiastical Peace, 1631-1633, n.d.

[108] HP, 20/11/15a-28b, Memo on Durie & Ecclesiastical Peace, 1631-1633, n.d; Hartlib Papers 5/57A-B, 7 February 1632, 'Clarissimo Viro Domino Iohanni Duro Herpiboli commoranti apud Iacobum Ramsay Chilearcham Scotum in dibus Gulielm. Nunsam Fautori plurimum honorando. Wurtzburg'.

[109] HP, 5/49/1A-2B, Philip Snabelius to John Durie, 25 January 1633. It is commonly held that it was Laud who persuaded Charles I to raise Edinburgh to a Bishop's See for Forbes after the king heard him preach in 1633. See Lippe, *Wodrow's Biographical Collections'*, p. 253.

we can surmise that he gained another ally in the Laudian camp prior to the meeting of Laud and Forbes in Scotland in 1633.

The untimely death of Gustav II Adolf at Lützen in 1632 left Durie negotiating with the Swedish Chancellor, Axel Oxenstierna, which opened up a new phase of interaction between Durie and the Swedish government.[110] This would find him eventually moving to Sweden for two years between 1636-1638 in a failed attempt to win support of the Swedish Lutheran establishment. Nonetheless, the very fact that Durie got so close to the Swedish king and Chancellor in 1631-1634 can only be attributed to his intimacy with his relatives and friends in Swedish service, Colonels David Drummond, Sir James Ramsay and Sir James Spens in particular.

Durie's Scottish network stretched across the military, diplomatic and intellectual disciplines. They not only brought his teachings into Swedish spheres of influence, but also into Danish-Norwegian and German ones as well. While working as Sir James Spens's secretary in 1628, Durie must have written and read many letters between Spens and his half-brother Sir Robert Anstruther. In April 1633, Charles I commissioned Anstruther to travel to a Diet of Protestant princes at Heilbronn.[111] Undoubtedly due to his relationship with Sir James Spens, Anstruther allowed Durie to travel with him as part of his retinue.[112] Indeed he is reported to have actively encouraged Durie and like minded people to co-operate at the Diet.[113] In Heilbronn, Durie again met with Chancellor Oxenstierna, his requests being supported by a private audience between Anstruther and Oxenstierna on his behalf.[114] Durie also made an important contact through the Swedish ambassador to Strasbourg, Josias Glaser.[115] In the

---

[110] In c.1632 Durie asked Oxenstierna for a document of permission and approval for his work of reconciliation which the Swedish Chancellor provided saying it was in accordance with the wishes of the late lamented king. See HP, 9/1/1A-6B.

[111] Turnbull, *Hartlib, Dury and Comenius*, p. 147.

[112] HP, 69/8/1A-2B, Bunickhausen to John Durie, 4 July 1633 addressed to 'Monsieur Jean Dure Ministre du St euangile, a la suite de Monsieur Anstruther Ambassadeur des Couronnes de la Grande Beretagne'.

[113] HP, 69/8/1A-2B, Bunickhausen to John Durie, 4 July 1633. 'Je n'ay neglig nullment de travailler en caste affaire Chretienne concerte entre nous a Heylbron, sur L'ouuerture que m'en fist [premiermenet?] Monsieur L'Ambassadeur Anstruther'.

[114] HP, 14/4/8A-8B, Sir Thomas Roe to the Archbishop of Canterbury, 20 July 1633; Turnbull believed that Oxenstierna had cooled towards Dury by this stage of his negotiations. See Turnbull, *Hartlib, Dury and Comenius*, p.147-8.

[115] Ibid., p.147-148.

period following the Diet, Anstruther and Durie undertook a pilgrimage around Europe's leading academics and theologians after which Anstruther returned to Hamburg and Durie to Britain.

Through Anstruther, Durie came into contact with another Scottish cleric, Samson Johnson, Anstruther's chaplain. Johnson wrote to Durie to inform him that he had travelled with Anstruther into Denmark. He noted that while Anstruther met with Christian IV at Glückstadt, he had managed to discuss Durie's ideas with Cluuerius, 'the chiefest man of note in that Kingdom [and] he professed that nothinge could be more acceptable to him then this long-wished-for vnion of the Church'.[116] Within a few months, Johnson wrote that he had left Anstruther at Schindeburg and

> Took a journey farther to that most famous monument of Danemarke, Oliger Rosencrantz, a man knowne through the world both for his great learning and piety in soe much that I thinke he hath few equals in the Christian world.[117]

In fact, Rosencrantz was important for several reasons. As the father-in-law of the Danish Chancellor, he promised he would use his influence to endeavour to introduce Durie's Irenicist teachings into the Danish universities of Sorø and Copenhagen.[118]

In the meantime, Durie had travelled to England where he believed he had gained the support of Archbishop Laud for further meetings with the Lutheran clergy in Scandinavia. Most historians ascribe Laud's support to be due to the influence of Sir Thomas Roe. When it comes to influencing Laud, the support of a fellow clergyman such as William Forbes is likely to have carried far more weight although both men probably had a role to play. John Durie also knew that in addition to any support he had in Britain, he could continue to rely on his family to use their influence with the Swedish government.

Sampson Johnson informed Durie in April that his cousin, Sir James Ramsay, had arrived in Frankfurt with Axel Oxenstierna and that Ramsay expected Durie to make contact with him in due course.[119] Armed with refreshed self-confidence, he left for the continent bearing what he believed to be letters of

---

[116]HP, 42/13/5A-6B, Sampson Johnson to John Durie, 19 September 1633.

[117]HP, 42/13/7A-8B, Sampson Johnson to John Durie, 21 December 1633; Turnbull, *Hartlib, Dury and Comenius.* p. 161.

[118]HP, 42/13/7A-8b, Sampson Johnson to John Durie, 21 December 1633; Turnbull, *Hartlib, Dury and Comenius.* p. 161.

[119]HP, 42/13/9A-10B, Sampson Johnson to John Durie, 8 April 1634.

support from Laud and Secretaries Coke and Windebank. Prior to his departure in 1634, Laud had also given Durie letters to give to the Lutheran and Calvinist parties in Germany. Laud also provided a letter for the Stuart ambassador, Sir Robert Anstruther, with whom Durie was to meet up at the Diet of Protestant Princes in Frankfurt.[120] Anstruther sponsored John Durie's attendance at the Frankfurt Diet in direct contravention of the orders of Archbishop Laud, who had expressly forbidden Anstruther to have anything to do with sanctioning Durie's teachings.[121] Roe believed that Anstruther had gone out of his way to hinder Durie's mission, but these charges were strongly denied by John Durie himself. Indeed he commented that it had been quite the reverse and that Anstruther had gone a long way to facilitating his mission.[122]

Sir Robert Anstruther certainly had the connections to promote Durie for, in 1634, he joined the select German organisation *Fruchtbringenden Gesellschaft* led by Prince Ludwig of Anhalt.[123] The main objective of this group was to win over the leading political, intellectual and military classes to the idea of establishing a national linguistic and cultural society in Germany. Yet the other stated aim of the society focused on developing Germany into a society based on denominational tolerance. It has been noted that to achieve this no theologians were asked to join the society.[124] Yet, doubtless due to his parallel agenda, Durie secured many important contacts among the members of the society. Some of them, such as Axel Oxenstierna, he already knew.[125] Others, like the Scottish officer James King, he probably met while travelling with Anstruther in Germany between 1633-1634.[126] Durie developed a close friendship with King

---

[120]PRO SP 75/13, f.196. Anstruther to Coke, 31 May 1634; Turnbull, *Hartlib, Dury and Comenius.* pp.148-65. Th. Fischer erroneously believed that this mission was led by Roe adding to confusion over the role of Sir Thomas in the promotion of Durie's business. See Fischer, *The Scots in Germany*, p. 178.

[121]Turnbull, *Hartlib, Dury and Comenius*, pp.159-63.

[122]Ibid., p. 165.

[123]K. Conermann, *Die Mitglieder der Fruchtbringenden Gesellschaft 1617-1650* (Weinheim, 1985), pp. 262-3; For more on the *Gesellschaft* see R.J.W. Evans, 'Learned Societies in Germany in the Seventeenth Century', *European Studies Review* 7 (1977), pp. 129-51. It is of interest to note that the society contained a number of Scotsmen but had no members from England or Ireland. All the Scots with the exception of Anstruther served in the Swedish army.

[124]Evans, 'Learned Societies in Germany', p. 131.

[125]Conermann, *Die Mitglieder der Fruchtbringenden Gesellschaft*, pp. 252-3.

[126]Conermann, *Die Mitglieder der Fruchtbringenden Gesellschaft*, pp. 239-40; DNB, XI, p. 135; *SSNE* no. 2814.

whom he repeatedly met and eventually introduced to Samuel Hartlib.[127] Certainly by the end of that year, a crucial round of network building had been completed by Durie which facilitated the next stage in his Irenicist career.

Conclusion

The purpose of this paper has not been to deliberate the life, theology or politics of John Durie. It has simply been to expose a deficit in the research surrounding the early years of his career. This has focused on illuminating 'the void', described in the introduction to this chapter, by building up a picture of the Scottish-Baltic world in which Durie operated. This has been achieved by evaluating the knowledge we have relating to Durie's Scottish origins which, though usually ignored today, was frequently recognised during his own lifetime.[128] Indeed, Durie was not unknown to be referred to as 'Ecclesiastae Scoto-Britanno', even while working for Oliver Cromwell.[129] That is not to say that we should now overstate the nationality of the cleric, but simply recognise it. For, as Edward Lane once told Durie, 'you love truth not as it is in Luther or Calvin, in Presbyterian or Independent, in Englishman or Scot, but as it is in Jesus'.[130]

Clearly Durie spent his life trying to break down all manner of theological and national divisions. Yet, had he not been related to Scottish members of the Swedish military élite, it is doubtful whether he would have gained the ear of the

---

[127] For Durie's introduction of King to Hartlib see HP, 2/2/11A-B, John Durie to Hartlib, 14 April 1640. Surviving letters from and to King, Durie and Hartlib can be found in HP, 2/2/28A-29B, John Durie to General King, 10 July 1640; HP, 27/11/3A-4B, James King to Hartlib, 6 May 1642; HP, 27/11/5A-6B, James King to Hartlib.

[128] HP, 42/13/3A-4B, Sampson Johnson to John Durie, 18 July 1633. Johnson, a fellow Scot, wrote to 'Monsieur Iean Dury, Gentilhomme Escossois, Ministre de la Parole de Dieu'. But foreign theologians thought of him in these terms as well. See HP, 5/49/1A-2B, Philip Snabelius to John Durie, 25 January 1633, 'Domino Iohanni Duro, verbi Dei ministro orthodoxo Scoto-Britanno; HP, 59/10/68A-69B, the Ministers of Metz to John Durie, 11 August 1633, 'Reverendum in Christo fratrem Iohannem Durum, Scoto-Brittannum'.

[129] For example, in November 1636 John Durie wrote *Consultatio Theologica de Tollendis in Negotio*, part 1, and signed himself Iohanne Duræo Ecclesiaste Scoto-Brittanno, HP, 19/11/54A-61b. The following year he wrote *Explicata Delineatio Mediorum Theologicorum* part 1, to the Swedish clergy and again used the form 'Ecclesiaste Scotto-Brittano', HP, 19/4/1A-4B. During his Cromwellian service, foreign theologians continued to refer to Durie as a Scot. See HP, 5/19A-B, Crocius to Durie, 8 January 1655; HP, 15/7/7A-8B, William VI of Hesse-Cassel to the Protector, 28 April 1656, referring to 'Iohanne Duro Theologo Scoto-Britanno'.

[130] HP, 1/32/7A-22B, Edward Lane to John Durie, 26 August 1651.

Swedish king or the credibility to continue a dialogue with Axel Oxenstierna after Gustav II Adolf died in 1632. The good reputation and strong recommendations of Scots working in Scandinavia guaranteed that when John Durie met the Swedish king there had been several years of careful preparation by his allies to ensure the meeting occurred in a positive atmosphere. It further did Durie no harm that Spens and Anstruther were half- brothers, for the relationship of one to the other undoubtedly influenced Anstruther's decision to support Durie in the face of a royal command to the contrary.

John Durie's Scottish network, based on ties of kith and kin, has been shown to have penetrated the very heart of the Swedish, Danish-Norwegian and Stuart governments. Bearing this information in mind, his rise from obscurity becomes less surprising. The extent of the network and some other important members of it can be seen in glimpses from surviving correspondence. Such correspondence can include well-known figures such as James 3rd Marquis of Hamilton from whom Durie sought help in 1634.[131] But the Durie network also included names less familiar to most historians. Sampson Johnson concluded one letter to Durie by passing on his 'best respects to that worthy and pious warrier Sir James Ramsay, to Sir Alexander Hamilton, the gouenour, mr Hinderson, mr Muat & the rest'.[132] The significant point here is that all the people Johnson equated with

---

[131] In 1633 the Archbishop of Canterbury gave Durie a benefice in Exeter in the king's name. When Durie reached it, he found the incumbent of the benefice still alive and in good health. He approached Hamilton to 'bee pleased to let his Matie know that his Royall favour intended towards me is disappointed' and that Hamilton might intercede to sort the problem out. See National Archives of Scotland, GD406/1/9251, John Durie to Marquis of Hamilton, 3 March 1634.

[132] HP, 42/13/1A-2B, Samson Johnson to John Durie, 16 June 1633.

Durie's circle in Frankfurt were, like Drummond, King and the Marquis of Hamilton, important Scottish soldiers or agents in Swedish service.[133]

What has not been answered here is how a man so immersed in Scottish Presbyterianism from an early age made the quantum leap to become a leader in the international Irenicist movement. Such a theological question must remain the subject for another paper. In the meantime, armed with new knowledge relating to John Durie's Scottish network, we can better understand how his English and continental contacts fitted into the jigsaw of his life once he stepped into the international limelight.

This case study of John Durie's network studied here barely covers a ten-year period of a remarkable career which spanned over half a century. It has also been the personal network of one Scotsman out of thousands, many of whom remain to be discovered by historians.[134] There must have been many more such networks operated by influential Scots and others of which we remain ignorant. There is clearly still much to be done researching the vast British and Irish diaspora of the seventeenth century. With the ease of utilising new resources such as the *SSNE* database, that work has been simplified but is still proving to be most rewarding.

---

[133] Sir James Ramsay has been discussed already. Sir Alexander Hamilton had served as a captain in the Danish army. After the treaty of Lübeck in 1629 he transferred to the Swedes where he received promotion to Colonel and became the Governor of Hanau 1631-3. Mr Henderson probably refers to Captain John Henderson who later became both Colonel and Governor of Gothenburg (1644). At the time this letter was written he served as a captain or Major in the regiment of Sir James Ramsay. Mr Muat is, in fact, Hugh Mowatt, the Stuart envoy mentioned already in this chapter in Danzig in 1624. He later worked as an agent for Sir James Spence in 1626. Durie would probably have met him during his time in Elbing. In 1629 he was sent to the Polish Court by Sir James Spens with the explicit brief of disrupting the official mission of Charles I's representative, Francis Gordon, whom Spens believed to be a traitor. Mowatt continued as Spens's agent and eventually became the official representative of the Scottish Covenanters at the Stuart Court and Swedish agent to the Solemn League and Covenant. For more on Hamilton see W. Fraser (ed.), *Memorials of the Earl of Haddington* (2 vols., Edinburgh, 1889), I, pp. 28-33; C.B.R. Butchart, 'Sir Alexander Hamilton, General of Artillery', in *Aberdeen University Review*, XLII (1968), p.298;. For Mr Hinderson see Stockholm Krigsarkivet MR 1628/14, 15; 1629/5-10; N.A. Kullberg, et al. (eds.), *Svenska Riksrådets Protokoll, 1621-1658* (18 vols., Stockholm 1878-1959), XI, p.1; Sv. Ra. Anglica 5, James Spens to Axel Oxenstierna, 29 July 1626. For Mowatt's diplomatic correspondence to and from Sweden see Sv. Ra. Anglica E.514.

[134] In the course of building the *SSNE* database several hundred high ranking officers and dozens of diplomats have been included who are not recorded in other biographical collections. To date articles on upwards of 30 of these individuals have been accepted for entry in the *New DNB*.

Chapter 3

The herring fishery and the growth of Britain's Baltic trade in the seventeenth and eighteenth centuries

Jerzy Litwin

Throughout the seventeenth and eighteenth centuries the herring fishery proved to be a key influence in the expansion of British trade and the growth of the British shipbuilding industry. It also helped to shape political and economic relations between the states of northern Europe. Numerous contemporary publications, many of them dating from the early years of the seventeenth century, testify to the significance of the Baltic trade for the growth of British commerce. These sources, together with others found in the John Carter Brown Library at Brown University, Providence, Rhode Island, USA, form the basis for the present paper. The main focus is on Gdańsk (Danzig), a city that was of great importance as a market for fish, as well as a source of imported timber.

The records of English commerce with Baltic countries go back to the Middle Ages when England imported a wide range of timber and other forest products, metals, linen and textiles from that region. In the sixteenth century even the occasional ship was purchased there. Cloth, salt, animal hides and wool were shipped in the opposite direction, to a very large extent in non-English bottoms, as historical sources testify. Hence, it was very rare to see an English ship in Gdańsk before the end of the fifteenth century; indeed, between 1460 and 1583 only 0.1 to 3.7 per cent of the vessels entering that port were registered as of English origin.[1] However, during the reign of Henry VIII (1509-1547), commerce between England and Gdańsk grew substantially, particularly in respect of increased timber imports for the construction of warships. This trade, in turn, brought about the expansion of the English merchant fleet, which gradually became a serious competitor to its continental rivals. Henry VIII even purchased vessels from cities of the Hanseatic League as a way of enlarging the Royal Navy. Three of these ships – the *Morion of Danzig*, the *Sepiar of Danzig* and the *Trinity of Danzig* – were purchased in Gdańsk.[2]

As English merchants developed trade relations with the Baltic region, Muscovy (Russia) gradually emerged as an attractive potential market. Cargoes were moved there via Narva and Novgorod, the second city in Russia after Moscow.[3] But voyages to Narva were by no means safe. Ships sailing there were constantly under threat from piratical raids sanctioned, amongst others, by kings of Poland like Sigismund the Old (Zygmunt Stary). In the late fifteenth and early sixteenth centuries, England was also interested in opening up alternative trade routes to the Far East and English mariners like John and Sebastian Cabot began to search for a North West passage to the Orient. In 1497, John Cabot, sailing under the flag of Henry VII, reached the coasts of Labrador and Newfoundland. In 1517, his son Sebastian was the first European seaman to enter Hudson Bay. Despite their efforts, however, the desired north-west passage could not be found and attention turned to the possibility of a north-east passage to Cathay (China).

The results of an expedition that began in the spring of 1553 turned out to have great significance for English trade with Muscovy. Three ships participated in the expedition led by Sir Hugh Willoughby. A few weeks after setting sail and following a severe storm in the Norwegian Sea near the Lofoten Islands, the flotilla was scattered. Two of the vessels, the *Bona Confidentia* and the *Bona Esperanza* ran aground on the Kola Peninsula and broke up; their crews perished in the freezing weather. The third ship, the *Edward Bonadventure*, commanded by Richard Chancellor, had more luck and, having sailed into the White Sea, eventually cast anchor off Archangel. For both English and Russians, this was a discovery as significant in its way as that of Christopher Columbus in 1492. The voyage demonstrated that Muscovy could be approached from the north. The

---

[1] H. Samsonowicz, *Historia Gdańska* (Gdańsk,1982), pp.139-142.

[2] J.S. Corbett, *Fighting Instructions 1530-1816* (Publications of the Navy Records Society, vol. XXIV, London, 1905), pp. 18-22.

[3] See Enn Küng's contribution to this volume.

fact that Chancellor and a delegation from his crew were given an enthusiastic welcome at the court of Tsar Ivan IV merely served to underline the importance of their discovery. Gifts were bestowed on the travellers and the Tsar offered the Englishmen attractive commercial privileges. On their return to England in 1554, they established the Muscovy Company, which thereafter enjoyed a monopoly of the trade with Russia.

During the second half of the sixteenth century England's trade with the Baltic was further influenced by a number of political and commercial developments. The decline of the Hanseatic League and conflict between the Polish king Stefan Batory and the merchants of Gdańsk in 1577 led to the establishment of an English trading post at Elbing.[4] Two years later, in 1579, Queen Elizabeth I consented to the establishment of the Eastland Company. The Company exercised a monopoly over Baltic commerce with Norway, Sweden, Poland and their possessions in Livonia, Prussia and Mecklenburg. English exports to Elbing were those traditionally sold in Baltic countries, i.e. cloth and hides. The principal imports from Elbing were primarily materials for the construction and fitting out of ships, i.e. linen, hemp, timber, iron bars, birch tar and pitch.[5] Gdańsk, however, remained the principal port from which shipbuilding timber was supplied to England. Specialising as it did in the Dutch trade, Gdańsk endeavoured in a variety of ways to restrict competition from Elbing and to close down or transfer the English counting house to Gdańsk, a move that eventually succeeded in 1628.

Herring fishery – the source of commercial success

The growth of Hanseatic cities such as Gdańsk during the Middle Ages was due to the herring fishery and the herring trade. In the fourteenth century, herring catches in the Baltic were crucial to the economies of the region; indeed, as local fishing fleets were unable to meet the demand for herrings, Hanseatic merchants bought them up in Scania.[6] In 1370 the League concluded a treaty with Denmark at Stralsund, by which it acquired almost sole rights to trade in herrings caught off the coast of Scania. Teeming with herrings, these waters were intensively fished. The rapid growth of the fishery was based on a commission system, similar to that already being used in Gdańsk. However, towards the end of the fifteenth century, the commission herring fishery fell into a decline largely

[4]   A. Groth, *Kupcy angielscy w Elblągu w latach 1583-1628* (Gdańsk,1986), p 9.

[5]   Ibid., p. 27.

[6]   A. Ropelewski, *1000 lat naszego rybolowstwa* (Gdańsk, 1963), p. 42.

because the increasing number of Dutch merchants in Gdańsk were not interested in sustaining it. It was this, rather than falling yields from the Baltic herring grounds, that explains the demise of the local, open-sea fishery.[7] In setting up their counting houses in Gdańsk, Dutch merchants pursued their own self-interest and adjusted the structure of cargo movements to their own commercial policies, which favoured the import of herrings.

By the end of the fourteenth century Dutch fishermen were catching substantial numbers of these fish in the North Sea, which had become the other main herring fishery in Europe. Catches rose dramatically after 1416, when the first specialised fishing vessel known as a herring buss was built. At the same time, fishing with drift nets became more common, as did the salting of herrings and the manufacture of barrels. Thus, by the end of the sixteenth century, herrings were Holland's chief export and substantial quantities were shipped to the Baltic. By a proclamation of The Generality in 1580, the herring fishery was raised to the status of an approved maritime activity. These developments coincided with an increased demand for herrings in the Baltic countries where, in the opinion of many historians, the species had been over-fished.[8] Considerable imports of grain, shipbuilding timber, hemp and pitch from Baltic ports to the Netherlands were counterbalanced by the export of herrings fished by industrial methods in the North Sea. This proved to be an important substitute for sailing to the Baltic in ballast.[9]

---

[7] S. Gierszewski, *Dzieje Helu w latach 1526-1919* (Gdańsk, 1969) p. 51.

[8] Ropelewski, *1000 lat naszego rybolowstwa*, p. 40.

[9] In 1583 36.6 per cent of the ships tying up at Gdańsk had sailed there in ballast. See M. Bogucka, *Historia Gdańska* (Gdańsk, 1982), p. 468.

A Buss taking a driftnet from the sea.[10]

Attempts at expanding the herring fishery in England

The emergence of the Dutch as the leading carriers into the Baltic, and the significance of their highly specialised fishery, soon attracted the interest of English merchants and mariners. They drew attention to the efficiency of the Dutch and suggested that the English would do well to develop something similar. One of the most ardent advocates of the expansion of the maritime fishery in England was Admiral Sir William Monson (1569-1643), author of *Naval Tracts*, published as a manuscript in 1703.[11] In this voluminous tome, intended initially only for the eyes of the Admiralty and His Majesty's ministers, there are numerous comments about shipbuilding and the importance of the

[10] All illustrations are taken from G. Groenewegen, *Verzameling van Vier en taching Stuks Hollandische Schepen geteekend en in Koper Gebragt* (Rotterdam, 1789).

[11] W. Monson, *Naval Tracts* (London, 1703).

Baltic trade to the Netherlands. Monson perceived it to be the source of that country's economic strength. He wrote: 'In four towns within the Sound, Koningsberg [Königsberg/Kaliningrad], Melvin [Memel/Klaipeda], Stettin [Szczecin] and Dantzick [Gdańsk], there is vented in a year betwix 30 and 40 thousand lasts of herring, which will amount to more than 620 000 pounds [sterling].'[12] Monson argued that Dutch success was due to their possession of industrial fishing vessels like the buss and the hooker and he suggested that England should start building them. Dutch busses, he wrote, had a capacity of 35 lasts (about 70 tons).[13] 'We will make a greater gain with a buss of 20 last, which is but 40 tun, than Hollanders do with their 70 tun, in re spects of the nearness of our harbours to put in upon all occasions.' He added: 'If at any time corn fails the countries, we will here after supply them at a reasonable rate with our trade to Dantzick with herrings.'[14]

Fishermen on the deck of a Hocker catching cod on long lines.

---

[12] Ibid., p. 516.

[13] Ibid., p. 519.

[14] Ibid., p. 523

Further arguments in support of an expansion of the English herring fishery can be found in *England's Way to Win Wealth, and to Employ Ships and Marriners* by Tobias Gentleman, published in London in 1614:

> We having in our own countries sufficient store of all necessaries to accomplish the like businesse. For the Hollanders have nothing growing in their owne land for that businesse, but they are compelled to serch all their wood, tymber, and planke, wherewith they build, & make all their ships of, out of divers countries, and their iron out of other places, their hempe & cordige out of the easterne countries, their hoopes and barrell-boords out of Norway and Sprucia, their breadcorne out of Poland & east parts, their mault, barley and best double drinke from England and also all their fish and chiefest wealth out of his Maiesties Seas. The which they doe transport unto the foresaid countries, & returne for the procedue of fish and herrings, the fore-named commodities, whereby their Ships and marriners are set on worke, and continually multiplied, and into their countries is plentifull store of money and gold daily brought, onely for the sailes of fish and herrings.[15]

Gentleman considered that the cost of one 30-40 last buss, with a lifetime of some 20 years, would be around £500, with an additional £80 for the fishing gear. The running costs of one buss, which during four months would catch 100 lasts of herrings, would be £225; with herrings selling for £10 a last, the profit would be £650 in a single summer. According to Gentleman, however, the herrings could be sold for as much as £15-20 a last in Danzig.[16] He also drew attention to the practice adopted by some Dutch fishermen of taking their wives and daughters to sea as crew members. Moreover, during the fishing season special vessels would collect the fish and supply the fishermen with provisions. The French, like the Dutch, usually returned twice to their home ports with their catches during the herring season.[17]

Tobias Gentleman ended with an assurance that if the decision to construct busses in England were taken, he would be prepared to give assistance in preparing drawings, demonstrating the geometrical principles of building ships, selecting the proportions of the chief dimensions, planning the interior and

---

[15] T. Gentleman, *England's Way to Win Wealth and to Employ Ships and Marriners* (London, 1614) pp. 5-14.

[16] Ibid., p. 31.

[17] Ibid., p. 43.

distributing the installations and catching gear, all in accordance with the Dutch tradition.[18]

The Jager, a typical transport and supply ship for the Dutch North Sea fishery fleet.

Another book which contained comment on the efficiency of the Dutch fishery and trade, was *The Trades Increase* by Robert Kayll, published in 1615. The author, reviewing the possibilities for the development of English trade with the Baltic stated that 'barely five or six vessels out of London are headed for Danzig, Memel and Königsberg each year. A few more sail out of Ipswitch, Hull, Linne and Newcastle for the Baltic, often making two voyages in a year and bringing back grain, linen, potash, hemp, iron, wax and sawn timber.'[19] Kayll considered the advantages of expanding the English herring fishery, describing the abundance of fish in British waters as the fishing grounds moved in accordance with the seasons. The shoals of herring always remained off the

---

[18] Ibid., p. 46.

[19] Robert Kayll, *The Trades Increase* (London, 1615), p. 11.

British Isles, providing opportunities for Scottish and Irish fishermen to expand their activities too.[20] He did not consider the recruitment of crews for the fishing vessels to be a problem. There were substantial numbers of such men in coastal fishing villages throughout the kingdom and an increase in the numbers of fishermen had the further advantage of providing a reserve of men for the Royal Navy.[21]

Two further publications dealing in part with the herring fishery and the Baltic trade appeared in 1615: *The Defence of Trade*, by Dudley Digges, and Edward Sharpe's unpaginated dissertation *Britaines Busse*. The latter contains a detailed description of a Flemish buss which was then being completed near Radcliffe on the river Thames. It gives a precise specification of all the materials required to build a buss with a capacity of 35 lasts on a 50-foot keel. The longest deck beam was 17 feet. Construction and fitting out costs amounted to £260. Detailed descriptions of the crew's living quarters and the catching gear provide invaluable information about the minutiae of life on board ships in those days. The ship's equipment included armaments: pikes, 6 muskets, powder and shot, costing a little over £7. Nets, each 30 yards long, were suspended one after another on a carrier rope or reep, giving a total net length of 345 yards. Further ropes and floats for servicing them, together with other nets, added to the outlay for the catching gear.

The estimated costs of provisioning the crew are interesting, although Sharpe stressed the fact that the rations he quoted were those obtaining on His Majesty's ships, while the rations on Dutch busses were barely half as large. Provisions for a 16-man crew for a period of 4 months cost £57. Each crew member was entitled to one gallon of beer, one pound of hard tack, 1/16 gallon of peas or oatflakes, ¼ pound of butter and ½ pound of Dutch cheese per day, regardless of rank. There was also a weekly ration of two pounds of bacon. These provisions were supplemented by as much fish as the crew could catch. A small amount of vinegar and fuel to heat the food were also included. Large quantities of beer for the crew were carried in the herring barrels, each with a capacity of 32 gallons, i.e. about 2 days' ration for the entire crew. Eight tons of beer were taken on board for a four-month voyage. The wage bill for a 16-man crew for four months was £74 (the skipper received £20). Sharpe estimated the annual running costs to be £1000 and the profit in the first year after delivering 72 lasts of herrings to Gdańsk, including construction costs and freight charges, about

[20] Ibid., p. 36.

[21] Ibid., p. 38.

£80. In addition, the carriage of grain and other goods as a return cargo might be expected to yield a further profit of £120. Profitability in the second year of operations was expected to be much greater. Sharpe concluded by estimating the cost of 100 busses which he believed could be built within a year if raw materials from Ireland or Scotland were used. Somewhat optimistically, perhaps, he believed that the English herring fleet might eventually be expanded to 500 or even a thousand busses. England had the advantage over the Dutch, he argued, because they had direct access to the raw materials for shipbuilding and seamen to man the ships.

Tracts such as Sharpe's, which advocated the expansion of the English herring fishery, were published at a time when the Netherlands was beginning to challenge England for the leadership in whaling. Hull merchants had been associated with whaling voyages since 1598 but the first really well organised whaling expedition, led by Thomas Edge, set out from Hull in 1611 for the coast of Spitsbergen. The first Dutch whaling expedition to Spitsbergen sailed in 1612 and conflict between the seamen of both countries seemed inevitable. In 1613, when King James I granted the Muscovy Company a monopoly to hunt whales and other marine animals off Spitsbergen, the entire Dutch fleet was driven out by the English. However, the Dutch were not so easily intimidated and in 1614 they founded whaling companies of their own in Amsterdam and other cities. In 1614, Dutch and British vessels deliberately avoided each other in the waters off Spitsbergen in order to minimise the risk of further conflict. The following year, the Dutch arrived in greater numbers, thereby securing the advantage. Disputes and conflicts were an inevitable result of the whaling activities of the two fleets and they were further aggravated by the arrival of another country – Denmark – which claimed the island of Spitsbergen for itself. The Danes regarded the offshore waters of Spitsbergen as a closed sea. In the end, a compromise was found: the English occupied the western and the Dutch the north-western coasts of Spitsbergen and each fleet did its best to avoid the other and keep to its own fishing grounds. As it turned out, however, whaling was not as significant to the British economy as it was to the Dutch, and British whaling remained spasmodic for much of the seventeenth century.

British commerce with Baltic and the growth of shipbuilding

Edward Sharpe's description of the construction of the first buss on the River Thames, as well as later sources, indicates that despite some interest in the herring fishery, the British were unable to mount a serious challenge to Dutch commercial supremacy until the eighteenth century. However, Maria Bogucka has shown that herring imports into Gdańsk undoubtedly enabled ships to be exploited more efficiently.[22] According to Bogucka herring imports into Gdańsk increased from 20 per cent in 1565 to 36 per cent fifty years later although imports in subsequent years declined. By 1646 herring imports stood at 22 per cent, marginally more than they had been eighty years before. Imports of textiles, however, doubled from 28 per cent to 56 per cent between 1565 and 1646. Jerzy Trzoska has also drawn attention to the overall rise in imports from Britain during the second half of the seventeenth century.[23] He notes, however, that imports of fish to Gdańsk in the years 1671-1700, 97 per cent of which were herrings, remained an important commodity of trade. The greatest proportion, 77 per cent, were supplied by the Dutch; in second place were the Scots with 12 per cent (equivalent to 6105 lasts), while 8 per cent of these fish arrived in Norwegian ships.[24]

British trade with the Baltic increased substantially during the first half of the eighteenth century. The total number of British ships sailing through the Sound between 1700 and 1730 rose from 8 per cent to 20 per cent during these years. Imports of timber, iron, linen and hemp also rose – by 77 per cent in the first half of the eighteenth century, compared with the period 1699-1701.[25] Supplies of fish from Great Britain, particularly from Scotland, increased during the same period. In the years 1701-50 the Baltic ports received 44 per cent from the Netherlands, 35 per cent (15,910 lasts) from Scotland, 18 per cent from Norway and 1 per cent (434.4 lasts) from England.[26] By 1770 the same proportion of British and Dutch vessels – 26 per cent each – were sailing into the Baltic; by 1791-3, the British, with 37 per cent, had overtaken the Dutch, who now enjoyed only a 16 per cent share.[27] The industrial revolution, population growth and an increased demand for foodstuffs seem to have been the primary reasons for the growth of the British Baltic trade during this period.

---

[22] Bogucka, *Historia Gdańska*, p. 468.

[23] Jerzy Trzoska, *Historia Gdańska* (Gdańsk, 1993), vol. I, pp. 84-5.

[24] Ibid., p. 86.

[25] Ibid., p. 343.

[26] Ibid., p. 378

[27] Ibid., p. 431.

Table 1: *Numbers of British, Dutch and Gdańsk ships entering the Baltic 1784-95*

Origin of ships	Year			
	1784	*1788*	*1792*	*1795*
British	3179	3277	4347	2539
Dutch	1362	1511	2187	2?
Gdańsk (Danzig)	192	169	208	176

Source: H.Ch. Johansen, *Shipping and Trade between the Baltic Area and Western Europe 1784-1795* (Odense, 1983), p.18.

As Table 2 shows, a number of British ports specialized in the Baltic trade. One of these, Whitby, was the home port of the *General Carleton*, the wreck of which was recently discovered at the mouth of the River Piaœnica in northern Poland. The shipwreck has been investigated by the Polish Maritime Museum since 1995. According to Lloyd's Register, the *General Carleton* was a large ship of 500 tons built at Whitby in 1777. She sailed to Riga on her maiden voyage and made numerous other voyages to the Baltic before she was eventually wrecked. The precise circumstances of her loss are, as yet, unknown. This is not unusual, however, in 1788, for example, the fate of 18 British ships – about 2 per cent of the overall number of vessels plying between Britain and the Baltic – was recorded as 'unknown'.[28]

Table 2: *Principal British Ports in the Baltic Trade, 1787*

	No. of voyages	Average tonnage of ship
Dundee	68	118
Newcastle	228	268
Whitby	223	304
London	149	295

Source: Johansen, *Shipping and Trade*, p.29.

---

[28] H. Ch. Johansen, *Shipping and Trade between the Baltic Area and Western Europe 1784-1795* (Odense, 1983), p. 26.

Gdańsk remained the principal Baltic port of destination for British ships until the second partition of Poland in 1793, after which it gradually declined in importance. Fewer British vessels called there as the Napoleonic wars advanced, and from 1807 to 1813 the port was barred to them altogether by Napoleon's continental blockade.

The expansion of Britain's Baltic commerce in the eighteenth century went hand in hand with the rise in the numbers and size of the ships that were constructed. This in turn led to a steady increase in the demand for ship timber. Much of it was imported from the Baltic countries and later from North America and the Mediterranean. By the end of the eighteenth century, the British merchant fleet consisted of some 15,000 vessels, while the Royal Navy had nearly 600 warships at its disposal.[29] It is hard to imagine the number of oaks and other trees that had to be felled in order to build such a powerful fleet. Estimates are possible, however, on the basis of the records of the royal dockyards. They indicate that some 3,400 fully-grown oaks were needed to build a single hull of medium size. At Woolwich Dockyard between 1751 and 1761, 40,000 loads of oak were used to construct 16 warships.

In British shipyards, various types of imported timber were carefully examined to discover their physical characteristics. It turned out that ships built in Britain of Polish timber were twice as durable as vessels constructed of Canadian timber.[30] By the end of the eighteenth century, Gdańsk timber had become so well known in Britain that its use was specially recommended for certain hull sections. Gdańsk oak was usually supplied to British dockyards in the form of beams and strakes and, though its deficiencies were known, it was a favourite timber for reasons of strength and economy. As late as 1852 specifications for the construction of His Majesty's warships given in John Fincham's four-volume work, *An Outline of Ship Building* continued to require the use of Gdańsk oak. He described it in detail: 'This timber is dense-grained, cohesive, sometimes with very short grains … but large splits are rare in thick planks and strakes. Indeed, as soon as it has been sawn, it can be immersed in water and can be left there for a long time.[31] These qualities predestined Danzig oak for use in ships' bottoms, for decks and the internal structures of the hull, even though it was of poorer quality than timber from Britain, southern Europe

---

[29] J. Dodds and J. Moore, *Building the Wooden Fighting Ship* (London, 1984), p. 13.

[30] Trzoska, *Historia Gdańska*, pp. 272-3.

[31] J. Fincham, *An Outline of Ship Building* (London, 1852), p. 24. Fincham was a master shipbuilder in the royal dockyards and, incidentally, author of one of the world's first books on the history of shipbuilding.

or Memel.[32] Fincham was equally critical of coniferous timber imported from Poland, yet despite its faults this timber had much in its favour, as long as it was carefully selected. It was considered the best material for decks because it was economical, durable and had a neat appearance. It was also suitable for roofs and platforms on ships, while the shorter pieces were used for railings and other fittings.[33] These comments were published in the mid-nineteenth century, at a time when timber shipbuilding was on the wane. The usefulness of the various types of timber was certainly well known much earlier, but was a well-guarded trade secret. This knowledge was thus published at a time when it had become of little industrial significance. Nevertheless it is testimony to the enduring importance of the Baltic trade to the rise of British maritime supremacy.

---

[32] Ibid., p. 16.

[33] Ibid., pp. 25-6.

Chapter 4

Britain and Sweden: the changing pattern of commodity exchange, 1650–1680[1]

Leos Müller

The years 1650–80 represent a crucial period in the development of Sweden's foreign trade. During these three decades Swedish trade went through deep quantitative and qualitative changes. The flow of bar iron, Sweden's most important export commodity, shifted from the Dutch Republic to England. However, the shift of the market for iron was also linked to a new pattern of trade organisation. The predominantly bilateral trade became multilateral. The reason was the unfavourable balance of trade between Sweden and England. Because the rising exports of Swedish iron to England were not balanced by English imports to Sweden, the balance of trade had to be settled by commodity and credit flows to and from a third party, the Dutch Republic. A 'triangular' trade thus became the predominant pattern.

The changes had a number of economic and political causes in western Europe, and Sweden, as an important part of the west European politico-economic system, was seriously affected by them. Perhaps the most significant economic consequence of this development was the decline of the Dutch dominance over Sweden's economic life and the rising importance of Swedish-English commercial connections. On an

[1] I wish to take this opportunity to express my gratitude to the Swedish Institute, Stockholm, whose grant made possible my participation in the conference 'Britain and the Baltic: East Coast Connections'.

actor level, one consequence of the changed commercial situation after 1650 was the growing engagement of merchants and factors from the British Isles in Sweden. Especially in the course of the Danish-Swedish conflicts, the English factors became deeply involved in Sweden's trade and shipping.

This paper has two related purposes: to describe the changes in Stockholm's foreign trade between 1650 and 1680 on a macro-economic level, and to analyse the role of wholesale merchants of Scottish and English origin engaged in this trade. The paper is founded on evidence of the Stockholm foreign trade, not the whole of Sweden's trade. However, Stockholm is fairly representative, as the Swedish capital completely dominated the kingdom's commerce.

The pattern of Stockholm's foreign trade in the course of the seventeenth century

It is impossible to understand the importance of the market shifts from the Dutch Republic to England without a general picture of Stockholm's foreign trade. The trade of Stockholm during the seventeenth century, as well as that of Sweden as a whole, was characterised by a deep discrepancy between exports and imports. Exports consisted of a very few staple commodities of which metals (iron and copper) constituted roughly 80 per cent in the middle of the century.[2] In the second half of the seventeenth century copper exports declined, but iron became even more important; thus the ratio between metals and the other export commodities did not change significantly. Imports, on the other hand, consisted of an endless number of commodities, from bulky salt and grain to highly valued textiles, luxury goods, wine and so on.[3]

The composition of foreign trade underlines the extreme dependence of Stockholm's commerce on iron. It was exported primarily in a form of bar iron, but there were also some highly valued iron products, for example steel and guns. Nor can bar iron be described as a homogeneous product: it came in many different kinds, each with a different price. Generally, the development of the Stockholm bar iron exports was characterised by steady increase. Exports rose from roughly 17,000 ship-pounds of bar iron in the 1610s to 150,000 ship-pounds during the 1660s and 1670s.

---

[2] Å. Sandström, *Mellan Torneå och Amsterdam. En undersökning av Stockholms roll som förmedlare av varor i regional- och utrikeshandel, 1600–1650* (Stockholm, 1990), p. 314.

[3] See the Stockholm tolagsjournaler. Stockholm City Archive, Stadskamrerarens arkiv, Verifikationer och specialer till Stockholms stads huvudbok (1573–1800) [hereafter SSA, Verifikationer och specialer].

The peak was reached in 1678 with an export of 189,000 ship-pounds.[4] However, the steady increase did not mean stable markets. The Stockholm iron exports in the seventeenth century went through three distinct phases. In the first phase, until the 1610s, the Stockholm foreign trade was focused on Baltic ports. Danzig and Lübeck were the most important destinations of iron, which was exported mainly as pig iron. At this time even Scotland was a more substantial purchaser of iron than the Dutch Republic or England.[5]

In the second phase, between the 1620s and the 1650s, bar iron exports increased rapidly and the market shifted from the Baltic ports to the Dutch Republic. Around 1650 the Dutch accounted for over 50 per cent of Stockholm's exports.[6] The Dutch period was characterised by an inflow of Dutch capital and industrial know-how, and by a rising number of Dutch merchants in Stockholm. During this time iron exports to England were negligible. In 1646, a tiny 2 per cent of the Stockholm iron exports went to England – a figure rising to only 3 per cent in 1648.[7]

The first marker of the future role of the English market came in 1659. Because of the Dutch involvement in the Swedish-Danish war, iron exports to Amsterdam were stopped. The English replaced the Dutch and took over 38 per cent of iron exports. The situation in this year was exceptional. However, in the following years, too, the English merchants were substantial buyers of Stockholm bar iron. They imported about one-fifth of the total export of bar iron. The next dramatic shift came during the war of 1675–9. The Dutch-Danish navy had complete control of the Baltic Sea, and Swedish shipping and foreign trade were paralysed. In this situation the Englishmen replaced both the Dutch intermediaries and the Swedish merchants. The share of the iron exports destined for England reached about 50 per cent. The pattern with England as the primary destination of the Swedish bar iron was established – and it was to change little over the next century.

---

[4] L. Müller, *The Merchant Houses of Stockholm, c. 1640–1800. A Comparative Study of Early-Modern Entrepreneurial Behaviour* (Uppsala, 1998), p. 85.

[5] Sandström, *Mellan Torneå och Amsterdam*, p. 335.

[6] Ibid., p. 337; Müller, The Merchant Houses, p. 89; S-E. Åström, *From cloth to iron. The Anglo-Baltic trade in the late seventeenth century* (Helsinki, 1963), p. 35.

[7] Åström, *From cloth to iron*, p. 35.

Table 1: *Destinations of bar iron shipments from Stockholm, 1620–87 (percentage)*

	1620	1646	1648	1659	1685	1687
Lübeck	29	21	13	25	3	5
Danzig	14	21	15	5	6	4
Scotland	10	4	5	6	5	4
The Dutch Republic	14	36	48	0	28	23
England	0	2	3	38	42	51
other destinations	33	16	16	26	16	13

Source: S-E. Åström, *From cloth to iron. The Anglo-Baltic trade in the late seventeenth century* (Helsinki, 1963), p. 35.

Roughly the same market shift from the Dutch Republic to England can be traced in other staple commodities, especially brass, tar and pitch. On the other hand copper seems, even after 1680, to have been exported primarily to Amsterdam.

Traditionally, these changes have been seen in the light of shifting market conditions in the Dutch Republic, Sweden and England. Thus, the Dutch interest in Swedish iron industries and the growth of exports destined for Amsterdam from the 1620s have been seen as a consequence of Dutch difficulties in obtaining iron from Spain and the German hinterland during the Thirty Years War. On the other hand, the stagnating exports from the 1650s have been explained by the fact that after 1648 the Dutch could again buy their iron from their traditional suppliers.[8]

The classical explanation of the English demand for Sweden's iron from the mid-seventeenth century relies on the scarcity of wood in England. Shortage of wood supplies limited the burning of charcoal and consequently iron production. S.E. Åström and K.G. Hildebrand argued instead for the importance of the internal shift

---

[8] K.-G. Hildebrand, *Fagerstabrukens historia. Sexton- och sjuttonhundratalen* (Uppsala, 1957), pp. 40–2.

of the English iron industry from the south-east of England to the north-west.[9] Other explanations include the boom in the English economy, rising colonial demand, shipping and the reconstruction of London after the fire of 1666. All these explanations stress supply and demand as the key factors in the market change, and they are surely right up to a point. However, such market-focused explanations miss important aspects of the historical truth. Here I wish to stress also the significance of political, institutional, military and diplomatic aspects for understanding the market shifts in the course of the century. I have been inspired by Jonathan Israel's model of the rise and decline of the Dutch Republic in the course of the seventeenth century.[10] Israel's explanatory model is based on the interaction between political and economic developments. So the Dutch success, according to Israel, cannot be understood without reference to the favourable political and military developments in western Europe. In the same way the Republic's decline from about 1670 must be linked to the deteriorating political and military situation and not only to economic decline. Thus, for example, Israel stresses the impact on Holland of the mercantilist policies pursued in France, England, Prussia, Austria – and Sweden.[11]

Applying a similar perspective to Swedish economic and political development one can differentiate between the phase of Dutch-Swedish friendship between 1614 and 1645, and the phase of Dutch-Swedish hostility from 1645 to 1679.[12] The first phase was also a phase of deep Dutch engagement in Sweden's economic life, with Dutch entrepreneurs settling in the country and investing in metal and other industries. The second phase, on the other hand, was characterised by rising Swedish hostility to Dutch influence and by efforts to diminish it.

As Dutch-Swedish relations deteriorated, English-Swedish relations improved. These relations were basically indifferent during the years of the English Civil War and problematical during the First Anglo-Dutch War (1652–4).[13] From the late

---

[9] Hildebrand, *Fagerstabrukens historia*, pp. 44–5; S-E. Åström, 'Swedish Iron and the English Iron Industry about 1700: Some Neglected Aspects', *Scandinavian Economic History Review 30* (1982). For another aspects of the debate see also A. Florén and G. Rydén, 'A Journey into the Market Society. A Swedish Pre-industrial Spy in the Middle of the Eighteenth Century', in R. Björk and K. Molin (eds.), *Societies made up of history*, (Uppsala, 1996), pp. 260–4.

[10] J.I. Israel, *Dutch Primacy in World Trade, 1585–1740* (Oxford, 1989).

[11] Ibid., pp. 383–6.

[12] T.J. Lindblad, 'Evidence of Dutch-Swedish trade in the 17th century', in J.Ph.S. Lemmink and J.S.A.M. van Koningsbrugge (eds.), *Baltic Affairs. Relations between the Netherlands and North-Eastern Europe 1500–1800* (Nijmegen, 1990), pp. 213–18.

[13] W. Pursche, 'Stockholms handelssjöfart och de engelska kaperierna 1652–1654', *Studier och handlingar rörande Stockholms historia*, vol. 3, (Stockholm, 1966).

1650s, however, Sweden and England had common interests. The contrasting development of relations between Sweden and the Dutch Republic and between Sweden and England is not difficult to understand. It followed closely the shifts on the international scene where England and the Dutch Republic were the main rivals in the decades 1650–80, fighting against each other in three naval wars (1652–4, 1664–7 and 1672–4). In the same period, Denmark and Sweden fought for control of the Baltic basin.

The development of Swedish political relations with the Dutch Republic and England should also be linked to the rising mercantilist policy in Sweden and England. For example, the worsening relations between the Dutch and Swedish may be seen in the light of Swedish mercantilism. Many mercantilist measures in Sweden were, more or less, directed against the Dutch. A system of free, half-free and foreign ships in the ordinance of 1645, which meant higher duties for the Dutch shipping than for Swedish shipping, was one of them. The founding of the Swedish Board of Commerce in 1651 may also be seen in this perspective.[14] Swedish mercantilism was naturally seen as a danger in the Dutch Republic. Of course, even England and Sweden had different commercial interests but generally these two countries followed the same mercantilist policy. The potential conflicts between Sweden and England were conflicts of interest, not of principle.

The role of political and military factors in commerce can be best illustrated by the situation during the war of 1675–9. In the initial phase of the war the Swedish navy suffered a terrible loss in a battle near the south cape of Öland in 1676. From that point the joint Danish-Dutch fleet gained complete control over the Baltic Sea. Stockholm's foreign trade was cut off.[15] The numbers of Swedish vessels in the Sound illustrate the dramatic decline of Swedish shipping (Table 2). In 1674, before the war, there were 65 Swedish vessels going westwards from Stockholm. Between 1676 and 1678 there were no Swedish vessels from Stockholm at all in the westbound traffic. On the other hand the number of foreign vessels from Stockholm rose from 32 in 1674 to 167 in 1678, the highest year for foreign shipping.[16] The majority of these foreign vessels were English.

---

[14] For a Dutch perspective on the Swedish mercantilism see J.E. Elias, 'Contract tot oprichting van een Zweedsch factorie-comptoir te Amsterdam in 1663', *Bidragen en mededelingen van het Historisch Genootschap* (1903), p. 380.

[15] It should be pointed out that the state of war between Sweden and the Dutch Republic did not mean a complete stop of Dutch commerce with Sweden. The countries had a special agreement concerning the commerce in spite of the war. Åström, *From cloth to iron*, p. 62.

[16] O. Bjurling, 'Stockholms förbindelser med utlandet under 1670-talets växlingar', *Forum Navale* 10 (1951), p. 5.

Table 2: *Westbound vessels from Sweden passing the Sound in the 1670s*

Year	Swedish	Dutch	English
1671	170	77	22
1672	158	16	1
1673	151	15	0
1674	153	43	8
1675	33	40	99
1676	0	33	148
1677	0	38	100
1678	0	82	125
1679	3	86	93
1680	99	74	93

Source: N.E. Bang and K. Korst (eds.), *Tabeller over Skibsfart og varetransport gennem Øresund 1661–1783*, vol. 1, (Copenhagen-Leipzig, 1930), pp. 12–21.

The English activity was not visible only in shipping. The English replaced both the Swedish and Dutch merchants during the war years, and strengthened England's role as a market. Perhaps most remarkable was the English success in imports which had previously been completely dominated by the Dutch.

However, with the peace of 1679 the favourable situation disappeared and commerce reverted to a more traditional pattern. This is correct as regards both shipping and imports. First the Dutch and then the Swedish shipping pushed aside the English vessels. In the course of the 1680s the number of English vessels passing Sound on their way from Sweden/Stockholm fell to about 60 and in the last decade of the century to a mere 10 vessels. At the same time the number of Swedish vessels on the same route rose from 99 (1680) to 261 (1696).[17]

---

[17] N.E. Bang and K. Korst (eds.), *Tabeller over Skibsfart og varetransport gennem Øresund 1661–1783*, vol. 1 (Copenhagen-Leipzig, 1930), pp. 20–41. See also S-E. Åström, 'The English Navigation Laws and the Baltic Trade, 1660–1700', *Scandinavian Economic History Review* 8 (1960), pp. 13–14.

In the import trade the Dutch replaced the English. The reason was the Dutch Republic's strong position in the most important import commodities: salt, wine and cloth. The only sector where the English kept their influence even during the 1680s was the iron export. England finally replaced the Dutch Republic as the most important market for Swedish iron and so it remained for the next hundred years. Despite the limited effects of the English dominance from the period 1675–9 the pattern of trade changed and England succeeded in keeping its role as the most important export market.

The British merchants in the Stockholm iron trade

In this section I shall examine more closely the role of the English merchants who took part in this development in Stockholm. Who were these men? How did they differ from their Dutch counterparts? The first merchants from the British Isles who settled in Stockholm were not Englishmen but Scots. The reason was Scotland's special role as a buyer of Swedish iron as early as the 1620s. As Table 1 shows, Scotland was a relatively significant iron importer around 1620. The Scottish merchants formed a very active business community in the whole Baltic area. The Leyels (Lyel, Leijel) were perhaps the best-known Scottish family in Sweden.[18] The Leyel brothers settled in Sweden in the 1640s. Through marriage the family was related to Adam Raddou, a successful Swedish merchant in Stockholm. Raddou and the Leyels built up a huge iron-works complex in central Sweden. Their combined iron exports in the decade 1651–60 were over 13,000 ship-pounds annually. Such exports made the Leyels and Raddou the leading iron export group in Stockholm.[19] Alexander Buchan, Alexander Waddell and Jacob Sempel were the other merchants of Scottish origin in Stockholm.[20] All three appeared frequently as big iron exporters in Stockholm weigh-books. Sempel was also engaged deeply in the tar and pitch trade.[21]

---

[18] *Svenskt biografiskt lexikon*, vol. 22, pp. 448–51. The Leyels also belonged among the big merchant families of London: for example Adam Leyel became in 1666 a member of the Eastland Company, an important and honourable membership. (Åström, *From cloth to iron*, pp. 137–40).

[19] Müller, *The Merchant Houses*, 86.

[20] Åström, *From cloth to iron*, pp.136, 140; Henry Roseveare, *Markets and Merchants of the Late Seventeenth-Century: The Marescoe-David Letters 1668–1680* (Oxford, 1987), p. 126.

[21] A. Hallberg, 'Tjärexport och tjärhandelskompanier under stormaktstiden', *Historiska och litteraturhistoriska studier* 34 (Helsinki, 1959), p. 121.

William Maister (of the Hull merchant family) and William Strang were the first two true Englishmen registered in Stockholm. Maister and Strang were already registered in toll books by 1636. However these two men cannot be seen as typical representatives of London Baltic merchants. As subjects of the Danish crown living in Elsinore they did not have to pay the Sound toll duties. They traded primarily with the Dutch Republic, and not England.[22] The members of the respected Eastland Company, the English privileged company in the Baltic trade, saw these men as interlopers. The engagement of these men in the Stockholm foreign trade was probably a strategy to broaden their operations in the Baltic area and diminish their commercial risks. The Maister family was big in the ports of Riga and Narva, where the English were traditionally stronger than the Dutch.[23]

A significant shift of Swedish iron exports to England occurred at the end of the 1650s, in connection with the Swedish-Danish wars of 1657–60. It appears that 1659 was a turning point. With English shipping came English factors who traded in a quite different way from the Scottish and Dutch merchants. William Blackett, in Swedish sources also mentioned as Blaccaert, was one of the first English factors.[24] His stay in Stockholm can be seen as a typical example of how the factor trade was carried on in the following decades. In contrast to the other merchants, Blackett did not buy iron directly from iron-works and he never engaged in the iron industry. As the following case shows, he bought his iron in Stockholm from other iron exporters. Blackett appears as a substantial customer in the accounting books of the leading Stockholm firm, the Momma-Reenstierna brothers, in the years 1656–7.[25] He purchased huge volumes of bar iron and he paid well. The prices paid by Blackett were significantly higher than those paid by the other customers of the Momma-Reenstiernas. After some years in Stockholm Blackett returned to England and settled in Newcastle. By 1670, he was again doing business with the Momma-Reenstiernas. He supplied the Momma-Reenstiernas' brass-works with coal from Newcastle.[26] Blackett continued to make his career in the Baltic trade and in the course of the

---

[22] Åström, *From cloth to iron*, p. 136.

[23] Ibid., pp. 122, 128, 131.

[24] Ibid., p. 139.

[25] Müller, *The Merchant Houses*, pp. 96–7.

[26] It should be pointed out here that Blackett was not the only English merchant supplying the Momma-Reenstiernas with coal. Samuel Sowton from London was another. Also it seems that coal was quite important commodity in Swedish imports from England. Müller, *The Merchant Houses*, p. 173.

1670s he was among the leading merchants in this trade in England. In this period he also had his own factor in Stockholm, named Johan (John) Strother.[27]

During the 1660s, the Dutch and English shares in Stockholm's exports were almost equal. In 1669, 28.6 per cent of the Stockholm exports were destined for the Dutch Republic, while 25 per cent of the total went to England. Including the exports to Scotland (6.3 per cent), the British market was therefore already bigger than the Dutch market.[28]

Despite some new names the group of leading merchants did not change very much in the 1660s. The same merchant families as in the 1640s and 1650s dominated trade. This meant that these men had to adapt their trade to changed market conditions, to shift at least part of their trade toward England. The Momma-Reenstiernas are perhaps the best example of such an adaptation. They built up their English connection on their relationship with the London firm of Charles Marescoe, a relationship which was already established by the early 1650s. However, during the 1660s this London connection became more and more important. As in the trade on the macro level, the commodity exchange between Charles Marescoe and the Momma-Reenstiernas was based on bar iron exports, but other commodities became to play an increasingly important role. This is evident especially in exports of brass and tar and pitch, in which both Marescoe and the Momma-Reenstierna were among the big players.[29] The Momma-Reenstiernas' business did not go well in the early 1670s but their failure did not depend on links with the English market. It was primarily the result of faulty investment decisions within Sweden.

As mentioned in the previous section, the real breakthrough for the Englishmen came in 1675, with the Swedish-Danish war. Allestree, a secretary of the English envoy in Stockholm, mentioned in a report of 1675 that the English colony in Stockholm had expanded to about thirty persons, some from London, but most from Hull and York.[30] These English factors replaced the established Dutch-Swedish families and dominated both the exports and imports. The rapid transition is reflected in the Stockholm weigh-books for 1677–80. The weigh-books for 1671–6 are missing but the books for1677–80 are sufficiently illustrative. English names occur in the weigh-books much more frequently than in the period before the war. There were names such as: Urban Hall, Ashton Nuttal, Gilbert Heathcote, Johan Strother, Johan

---

[27] Roseveare, *Markets and Merchants*, p. 401.

[28] The figures are based on SSA, Verifikationer och specialer, 1655 and 1669. See also Åström, *From cloth to iron*, pp. 34–5.

[29] Roseveare, *Markets and Merchants*, p. 29; Müller, *The Merchant Houses*, pp. 103–9.

[30] Åström, *From cloth to iron*, p. 140.

Green, Philip Nisbett, John Harvey, William Mauldt, George Marioribank, Patrick Thomason, Robert Watson, Alexander Patilock, Simon Story, and many others.[31]

Table 3: *The leading iron exporters of British origin in Stockholm (ship-pounds)*

1677	
Urban Hall	15,658
Gilbert Heathcote	7,751
Simon Story	5,689
Johan Green	4,474
Johan Strother	3,834
Ashton Nuttal	3,803
Johan Zederitz	2,191
Johan Harvey	1,534
William Helleday	1,488
Patrick Thomason	1,258
William Mauldt	1,118
Robert Born	974
George Marioribank	685
Robert Watson	669
Alexander Patilock	584
Philip Botte	584
Robert Gardin	523
Total exports by above mentioned	52,817
Total Stockholm iron exports	133,665

---

[31] National Archives of Sweden, Stockholm, Stockholms vågböcker II, reviderade vågböcker, 1544–1722, [hereafter RA, Stockholms vågböcker II] (1677–80). See also Åström, *From cloth to iron*, pp. 96, 160.

1678	
Ashton Nuttal	13,859
Johan Strother	10,780
Gilbert Heathcote	7,846
Simon Story	5,260
William Helleday	3,738
Johan Green	3,595
William Mauldt	2,893
Urban Hall	2,862
Johan Zederitz	2,737
Johan Harvey	2,137
Philip Nisbett	1,571
George Marioribank	1,122
Robert Gardin	978
Total exports by above mentioned	59,378
Total Stockholm iron exports	189,445

1679	
Ashton Nuttal	10,299
Gilbert Heathcote	8,334
Johan Strother	6,907
Simon Story	5,892
William Helleday	4,153
William Mauldt	3,216
George Marioribank	1,892
Johan Green	1,594
Johan Zederitz	1,175
Robert Born	872
Johan Harvey	813
Total exports by above mentioned	45,147
Total Stockholm iron exports	146,203

Source: National Archives of Sweden, Stockholm, Stockholms vågböcker II, reviderade vågböcker, 1544–1722, (1677-9).

Note: The exports include bar iron, steel, copper and brass, however bar iron dominated completely (e.g. in 1677 Stockholm exports consisted of 127,000 ship-pounds of bar iron). The names mentioned are 'British-sounding'. It means that some important names may be missing, while some other may be misunderstood. There are some merchants of British origin (e.g. Leyels) who are not mentioned because of their long establishment in Sweden.

With the peace between Denmark and Sweden the Dutch returned to some extent. They came back as carriers of Swedish commodities and also as importers. But in the iron trade the English factors kept their position. Generally, we find in the 1680s the same men who had established themselves in the course of the war: Philip Nisbett, William Mouldt, Johan Strother, Thomas Cutler, William Maister, Henry Moxon, Johan Green and Ashton Nuttel. But in the course of the 1690s, during the English war with France, the English factors left Stockholm. They were simply replaced by the Swedish merchants. An indication of the decline is the number of factors hiring storehouses in Stockholm. In 1686 there were at least ten English factors hiring storehouses in Stockholm. In the late 1690s, there were only three such men with English-sounding names: Geoffrey Liddel, Jacob Herter and Philip Forster. All became Stockholm burghers.[32]

The disappearance of the English factors from Stockholm does not mean any change in England's role as a destination for iron. England had been established as a key market for Swedish bar iron, with roughly 50 per cent of Stockholm iron exports going there – and this situation did not change seriously in the next 100 years.

In the period 1650–1680 Stockholm merchants and factors established a new trade pattern. A 'triangular' exchange pattern replaced the traditional bilateral pattern. England became the main importer of Swedish bar iron. In parallel, English textile exports to the Baltic area declined. This new Baltic-English, or more properly Swedish-English, pattern of exchange resulted in an unfavourable balance of trade for Britain. Thereafter English exports to the Dutch Republic paid for iron imports from Sweden, and Swedish imports from the Dutch Republic completed the triangle. Another way to organise payments was bills of exchange. Amsterdam played a role in the triangle as the financial centre where the balance of trade between the countries was restored. Nevertheless, the Dutch dominance of the Baltic trade belonged to the past.

Typical English factors

It has been argued that the English merchants played an important role in the change of the Stockholm foreign trade in 1650–80. They partly replaced the Dutch as intermediaries in the Stockholm commerce and they linked Swedish and English markets. In many ways, they fulfilled the same functions as the Dutch had, but they were also different. In comparison with the Dutch or even

---

[32] Åström, *From cloth to iron*, p. 143.

Scottish merchants the majority of English merchants apparently had a different entrepreneurial behaviour. They did not plan for a long stay in Sweden, they did not invest in iron-works and they did not apply for Swedish citizenship. Very few of them became Stockholm burghers. To exemplify the different patterns of their entrepreneurial behaviour I shall pay attention to three of these men, Urban Hall, Gilbert Heathcote and William Hodgkinson. Each of them in his way made a different career and reached a different position back in England.[33]

Urban Hall established himself as a factor in the Stockholm iron trade from the late 1660s. In 1668, he registered a quite substantial volume of bar iron, over 900 ship-pounds.[34] He was one of the factors who most successfully utilised the commercial opportunities created by the war of 1675–9. In 1677 he registered at the Stockholm weigh-book an export of over 15,000 ship-pounds of iron, copper and brass, a huge volume by contemporary terms.[35] His total metal exports were bigger than those of Louis De Geer, the best-known merchant tycoon and industrialist in seventeenth-century Sweden.

Just two years later Hall disappeared from Stockholm's trade statistics. He returned to London and he became a member of the Eastland Company. Membership in this company seems to have been the ultimate aim and a marker of success of the leading Baltic merchants in London. George Shuttleworth and Samuel Sowton, mentioned earlier, were other big Baltic merchants in England who obtained membership in the Company.[36] In the 1680s Hall belonged among the biggest Baltic merchants. However, he seems never to have reached the top of London's mercantile élite and he never acquired a title.

Like the majority of wholesale merchants, Hall dispersed his investments in company shares and land. He owned shares in the East India Company and, in 1699–1700, he acted as Sub-Governor of the Royal Africa Company, a favourite investment object of Baltic merchants. He owned shares in the Bank of England and was among the founders of 'The Company of Copper Mines in Wales'. This engagement was surely linked to his experience in the metal trade. He owned land in Chatham). It is a rather surprising fact that the Fishmongers were the only City guild of which Hall was a member.

---

[33] Sources of biographical information about Hall and Heathcote are Åström, *From cloth to iron*, pp. 158–65. On Hodgeson see, P. Riden, 'An English Factor at Stockholm in the 1680's', in *Scandinavian Economic History Review 35* (1987), pp. 191-207.

[34] RA, Stockholms vågböcker II, 1668.

[35] RA, Stockholms vågböcker II, 1677.

[36] Roseveare, *Markets and Merchants*, p. 41.

Gilbert Heathcote was perhaps the most outstanding member of the London merchant élite engaged in the Stockholm iron trade. He had to do business in Stockholm as early as in 1674, because in this year his goods were confiscated by Swedish customs. In 1677, he was the second biggest iron exporter in Stockholm, with an export of 7,800 ship-pounds of iron, and he belonged also among the top exporters in 1678 and 1679 (see Table 3). In 1681, Heathcote was already back in London. In the following decade he made his fortune as an importer of Baltic staple commodities. In 1690, he left the Baltic commerce and went into more lucrative and speculative trading activities, in the African and East Indian trade. He became a member of the new East India Company in 1698. He is also known as a vociferous critic of the Royal Africa Company's monopolistic policy. His career reached its peak after 1700. He became a Member of Parliament and Lord Mayor of London. In 1702 he was knighted. The Heathcote family belonged to London's commercial élite during the eighteenth century and in time they merged with the English land-owning aristocracy.

William Hodgkinson, the third factor mentioned here, arrived in Stockholm later than Heathcote and Hall. He probably came to Stockholm in 1678 and the main period of his activity in Sweden was the mid-1680s. Hodgkinson was a member of an old Hull merchant family so his main connection in England was his father's firm in Hull. Like the other English factors he was mainly engaged in the iron trade. His accounts show his partnership with both his countrymen and Swedish merchants. For example, both Heathcote and Mauldt appeared among his partners in London.[37] However, Hodgkinson never belonged among the top iron exporters such as Hall and Heathcote. In 1689 he returned to England and established himself as a merchant in Hull. After his father's death he settled at Overton and took over the family business. For the next forty years he traded in iron, other Baltic staple commodities and lead – the family's speciality. The Stockholm period, apparently, was just a prologue to his merchant career at home.

Stockholm was just a step in the successful business career of the English Baltic merchants. They stayed a few years as factors of some other English merchants, before they returned to London, Hull or Newcastle to make their proper careers. Obviously, they had use of their knowledge of the market and their contacts in Sweden, because they frequently continued in the Baltic trade. However, the colonial trade was clearly regarded as a very attractive alternative. A remarkably large number of Baltic merchants invested in colonial trade. An

---

[37] Riden, 'An English Factor at Stockholm', p. 204.

important factor in such a move may have been the supplies of Baltic staple commodities, which were re-exported to colonies. But any firmer conclusions as regards the link between the Baltic and colonial trade require further research.

Conclusions

The period 1650–80 can be characterised as one of deep changes in Swedish foreign trade. As relations with the Dutch deteriorated and mercantilism began to dominate Swedish trade policy, iron exports shifted from the Dutch Republic to England. The shift was caused by a combination of political and economic factors. England became at the end of the period the most important market for Swedish iron. The shifts between markets, however, resulted also in a new pattern of trade, in which the old, bilateral pattern was replaced by a 'triangular' trade. The link between London and Amsterdam balanced commodity flows between Sweden and the Dutch Republic and between Sweden and England.

A very interesting aspect of the shift from the Dutch Republic to England is the role of British merchants. The first Scottish merchants were already trading with Stockholm at the beginning of the seventeenth century, but they did not play a very significant role in Stockholm's foreign trade. The situation changed around 1650 when the British market became more important. Then the English joined the leading Dutch-Swedish merchants who dominated the Stockholm trade. As the importance of English market rose, the number of English merchants engaged in the Stockholm iron trade also increased. In the 1670s, the English factors did play a more important role in replacing the established merchant families. However, a typical English business career in Stockholm was different in comparison with the Dutch and even the Scots. For an English factor Stockholm was just a prologue to his proper business career in England. So the English factors returned after a few years to Britain. The English engagement in iron trade was not steady and, in the course of the 1690s, the Stockholm iron trade was taken over again by Swedes, or by merchants living in Sweden.

Chapter 5

English commercial activity in Narva during the second half of the seventeenth century

Enn Küng

By the sixteenth century English traders had long been active in the Baltic area, selling mainly cloth and returning with corn, timber, forest products (tar, pitch), flax and hemp. In 1553 the English established a new trade route to Russia via the Arctic Ocean but as long as Narva was in Russian possession (1558-1581), they preferred to sail to Narva than to the shores of the White Sea, despite the obstacles set in their way by Sweden and Poland. The Muscovy Company, or Russia Company, was founded in 1555. Its area of activity first involved only the shores of the White Sea, but in 1560 the Englishmen arrived in Narva. Tsar Ivan IV had given the English the right to trade all over Russia in 1555, and in 1569 they also obtained the right to open a warehouse for goods in Narva.[1] After the Swedish occupation of Narva in 1581, English interest turned towards the Arctic Ocean. The Arctic sea route to Russia seemed to the Muscovy Company to be more convenient than to continue shipping to Narva. Besides, in the north it was possible to have direct trade contacts with Russians and thus maintain

---

[1] Artur Attman, *Den ryska marknaden i 1500-talets baltiska politik: 1558-1595* (Lund, 1944), pp. 153-7; Artur Attman, *The Struggle for Baltic Markets. Powers in Conflict 1558-1618* (Gothenburg, 1979), pp. 33-7; Arne Öhberg, 'Russia and the World Market in the Seventeenth Century. A Discussion of the Connection between Prices and Trade Routes', *Scandinavian Economic History Review* 3 (1955), pp. 126-7; T.S. Willan, *The Early History of the Russian Company, 1553-1603* (Manchester, 1956), pp. 67-97.

mercantile privileges obtained from the Tsar for the Company.[2] So the first phase of Narva's special importance in the trade relationship between western Europe and Russia lasted only for about twenty years. By the middle of the seventeenth century a few English and Scottish merchants had settled in Narva[3] but, according to the customs registers preserved for Narva and partly for Tallinn, the English shipments had entirely stopped at a time when not only the traditional Lübeck and other North German towns, but also merchants from the Netherlands, continued their journeys to this area.[4] Therefore two London merchants, John and William Rowley, could not make use of the privilege of exemption from duty in Narva, given to them by Gustav II Adolf in 1629.[5]

The Governor General of Livonia and Ingria, Johan Skytte, gave more serious attention to attracting English merchants to the towns along the shore of the Gulf of Finland. In the autumn of 1630 he concluded an agreement with the Moscow-bound diplomat Alexander Stuart to the effect that the latter would alert the members of the Muscovy Company, residing in Moscow, to the advantages of Narva over Archangel. When the envoy returned in the spring 1631, he announced that one part of the Company was willing to transfer its trade to Narva. Skytte sent his son Bengt to Moscow to find out under what conditions the English would transfer their warehouses to Narva or Tartu.

---

[2] Attman, *Struggle*, p. 196; Eric H. Wijnroks, 'Anglo-Dutch Rivalry in Russian Trade in the Latter Half of the 16th Century. A Historiographical Essay', *Baltic Affairs. Relations between the Netherlands and North-Eastern Europe 1500-1800* (Nijmegen, 1990), pp. 426-31.

[3] On 8 August 1612 Thomas Köllner from York, England, became a citizen of Narva; on 11 May 1614 Peter Lessle(y) from Aberdeen in Scotland; on 17 April 1615 Carl Bock from Douglas in Scotland et al.: EAA (= History Archives of Estonia), 1646-1-74, pp. 222, 314, 318, 361.

[4] For the maritime connections of Tallinn in the first third of the seventeenth century see: Evald Blumfeldt, 'Statistilisi lisandeid Tallinna kaubaliikluse ja meresõidu ajaloole aa. 1609-1629', *Ajalooline Ajakiri* 1-2 (1935), pp. 8-14; Wolf-Rüdiger Rühe, 'Revals Seehandel 1617-1624', *Zeitschrift für Ostforschung* 38 (1989), pp. 204-6. For Narva: Helmut A. Pijrimjaë, 'O sostojanii Narvskoj torgovli v nacale XVII veka', *Skandinavskij sbornik* XI (1966), p. 87 (table 1).

[5] Arnold Soom, 'Die Politik Schwedens bezüglich des Russischen Transithandels über die estnischen Städte in den Jahren 1636-1656', *Õpetatud Eesti Seltsi Toimetused* XXXII (1940), p. 19; Dirk-Gerd Erpenbeck '"Die englischen in Liefflandt negotierenden Kaufleute". Reval und der englische Handel im späten 17. Jahrhundert', in Norbert Angermann and Wilhelm Lenz (eds.), *Reval: Handel und Wandel vom 13. bis zum 20. Jahrhundert* (Lüneburg, 1997), p. 210; Stefan Troebst, *Handelskontrolle - "Derivation" - Eindämmung: schwedische Moskaupolitik 1617-1661* (Wiesbaden, 1997), pp. 148-9.

However, Bengt Skytte reported that the English merchants in Russia were neither interested in the Narva trade route nor considered it profitable.[6]

The English merchants' interest in Narva was restored only in the second half of the seventeenth century. Up to that time English mercantile interest had focused on Prussian ports of Danzig, Elbing and Königsberg on the shore of the Baltic Sea but in the 1650s the Englishmen appeared quite unexpectedly at Riga and other Swedish ports. These areas were then under the Eastland Company which had been founded in 1579.[7] One of the reasons for re-orientation was that the Prussian ports served the Polish hinterland which was undergoing a deep economic and political crisis in the second half of the seventeenth century. Thus, for instance, traditional Polish and Russian goods, formerly shipped via Danzig, were later procured from neighbouring towns.[8] On the other hand, the English faced increasing Dutch competition in Archangel. A yet more important role in the re-orientation was played by the anti-English policies adopted by the Russian Tsar in the mid-1640s. When Tsar Aleksei Mikhailovitch came to the throne, he began to reorganise Russia's foreign and domestic trade. One way to increase the state revenues was to remove the privileges given to foreign companies and merchants. One of the first to be affected was the Muscovy Company which was deprived of exemption from duty on 1 July 1646. The elimination of foreigners from domestic trade was in the first place in the interests of Russia's own merchants – *gosts*. Their attacks on foreigners continued and, under the pretence of the execution of King Charles I, the Tsar completely cancelled the Englishmen's privileges on 1 July 1649.[9]

---

[6] Ragnar Liljedahl, *Svensk förvaltning i Livland 1617-1634* (Uppsala,1933), pp. 476-7; Soom, 'Die Politik Schwedens', p. 19; Troebst, *Handelskontrolle*, pp. 146-7.

[7] R. W. K. Hinton, *The Eastland Trade and the Common Weal in the Seventeenth Century* (Cambridge, 1959), p. 5; Erpenbeck, *"Die englischen in Liefflandt"*, pp. 209-10. See also J. K. Fedorowicz, *England's Baltic trade in the early seventeenth century. A study in Anglo-Polish commercial diplomacy* (Cambridge, 1980).

[8] Elisabeth Harder-Gersdorff, 'Lübeck, Danzig und Riga. Ein Beitrag zur Frage der Handelskonjuktur im Ostseeraum am Ende des 17. Jahrhunderts', *Hansische Geschichtsblätter* 96 (1978), pp. 110-12; Maria Bogucka, 'Danzig an der Wende zur Neuzeit. Von der aktiven Handelsstadt zum Stapel und Produktionszentrum', *Hansische Geschichtsblätter* 102 (1984), pp. 91-103.

[9] S. I. Arhangel'skij, 'Anglo-gollandskaja torgovlja s Moskvoj v XVII v', *Istoriceskij sbornik* V (1936), p. 17; L. A. Nikiforov, *Russko-Anglijskie otnošenija pri Petre I* (Moskva, 1950), p.10; Arnold Soom, *Der Handel Revals im siebzehnten Jahrhundert* (Wiesbaden, 1969), pp. 2-3, 87; Troebst, *Handelskontrolle*, pp. 256, 265-70.

The reason why the English merchants appeared on the Baltic Sea and the Gulf of Finland was therefore the need to find new ways of procuring Russian raw materials. The resources of the English North American colonies could not replace the goods from the Baltic area. Instead of growing flax and hemp or making forest products the American colonists preferred to produce tobacco. The scope for providing domestic strategic raw materials was also limited in England. As a result, during the latter half of the seventeenth century, the governments of England and Sweden came closer both economically and politically since access to Russian goods was possible only via the ports under Swedish rule.[10] It was also essential to find new markets for the goods such as cloth and tobacco produced in England and her colonies.[11]

English interest in the Baltic trade was welcomed by Sweden. The English merchants would assist the commercial policy of the state as it was hoped that with their help Russian consignments would be sent to the Baltic ports instead of Archangel. It was also hoped that the English would reduce the role of the Dutch merchants in the Baltic trade.[12] As early as 1649 the Governor of Estonia, Erik Oxenstierna, understood that the Tsar's decree could serve the interests of the state commercial policy if, for example, the English merchants were provided with a yard for storing goods in Tallinn. In December 1649 negotiations were held between the Swedish resident in Moscow, Jacob de Moulin, and the Tallinn Town Council at which the latter agreed to bestow great commercial privileges in the city.[13] On 12 December 1649 the Tallinn Town Council contracted a legal statement in accordance with which the Englishmen were promised: (1) to be given a convenient construction site for building dwelling houses and a packing room (2) in questions of religious liberties to consult the tutelary government of Queen Christina (3) to share the citizens; right to be free from excise on wines and beer (4) to open their packing room as often as they wished and sell *Laken* (linen material) by wholesale both to retailers and foreign merchants but not ell- or piece-meal to the nobility (5) to receive justice similar to that of the citizens in their legal affairs.[14]

---

[10] Sven-Erik Åström, *From Stockholm to St. Petersburg. Commercial Factors in the Political Relations between England and Sweden 1675-1700* (Helsinki, 1962), pp. 15-16.

[11] Jacob M. Price, 'The Tobacco Adventure to Russia. Enterprise, Politics, and Diplomacy in the Quest for a Northern Market for English Colonial Tobacco, 1676-1722', *Transactions of the American Philosophical Society* 51 (1961), p. 20.

[12] Birger Fahlborg, *Sveriges yttre politik 1660-1664* (Stockholm, 1932), p. 53.

[13] Soom, *Die Politik Schwedens*, p. 251.

[14] RA (= Svenska Riksarkivet), Livonica II, vol. 668.

The Swedish diplomats in Moscow Karl Pommerering and Johan de Rodes attempted during the winter of 1649-50 to persuade the English merchants in Moscow to transfer their storage places to Tallinn, informing them about the promises of the Tallinn Town Council to give them great privileges. The Englishmen's reaction was positive but, first and foremost, they demanded the liberty to worship in accordance with their own confession. If that was guaranteed they had no doubts about their move to Tallinn. Only the permission of the Muscovy Company was required. However, the English merchants' representation was not allowed to cross the border to Sweden and further to England because the Tsar had forbidden it. Although that particular attempt to obtain a place for storing English goods in Tallinn failed, the Muscovy Company understood quite clearly by the spring of 1650 that the Tsar would not restore their privileges on the White Sea. Therefore their interests in the possibilities offered to them by Sweden grew significantly.[15]

However, in the 1650s all the talks and signed contracts (1654, 1656) between Sweden and England did not lead to concrete commercial agreements. Although the Swedes were willing to give the English merchants special privileges in its ports, Cromwell turned them down.[16] The wars waged in the mid-1650s (including the first English-Dutch naval war of 1652-4; the Swedish-Polish war of 1655-60; the Danish-Swedish wars of 1657-60; the Russian-Swedish war of 1656-61) all had a negative impact in blocking access to the Baltic for English ships. A breakthrough in the relationship between the two countries came only after the Restoration.

In the second half of the seventeenth century political and economic relations between Sweden and England were based on various treaties. The friendship and trade treaty which was signed on 21 October 1661 was essentially an alliance treaty between Charles II and the tutelary government of Karl XI. Charles II consented to support Swedish ambitions in Poland. In return the English merchants enjoyed as favourable trading conditions in Sweden as the Dutch merchants. Gothenburg and Plymouth were declared free ports for the merchants of both parties. The mutual transit trade through each other's countries was also guaranteed and for England this meant trading via Swedish-governed areas to Russia. The English could establish their residences in Stade, Landskrona and Narva. Soon the treaty of 1661 was replaced by a treaty of friendship, defence, trading and navigation concluded on 1 March 1665. Article

---

[15] Troebst, *Handelskontrolle*, pp. 333-4.

[16] Michael Roberts, 'Cromwell and the Baltic', in *Essays in Swedish History* (London, 1967), pp. 152-3, 172-3.

23 facilitated the Englishmen's purchase of stock in trade in Sweden and Article 24 enabled the English to establish trade companies in Stade, Landskrona and Narva, as mentioned above, as well as have their warehouses. When in 1672 the Swedish-English alliance was renewed, the liberties of the English merchants as in Narva as well as elsewhere in Sweden were again acknowledged.[17] In the mid-1660s a number of propaganda writings were published in Stockholm to coax both English and Dutch merchants to come to the towns on the Gulf of Finland.[18] In 1665 a special booklet in English was issued and circulated all over England by the Swedish authorities.[19] The ideas, how to get the trading by the English, Dutch and other foreigners to Tallinn, Narva and Nyen so that they would settle down as wealthy new residents in the towns, were presented to the tutelary government by the Royal Board of Trade on 12 May 1669,[20] and even later.

The concentration of the English trade on Narva in the 1660s and 1670s

Although Narva was mentioned in the Swedish-English treaties of 1661 and 1665, English merchants – first of all the members of the Eastland Company –

---

[17] Fahlborg, *Sveriges yttre politik*, pp. 187-210, 480 ff.; Birger Fahlborg, *Sveriges yttre politik 1664-1668*, vol. I (Stockholm, 1949), pp. 87-91; Georg Landberg, *Den svenska utrikespolitikens historia. 1648-1697*, vol. I:3 (Stockholm, 1952), pp. 131-3, 141; Hinton, *Eastland Trade*, p. 145; Åström, *From Stockholm*, pp. 301, 76; Enn Küng, 'Trading Conditions of the English in Narva in the Second Half of the 17th Century', *Kleio. Estonian Historical Journal. Special Issue in English* (1994), pp. 18-19.

[18] *Remonstration, att dhe Engelskes seglation och handell på Rysslandh mycket bättre och beqvämmare kan skee gienom Östersiön och deri belägne Svenske hambner och städer, än på och gienom Archangel. Actum Stockholm, den 10 aprillis a:o 1665: EFMSoR (=Ekonomiska förbindelser mellan Sverige och Ryssland under 1600-talet (Dokument ur svenska arkiv))* (Stockholm, 1978), pp. 161-2.

[19] Per Nyström, *Mercatura Ruthenica. Die schwedischen Ostseeprovinzen Estland und Livland im 16.-18. Jahrhundert* (Uppsala,1993), p. 144; Helmut Piirimäe, 'Kaubanduse küsimused Vene-Rootsi suhetes 1661-1700. a' *Tartu Riikliku Ülikooli Toimetised* 113 (1961), p. 91; Stefan Troebst, 'Stockholm und Riga als "Handelsconcurrentinnen" Archangel'sks? Zum merkantilen Hintergrung schwedischer Großmachtpolitik 1650-1700', *Forschungen zur osteuropäischen Geschichte* 48 (1993), p. 275.

[20] *Kommerskollegiets förslag till svenska regeringen rörande handelsfrihet för engleska, holländska m. fl. främmande köpmän i fråga om handeln i Reval, Narva och Nyen. Stockhom, den 12 maj 1669:* RA, Handel och sjöfart (utrikeshandel, Ryssland 1500-1600-talet), vol. 15; samas, Kommerskollegiets underdåniga skrivelser till K. Maj., vol. 2 (1666-1669); EFMSoR, pp. 171-173.

arrived in the towns of the Gulf of Finland only at the beginning of the 1670s.[21] Narva was not their first choice: they had first attempted to settle in Tallinn. This was logical, since Tallinn was located immediately on the territory of the Eastland Company and so no licence had to be purchased from the Muscovy Company as was the case for Narva up to 1698. It was also important for the English that, in comparison with the three towns on the Gulf of Finland, Tallinn had a more developed infrastructure. A breakthrough in the arrival of the English in Tallinn took place in about 1675.[22] The residents as representatives of the Eastland Company arrived in Tallinn and, while engaged in their own business, managed from there the trading links for other members of their Company via Narva to the Russian market. Men who were simultaneously merchants, owners of warehouses and residents in the 1670s included John Brawn, Henry Hoyle and, at first, also Thomas Loftus. The latter soon moved to Narva where he was joined by similar intermediaries such as Richard Bacon, Alexander Gilbert and William Kettlewell. But in Tallinn the English faced some serious problems, concerning local laws, such as the 1679 regulation of street trading (*Straßen-Ordnung*), which affected their commercial interests.[23] The fact that Tallinn was first a coordination centre for the English-Russian staple products via Narva appears in the reports on import-export figures by the English merchants in Tallinn which are surprisingly low, particularly when compared to respective Dutch figures.[24] Thus, as far as the last quarter of the seventeenth century is concerned, the statement by the secretary of

---

[21] One of the obstacles to English navigation to the Baltic Sea was the second English-Dutch Naval War of 1665-7 during which their trade routes via the Sound were blocked: Hinton, *Eastland Trade*, p. 103; Roberts, 'Cromwell', p. 148; Jonathan I. Israel, *Dutch Primacy in World Trade 1585-1740* (Oxford, 1989), pp. 273-9.

[22] The year of 1675 was described as a miracle for the English, as their trade with the Baltic had doubled: Hinton, *Eastland Trade*, p. 108.

[23] Sven-Erik Åström, *From Cloth to Iron. The Anglo-Baltic Trade in the Late 17th Century* (2 vols., Helsinki, 1963-5), vol. II, pp. 126-127; Erpenbeck. "*Die englischen in Liefflandt*", pp. 214-48.

[24] Helmut A. Pijrimjaé, 'Udel'nyj ves razlicnyh stran Zapadnoj Evropy v torgovle Éstonskih gorodov v XVII veke', *Skandinavskij sbornik* XV (1970), pp. 14-17. In 1682 the proportion of the English trade in the export from Tallinn was 1.3%; in 1686 0.8%, in 1695 0.2% and in 1700 0.4%. The figures for Dutch exports in the same years were 84.4, 37.7, 60.8 and 17.9%. The English import to Tallinn in 1695 was 6.6% and the Dutch one -545%: ibid., Tables 3 and 4; Soom, *Der Handel Revals*, pp. 1-45, 105-25.

the English Embassy, William Allestree, in 1675 that Tallinn was only a passage for English trade to Narva was not quite true.[25]

As in Tallinn so also in Narva, the rising interest of the English merchants could be observed in the 1670s. During the last quarter of the seventeenth century the English import from Narva took a solid second place after the market leaders from Lübeck.

Table 1: *The proportion of the English merchants in the trade of Narva in 1662-1696 (%).*[26]

Year	Export	Import
1662	14.9	-
1668	6.0	4.9
1671	18.2	2.9
1675	5.1	5.3
1677	33.8	47.1
1679	28.4	21.2
1696	20.4	24.3

The rise of the English merchants' interest in Narva is also indicated by the increasing number of ships sailing from Narva to western Europe via the Sound. In 1661-1674 there were fewer than ten ships per a year; in some years there were none (1666, 1667, 1672, 1673), in others only from one to three (1661-1663, 1665, 1668). However, 25 ships sailed from Narva via the Sound to England in 1675, and thereafter the numbers rose gradually from year to year. The record years were 1683 and 1700, with 50 and 69 ships respectively. Already during the Great Northern War in 1701 only two English ships sailed from Narva via the Sound, thereafter there was a longer pause. The data on Narva are very interesting to compare with the respective data of Tallinn and

[25] Åström, *From Cloth to Iron*, p. 127; Dirk-Gerd Erpenbeck, 'Die Engländer in Narva zu schwedischer Zeit', *Zeitschrift für Ostforschung* 38 (1989), p. 486.

[26] Pijrimjaé, 'Udel'nyj ves', pp. 10-13, tables 1 and 2.

Nyen. The comparison clearly indicates the small share of the English-Russian trade held by the neighbouring towns of Narva (see Table 2).[27]

Table 2: *The number of Dutch and English ships coming from Riga, Tallinn, Narva, Nyen and Pärnu to Western Europe via Öresund in 1661-1704*

Year	The Netherlands					England				
	Riga	Tallinn	Narva	Nyen	Pärnu	Riga	Tallinn	Narva	Nyen	Pärnu
1661	57	25	3	0	15	3	1	1	0	0
1662	45	33	3	3	17	8	2	2	0	0
1663	62	17	8	1	9	14	0	2	0	0
1664	58	15	9	1	11	9	0	7	0	0
1665	16	10	0	0	1	6	0	1	0	0
1666	59	20	4	0	6	0	0	0	0	0
1667	41	19	10	0	5	1	0	0	0	0
1668	92	41	10	2	12	13	0	3	0	0
1669	152	63	17	3	16	14	0	5	0	0
1670	113	26	8	0	24	19	0	6	0	0
1671	151	36	8	2	22	19	2	9	0	0
1672	21	8	2	0	4	1	0	0	0	0
1673	51	7	0	0	4	4	0	0	0	0
1674	156	25	5	1	20	19	1	7	0	0
1675	33	8	0	0	2	72	9	25	1	3
1676	86	12	1	0	10	86	11	29	0	6
1677	131	38	12	2	15	76	2	25	1	1
1678	61	17	10	3	14	44	2	22	1	0
1679	131	22	9	5	12	34	5	23	1	1
1680	180	32	14	10	17	30	3	22	1	0
1681	147	49	20	16	22	31	20	32	1	1
1682	228	78	20	25	22	70	3	46	6	1
1683	234	50	42	21	23	90	5	50	1	0
1684	186	72	35	18	18	48	4	29	0	0
1685	207	34	31	23	18	73	0	35	0	0
1686	248	16	43	13	24	77	1	43	0	1
1687	248	20	60	16	32	70	2*	49	0	0
1688	206	10	56	46	41	85	1	43	0	0
1689	159	34	16	17	9	67	2	24	0	0
1690	111	39	32	29	12	36	0	20	0	0
1691	120	40	26	19	10	53	0	25	1	0
1692	106	42	26	24	10	55	0	26	0	0
1693	173	57	31	31	11	51	0	29	0	0
1694	204	36	16	19	11	41	0	27	0	0
1695	160	30	49	10	14	39	1	26	0	0
1696	77	1	25	19	14	43	0	23	0	0
1697	104	2	30	15	23	32	1	10	0	0
1698	189	3	51	23	24	44	0	27	0	0
1699	204	5	80	33	22	80	0	47	4	0
1700	16	12	72	49	18	3	3	69	1	0
1701	44	3	8	13	16	0	3	2	0	0
1702	71	1	10	28	11	14	3	0	1	0
1703	64	1	11	1	16	13	0	0	0	0
1704	107	0	0	0	15	28	2	0	0	0

*one of them from Narva

Based on: N.E. Bang & K. Korst (eds), *Tabeller over Skibsfart og Varetransport gennem Øresund 1661-1783 og gennem Sturebelt 1701-1748*, vol I (Copenhagen, 1930).

---

[27] Tabeller over Skibsfart, pp. 2-45; Åström, From Stockholm, p. 24.

Information about the trade treaty concluded between Sweden and England on 1 March 1665 reached Narva relatively quickly. On 26 April 1665 the tutelary government of Karl XI informed Governor General of Ingria S. Grundel-Helmfeldt, who, in his turn, forwarded that information to the Narva Town Council on 31 May. Thus, in accordance with the information forwarded by Governor General, (1) the merchants of Narva who were going to sail to England needed a marine passport issued by his office (2) the ships which took the merchants from Narva to England had to be *clear* (of debt, mortgages?), and their skippers had to be Swedish subjects whilst the crew could be international. Likewise, the ships were not to carry illegal goods, therefore the authorities had the right to inspect the vessels (3) the merchants of Narva, like any other Swedish subjects, had the liberty of loading and transporting goods in Plymouth free of import duty (4) despite the principles of the Navigation Act revised by the king of England in 1660, the subjects of Sweden had the right also to import to England hemp, pitch, bacon, masts and copper which had not been grown or produced in Sweden, i.e. possibly Russian goods which were not carried by Swedish ships and seamen. These goods did not to have to be charged higher in England than the goods imported by the Englishmen themselves. At the same time the king of England had allowed his subjects also to freight and use Swedish ships for transporting goods to England as well as to her colonies and back. The only restriction was that the skippers and crews of Swedish ships had to be friendly towards England and in the case of such voyages did not to have to sail elsewhere but to England.[28]

The above-mentioned document refers only to the rights and obligations of the subjects of Sweden, including those of the citizens of Narva, in their commercial relationships with England. No reference is made to the liberties and special privileges given to Englishmen in Narva in accordance with the treaty of 1665. However, the propagandist statement compiled by the Royal Board of Trade of 10 April 1665 about the question how to induce the Englishmen to transfer their Russian trade from Archangel to the Baltic Sea clearly states:

> *Hafver H:s Kongl. Maij:t, vår allernådigste nu regerande konungh och herre, dhe Engelske i Narwa medh een court privilegerat, hvarest dhe kunna hafva sin egen consul, exercitium religionis och flere önskelige vilkohr och commoditeter, så at dhen Archangelske fahrten med denne icke står till förlijkna.*

---

[28] EAA, 1646-2-253, l. 89-90.

Apart from the role of Narva in the English Russian-oriented trade, the Board discussed the advantages that the Englishmen were given when they began to sail the Baltic Sea route and, on the other hand, the local hardships to be overcome on the spot when their commercial activity was transferred from Archangel to the Gulf of Finland.[29]

The late 1660s and early 1670s were nevertheless, from the Swedish point of view, a period of waiting for the English to arrive in the Baltic area. Reorientation was hindered not only by international complications such as the English-Dutch naval war, but by the English hankering after a possible restoration of their former privileges in Russia. Swedish residents in Russian towns keenly observed how the Russian authorities treated the Englishmen and what the latter strove to obtain there. For instance, the former Swedish resident J. von Lillienthal in Moscow reported in 1665 rumours in Russia that the English privileges would soon be restored and that the King of England was willing to establish friendly relations with the Tsar if this happened.[30] However, the Tsar did not revise his attitude towards the English merchants and their former privileges were not reinstated. The attitude of Russia towards the subjects of England is eloquently expressed in a report by a Swedish resident in Novgorod in 1669 that an English envoy on his way to Moscow had been very badly treated in Novgorod in a manner which was extremely unconventional.[31]

English trading conditions in Narva in the last quarter of the seventeenth century

By the beginning of the 1670s coaxing English merchants to the towns on the Gulf of Finland was a goal of Swedish economic policy. However, as soon as the English appeared *en masse* in Narva they were bitterly resented by the citizens. Wealthier than local entrepreneurs, they began to conclude trade contracts with the subjects of the Russian Tsar. In the summer 1672, when complaining about the merchants from Lübeck, both the commander of the Narva fortress and J. von Lillienthal accused the Englishmen of causing great harm to the trade of local Narva citizens. Like the Lübeckers, they preferred to deal directly with the Tsar's Russians who came to Narva, rather than with local citizens as was expected by central authorities (the customs rules of 1648 gave the latter a monopoly on the trade in salt, herring

---

[29] EFMSoR, s. 161-162.

[30] RA, Livonica II, vol. 178 (J. von Lillienthal to J. J. Taube from Moscow, 23 July and 4 October 1665).

[31] Ibid., Livonica II, vol. 179 (Letters to S. Grundel-Helmfeldt from Swedish residents in Novgorod and Pihkva (Pskov),10 June and 3 August 1669).

and corn). Although the merchants from Lübeck and England offered their commodities to the merchants of Narva, they raised the price for the local merchants. After that they went to Russians and sold the goods at a more favourable price. In Lillienthal's opinion it was a way of devastating the local market. The commander also blamed the foreigners for not hiring the citizens of Narva as shop assistants and thus not letting them make profits as they preferred sending their own salesmen to the spot. Nor did the foreigners become citizens of Narva, even though they wanted to engage in retail as well as wholesale trade. This possibly refers to the English who traded with Karelians in the hinterland of Narva, selling them tobacco and so violating the privileges of the local merchants who considered it their sole right.[32]

The commander's report deserves attention since it is one of first documents to describe the dispute over tobacco trading between the Narva and English merchants which was to increase in the years that followed. It is also noteworthy that when criticising the activity of Lübeck and English merchants, von Lillienthal recommended inviting merchants from the Netherlands to live in Narva and even allowing them to worship in the Reformed Church. On the other hand, he had to admit that in Narva the Englishmen had no motivation for committing themselves, while they preferred to link their shipping and trade routes with Tallinn.[33]

The Swedish Board of Trade discussed von Lillienthal's complaints about foreign competition towards the end of 1672.[34] In the early spring of 1673 the commander was supported by Berend Strahlborn, the envoy of the Narva Merchant Guild. Their report together with the views of the Board were forwarded to Karl XI on 13 March 1673. The document in question reveals a number of other thoughts by J. von Lillienthal. The commander held that the merchants from England and Lübeck who ignored the merchants of Narva and traded directly with the subjects of the Tsar should not be given greater privileges in the towns of Ingria than the subjects of Sweden had been given in England or Lübeck (i.e. they could do business with the citizens, not with other foreigners, and if they could not sell all their goods, these had to be left for commission). He was the first to demand that tobacco trade should be proclaimed as an exclusive privilege for the citizens of

---

[32] RA, Handel och sjöfart; vol. 17 (Berättelser och förslag angoende handeln på Ryssland), (J. von Lillienthal's report to the tutelary government of Karl XI in Stockholm, 31 July

[33] Ibid.

[34] RA, Kommerskollegium, huvudarkivet, protocol, A.I.a.1, vol. 18 (1672) (the session protocol as of 5 September 1672).

Narva, a demand which he justified by the prohibition on the importation of tobacco to Russia.[35]

The Board of Trade did not support the commander's proposals, which they regarded as contradicting the understanding that Russia could trade without any limitations in Narva in order to bring the trade of Archangel back to Baltic waters. This was also the position of the Swedish embassy which was due to be located in Moscow in 1673. However, the Board insisted that foreigners could trade directly only with the Tsar's Russians in these three towns on the Gulf of Finland and not with Karelians and other Ingrian inhabitants in the hinterland of Narva. It did not agree with the commander's demands concerning tobacco trade, considering that despite the prohibition great quantities of tobacco were imported to Russia and that the Russian trade was not to be restricted in any way. On the other hand, the Board did not accept the demand by Strahlborn to limit the English tobacco import to Narva.[36]

King Karl XI endorsed these recommendations in resolutions forwarded to the commander of Narva, von Lillienthal and Berend Strahlborn on 12 July 1673. He advised the Commander that the commercial interests of the state were more important than those of only one body of merchants, those of Narva. Far from setting any restrictions, the king advised the commander to co-operate with the town council to ensure that foreigners used all their liberties to the full and settled down in Narva. That was also the reason why tobacco trading was not privileged to the merchants of Narva.[37] The king reminded Berend Strahlborn that the English, above all, had been very successful in advancing the Russian Baltic trade. He pointed out that Narva had benefited more from the English trade than it would have from the privileges the locals demanded.[38] As a result, English subjects could trade relatively freely in Narva after the 1673 resolutions. They could trade in all transit commodities apart from corn, salt and herring, and hold direct contacts with the subjects of the Tsar. The only restrictions were the obligations of the 14-day warehousing and offering goods first to local merchants. The latter obligation was ignored by selling higher than the market price.

Tobacco was the main bone of contention between local merchants and the English. Given the increasing popularity of tobacco smoking in the second half of

---

[35] RA, Kommerskollegium, underdåniga skrivelser till K. Maj., vol. 4 (1673-5).

[36] Ibid.

[37] EAA, 1646-1-1, 1. 113.

[38] Ibid., 1. 117-117p. §4. The same resolution was addressed to the Great Guild of Narva merchants on 8 September 1673: ibid., 1646-1-5, 267-70, §4.

the seventeenth century, the citizens of Narva were vitally interested in their sole right to trade in tobacco in their own town and its hinterland. In the mid-seventeenth century the Narva tobacco trade was in the hands of state-subsided tobacco companies, but in the second half of the 1660s the central authorities gradually handed the trade over to the citizens of Narva. On 14 May 1666 the tutelary government of Karl XI allowed Narva merchants to trade with tobacco *en gros*.[39] On 26 May 1669 the same government gave tobacco trade permit to Narva merchants to sell tobacco also by retail.[40] Since the tobacco trade was banned in Russia, Karl XI resolved on 14 October 1675 under this pretence to privilege tobacco trade to Narva merchants alone. On their arrival in Narva all foreign merchants had to sell their tobacco immediately to local merchants. Since Narva merchants were not able to buy up the tobacco quickly, the town council resolved in 1678 to provide storage in its vaults, where the foreign merchants were obliged to offer it to local merchants within two months.[41] This regulation was valid in Narva until the end of the century[42] and caused misunderstandings among many foreigners, first and foremost the English. Before the establishment of the tobacco monopoly in 1675, the Mayor of Narva Jürgen Tunderfeldt had complained to the Royal Board of Trade in Stockholm that Narva merchants were not able to compete with the English in tobacco trade. However, he also admitted that despite the Tsar's veto it was possible to export tobacco to Russia illegally.[43]

As Table 3 shows, the English indisputably enjoyed the leading role in the tobacco import to Narva from the 1670s. It was therefore important for the English not only to import tobacco to Narva but to exchange it, then and there, without intermediaries, with the subjects of the Tsar and the inhabitants of Ingria for flax, hemp and other Russian commodities. Since the merchants of Narva were not able to participate in the tobacco import, they wished at least to hold the monopoly in re-exporting it.[44] Only after the promulgation of tobacco privilege in 1675 did the Narva Town Council begin to apply the law to the English. In October 1677 three English merchants (W. Kettlewell, Al. Gilbert and R. Bacon) trading in Narva, made a written complaint against Narva Town Council to the Governor of Ingria, General J.

---

[39] EAA, 1646-1-1, l. 101p.

[40] Ibid., l. 111.

[41] Ibid., 127p.

[42] Ibid., 1646-2-38, l. 68-69.

[43] See e.g. the Commercial Bills of the Narva Town Council of 4 July 1694: EAA, 1646-2-38, l. 88p.

[44] RA, Kommerskollegiets underdåniga skrivelser till K. Maj., vol. 4 (1673-1675) (The Board of trade to Karl XI on 5 June 1675.

J. Taube. The English argued that the town council ignored the trade treaty concluded between England and Sweden. The merchants assumed that the treaty gave them the right either to sell all the goods on the spot or take them wherever they wished. However, the Narva Town Council had banned them from taking a parcel of tobacco to Nyen and had had it unloaded from the barge despite the fact that they had paid duty on the consignment. In their appeal the English merchants referred to an incident a few months before when they had wished to unload a part of consignment of tobacco at Kudruküla and to ship another part to Nyen. On that occasion the Narva Town Council had let them pay duty on the latter but had not banned the shipping of the tobacco. They also noted that in Tallinn they had had no problems such as those in Narva. Thus the Governor General was asked to kindly see if their confiscated goods could be retrieved and if the Narva Town Council would allow them to freely transit tobacco.[45]

On 22 October 1677 Albertus Tretzel, the port and licence inspector of Narva, reported on the incident to Taube. According to his information W. Kettlewell, after having paid the duty on the 20th of that month, wished to take 12 barrels of tobacco to Nyen, for which purpose he had asked to be given a marine passport after he had paid the license and port duties as well as other taxes. But the commander of the Narva fortress and the town councillors had refused to issue the passport, wishing first to consult the Governor General. Since the latter was ailing and could not be approached, the town council had had the tobacco removed from the barge without the knowledge or agreement of the port inspector.

The Narva Town Council discussed the English merchants' complaint on 25 October. The question was raised whether English subjects could transit the tobacco they had brought to the town further to Nyen or Viborg. Almost the whole town council believed that they had the right to ban it. Only councillor J. C. Schwartz held a different opinion, considering it more profitable for the town to allow the English to transit tobacco to Nyen. The Narva Town Council decided that foreigners had to weigh tobacco immediately after unloading and thereafter leave it either at the shop at the weighhouse or in the vaults of the town council for four weeks to sell it to the merchants of the Great Guild. The days of the week when the shop could be open were also fixed. These were Monday, Wednesday and Friday. If the merchandise had not been sold by the time fixed, the town treasury clerk would make it available for sale to anybody interested in buying.[46]

---

[45] At the time when the import and consumption of tobacco was banned in Russia, English merchants considered Narva as a smuggling centre: Price, *The Tobacco Adventure*, p. 9.

[46] EAA, 1646-1-91, l. 157p-158.

Table 3: Tobacco import to Narva in the second half of the 17th Century (in ship pounds)

Town/Country	1657	1660	1662	1666	1668	1670	1671	1672	1675	1677	1679	1689	1690	1694	1695	1696	1699*
England	-	-	-	-	-	-	8750	8850	-	130,126	71,152	103,296	93,276	58,381	109,569	164,123	20,071
France	-	-	-	-	-	-	17,857	-	-	10,132	18,863	-	-	-	690	-	-
Amsterdam	-	-	8820	2000	15,711	-	5154	-	-	7419	700	27,767	15,025	30,090	28,430	19,183	43,342
Lübeck	-	-	19,331	41 189; 5,5 for state thalers	32 576; 4 for state thalers	-	32,126	13,688	-	441	9553	525	7354	1167	33228.5	35,533	715
Stralsund	-	-	-	-	-	-	-	-	-	200	-	-	-	-	-	-	-
Danzig	-	-	-	500	-	-	42,292	-	-	-	13,921	17,172	24	2725	6648	-	42,742
Swedish towns	-	-	-	146 rolls	-	-	-	-	-	-	60	-	2870	200	804	2570	-
Riga	-	-	20 rolls	-	-	-	-	-	-	-	-	-	-	-	-	-	1774
Tallinn	-	-	2520; 128 rolls; 8 cases	2171	-	-	-	-	-	300	41,055	-	-	1900	-	1003	-
Total amount	19,208	3411	30 671; 128 rolls; 8 cases	45 860; 146 rolls; 5,5 for state thalers	59 787; 4 for state thalers	89,349	106,179	22,538	158,085	148,618	155,304	148,760	118,549	94,463	179,370	222,412	108,644

Years

* incomplete data

Based on: EAA, 1646-1-1073, 1074, 1083, 1086, 1089; 1646-2-342...249;
RA, Östersjöprovinsernas tull- och licenträkenskaper 1583-1707, Vol. 43.

The English were not satisfied with the municipal authorities' decision. On 21 March 1678 the town council discussed a new request by the English in connection with transit trade and resolved that they were allowed to offer three kinds of merchandise - wines, tobacco and herring – only to locals from the vaults of the town council within two months.[47] However, such a strict regulation of tobacco trade did not exclude deception. Thus, for instance, on 23 March 1680 the Narva magistrate's court accused the Englishman John Loftus of having smuggled his tobacco out from the vaults guarded by the town council and selling it to a merchant from Nyen.[48] Apart from the obligation to store their goods in the town council's vaults, the English found it hard to cope with the time limit. The main problem was that Narva merchants did not have enough money to buy up the tobacco, so that by the time set for the English to sell had passed their goods remained unsold. Therefore the English were compelled to sell their tobacco to local merchants on credit without any guarantee of getting the money quickly.[49]

This was the way in which the Narva Town Council tried to hinder the English merchants' tobacco trade with the hinterland of the town. With some reservation one could claim that in the years 1680-90 the town council and merchants of Narva succeeded in forcing upon the English their way in tobacco trade. It was so at least until the autumn of 1698 when Tsar Peter I set the tobacco import to Russia free for English merchants and the first consignments were shipped there via Narva (to be discussed in greater detail below). The neighbouring town of Tallinn also had problems with the English concerning the tobacco trade. Tallinn, for instance, imposed on the English the 1679 regulations of street trading as a result of which the English agents could not receive goods from their own companies but the latter were obliged to sell them to local citizens. The Englishman J. Brown thus came into conflict with the Tallinn Town Council, which prohibited him from sending tobacco from Tallinn to Narva, and forced him to offer it to Tallinn merchants. The Englishman protested even to the Governor General of Estonia, A. Torstenson.[50]

---

[47] Ibid., 1646-1-92, l. 515.

[48] Ibid., 1646-1-805, l. 57p.

[49] For example, the English trade agent Th. Meux told the Narva Town Council on 11 February 1698 that a citizen of Narva, Philipp Wichmann, had owed him money for tobacco for eight months: ibid., 1646-2-263, l. 104-104p.

[50] Ibid., 1-2-409, l. 144-147 (J. Brown to A. Torstenson, 31 August 1680); Erpenbeck. *"Die englischen in Liefflandt negotierenden Kaufleute"*, pp. 244-8.

The 1679 regulations were among the reasons why the Russian-trade focus of English merchants shifted from Tallinn to Narva in the following decade.

No concessions to the English were made in wine trading, either. A royal resolution of 22 December 1675 gave the monopoly of the trade to the Narva Merchants' Great Guild in 1675, decreeing that all foreigners arriving in Narva must immediately sell the wines they carried to local merchants.[51] Thus, for instance, the Narva Town Council suspected that a group of English merchants in the spring of 1678 were reselling various wines to Russia. It appeared, though, at the interrogation of the local merchants H. Ranie and H. Wiens who were accused of participating in the transaction, that before forwarding the suspicious wines to Russia the English had sold them to local citizens of Narva.[52] The English in Narva had disputes with local merchants over other commodities. In 1676 the English had requested the Royal Board of Trade to be given the right to trade in salt in Narva, i.e. in salt transit to Russia. The Board refused, stating that otherwise the merchants of Narva would lose all their income.[53] In 1678 some of the merchants of Narva founded a tar company which had a monopoly in buying up the forest product and selling it to foreign merchants.[54] In the spring of 1680 the English applied for permission from the Narva Town Council to buy up tar from the nobility and peasants in the hinterland. The town council refused, arguing that they had the right to procure the goods produced in Ingria only through the medium of local citizens.[55]

To remind the English of their privileges and liberties in Narva, the town council summoned the English merchants who where in town on 25 February 1688 to notify them that: (1) the liberties permitted to them by His Royal Majesty applied only to Russian trade (2) they must therefore immediately take all the retail goods which did not belong to Russian trade from their ships or sledges into a public packing house. The rest of the goods could be kept in rented cellars and packing houses (3) they were not allowed to trade directly with the citizens of neighbouring towns such as Tartu, Viborg and Nyen, but could do so only through the medium of Narva merchants. The English were also

[51] Ibid., 1646-1-2, l. 551-552, §1.

[52] Ibid., 1646-1-92, l. 479, 487-488.

[53] RA, Kommerskollegium, huvudarkivet, protocol, A.I.a.1. vol. 22 (1676) (protocol of session of 19 February 1676).

[54] Minutes of Narva Town Council, 26 August 1678: EAA, 1646-1-92, l. 601.

[55] Ibid., 1646-1-94, l. 52p, 62p (minutes of Narva Town Council, 20 March and 8 April 1680).

reminded of the prohibition on doing business with people from the border areas of Russia.[56]

The Narva Chamber of Trade repeated the same principles on 25 August 1698 when it discussed the complaints of the municipal treasury clerk Zacharias Falck against the English trade agents Thomas Meux, Randolph Knipe, Abraham Hoyle and William Beaumont concerning their offences against local trade regulations. According to the clerk's report, Meux had sent tobacco to Tallinn, by-passing the citizens of Narva. At the same time Meux, as well as Knipe and Hoyle, had sent various Russian commodities in the name and account of other strangers, e.g. the citizens of Tallinn, from Narva to Amsterdam, showing that they had previously had contacts with Russians in border areas. Beaumont was accused of storing various retail goods at home and selling them by retail. In the course of the discussion the positions of both the English merchants and the Chamber of Trade were made clear. Although the English denied their direct contacts with the Russian peasants of the border areas, they argued that *in connection with worshipping in their own religion* in Narva, the Swedish king had allowed them in *wholesale to make contact with whom they chose and do business wherever they wished*. First and foremost this referred to their wish to communicate directly with other foreigners. However, the Chamber of Trade remained firm in its demand that the English, like all other foreigners, had to take into account the regulation of trade in town, in particular the council's most recent commercial bill of 4 July 1694. Special emphasis was laid on the fact that although the Swedish crown had permitted the English to enjoy *their own religion* in Narva, it did not mean any compliance as regards commercial laws. The English were reminded once again of the requirement that they must trade with Russians and other foreigners only through the medium of the merchants of Narva.[57]

S.-E. Åström is certainly right to assert that the attitude of the state authorities towards English trade in Narva did not coincide with that of the local town council and merchants. The citizens of Narva stubbornly continued to exert pressure on the central authorities with the aim of avoiding excessive favour to both the English and other foreigners as well as their violating local commercial regulations.[58] Sweden, by contrast regarded it as important from the aspect of the development of international relationships that the commercial

---

[56] Ibid., 1646-1-100, l. 43-43p.

[57] Ibid., 1646-2-255, l. 25-26p; 1646-2-263, l. 98-98p.

[58] Åström, *From Stockholm*, p. 76.

activity both by the English and other foreigners should smoothly proceed across the Gulf of Finland and via Narva.

Proof is provided by an incident from the late autumn of 1696. On 11 November a ship from Lübeck, the *St. Johannes* ran upon the rocks on the north Estonian coast on its way from western Europe to Narva. Based upon the *shore rights* both the local peasants and even far-away peasants plundered the ship. Since the ship was carrying mainly goods belonging to Persian Armenians, the English and citizens of Narva, this raised a major scandal. An investigation and the punishment of the culprits were required by King Karl XI and, subsequently, by the tutelary government of his son. The fact of the plunder itself did not present a problem to the king, but rather the fact that Estonian peasants supported by tenants of estates and even landlords had interfered with international relationships. The Swedish state had finally gained, after lengthy diplomatic exchanges, an agreement from the Tsar of Russia to make possible for Armenian merchants to sail in Baltic waters instead of Archangel. The same applied to free and unhindered navigation for the English to towns along the Gulf of Finland.[59] That the English were aware of their special privileges is apparent through frequently occurring remarks in their letters emphasising that in case of need they could turn to the English resident in Stockholm or directly to the Swedish king.

The tobacco trade in Narva after the 1698 English-Russian commercial treaty

Throughout the seventeenth century smoking tobacco was prohibited in Russia. During the reign of Tsar Aleksei Mikhailovitch the tobacco ban became particularly strict. By his 1649 ukase the tobacco-smokers could be sent to Siberia and in 1655 the law became even more severe, leading to capital punishment. The lifting of the tobacco ban occurred only at the beginning of 1697, i.e. a short while before Peter I started his travels to western countries. By his ukase the Tsar decreed that tobacco could be publicly sold and consumed

---

[59]RA, Livonica II, vol. 268 (Governor General of Ingria O. W. Fersen to Karl XI , 7 December 1696, forwarding letter from Armenian merchants to Karl XI, undated, letter from Narva Town Council to Karl XI, undated, and letter from the English merchants to Karl XI , 5 December 1696); ibid., (Karl XI to Governor General of Estonia A. J. De la Gardie, 14 January 1697). For the investigation into the incident and punishment of Estonian peasants, see: Otto Liiv, 'Ühest suurprotsessist 17. sajandi lõpul, *Ajalooline Ajakiri* 3 (1932), pp. 129-49; Otto Liiv, 'Den hävdvunna strandrätten i ljuset av en stor process från 1600-talets slut', *Svio-Estonica* (1938), pp. 183-98.

throughout the country. The issuing of the ukase was motivated by an extensive consumption anyway as well as by rapidly growing smuggling. New high revenue taxes were instituted, depending on the quality of the imported tobacco.[60]

It was vital for England to find markets for tobacco. The production of tobacco in the American colonies was continuously increasing. When Peter I came to England in January 1698, English merchants compiled a memorandum to the Board of Trade to make use of the Tsar's stay in England to gain the right to export tobacco to the countries under his rule. On 16 April 1698, a short while before his departure from England, the Tsar granted the tobacco monopoly for seven years to Peregrine Osborne, the Marquis of Carmarthen, and his assistants. Behind the Marquis' name were about 60 entrepreneurs who were all connected with the Eastland Company.[61] The treaty concluded between Peregrine Osborne and Tsar Peter I marked a breakthrough in the return of the English to Russian trade. Between 1697 and 1704 English-Russian trade is estimated to have grown three times.[62]

The treaty guaranteed Osborne and his associates the sole right to import tobacco to the whole empire, to display and sell it and to buy appropriate Russian goods in return. Tobacco importers were to send to Russia in the first year (which by the Russian calendar ended on 1 September 1699) a total of 1,500,000 pounds or 3,000 barrels of tobacco, in the second year 5,000 barrels and in each following year at least 1,000 barrels more. The Tsar in his turn pledged to fight against both tobacco contraband and the growing of tobacco in Russia.[63]

News of the treaty reached Sweden rapidly. Osborne's partners compiled a commentary on the main points of the treaty. The most important message for the Swedes was in item 11, which explicitly declared that only the English could import tobacco to Russia, either via Narva or any other place.[64] On the other

---

[60] Price, *Tobacco Adventure*, pp. 18-20.

[61] Samas, pp. 20-27; Arhangel'skij, *Anglo-gollandskaja torgovlja*, pp. 31-3; A. I. Andreev, 'Petr I v Anglii v 1698 g.', *Petr Velikij* (1947), p. 78; N. N. Molčanov, *Diplomatja Petra Pervogo*, (Moscow, 1984), pp. 101-2.

[62] L. A. Nikiforov, *Russko-Anglijskie otnošenija pri Petre I* (Moscow, 1950), p. 17.

[63] Price, *Tobacco Adventure*, p. 28. Text of English-Russian tobacco treaty in *Polnoe sobranie zakonov' Rossijskoj imperii*, III, pp. 447-50.

[64] Extract *af de ryske gesanternes avhandling och contract med en engelsk Marquis och des medinteressenter angående tobakhandeln i Ryssland, slutit d. 16. apr. 1698*: RA, Handel och sjöfart, vol. 15 (utrikeshandel, Ryssland 1500-1600-talet).

hand, the English tobacco trade to Russia was welcomed in Sweden. It was seen as an additional chance for stimulating the trade of Narva and, more broadly, of the whole region of the Gulf of Finland. However, the new tobacco trade brought about a variety of problems at the national as well as at town levels.

One of the first misunderstandings was related to the imposition of duties on tobacco. Unlike other goods, tobacco had not been among the transit commodities subject to duty, and therefore the low customs tariffs (1% licence and 1% port duties) had not been collected on it. Duty had only been imposed on goods carried to the hinterland of the town (over 6% licence duties). Here it is important to note that charging duties and collecting customs were not the responsibility of the Narva Town Council but were the privilege of the state. In response to the complaint submitted by English merchants, the Swedish resident C. Leijoncrona reported from London on 23 August 1698 to Karl XII that English merchants had soon after the conclusion of the English-Russian tobacco treaty sent a larger amount of tobacco to Narva.[65] On reaching Narva the local customs service demanded paying customs to the full extent. Since in Narva the tobacco was received by the English factors only for selling it, they failed to pay duty. But as long as they had not paid duty, they were not allowed to unload their ships. Leijoncrona did not directly condemn the work of the Narva customs service but advised the king that the problem should be solved as soon as possible. He pointed out that if the commodities were carried to Moscow via Narva, their return journey would also pass through that place, and he considered this useful in the rivalry with Archangel. Leijoncrona also hoped that, along with the English, Swedish subjects would also get an opportunity to convey tobacco to Russia. One way or the other, he considered it profitable for the citizens of Narva if they had a possibility of unloading, storing, re-carrying etc. the English commodities.

In September or early October the English Stockholm resident John Robinson informed Karl XII that some of English merchants had conveyed a few hundred *oxhofts* of tobacco, both twined and in sheaves, to Narva, supposing that in transit it would not be charged higher than other transit commodities. However, on reaching Narva with their goods the local customs inspector had told them that there were no regulations for charging duty on tobacco other than those concerning consumption in the country. Robinson knew that this was also the standpoint of Narva municipal authorities. The resident reported that the

---

[65] In 1698 180,000 pounds of rolled and cut tobacco, together with tobacco pipes and boxes, were conveyed via Narva to Russia. This proved a very unprofitable undertaking, since they were charged duty of 17% on rolled and 34% on cut tobacco: Price, *Tobacco Adventure*, p. 43.

town council wanted to obtain the privilege on tobacco and charge its transit as well as keep it under their lock and key. The town council explained their standpoint by arguing that tobacco trade was a new development and so far Russia had banned its import. Robinson wished Karl XII to reduce the duty on tobacco to the level at which other transit commodities were charged.[66]

In Narva the problem of English tobacco trading was discussed at the beginning of November 1698, in response to a proposal by the Swedish Board of Trade that the Narva merchants should be allowed to submit their views on the English-Russian agreement. The Narva Merchants' Great Guild recalled, in a letter to the Board of 5 November, their anxiety during the summer on hearing that the English had been given permission to import tobacco into Russia – an anxiety heightened by a letter from the Board of Trade of 18 July which noted that the Board did not see any reason to prevent the English tobacco transit to Russia.[67] This had contradicted their understanding that the agreement reached by England and Russia contravened the tobacco monopoly guaranteed to them by Karl XI in 1675. The monopoly had enabled the Narva merchants to make a good profit, especially from Karelian Russians; but now the latter did business with the English instead. The letter also noted that in accordance with the treaties concluded between Russia and Sweden the subjects of both states were allowed mutually to trade in all kinds of commodities. However, now that the consumption of tobacco in Russia had been set free, its import was banned for the Swedish subjects. The merchants were therefore worried that while the officials of the Tsar banned their tobacco transit, they had to allow Russians to trade in all commodities in their town as well as let them conclude business agreements with other foreigners. The Merchants' Great Guild concluded that if the foreigners obtained all the privileges in their town and the privileges of the citizens of Narva were gradually cancelled, the foreigners would lack the motivation to apply for citizenship. Thus they appealed to the Board of Trade not to cancel the privileges which the citizens of Narva had enjoyed before the foreigners came.

Probably after having received the letter from the Narva Merchants' Great Guild, the Board of Trade resolved on 13 December 1698 to present to Karl XII a thorough analysis of the appeal of John Robinson, the English resident. The Board did not agree with the Narva merchants' assertion that the monopoly of

---

[66] EFMSoR, pp. 286-7.

[67] RA, Kommerskollegium, huvudarkivet, kungl. brev och remisser, E.I.a., vol. 20 (1698) (Great Guild of Narva Merchants to Board of Trade, 5 November 1698, forwarded to Board by commander of the Narva fortress Chr. von Kochen, 6 November).

the tobacco trade belonged to them, pointing out that it had existed only as long as the commodity had been banned in Russia. Now that the situation had changed – with the English privilege of importing tobacco to Russia – the Board declared the monopoly null and void. The interests of the Swedish state must not be outweighed by earlier privileges enjoyed by Narva.

On the other hand, the Board advised that along with the English, Swedes could also trade in tobacco with Russia. If they were prevented form doing so, there was no reason to reduce customs duties, since Sweden would privilege only foreigners without making any profit from the trade. The Board argued, further, that somewhat higher customs than usual were not likely to make the English leave the towns of the Gulf of Finland for Archangel.[68] Since a legation was on its way from Sweden to Russia in 1699,[69] Stockholm decided to negotiate the tobacco trade via Narva with the Russian. However, once in Russia, the legation failed to raise the subject.[70]

Generally it seems that Sweden did not reduce customs duties and that English tobacco was continuously charged in Narva over 6% of licence duty. When in the spring of 1700 Narva Town Council asked all the English merchants to put all their claims and demands in writing, Abraham Hoyle informed them that the English had nothing to complain about or anything to demand.[71] Thereafter the problem of tobacco trade via Narva related to the English disappears from respective archival sources. Probably before the Great Northern War broke out it developed a certain routine. However, the Narva customs statistics show that in 1699 the English commissioned 20,071 pounds of tobacco, while at the same time 43,342 pounds were imported from Amsterdam and, surprisingly, 42,742 pounds from Danzig. Concerning Danzig it is possible to suppose that it was the English re-export. On the other hand, by way of comparison, in 1696 the English shipped to Narva 164,123 pounds of tobacco and Lübeck took the second place with 35,533 pounds (see Table 3).[72] In August 1700, with the Great Northern War approaching Narva, the English

---

[68] RA, Kommerskollegiets underdåniga skrivelser till K. Maj., vol. 15 (1698) (Board of Trade to Karl XII, 13 December 1698).

[69] RA, Muscovitica, vol. 121 (instruction to Swedish embassy in Moscow).

[70] RA, Muscovitica, vol. 118 (report by Swedish embassy in Moscow to Karl XII, §20).

[71] RA, Livonica II, vol. 360 (Trade Board of Narva to Governor General of Ingria Otto Velling, 4 May 1700).

[72] Enn Küng, 'Tubakakaubanduse riiklik reguleerimine', p. 5;Enn Küng, 'Die staatliche Regulierung des Tabakshandels in Narva in der 2. Hälfte des 17. Jahrhunderts', *Estnische Historische Zeitschrift* 1 (1998), p.80.

temporarily left the town. As far as is known, they fled to Tallinn.[73] After the Swedish victory some of the English returned to Narva but with the general decline in trade their business was no longer successful.

The English citizens in Narva

In 1672 Count Johan von Lillienthal reproached the English for not wishing to become naturalised in Narva and preferring to associate themselves with Tallinn. From the beginning of the 1680s, however, a great number of merchants and skippers of English origin became citizens of Narva. There were various reasons for this change. As indicated above, the English confronted difficulties when trading in Tallinn after the adoption of the 1679 regulations of street trading, and there were other legislative acts which worked against the interests of foreigners. Thus the town lost its attraction in the eyes of the English. Moreover, the citizens of Tallinn were more capable in competition than the inhabitants of Narva. At the end of the 1670s the idea of coordinating from Tallinn the English-Russian trade passing through Narva was dropped. Although Narva also imposed various restrictions on their mercantile activities, it was essentially more open to foreigners. Both at the state and local levels Narva was interested in wealthy, experienced new citizens who had had close business contacts with western Europe. New settlers were offered various advantages.[74]

In the last two decades of the seventeenth century the English made up a remarkable minority group among the inhabitants of Narva. Why did they choose to become naturalised in Narva? The most obvious answer is that it resulted from a situation in which the English, despite their large volume of transactions, did not enjoy unhindered transit trading with Russia. As we have seen, tobacco had to be sold to local citizens. As long as the English traded in Narva as foreigners, all the restrictions on foreigners were also imposed on them. As citizens, by contrast, they were guaranteed all the privileges and liberties

---

[73] There are several references to the departure of the English for Tallinn in the autumn of 1700. In December 1700 ten Englishmen joined the Tallinn Blackheads' Brotherhood, donating a large silver goblet as a present for their admission (Erpenbeck, 'Die Engländer in Narva', p. 481). The Narva Anglican congregation also left Narva for Tallinn because of the war (Enn Küng, 'Anglikaani kogudusest Narvas 17. sajandi lõpukümnenditel', *Ajalooline Ajakiri* (1998) 4 (103) (Tartu, 1999), p. 35). It is also known that during the siege of Narva the Russians allowed around ten Englishmen to leave the town for Tallinn: Margus Laidre, *Lõpu võidukas algus. Karl XII Eesti- ja Liivimaal* (Tartu, 1995), pp. 143-4.

[74] Enn Küng, 'Narva kodanikkonnast 1581-1704', *Rootsi suurriigist Vene impeeriumisse. Artiklid* (Eesti Ajalooarhiivi Toimetised 3(10)) (Tartu 1998), pp. 16-18.

enjoyed by Swedish subjects, including duty-free trading in the Sound, the most important liberty from the point of view of seventeenth-century Baltic commerce. Apart from the subjects of the Netherlands and England, the Swedes had the right, since the 1645 Brömsebro peace treaty, to sail Swedish-owned ships and carry goods which belonged to Swedish subjects duty-free through the Danish straits. This liberty was confirmed also in the following Swedish-Danish peace treaties.[75] This way the English, having naturalized in Narva, built a bridge for conveying Russian commodities to England and *vice versa*. They informed their trading partners about the business situation both in Narva and in neighbouring towns as well as in Russia, attempted to unload ships quickly, obtain new cargoes and so on. The English as citizens continued to be factors for the members of the Eastland Trading Company. So, for instance, English tobacco was commissioned to an Englishman as a citizen of Narva. Being citizens of Narva, they could successfully compete with other citizens of Narva who were generally less wealthy.

Apart from merchants and a few handicraftsmen, a number of skippers also became naturalised in Narva. The latter, in particular, clearly wished to enjoy the privileges enjoyed by Swedish subjects in navigation. Their ships sailed, as a rule, between Narva and the ports of England just as the skippers who came from the Netherlands held their course to Amsterdam. Several Narva Englishmen (e.g. W.

---

[75] Nilsson, *Sundstullsräkenskaperna*, pp. 14-16, 31.

Kettlewell and T. Loftus) were shipowners and/or joint owners of vessels,[76] as well as owners of dockyards or other manufactures.[77]

Table 4: *The Englishmen as citizens of Narva*[78]

07.11.1681	John Langerwood	rope spinner	Nottingham
14.12.1682	Henry Brown	merchant	England
24.09.1683	William Kettlewell	merchant	England
27.01.1687	Thomas Loftus	merchant	England
14.06.1688	John Russel	skipper	Margate in Kent in England
23.09.1689	Alexander Gilbert	merchant	England
18.01.1692	George Peirsson	merchant	England
18.01.1692	Johann Wricht	tailor	England

[76] For example, W. Kettlewell owned in 1686-1692 1/2 of the ship *St. Johannes*; in 1688 a part of the ship *Der Grosse Christoffer*; in 1689-1693 he was a joint owner of the *Carolus von Narva* (also called *Carolus XI*); in 1691-1692 he owned 1/4 of the *St. Petrus*; in 1691-1697 1/8 of the *Rådhuset af Narven*; in 1692-1695 1/2 of the *Slåttet av Narvfen*; in 1692-1694 1/8 of the *Ivangorod ifrån Narva*; in 1692-1697 he was a full owner of the ship *Wapen af Narva*; in 1693-1695 1/2 of the *Printz Carolus I*; in 1695 1/3 of the *St. Helena*; in 1696-1697 1/2 of the *Printz Carolus II*; in 1693 1/3 of the ship *Die Hoffnung von Narva* . In 1694 he owned a part of the *Carl von Refwell*; in 1694-98 a part of the *Fortuna von Narva*; in 1696-1697 he had 1/32 of the *Concordia Narvensis*; in 1696 1/16 of the *Dorothea von Narva*; in 1698 he was a sole owner of the *Engel Raphael*; in 1699-1701 a part of the *Patientia*: EAA, 1646-1-103, 104, 105, 107, 810, 811, 813, 814, 815, 817, 1976, 1977, 1978, 2408, 2411, 2413, 2415; 1646-2-157. Data found also in: Rigsarkivet København, Øresunds toldkammers arkiv, Sundtoldregnskaber 1686-1701.

[77] On 30 December 1686 Karl XI granted W. Kettlewell the right to establish a tobacco spinning workshop in Narva: Anders Anton von Stiernman (ed.), *Samling utaf Kongl. Bref, Stadgar och Förordningar etc. angående Sveriges Rikes Commerce, Politie och Oeconomie* IV, p. 701 (Karl XI to Board of Trade, 30 December 1686). W. Kettlewell's tobacco spinning manufacture was operating in 1689 since in that year he requested a licence to sell his production in Finland, otherwise provided for by the state tobacco company: RA, Kommerskollegium, huvudarkivet, kungliga brev och remissar, E.I.a. vol. 10 (1689) (letter from Karl XI is undated). From 1694 Kettlewell is known to have possessed a sawmill in Narva: ibid., Kommerskollegium, huvudarkivet, protocol, A.I.a.1, vol. 40 (1694) (protocol of the Board, 13 September 1694). Kettlewell himself has described his activities in Narva best in his letter to Karl XI in the late autumn of 1696: ibid., Livonica II, vol. 191. See also Erpenbeck, 'Die Engländer in Narva', p. 492. In 1697 Kettlewell wished to establish a purifying workshop for raw flax and hemp: RA, Kommerskollegium, huvudarkivet, inkomna skrivelser, E.III.a. vol. 23 (1697).

[78] Data from: Dirk-Gerd Erpenbeck and Enn Küng, 'Narvaer Bürger- und Einwohnerbuch 1581-1704' *Veröffentlichungen der Forschungsstelle Ostmitteleuropa an der Universität Dortmund*, series B, vol. 64 (Dortmund, 2000).

01.02.1692	John Elers	merchant	England (?)
05.07.1692	John Russel	skipper	England
18.06.1692	John Nothon	skipper	Newcastl -England
18.06.1692	Philipp Woodhouse	skipper	Hull - England
15.08.1692	George Burges	skipper	Hull - England
27.03.1693	Nicolaus Russel	skipper	(John Russel's brother)
20.11.1693	William Walcker	merchant	York England

As was mentioned above, along with the citizens of the English origin there were numerous English trade agents active in Narva. Altogether they organised a business system whose management was in England and mainly associated with the Eastland Company and whose representatives had settled in Narva as they had, in earlier times, in Danzig, Elbing, Tallinn and elsewhere. As well as the Englishmen – the citizens of Narva – listed in Table 4, numerous non-citizens, i.e. representatives of their companies (factors), also operated in Narva: men such as R. Bacon, W. Beaumont, Richard Darwin, Thomas Dowker, A. Hoyle, H. Hoyle, R. Knipe, William Linch, Leo[nard] Lydes, Gilbert Metcalfe, Th. Meux, Thomas Moore, William Ramsay, Thomas Stanniland, Thomas Remington, John Taylor, John Tyreman and many others. Consequently, only a minority of the Englishmen trading in Narva became citizens of the town.

Citizens of both English and other foreign origin practised a certain amount of deception in pursuit of their business interests. A number of new citizens maintained their economic interests in their native countries. A clear case of deception consisted in the fact that many new citizens did not send for their families at home. For that reason, Narva Town Council put pressure on foreigners trading in town for a longer period to settle down as citizens. For example, when the Englishman Th. Loftus married in Narva in 1678 and founded his individual household, the town council started to hinder his activities and demand that he should bear all the fiscal burdens as a citizen.[79] As Table 4 indicates, Loftus became naturalised only on 27 January 1687, having been a trade agent for the Eastland Company for many years both in Tallinn and in Narva. A similar incident concerns G. Peirsson, to whom Narva Town Council in 1689 suggested that he became naturalised. The Englishman asked the town council to wait for some time since all his household was yet in

---

[79] RA, Livonica II, vol. 210 (Th. Loftus to Karl XI, 15 October 1678).

England and he had planned to return there in the coming summer and decide there where he would settle down in future.[80] Up to that time he wished to operate in Narva as a foreign merchant. G. Peirsson became naturalised in Narva on 18 January 1692. On the other hand, there were also local citizens ready to cheat. For instance, employing skippers from England, Netherlands and elsewhere to their ships, they promised to refer to them as citizens of Narva and so guarantee a duty-free carriage for their goods in the Sound. As Table 4 shows, one skipper, J. Russel, became a naturalized citizen of Narva twice – evidently for sound commercial reasons.

A notable phenomenon was that, in a strictly Lutheran state, the English were allowed, from 1684, to *enjoy their own religion.* Hitherto the Swedish authorities' attitude towards the possibility of religious liberty for the English in Narva had been as hostile as to other 'foreign' religions. It was only in the summer of 1681, when a new commercial treaty between Sweden and England was under discussion, that the Royal Board of Trade presented to Karl XI a long list of items, submitted by the English envoy in Stockholm Ph. Warwick. One of these appealed for religious liberty together with the appointment of an appropriate clergyman. The Board advised against the request since it might lead other foreigners to apply for the same freedom.[81]

However, a change of attitude came about with the appointment of Jöran Sperling as Governor General of Ingria in 1683. On 16 June 1684, speaking before the Board of Trade in Stockholm, Sperling made a number of suggestions to improve commercial conditions in Narva and Nyen, including the possibility of giving the freedom of religion to the members of the Reformed Church.[82] On this occasion the Board must have changed its mind, because in a letter to King Karl XI of 1 July 1684 the Governor General noted the fact that his proposal had been thoroughly discussed and approved from the point of view of encouraging the development of commerce. Nevertheless, on the very same date, king noted in his own hand on Sperling's letter: '*His Royal Majesty finds the matter harmful, therefore it remains as it was before*'.[83] In government circles the issue of freedom of religion for the English continued to be discussed because

---

[80] EAA, 1646-2-268, l. 111 (G. Peirsson to Narva Town Council, 22 April 1689).

[81] RA, Kommerskollegiets underdåniga skrivelser till K. Maj., vol 6, (Board of Trade to Karl XI , 9 July 1681).

[82] RA, Kommerskollegium, huvudarkivet, protokol A.I.a.1, vol. 30 (1684).

[83] RA, Livonica II, vol. 186; Lars Hagberg, 'Johannes Gezelius d.y. och engelsmännens religionfrihet i Narva 1684', *Kyrkohistorisk årsskrift* 48 (1948), pp. 114-15.

almost two months later, on 20 August 1684, Sperling unexpectedly received a favourable answer from the king. Karl XI now stated that it would be very profitable for Narva if the English were allowed to practise their own religion.[84]

Sperling negotiated subsequently with Johannes Gezelius the Younger, the Superintendent of Ingria in Narva. The Governor General sent his own opinions as well as Gezelius's longer report to Karl XI in Stockholm on 14 November 1684.[85] Sperling stated that by allowing the English freedom of worship and increasing their interest in trading in Narva it would be possible to improve the local economic situation and thus to reduce or even defeat commercial competition from Archangel.[86] Gezelius emphasised that the freedom granted to the English should not be treated as a precedent for the treatment of other foreign religions. On the contrary, he admitted that *'undoubtedly it would have been better if it had been so that the local circumstances did not need some [people] from foreign religions amongst us, however, since the whole trade and navigation would fall apart without those who are here at present, then His Royal Majesty found it reasonable to consider the above proposition.'*[87]

The two leading figures in Ingria thus supported the establishment of the Anglican Church in Narva. Karl XI approved their proposals on 16 December 1684 in a special resolution which also underlined the restrictions under which the English were to practise their religion. They must remain separate from other inhabitants; they were not allowed to erect their own church but had to use some other appropriate edifice in the town. At their services they could speak only English, and they were only to worship God, not create tensions among the town population by their sermons.[88]

Sperling wrote to Karl XI from Narva on 30 January 1685, reporting that he had informed the English of the king's decision. They had received the news with great joy and promised to observe the restrictions set. They had also confirmed their conviction that the resolution would advance trade in Narva and bring prosperity.[89] A letter of 5 February from the English merchants informed

---

[84] RA, Riksregistraturet, 20.08.1684; Hagberg, 'Johannes Gezelius d.y.', p. 115.

[85] RA, Livonica II, vol. 186; Hagberg, 'Johannes Gezelius d.y.', p. 115.

[86] RA, Livonica II, vol. 186 (Governor General of Ingria Jöran Sperling from Narva to Karl XI, 14 November 1684).

[87] RA, Livonica II, vol. 186; Hagberg, 'Johannes Gezelius d.y.', pp. 116-17, 121-5.

[88] Matthias Akiander, *Bidrag till kännedom om Evangelisk-lutherska Församlingarne i Ingermanlands stift* (Helsingfors, 1865).

[89] RA, Livonica II, vol. 186.

the leaders of the Eastland Company, Sir Benjamin Ayloff and Peter Joy, that at their audience with the Governor General on 23 January, the latter had declared that *'for enlivening the local English trade and for the Englishmen who wish to permanently live and trade here, His Majesty has graciously given the liberty to get themselves an English pastor from England. That he could perform his duties in serving God he has to observe the following restrictions, namely: he has to be a reasonable Orthodox servant of God, in accordance with the instituted Church of England and must not be involved in any sect, he must be a clergyman of commendable conduct and not use insolent words or deeds against the local subjects of His Majesty. If these conditions are observed, His Majesty wishes to confirm these privileges in an appropriate manner and form.'*[90] Thereafter the Anglican Church was established in Narva. In September 1685 the priest Charles Thirlby arrived in Narva and remained associated with the town until 1703 when his congregation also ended their activity there.[91] In other Swedish towns the English were not allowed to establish their own church congregation.

In order to establish better contacts with the whole English community and link them more to the town, the Englishman Thomas Loftus was appointed on 30 April 1688 to the vacant position of alderman in the Narva Town Council by the Governor General.[92] The English had also language privileges. For instance, in 1692 when the English skipper John Russel became a citizen of Narva for the second time, he swore his civic oath in front of the town council in English.[93]

Conclusion

Sweden was vitally interested in attracting English merchants to the country and its provinces. They were expected to help beat the commercial competition from the merchants of the Netherlands, but it was still more important to make use of the English interest in Russian trade. Hence, various privileges were guaranteed by international treaties to English merchants in Swedish towns which other foreign merchants did not enjoy, for instance, merchants from the Netherlands, France and elsewhere. Lübeck merchants were even deprived of their earlier privileges. On the other hand, the interests of the state did not coincide with

---

[90] EAA, 1646-1-1997, unpaged. Letter signed by: Th. Dowker, H. Hoyle, W. Linch, L. Lydes, G. Metcalfe, G. Peirson, W. Ramsay, Th. Remington, J. Taylor, J. Tyreman.

[91] For more on the activities of C. Thirlby and the Anglican congregation in Narva see Küng 'Anglikaani kogudusest', pp. 25-39.

[92] EAA, 1646-1-100, l. 107-109.

[93] Ibid., 1646-1-103, l. 126p.

local interests, i.e. those of the town council and merchants of Narva. First of all, the state had created conditions which made its towns attractive trading centres: reducing customs duties, making it possible to establish commercial societies and have warehouses etc. Since the English were most interested in selling their commodities in this region (tobacco) and procuring Russian goods (hemp, flax), several trade agents became citizens of Narva. This was a matter of interest to both the state and the municipal authorities. Wealthy English merchants as citizens of Narva increased commodity circulation of the town, built a *bridge* between Russian and West European markets, and guaranteed extensive commercial relationships, commercial treaties etc. At the same time they could also enjoy all the liberties of Swedish citizens both at the local Narva market and when passing through the Sound.

The attitude of the Swedish state to the English tobacco trade at the end of the seventeenth century was somewhat ambivalent. As shown by the implementation of the 1698 English-Russian treaty on tobacco trade, Sweden did not intend to hinder commodity flows of English merchants: on the contrary, they were ready to revise the privileges given to the merchants of Narva in 1675. On the other hand, since only the English could import tobacco to Russia, and the Swedes were not allowed to do it, then the English did not get any preference. Giving a licence to the Anglican Church congregation in 1684 was a successive step by Swedish economists to enliven the trade in Narva and in region of the Gulf of Finland as a whole. In all the letters establishing the freedom of religion a special emphasis was laid on commercial-political aspects.

Part II: 1700-1850

Chapter 6

Economic warfare or piracy? Swedish privateering against British and Dutch trade in the Baltic during the Great Northern War 1710-21[1]

Lars Ericson

The Great Northern War was the longest and most intensive war ever fought by Sweden. When the alliance of Saxony-Poland, Russia and Denmark-Norway attacked Sweden in 1700, it was an assault on a country that dominated large parts of the shores of the Baltic Sea. Sweden's empire extended from north of the Gulf of Bothnia to Pomerania in the south, and along the east coast of the Baltic from the metropolis of Riga to the commercial centre of Narva deep in the Gulf of Finland. Some 21 years later Sweden had lost most of her empire: parts of Pomerania, Livonia, Estonia and Ingermanland in the east, while the eastern part of the realm, Finland, had been occupied by Russian troops for seven years. The result was not only devastating for Sweden's imperial position, but the war had also cost the country severe casualties. During the two decades of war some 200,000 Swedish and Finnish soldiers had been killed in action, of whom 50,000 were Finns and 150,000 Swedes. The peace treaties with her numerous enemies in 1719-21 definitively ended Sweden's age of greatness. Much of the historical debate on this subject in Sweden in recent years has revolved around the question whether

---

[1] References to archival sources and literature are given in my book *Lasse i Gatan. Kaparkriget och det svenska stormaktsväldets fall* (Lund, 1997).

Swedish society was really in such a severe condition at the end of the war. Some historians argue that the army and navy were still relatively strong, their ranks far from filled only with young boys and elderly men. Peter the Great's navy, although large in size, was qualitatively weak despite the presence of a number of western European officers and sailors on Russian ships of the line. Swedish civilian society, both urban and rural, had suffered greatly, but the situation was not as critical as many early twentieth-century historians have argued. It is nevertheless fair to conclude that during Sweden's age of greatness, from the conquest of Riga from the Poles in 1621, via participation in the Thirty Years War to the end of the Great Northern War, about one third of Sweden's male population died in the service of the army and navy. This fact underlines Michael Roberts's argument that the important question is not *why* the Swedish empire collapsed, but rather *why it lasted as long as it did*, for almost a century.

It is only against this background that Swedish policy in the last decade of the Great Northern War can be understood. The political and military measures employed by Stockholm in the great clash not merely with the three main enemies, but with their supporters Hanover and Prussia, also explains why privateering became an economic and military weapon on a scale and of an intensity never seen before or later in Swedish history. Of course privateers had been seen in Baltic waters before: during the late medieval period and during the war between Sweden and Denmark in the 1560s. They were to be seen again for the last time, on a much smaller scale in the Swedish-Danish conflicts of the early nineteenth century. During the second half of the seventeenth century Sweden, like many other neutral countries, became a victim of British privateers during the Anglo-Dutch wars, and in the first years of the Great Northern War a few Polish privateers managed to make the Baltic waters uncertain for Swedish ships. But such naval warfare escalated dramatically in 1709-10.

The collapse of the main Swedish field army at Poltava in the Ukraine in June 1709 was followed by Russia's capture of Sweden's Baltic provinces in 1710. Sweden's positions on the southern shore of the Gulf of Finland had been taken by the Russians as early as 1702-4. The first to fall was Nöteborg, where the River Neva met Lake Ladoga; it was followed by the fortress of Nyen (on whose ruins Tsar Peter in 1703 founded the new city and later capital, St Petersburg) and then by Narva and the island of Retusaari, soon to be transformed into the growing Russian naval base of Kronstadt. In 1710 the important cities of Reval (Tallinn), Pernau and Riga came into Russian hands. At the same time, Denmark-Norway rejoined the war, after having been forced by a Swedish invasion in 1700 to a non-participant position. Although a Danish invasion of southern Sweden, the province of Skåne - before 1658 eastern Denmark - failed in February 1710, the Danish-Norwegian navy represented a serious threat to Sweden, and the fear of a new invasion over the Sound or from Norway against western Sweden was a real possibility. A number of Danish and Russian ships acted as privateers, especially along Sweden's western coast and in the North Sea. In these two years, 1709 and 1710, a large number of Swedish privateers joined the battle of the seas, both in the Baltic and the North Sea. Although directed against the main enemies, Denmark-Norway and Russia, the repercussions of this campaign, as so often in trade wars, were felt mainly by neutrals. Its effects were soon seen in the anger it aroused in London and The Hague.

Sweden's attacks on the interests of Denmark-Norway had two main purposes. The first aim was to cut off communications between Denmark and Norway. In one direction large quantities of naval goods as well as skilful sailors came from Norway to the Danish navy based in Copenhagen. The importance of Norwegian manpower for the Danish ships cannot be underestimated. In the other direction arms and other military supplies as well as army units were sent to Norway. If this could be stopped, the threat from the land forces in Norway to western Sweden could be reduced. Secondly, a halt to the valuable Norwegian timber trade with western Europe would be a severe blow for Copenhagen's economic capacity to continue the war. In November 1710, from his exile in Turkey, King Karl XII ordered the Admiralty, if it had not been done already, to encourage private individuals to equip privateering ships at their own expense. The purpose was, in the king's own words, 'to inflict damage on the Danes'.

When it came to Russia, Karl XII, from a legal point of view, regarded Sweden's Baltic provinces as his dominion. He himself was the one who had the right to decide what country or what ship should be allowed to trade with Narva, Reval, Pernau or Riga, regardless of the fact that the cities were controlled by Tsar Peter's troops. The king ordered that the trade with all those cities that the Russians controlled on the Baltic Sea must be totally stopped. When the Russians in 1710 also conquered the Finnish city of Viborg and in 1713 even Helsinki, the Swedish blockade was extended also to these ports. A number of instructions were published during 1710 and 1711, with regulations for the privateering. In addition to the naval ships, private captains were given letters of marque by the crown. The ships were equipped and manned by civilians, and all use of sailors from the navy was forbidden to the privateers. All ships taken at sea were to be transported to a Swedish harbour – in the west Gothenburg – where an Admiralty court would decide whether the ship and cargo had been taken legally and could be declared a legal capture or, as sometimes occurred, should be released to continue its journey. The reward for the privateers was the value of the captured ships and cargo, when sold or used by the privateers, although the crown took a certain percentage of the value. After some years the crown gave up all these demands in order to encourage the privateering activities still further. Now the ship owners, their captains, officers and sailors could share the whole profit themselves. Of course all ships from enemy nations were regarded as legal capture, as well as all ships headed to or from ports controlled by the enemy nations, as well as ships travelling between two neutral ports if the cargo, or at least some part of it, could be proved to belong to, say, a Danish or Russian merchant.

From the start of privateering in 1709 to the end of the war twelve years later, at least 156 Swedish ships were used as privateers. Together with units from the regular navy, they attacked trading ships from their bases in the ports of Gothenburg, Karlskrona, Stockholm and Helsinki. Most of the privateers had Gothenburg as their home port, and many of them were owned by wealthy merchants in Gothenburg or by wealthy farmers in the countryside, especially in northern Halland, just a few miles south of Gothenburg. In this area there were long traditions of a combination of farming with small- scale trading at sea, often with the British Isles. These traditions dated back to the province's Danish time, before 1645.

Many merchants and farmers were involved in these activities, and they often owned shares of several ships instead of a whole ship, in a system of spreading the risks. However, one person owned partly or totally more than every third Swedish privateering ship, namely Lars Gathenhielm. He was born in 1689 just south of Gothenburg in one of the most important families connected with both farming and sailing, and as a young man he spent a number of years on both English and Dutch ships. During these years he not only learned English, but obviously also made a number of important business contacts in England and Scotland which proved to be of use later in his career.

Together with his brother Christian and his wife Ingela, Lars Gathenhielm was one of the successful privateering captains in the western seas, between 1710 and 1713, before he had to leave the sea for health reasons and continued his work as a manager of a growing privateering company from land. Although he was taken by the Swedish customs for smuggling a couple of times, and was also accused of illegal activities by German, Dutch and English crews, the king obviously favoured him. Lars Gathenhielm was ennobled and in 1717 he was promoted to command all privateers along the western coast, in order to make the war effort more efficient. However, he was to die in the spring of 1718 from a tuberculosis of the bone that had crippled him for several years. But in the last years of the war, his widow Ingela continued to lead the privateering activities with even greater intensity.

What was the result of these activities? Here the source material available to the historian is unfortunately very poor indeed, for obvious reasons. Lars Gathenhielm and his colleagues never left any private account or presented their results to the crown. This is a fundamental problem for the historian, who has to study the protocols and correspondence of the Admiralty court in Gothenburg, as well as diplomatic correspondence between Stockholm on one side and London and The Hague on the other. The result can be presented in figures that give some idea of the scale of privateering, but do not allow us to quantify its effects. In economic terms the privateering war undoubtedly had real effects on Tsar Peter's Russia, who never managed to use the new Baltic ports on a full scale during the whole war, although we shall never know the exact figures of the direct and indirect casualties in terms of men, ships, goods and values.

The Swedish ships established positions west of Jutland, along the Dogger Bank. Here ships heading for the Baltic were stopped, their cargoes and papers checked, and the ships often taken to Gothenburg. In these positions Swedish privateers also attacked the trade between Denmark and Iceland, especially cod and other fish transports.

Anger grew in Britain and the Netherlands. Neither of these countries wanted a growth of Russian influence in the Baltic region, and this was an important factor for Sweden which was intensively used by the country's diplomats. But it could not excuse everything. The Baltic region was, together with North America and Russia (Archangel) an important source of naval goods for the Royal Navy. The port of Riga in particular exported great quantities of pitch, tar, hemp and timber for ships' masts. During the Great Northern War Britain bought pitch and tar from the North American colonies for some £15,000, from Norway for £1,500, from Russia for £44,000, from the southern ports in the Baltic for £1,150 and from Sweden for over £61,000. It was understandable that the secretary of the Admiralty in London, Josiah Burchett should note that 'There are not any People better furnished with Materials for Shipping than the Swedes, their country abounding not only with useful Timber of all kinds, but with numerous Mines of the best Iron in the World, and producing great quantities of excellent Tar and Hemp.' The British need for Swedish iron was so great that King George I had to lift the prohibition on import from Sweden imposed in 1717 because of the activities by the Swedish privateers, as early as February 1718.

London's official policy towards Sweden could differ from time to time but the trade in iron and naval goods was of fundamental importance for Britain. As early as July 1711 the British minister in Stockholm, Jackson, gave Chancellor Arvid Horn – in effect Sweden's prime minister when the king was abroad with the army – a very clear warning of where the limits for British interests were to be drawn. The neutral trade with the former Swedish harbours in the Baltic provinces, which Sweden had now prohibited in order to blockade the Russians, 'was of high importance, both in respect to Her Majesty's particular service [i.e. the Royal Navy] as well as the general interests of all her subjects, that we could never suffer any interruptions of it'.

The two western maritime powers argued that they must be allowed to trade with the Baltic ports controlled by the Russians, as long as no contraband was traded, but this point of view was never accepted by Karl XII. In the early days of 1715 the Swedish minister in London, Carl Gyllenborg, reported that four ships had been built in England for Russia, and were now ready to set sail for Kronstadt. A Swedish ship, *The Lobster*, left Harwich with his report and out on the North

Sea, close to the Dogger Bank, she met two Swedish frigates, *Kalmar* and *Varberg*, whose commanders also read Gyllenborg's report. This little squadron never met the Russian ships, but instead took four other ships into Marstrand, just south of Gothenburg. However, a number of Swedish privateers and regular naval ships began to sail between the Swedish coast and the northern shores of Jutland, waiting for the four Russians. The Russian ships arrived in early June, but they were not alone. In all some 450 ships of different size, forming a huge convoy heading for the Baltic Sea, approached the Sound. This huge convoy was never attacked by the Swedes, for a very good reason. The merchantmen were escorted by twenty British warships under the command of Sir John Norris, together with a further ten Dutch warships. The four Russian ships were therefore able to reach their new home base in safety, and instead the Swedish ship *The Lobster* was captured by a Norwegian privateer.

The situation could easily have developed to something very much worse for Sweden, since Denmark urged the British force to attack all Swedish naval ships they met, and if possible also to attack and destroy Sweden's main naval base at Karlskrona. Tsar Peter was also very much interested in British support along the Baltic coast and asked London for more units. Another proposal was that Norris's force should advance northwards up into the Gulf of Bothnia, where it could protect the shipment of a Russian army from occupied Finland to mainland Sweden, a deadly threat to Sweden. However none of these offensive plans were carried out, and Norris's instructions were clear: to protect British trade, but not engage actively in the ongoing war. But the expedition of 1715 finally meant that British involvement in the Great Northern War – described by an English writer as late as in 1703 as 'distant Battles of the Pole and Swede' – had now been placed high on the agenda both at Westminster and at the Admiralty. In Sweden this large expedition also led to a more radical warfare, with instructions issued by Karl XII that no foreign warships, 'of what nationality they might be', should be allowed to search for safe haven during bad weather along the western coast.

The king also described the activities of the Dutch navy as illegal. Dutch attacks on neutral Swedish ships heading for France were now used as an argument for Swedish attacks on neutral Dutch ships heading for Russian harbours. The Netherlands issued regulations against all trade in contraband with Russia, but they also described Swedish privateering as plain piracy. The Swedish ambassador in The Hague had a very difficult task maintaining diplomatic and political relations between the two countries. In October 1715 Britain declared war on Sweden, although it was never to become a open and intensive war. Only some minor British ships were sent to assist the allied siege of the Swedish positions at Stralsund in Pomerania. Apart from the privateering there, British anger at Swedish contacts with Jacobite groups and the prospect of total Russian dominance in the Baltic region were seen as threats to British interests throughout the war. When Admiral Norris once again led a large force into the Baltic in 1716, there were some who argued for a preventive British attack on Russia's troop transports between the Baltic coast and Mecklenburg. In this way Russian power could be swept out of the Baltic before it grew too great.

But it was the Swedes who had the greatest difficulities in London. In January 1717 minister Gyllenborg was arrested by the British authorities, after having informal contacts with Jacobites. An intense anti-Swedish propaganda was conducted in papers, pamphlets and books which described King Karl XII as 'the refuse of mankind'. One of the writers engaged in this campaign was Daniel Defoe. Despite all the efforts of the Swedish ministers in the Netherlands and Britain the activities of Swedish privateers led to a deterioration in the relations with these two countries. Privateers also attacked trade off the eastern coast of Sweden. In 1714 nine Dutch ships and their cargoes were sold in Stockholm, together with 13 British ships and one ship from Hamburg. The importance of Stockholm as a base for privateers is revealed even more clearly by a list of ships that were in the harbour in late January 1716 owing to severe ice conditions in the Baltic. Of the 202 ships that were there, no fewer than 25 had been taken by privateers and eight were privateers. However, privateering brought the anarchy of war to the Swedish capital. In 1716 a British ship sailing from Danzig arrived, was cleared by the Swedish customs and anchored in the harbour. On its third day in Stockholm the British ship was attacked, deep in the harbour of central Stockholm, by a privateer, an assault that was later declared legal by the Admiralty court.

Some figures give an idea of the scale and nature of the privateering war. Between 1710 and 1714 110 foreign ships were taken in to Gothenburg by Swedish privateers, and only 11 were released by the Admiralty court. Of the 99 taken, 35 came from Denmark and Norway, two from Russia and one from England and no fewer than 61 from the Netherlands and Lübeck. In Amsterdam it was reckoned that the privateers took goods to the value of 965,000 florins from Dutch ships between 1710 and 1719, while the British estimated that in total 136 British ships to the value of £170,000 were captured. France, too, suffered some losses, leading to diplomatic clashes between the two traditional allies Sweden and France. Many of the privateers did not take the ships and goods they captured home to Sweden: sometimes they argued that it was impossible for safety reasons, sometimes they didn't bother to argue at all. Many neutral, as well as Danish and Norwegian ships, were taken to Dunkirk and sold there. Many Swedish privateers also recruited new sailors and officers among the semi-pirates in that port.

Some captains and sailors even came from the British Isles. The most famous, and unscrupulous, of them was John Norcross, born in Liverpool in 1688. He had sailed as a teenager with the Royal Navy against Spain and the Netherlands but, being a Jacobite, he left Britain and came in 1716 to Gothenburg, where he made good personal contacts with leading Swedish military officers as well as Lars Gathenhielm and other privateers. Norcross was given the command of one of Gathenhielm's best privateer, *La Trompeur*. In 1717 Norcross took a Dutch ship sailing from Bordeaux off the Dutch coast and later managed to escape arrest by the French authorities. Norcross's most spectacular attack took place in March 1717, when *La Trompeur* attacked and captured the regular post boat between the Netherlands and Britain. The ship was taken all the way to Gothenburg, where the Admiralty court was extremely disturbed to realise that the ship not only carried a number of British and Dutch mail bags, but also personal mail addressed to George I and other members of the royal family in London. The diplomatic problems created by this seizure, especially because it was a privateer commanded by an Englishman in Swedish service and crewed by English and Scottish sailors, illustrates the complexity of privateering warfare during the Great Northern War. In 1718, again with an almost entirely British crew, Norcross commanded the *Post Boy*, privateer. He attacked ships in the Irish Sea sailing between Cork and Inverness, then, flying a Danish flag, he captured a Dutch merchantman in the English channel as well as a number of British vessels in the North Sea. All of these ships were a long way from the blockaded Russian ports in the Baltic. It was not until 1726 that the Danes were able to capture him, and thereafter Norcross spent the remaining 32 years of his life in a Copenhagen prison.

It is no accident that the most provocative activities of the Swedish privateers were carried out in the late 1710s. This period saw international piracy reach its peak, especially in the West Indies, before the Royal Navy was able to gain the upper hand during the 1720s. Privateering operations in the Irish Sea and the Bay of Biscay during the Great Northern War were spectacular but irregular. The main effort was conducted in the North Sea and the Baltic. In quantitative terms we still know relatively little about the effects of privateering, though some figures can be found in the archives. However, thanks to archival studies we now know a great deal more about the ships and men, as well as the operations they carried out and the diplomatic consequences of their activities. Conflicts over privateering reflected the strategic interests and actions of Sweden, the Netherlands, Britain, Denmark-Norway and Russia as well as France and other states. They were also an expression of the changing principles of international law and rules of warfare as they continued to evolve until the abolition of privateering in 1856.

Chapter 7

English east coast trade with the Baltic in the closing years of the Great Northern War 1714-21[1]

David Aldridge

From 1710 through to his death in late 1718 Charles XII of Sweden conducted a privateering war in the Baltic. The target of his campaign was merchant shipping trading with those east Baltic ports which had been in Swedish ownership for a century but which were now in process of being wrested from her by Tsar Peter I of Russia. The arrest of this traffic along a seaway integral to the supply of all shipbuilding materials of prime quality – mast timber, hemp, tar – became a component of Charles XII's strategy in his war for the Swedish Empire's survival. It was bound to affect all European states with maritime interests, whether or not they were otherwise well disposed towards the Swedish cause. The privateering intensified after February 1715, when Charles XII issued an edict giving commanders a virtually free hand with any ships seized, and the offensive was given a new focus because of the need to replenish Swedish naval stores. Further disruption was caused by Danish privateering against traffic with Sweden after 1710, in the approaches to the Baltic and in the Elbe estuary,

---

[1] All cited dates are Old Style.

which was compounded by the control Denmark exerted historically on all traffic passing into or out of the Baltic via the Sound or the Great Belt.[2]

This forms the background to the survey of Britain's east coast trade which follows. It is centred, by means of the surviving port books in the Public Record Office and the *original* registers kept by the Danish Sound Toll officials at Elsinore, on Newcastle, Hull, King's Lynn and Yarmouth, and such associated ports as Stockton and Bridlington. The exclusion of London, owing to the destruction of the capital's port books at the end of the nineteenth century in the erroneous belief their contents were duplicated elsewhere, can only be deplored. However, to an important extent this lost information is recoverable, as regards London's Baltic traders, from the Sound Toll registers as distinct from their printed form, *Øresundtabeller*, in which the editors' permutations do not disclose convoy arrivals or departures, or their dates.[3] As it happens, for 1714 we have a microcosm of British merchant shipping in the Kattegat and Baltic. This year was much the most severe in losses to Swedish privateers suffered by the Maritime Powers and – as I have shown elsewhere – it had important consequences in British government action.[4] Through May and June 29 British merchantmen were seized, all but six within the Baltic, the exceptions being taken into Gothenburg. They were all furnished with papers affirming non-contraband cargoes, but eleven of them were bound for Russian or Russian-held ports, above all St Petersburg. Hence they fell within the category it was Charles XII's purpose to ban. The list of ships, of which seven were out of Newcastle, Stockton and Hull, and which had a total value of £65,000, was presented at Stockholm by a protesting British government in June 1715. From that year, up to the end of privateering in the spring of 1719, probably fewer than a dozen British merchantmen were seized, almost all of them by Gothenburgers, though the *Adventure* out of Wells was taken into Karlskrona early in 1716. This modest number was essentially owing to an annual presence of Royal Navy warships

---

[2] See my paper 'Swedish privateering 1710-1718 and the reactions of Great Britain and the United Provinces', Proceedings of the Maritime History Section of the International Congress for Historical Sciences, San Francisco, 1975, vol. I, *Course et Piraterie*, pp. 416-40.

[3] N. Bang and K. Korst (eds.), *Tabeller over Skibsfart og Varetransport gennem Øresund* (Copenhagen, 1906-53). The appropriate volumes are I and III but the limits of their usefulness, at least for this period, need to be emphasised. For each of the following Port Books (all in Public Record Office [PRO]) the period covered was 1715-18: Newcastle and associated ports: E190/220/1, 220/5, 222/1, 221/4; Hull and Bridlington: E190/348/12, 350/8, 351/7; King's Lynn: E190/448/10, 447/5, 445/1, 448/9; Yarmouth E190/529/13, 530/18, 531/14, 532/2.

[4] 'Admiral Sir John Norris and the British naval expeditions to the Baltic Sea 1715-1727', PhD thesis, University of London, 1971.

affording convoy within the Baltic as distinct from past practice, which had been to convoy only as far as Copenhagen with two or three warships only.[5]

From the Sound Toll registers it can be learnt that eight of the 29 ships had begun their voyages in London and were bound for Petersburg. Two were in ballast and two with miscellaneous cargoes, and roughly the same proportions apply to the shipping out of Newcastle and Hull. Three of the skippers and their ships, impounded in Stockholm in 1714, were sailing out of their home ports on the same runs, though of course now under the Royal Navy's protection, in 1716, so they must have obtained release, perhaps in the spring of 1715. For these releases I have no corroborative evidence, and there is no clue in the lists, far from complete it must be supposed, of Stockholm prizes in Riksarkivet, Stockholm. I can give no indication of Gothenburg's archival holdings in this respect, though this port became the most notorious of the privateering bases partly owing to the peculiar resource of the privateer commander Lars Gathenhielm.[6] Gothenburg's offensive spirit was due as much to resentments at the suffering of its shipping at Anglo-Dutch hands since 1689 as to the directives of Charles XII who was exclusively in southern and western Sweden for the last three years of his reign 1716-18. During this time the king was bending all his energies in planning a knock-out campaign against Denmark in Norway, for which supplies were critically needed, and in seeking viable channels through which a peace with Russia might be accomplished. A British embargo on all trade with Sweden, imposed in February 1717, with which Britain tried unsuccessfully to associate the Dutch, only made Swedish agents the more resourceful in encouraging grain shipments into western Sweden.[7] Passes for such shipments were made readily available in Dutch and north German ports, but in the Baltic such equally needed commodities as hemp and mast timber could only be secured through attacks on unescorted traders or from those driven on to Swedish shores by stress of weather, such as occurred in 1718.

---

[5] Copy of list of seized ships: British Library, Add.MSS 28144, ff. 19-20; the British protest is analysed in J.J. Murray, 'Robert Jackson's mission to Sweden 1710-1717' *Journal of Modern History* 21 (1949), pp. 1-16.

[6] Riksarkivet, Stockholm, 'Svenska uppbringingar (kaperier)', vols. VII, VIII, XII, XV-XVIII, compiled by G. Cliff, 1952. The most recent treatment of Gathenhielm's career is in Lars Ericson, *Lasse i Gatan: Kaparkriget och den svenska stormaktsväldets fall* (Lund, 1997). See also Ericson's contribution to this volume.

[7] D.D. Aldridge, 'Sweden's Grain Importations 1717-1718', in W. Minchinton (ed.), *The Baltic Grain Trade* (Exeter, 1985).

The British naval force sent to the Baltic in 1715 under Sir John Norris's command was without precedent. It was to operate in conjunction with a Dutch squadron to protect merchantmen from both countries intending to trade into the east Baltic, and was thus an indicator of the extensive disruption the Swedes were causing to the trade in naval stores. But George I, as Elector of Hanover, was in uneasy alliance with Denmark and Prussia in aiming at the expulsion of Sweden from her north German territories. These included the fortress of Stralsund where Charles XII was present throughout 1715 and whence he directed the privateering war. To assuage Copenhagen and Berlin George was prepared to contravene one of the conditions of his kingship by secretly authorising Norris, once convoying had been completed for the outward voyages, to place his ships athwart Charles XII's supply routes between Karlskrona and Stralsund. In the event, such were the demands of convoy there was no time to make this movement, even had the Dutch commander been prepared to follow suit: between 30 May and 2 June 85 British merchantmen cleared at Elsinore for the Baltic, practically the largest number over to do so over so short a period between 1700 and 1729. The trading season was uneventfully completed because the privateers raced for cover and Charles XII ordered his naval commanders to avoid all hostilities with English warships, both to preserve the Anglo-Swedish alliance and to deprive Hanover of a pretext for less covert hostilities than hitherto. Of the 61 merchantmen now enabled to break the Swedish blockade of Russian-held ports perhaps a dozen ships were from the Tyne and Tees. The remaining 50 ships were predominantly from London, including ten under contract with the Navy Board to import critically needed hemp. Whatever the extent to which the naval stores trade was disrupted by Swedish action in these years, deceitful Russian survey and packaging of hemp, felt especially after the capture of Riga in 1710, was a pernicious abuse whose consequences emerge starkly from the Navy Board's records.[8]

It is difficult to generalise about the overall effect for Baltic trading of the Anglo-Dutch naval presence in 1715. However, because this show of force was without precedent, it may have ensured a normality for trade with Norway as well. The Newcastle, Stockton and Sunderland port books reveal a predictable volume of trade with Norway in 1715. Some ships made two or three round

---

[8]   For the 1715 season overall see Aldridge, 'Admiral Sir John Norris', pp. 25-70. See also R.M. Hatton, *Diplomatic Relations between Great Britain and the Dutch Republic 1714-1721* (London, 1950), pp. 75-80; J.J. Murray, *George I, the Baltic, and the Whig Split* (London, 1969), chapters VI-VII. Fair copy of Navy Board minutes, kept by the secretary, Charles Sergison, in National Maritime Museum, vol. 70 to end (unindexed).

trips during the season, freighting out coal, lead, salt, textiles, glass, grindstones, tobacco and malt. Homeward freights from ports such as Bergen, Kristiansand, Langesund and Kragerø were invariably timber. Ships from north-east ports undertook some 125 voyages, 25 of them either to or from Gothenburg with iron as well as timber. Hull and Bridlington ships undertook 60 voyages, 42% to or from Gothenburg with freights similar to those carried by the Newcastle ships. For ships out of Lynn there was a total of 40 voyages, predominantly for timber importation with some export of malt and textiles. Yarmouth ships undertook 60 voyages, revealing a more significant connection with Drammen and Frederikstad than with other timber ports. Among the cargoes carried by Yarmouth vessels were 26 great masts, a valuable import but difficult to stow, which were shipped from Drammen and Langesund. Though Danish privateers were not beyond operating from Norwegian ports (which of course were under Danish sovereignty) they were usually located in the Kattegat and the Elbe estuary, at least until the early summer of 1716. No later than October 1716 Swedish privateers were operating on the Dogger Bank seizing herring freights in any case destined for Sweden but also to watch for any merchantmen bold enough to break from convoy once the Skagerrak had been cleared. They may also have assisted fugitives from Scotland following the failure of the 1715 Jacobite Rebellion.[9]

Late May 1716 witnessed a more staggered arrival of British merchantmen at the Sound than there had been the previous year. In the course of March and April, seven Newcastle ships, bound mostly for Danzig and Lübeck, preceded the main convoy. Interestingly these included Henry Shadforth in the *Margaret* who had been taken up in 1714. The 40 merchantmen which arrived on 27 May were almost exclusively from London, and the same number arrived from Newcastle under separate convoy on 17 June, clearing at Elsinore over two days during which the good offices of the British representative there, Robert Tigh, were important. Almost all these 80 odd vessels were bound for Russian-held ports, and their numbers were swollen to around 300 after the arrival of the Dutch at the beginning of July.

That there was now no forward movement into the Baltic was because Sir John Norris, again commanding the British squadron, was under orders from George I to make none until an answer was received to a letter of protest to Charles XII about privateering seizures. Such an answer was unlikely given that Hanover was in *de facto* possession of the Swedish duchies of Bremen and Verden and had indeed declared war on Sweden, while Britain remained at

---

[9] See Aldridge, 'Sweden's Grain Importations', p. 39-41.

peace with her. However it was not George I's intention to impede his subjects' trade into the Baltic, but to rely on the Dutch warships to provide convoy exclusively. With only six warships the Dutch commander was in no position to oblige George I, and it was not until 6 August that the English merchantmen could end a two-month wait. By this time there was sufficient evidence of Swedish links with the Jacobite cause for Norris to be made free to cooperate with the Danes and detach some warships for convoy.

What is instructive in a trading context is not the exceptionally complex events which unfolded at Copenhagen over the next month bearing on British-Hanoverian, Danish and Russian relations,[10] but how merchantmen masters coped with the consequences of a delay which was directly attributable to George I's dilemma as an Elector/King of which they could know nothing. Robert Grundy achieved a turn-round at Königsberg in the *William and Robert* of about six weeks by not awaiting the general movement eastwards: he was back at the Sound, bound for Newcastle with flax, on 16 August. Alan Pearson in the *Happy Return* from Hull was back at the Sound from Stockholm with a cargo of iron on 29 July, and home by 26 August. Such voyages should be contrasted with those of some 20 other Newcastle and Hull ships, freighted with hemp from Riga or Petersburg and not clearing the Sound until 31 October. They had to meet very heavy weather in the Skagerrak, but all of them reached their home ports by the end of the year, a month to six weeks later than was customary. The last ship to arrive was the *Success* from Riga, which reached Hull on 20 December.

How many shippers failed in their contracts as a result of George I's political miscalculations? There may be no good answer to the specific question, but it is legitimate to place it in a wider context. Jacobite sources in London gleefully forecast that the delay at the Sound would contribute to the difficulties in which George I's first British ministry was enmeshed, partly owing to internal rivalries. But at Copenhagen in September and October 1716 British and Hanoverian interests stridently clashed, and animosities were also heightened which must postpone a much-coveted commercial treaty with Russia. The ministry's collapse, an accomplished fact by April 1717, had been pushed on at Copenhagen, though it had already been compassed by one of its members. The First Lord of the Admiralty, Edward Russell, Earl of Orford, was a veteran of William III's political struggles who in 1701 had narrowly escaped impeachment

---

[10] The fullest treatment in English of the events at Copenhagen is in Aldridge, 'Admiral Sir John Norris', pp. 140-60; see also W. Mediger, *Mecklenburg, Russland und England-Hannover 1706-1721* (Hildesheim, 1967), vol. I, pp. 300-40.

after his first spell as First Lord. Profoundly distrustful of Hanoverian exploitation of the Royal Navy's presence in the Baltic, Orford was a traditionalist who saw its role there only in terms of power-broking and trade protection. In the autumn of 1716 he may have been lobbied by merchant interests; certainly he queried every disposition Norris had made during the 1716 command, and vetoed Norris's either entering the Admiralty Board or receiving the senior Baltic command in 1717. This command instead went to Orford's favourite Sir George Byng, under whom Norris refused to serve. Orford may have been sceptical about the effectiveness of the beleaguered government's embargo on all trade with Sweden, since he was in a position to know how grain exports at a time of surplus in England would suffer. He may also have taken seriously the government's claim – in fact fictitious – that a Swedish invasion on the east coast was imminent. The end result of Orford's measures was a Baltic squadron of exceptional size which provided extensive convoy throughout the season even in the absence, this year, of a Dutch squadron.[11]

Three weeks, 18 June and 9 July separated the largest concentrations of merchantmen entering the Baltic in 1717. The first comprised about 40 vessels and the second 96. About 10 ships from the east coast ports arrived in the Sound on 18 June, but the majority came from the Iberian salt ports to which they may have originally sailed from home in ballast. They all declared for Danzig, Königsberg, and Riga. The larger convoy in July included about 20 Newcastle ships which had been detained for up to six weeks in the Tyne owing to vigilance over all sailings following the invasion scare. There were a further six from Hull and Bridlington, and perhaps three from Lynn and Yarmouth. Most of these ships declared for Petersburg and Riga, a good index of the need for hemp which was continuing in English dockyards. The first group cleared westwards from the Sound in early September, and some 75 of the ships in the second cleared over two days, on 26 and 27 October. Such a rapid clearance may have been due to the trust Robert Tigh enjoyed from Danish officials, since in January 1719 he reported that the 'Danish searcher, being an old man, does not venture to go on board in blowing weather' to verify declarations. The toll officials themselves however, through long usage, did not hesitate to alter the rates paid on the various commodities, and they discriminated against Petersburg

---

[11] For Orford's role in the ministerial collapse see D.D. Aldridge, 'Admiral Edward Russell: pre- and post- Barfleur', *Guerres maritimes 1688-1713* (Vincennes, 1996), pp. 169-71. For the government's dissemination of an invasion scare in 1717 see J.J. Murray, 'An eighteenth century Whitebook', *Huntington Library Quarterly* XIII (1949/50).

rather than Riga hemp because of the crudeness and dishonesty of Russian manifests. Although the Danish government supported the British imposition of a trade embargo on Sweden, it proved costly for takings at the Sound. For 1717 the yield was 59,335 rixdalers, the lowest since 1709. In 1718 the figure was improved by 20,000 rixdalers because of a deafening clamour in England by the end of 1717 for a restoration of Swedish iron imports, which compelled the government to permit importation at second hand from Dutch middlemen.[12]

The Dutch refused to be impressed by threats from London if they did not comply with the trade embargo. Britain therefore imported only one-fifth of the quantity of Swedish iron that came into Dutch ports, either by blockade runners or by merchantmen which, ironically, took full advantage in the Baltic of Sir George Byng's convoying arrangements. The 1717 figure for Swedish iron was a mere 1,850 tons whereas in 1718, the government having bowed to pressure and relaxed the Navigation Acts, the figure rose to 11,200 tons, almost two-thirds of which came from stockpiles in Dutch ports.[13] The balance was imported through Königsberg and Danzig from stocks accumulated there by Dutch merchantmen which had made the trans-Baltic crossing from ports such as Stockholm and Norrköping. Ships from the east coast ports carried about 2,500 tons (computed from the port books), rather more than a third of the total. Lynn, which in 1717 had imported a fractional quantity, imported 500 tons in 1718. Yarmouth ships, which had imported 60 tons of unspecified bar in 1717, carried 210 tons a year later, most of it from Rotterdam. The figures speak for themselves, for the embargo had had the effect of stimulating extraordinarily high levels of iron exportation from Sweden in 1718.[14] Given Hull's pre-eminence amongst the out-ports as an iron importer, 1,100 tons in 1718 comes as no surprise, but how much of it really came from Amsterdam and Rotterdam, as stated in the Hull port book, may be questioned, for the traditional source of Hull's iron was of course Gothenburg. Here the great Hull iron merchant Henry Maister was periodically resident and, though a Whig, Maister labelled the original embargo and its alleged causes 'childish' (*barnsligt*). In 1718, in exchange for iron, he undertook to import into Sweden 'just as soon as possible' (*så snart som möjligt*)

---

[12] For Tigh's report from Elsinore to Commissioners of Trade, 17 January 1719, see PRO Colonial Office Series 389/27, pp. 82 et seq. Figures of gross takings in Tigh to Commissioners, 7 November 1719, ibid., p. 300.

[13] According to the Customs 3 series in the PRO.

[14] This successful Swedish venting of iron is analysed in G. Lindeberg, *Svensk ekonomisk politik under den Görtska perioden* (Lund, 1941), pp. 36-9, 120-40, 387-91, and chapter XII.

corn and clothing for Charles XII's army 'or other necessary items' (*eller andra nödiga waror*).[15]

Britain's 1718 Baltic squadron, again commanded by Norris following changes at the Admiralty on the formation of a new ministry, reached the Sound on 14 May. He had less than ten in convoy from the east coast ports. The main convoy, about 90 strong, did not arrive until 20 June and 70 of these were destined for the east Baltic, to Königsberg for iron or Riga and Petersburg for hemp. The Dutch, nine of whose warships convoyed an enormous merchant fleet of 230 vessels to Copenhagen on 26 June, agreed to carry out the convoy duties without looking to Norris for assistance. Norris had known the Dutch commander, Van Koperen, since at least 1710, but the two men now found themselves in a novel situation. This was only partly because a feared junction of the Swedish and Russian fleets (should there be an accommodation between Charles XII and Tsar Peter) necessitated Norris's force blockading Karlskrona alongside Danish warships. More importantly, the very absence of the British force from the eastern Baltic would make it the easier for Dutch merchantmen, under Van Koperen's protection, to breach the embargo. Norris himself forecast this scenario on 9 June, before Van Koperen's arrival, when he addressed British representatives at The Hague: 'While there is an open trade with Danzig, Königsberg and other ports the wants of Sweden will be supplied. I should be glad to know whether, when the States propose *our* acting against Sweden [i.e. the Karlskrona blockade] they have forbid *their* commerce to that country'.[16] While circumstances enabled the Dutch to increase stockpiles of Swedish iron, fewer than ten east coast ships returned directly to their home ports at the end of October because of the attractions of calling first at Dutch ports for iron for onward sale in London. Dutch opportunism as well as resource dissolved George I's hopes of starving Sweden into submission.

After the death of Charles XII in December 1718 the new regime in Sweden suspended privateering in April 1719 and so enabled the British government to rescind an embargo which had long been an object of ridicule. Despite commitments in the Mediterranean, the renewal of the Anglo-Swedish alliance of 1700 resulted by August 1719 in a strong British squadron under Norris's command leaving Copenhagen to deter the Russians from continuing their galley attacks on the Stockholm coasts which had begun in June. The reduced

---

[15] For Maister's reactions See H. Almquist, *Göteborgs historia 1680-1718* (Gothenburg, 1935), pp. 319-20; other quotations from Lindeberg, *Svensk ekonomisk politik*, p. 310.

[16] My italics. Norris to Whitworth and Cadogan at The Hague, 9 June 1718, BL, Add. MSS 28145, f. 156.

need for convoy meant that around 60 east coast merchantmen preceded Norris into the Baltic, and those which sailed into the east Baltic achieved very reasonable turn-around, some 48 days. To some extent this was due to Tsar Peter's concern that his continuing war with Sweden should not disrupt merchant traffic. It may be significant that in 1720 two Yarmouth ships took malt into Reval, much the most formidable of Russia's naval bases, and that one of them then went on to Stockholm to bring home a cargo of iron. Those bound for Stockholm in 1719 from the Sound had to pass through an archipelago devastated by recent Russian attacks but evidently traded uneventfully.[17] In 1720 the Tsar's assurances of safe passages for merchantmen still obtained, though he chose to regard Norris as the satrap of a vengeful Hanover. The squadron this year arrived at Copenhagen in early May with a convoy of over 80 vessels, but Norris carefully avoided any delay there because of Danish resentment at British-Hanoverian representatives at Stockholm negotiating peace terms for Denmark without Copenhagen's concurrence. Rather than fearing for the security of the British merchantmen, London thought it likelier the Danes might take Norris as a hostage. Two dozen east coast ships had sailed with Norris, but the same number had preceded him since the start of the year, and these were intending to distribute themselves all over the Baltic. Almost all of them cleared the Sound for home by early November, though they were to meet with severe weather in the Kattegat and again in the southern North Sea.[18]

In 1721 about 20 ships from east coast ports came with Norris's squadron at the end of April, although less than ten of them appear to have left with it in early October. The majority, some 35 ships, arrived in the Sound during May and June, clearing for England in September and October, though ten were as late as December. The substantially larger volume of British shipping sailing into the Baltic in 1720-1, almost 400 vessels over these two seasons, was indicative of the more settled conditions that then prevailed. In January 1719 it had been Robert Tigh's informed opinion that trade in 'this last and former years has been very dull', but he supposed Charles XII's death would make an important difference. On this point he could only be right.[19] Yet the remarkable regularity of voyages into the Baltic from the east coast ports does seem to question *how*

---

[17] For the 1719 season overall see Aldridge, 'Admiral Sir John Norris', chapter IV.

[18] For Tsar Peter's declarations favouring merchant traffic see L.N. Nikiforov, *Russische-Englische Beziehungen unter Peter I* (Weimar, 1954), pp. 272-3, 299-300.

[19] See note 12 above for source of Tigh's opinion. Transcriptions from the Sound Toll registers for the three years 1719-21, provided to the Trade Commissioners by Tigh, are in PRO, CO 388/23, numbers R 14-15, R 17-18, R 87-88.

dull the trade had been during these years, especially after the inception of a British naval presence in 1715. In 1716 British traders had been as much interrupted by Hanoverian concerns as by Charles XII's privateers; and the trade embargo of 1717-19 seems if anything to have enhanced Swedish-Dutch trade at *British* expense. Finally it may be suggested that, whatever was attempted and achieved by Swedish privateering during these years, Denmark's near stranglehold on Baltic traffic, and an often studied neglect of provisions in past commercial agreement, denied her much goodwill among Britain's northern traders. At the same time Britain's long-standing links with Denmark's Norwegian subjects, and the great timber ports, stayed relatively unimpaired.

Chapter 8

Baltic iron and the organisation of the British iron market in the eighteenth century[1]

Åsa Eklund, Chris Evans and Göran Rydén

The rapid growth of metalware manufacturing in Britain in the later seventeenth century was to affect the Baltic profoundly. Nails, hinges, bolts, knives, locks, scythes and edge tools of every description were produced in greater and greater quantities, particularly in the specialised manufacturing zones that were emerging in the West Midlands, the West Riding of Yorkshire and the North East of England. Bar iron was essential for the production of these commodities, but as the output of metalwares surged upwards English ironmasters were unable to meet the rising demand for malleable iron. Charcoal was in short supply and although ironmasters tried every measure of fuel economy they found themselves constrained by a fundamental shortage of energy. There was, it was clear, a ceiling to bar iron production in the British Isles. By the early eighteenth century some 30,000 tons was made annually in British forges, yet domestic consumption of bar iron was twice that and rising. The shortfall had to be made up by imports from the Baltic, initially from Sweden, the most important iron-exporting region in Europe, but later from Russia as well.

Swedish iron first entered the British market in substantial quantities in the 1660s. At that time the Dutch market was the main destination for Swedish bar

---

[1] This paper is based upon research supported by the University of Glamorgan in the UK and the *Axel och Margaret Ax:son Johnsons Stiftelse för Almännyttiga Ändamål* in Sweden.

iron. By 1700, however, British consumption was paramount, accounting for 60 per cent of Swedish iron exports. Thus, the trade in iron between Sweden and Britain became one of the defining features of commercial life in northern Europe in the eighteenth century. Yet Swedish pre-eminence did not go unchallenged. A major export-orientated iron industry was established in Russia by Peter the Great. By the 1720s iron from the Urals was being shipped from St Petersburg in large quantities and was to be found stacked alongside the Swedish product on the quays of London, Hull and Newcastle.

The rapidly expanding British market was something of a novelty, for which the Dutch Republic, centre of the European trade in iron in the seventeenth century, offered the only precedent. It was not at all usual for iron to be exchanged on a large scale across long distances. Iron was a bulky commodity with a relatively low value-to-weight ratio which tended to be consumed close to the point of production. The standard pattern was for most regions of early modern Europe to be self-sufficient in iron, and for iron to be traded in the form of manufactured articles rather than as a raw material.[2] But Britain, whilst becoming a significant iron producer in its own right (unlike the Dutch Republic), imported bar iron in the eighteenth century on a quite unheralded scale and by doing so supplied the dynamo that drove forward industrial development in Sweden and Russia. The British market became an arena in which domestically produced bar iron jostled with imported bar iron made under quite different social conditions.

Ironmaking regimes in northern Europe 1600-1800

If the relationship between Britain and her Baltic partners in the iron trade is to be understood it is important to grasp the different social regimes which governed iron production in the three countries under consideration. To begin with Britain, it should be stressed that iron had been imported into the British Isles for several centuries, most notably from the Basque country.[3] Indeed, imports were essential because most British ores were phosphoric in character and yielded a metal that was too brittle for some purposes. Nevertheless, Britain had a sizeable iron industry of her own. The forge sector in the first half of the

---

[2] See Philippe Braunstein, 'The forest, the iron and the water: perspectives on the development of European economies in the end of the middle ages', in Gert Magnusson (ed.), *The importance of ironmaking: technical innovation and social change* (Stockholm, 1995), II, pp. 159-62.

[3] W.R. Childs, 'England's iron trade in the fifteenth century', *Economic History Review*, XXXIV (1981), 25-47.

eighteenth century numbered about 130 forges, employing about 1,000 forgemen. The structure of this industry followed the classic 'triad' formula for industrial activity in early modern Britain whereby different factors of production were drawn from different social groups: landowners (land), capitalists (capital) and wage labourers (labour). Professional ironmasters played the central coordinating role, leasing industrial sites and combining resources from the land (ore and charcoal) with the skills and muscle-power of a hired labour force. Typically, these ironmasters were grouped in extended partnerships, usually bonded together by ties of kinship, in which all elements of the production process were combined. Ore was smelted, pig iron was refined, and bar iron was rolled into plates or slit into nail rods by different members of the great dynastic partnerships which dominated the iron trade in the early eighteenth century. Because of this, it might be thought that ironmaking in Britain, as a large-scale enterprise, was organised along lines familiar from a later capitalism, and that the major ironmaking partnerships were precursors of the modern integrated firm. Nothing could be further from the truth. Interlinked ownership did not imply an integration of production. Different furnaces, forges and processing mills were grouped together loosely in order to protect the interests of the iron dynasts: pig iron, bar iron and nail rods were bought and sold amongst members of the major combines in order to ramify their control over regional markets, not to achieve a rational pattern of production.

In our view, the traditional way of analysing the British iron industry, with its emphasis upon the partnerships of the Foley or Knight families as predecessors of modern firms, overlooks the importance of the market. The great partnerships were not coherent organisations within which the sequence of productive processes (fuel processing-smelting-forging-rolling-slitting) was internalised, rather they should be seen as alliances of semi-autonomous associates who governed different parts of the productive process and who exchanged semi-finished articles on preferential terms. This does not mean that we want to see the industry as governed by a 'harmonious' market in which issues of power and control were absent. On the contrary, we wish to underline the question of power by stressing the role of the ironmaster as a controlling agent within the market. Ironmasters employed the partnerships in which they were involved to control the flow of raw materials and semi-finished commodities (pig iron, bar iron, nail rods). The partnerships which typified the organisation of the early eighteenth-century iron trade should be seen as networking arrangements designed to set prices and to confirm market shares, not to facilitate an efficient form of production.

The structure of the industry in Sweden was quite different. Professional ironmasters did not exercise control over the entire sequence of production and market exchanges were far less prominent. Instead, we can talk of a multiform organisation of production, with at least four important elements: *peasants* who were responsible for supplying charcoal and pig iron; *ironmasters* who were responsible for producing bar iron; *wholesale merchants* who had charge of the export of bar iron; and a powerful *state* which regulated production. The Swedish iron industry was also far bigger than its British counterpart. Next to agriculture, ironmaking was the most important sector of the Swedish economy. In the mid-eighteenth century Sweden could boast about 420 ironworks, each with at least one forge, to compare with the 130 forges in Britain. More than 2,500 forgemen were required to man these forges, as against the 1,000 or so forgemen in Britain.

Traditionally, peasants in *bergslagen* (the mining district of central Sweden) had been entrusted with all the stages of bar iron production. In the medieval period they had mined ore, prepared charcoal, and smelted and refined iron themselves. This iron was then bought by merchants based in Stockholm and other Baltic ports and launched into the international market. The ironmaking peasantry and the urban merchants remained important actors within the Swedish iron trade, but the early modern period saw the emergence of a class of professional ironmasters. It also saw the state intensify its regulation of the trade with the aim of expanding exports (and thereby export revenues). The state imposed a strict division of labour on the trade, in which different parts of the productive process were separated out socially and spatially. Ironmaking peasants, living within the traditional mining districts, continued to mine and smelt ore, but the refining of pig into bar iron was allotted to the new class of ironmasters who were to operate ironworks outside the mining districts.

This policy bore fruit in the seventeenth century. The Swedish iron industry acquired a dual structure in which peasants and ironmasters assumed responsibility for different links of the production chain under the supervision of the state. There was only one exception to this structure, that of ironworks in the very east of Sweden which drew upon the rich ores of the Dannemora mine. In the early seventeenth century a number of wealthy Dutch merchants acquired concessions to make iron in this area. Between seven and eight hundred Walloon workers followed in their footsteps, bringing their own ironmaking techniques with them. As a result, a quite distinct way of organising iron production arose in the county of Uppland, overriding what had been a weak tradition of peasant ironmaking. Large, integrated ironworks were built, combining blast furnaces, forges and (sometimes) workshops for metalware production. Swedish historiography has conventionally distinguished between this pattern of ironmaking and the form which dominated elsewhere in *bergslagen* according to the forging technique that was used. By far the greater part of Swedish iron was made by the so-called German forging technique, but in Uppland the Walloon forging method was employed, using pig iron made from Dannemora ore to produce a high-quality iron, Öregrund iron, that was amongst the most highly priced in Europe.

Ironmasters occupied a powerful position within the framework for production imposed by the Swedish state, but they did not have access to international markets. They were obliged to deliver their iron to certain designated ports, Stockholm and Göteborg above all, where the bar iron had to pass through state-regulated weigh-houses. The actual export of the iron was handled by an elite of wealthy wholesale merchants. Hence the multiform character of the Swedish iron trade in the eighteenth century with four social actors undertaking different roles. The means of production in ironmaking was divided between peasants and ironmasters, with the ironmasters controlling the high value-added sector of bar iron making. The state played a critical role as supervisor of the entire trade, whilst the wholesale merchants of the ports monopolised the export of iron. All in all, the Swedish iron industry differed radically from the more uniform organisation of its British counterpart, where the ironmaster had a controlling interest in all stages of the production process.

In Russia, Sweden's chief competitor on the international market, we are once again dealing with a more uniform organisation of production. But whereas the social homogeneity of production in Britain was supplied by a class of ironmasters enmeshed in market relationships, the Russian iron industry was bound together by feudal links. All aspects of ironmaking took place within the context of the feudal estate. The ironmaster, or more accurately feudal lord, had all the means of production at his disposal. Raw materials, extracted from his estate, were his personal property. The same could be said of his workforce, made up of serfs who were bound to the estate. Ironmaking was a matter of forced labour, not only when it came to auxiliary tasks like charcoal making and transportation, but in the central workshops as well. Furnacemen and forgemen had serf status.

Forced labour and abundant forest resources were the foundation for a gigantic iron industry in the Urals, on the frontier between Europe and Asia. The first Urals ironworks was founded at Neviansk in 1701. Fifty years later there were more than thirty works, equipped with forges that were far larger than those in Britain and Sweden. In mid-century total bar iron production amounted to close on 20,000 tons, still far behind the annual Swedish make of 50,000, but in the second half of the eighteenth century the Russian industry entered a period of explosive growth. Annual production was approaching 100,000 tons by the century's end.[4]

The British market absorbed iron that was made under three very different social regimes. We wish to make a more detailed examination of how changes on the British market affected production and policy in the Baltic by tracing the shifting relationship between Britain and Sweden. More specifically, we wish to focus upon the trading links between Francis Jennings, a member of Stockholm's 'quayside nobility', and Graffin Prankard, the Bristol merchant who was a leading importer of Baltic iron between the 1720s and 1740s. The activities of both merchants are well documented and provide an intimate view of the trade in iron, illuminating the wider issues of policy during a critical phase.

Swedish iron on the British market

Although part of Sweden's iron production was consumed domestically, by far the greater part was exported.[5] Indeed, iron completely dominated Sweden's export trade. Bar iron's share of the total value of exports routed through Stockholm in the eighteenth century never fell below two-thirds, and between 1730 and 1760 it exceeded three-quarters.[6] Moreover, there was a long tradition of selling iron overseas. As early as the sixteenth century significant quantities were sent to northern German towns. But it was the increasing demand for iron in the Netherlands in the first half of the seventeenth century that led to the rise of Sweden as one of the foremost iron exporting regions of Europe. As we have seen (and as discussed in Leos Müller's chapter in this volume), in the second half of the seventeenth century Swedish exports shifted away from the Dutch Republic towards Great Britain, and it was the expansion of the British market that underwrote a further growth in Swedish exports that lasted until the first decades of the eighteenth century. Thereafter, though, a policy of restricting exports was introduced (to which we will return), so that iron exports stabilised

---

[4] See Anders Florén and Göran Rydén (with Ludmila Dashkevich, D.V. Gavrilov and Sergei Ustiantsev), 'The social organisation of work at mines, furnaces and forges', in Maria Ågren (ed.), *Iron-making societies: early industrial development in Sweden and Russia , 1600-1900* (Oxford, 1998), pp. 61-138. For production figures see Hugh D. Hudson, *The rise of the Demidov family and the Russian iron industry* (Newtonville, MA, 1986), pp. 44, 83.

[5] K.-G. Hildebrand, *Fagerstabrukens historia. Sexton- och sjuttonhundratalen* (Uppsala, 1957), p. 161.

[6] Kurt Samuelsson, *De stora köpmanshusen i Stockholm 1730-1815. En studie i den svenska handelskapitalismens historia* (Stockholm, 1951), p. 77.

at around 43,000 tons in the mid-1730s and remained at that level for the next forty-five years. A renewed period of growth in the 1780s and 1790s proved short-lived. Iron exports fell in the new century, unable to compete with British-made iron produced by puddling and rolling.[7]

The British Isles remained the most important market for Swedish iron throughout the eighteenth century. The relative share taken by Britain varied, however, reflecting significant changes in the overall composition of Sweden's export markets. Britain's share of Swedish iron output declined from about 60 percent in 1700 to around 40 per cent at the end of the century. The Netherlands, once the main market for Swedish iron, declined from about 10 per cent to a mere 2-3 per cent, yet remained of great importance for the financing of the Swedish iron trade. The southern Baltic held its own, generally accounting for between a quarter and one-fifth of exports. The greatest change was to be found in the Latin-Levantine market, which until the end of the 1760s had taken no more than 10 per cent of Swedish exports. From the 1770s, however, exports to southern Europe, to France and Portugal in particular, grew quickly, with the result that one-third of exports went to the Latin-Levantine market at the end of the 1780s. There was then a sharp decline to about 20 percent at the century's end. The pressure which Swedish exporters found themselves under by 1800 was relieved to a certain extent by the opening up of new markets in the United States and the West Indies, which took 17 per cent of Swedish iron exports by the end of the first decade of the nineteenth century.[8]

Different markets took different irons. The small proportion of bar iron still manufactured by *bergsmän*, the ironmaking peasants, was generally regarded as of uneven quality and was mostly destined for the Baltic area or southern Europe. At the other end of the scale was the much sought-after Öregrund iron, almost all of which went to Britain for steelmaking.[9] The British market took such large quantities of Swedish iron – 15,000 tons in 1699, rising to about 19,000 tons fifty years later – that it is necessary to distinguish between different regional markets within the British Isles.[10] London, as Britain's leading commercial centre and with no significant iron-producing area within its

---

[7] E.F. Heckscher, *Sveriges ekonomiska historia från Gustaf Vasa, del II* (Stockholm, 1949), p. 398; Hildebrand, *Fagerstabrukens historia*, pp. 35-43.

[8] Hildebrand, *Fagerstabrukens historia*, pp. 94-8; Heckscher, *Sveriges ekonomiska historia*, appendix, p. 30.

[9] Richard Ringmar, *Gästriklands bergsmän, Kronan och handelskapitalet. Aktörer och institutionella spelregler i bergsmansbruket, 1650-1870* (Uppsala, 1999), p. 145; Hildebrand, *Fagerstabrukens historia*, pp. 35-43.

[10] Heckscher, *Sveriges ekonomiska historia*, pp. 401-02.

hinterland, was the single most important destination. In the first decades of the eighteenth century London received about 70 per cent of Swedish imports.[11] From then on London's relative share decreased, falling to 40 per cent at the end of the century, whilst the outports grew in importance. Hull, serving the Sheffield steel industry, expanded its share of Swedish imports (although Newcastle, port for the less buoyant steel centres of the Derwent valley, did not). Above all, west-coast outports began to attract Swedish iron in significant quantities. This was especially true of Bristol, *entrepôt* for the metalware manufacturing zones of the English Midlands, which for a period ranked second behind London. Thus, the relationship between Bristol and Stockholm came to be one of the major axes of trade between the Baltic and Britain in the mid eighteenth century. Fortunately, for a period in the second quarter of the century, this relationship can be explored in detail, by scrutinising two complementary archives: those of Francis Jennings and Graffin Prankard.

Francis Jennings, Graffin Prankard and the organisation of the iron trade

Francis Jennings, a native of Dublin, had settled in Sweden in 1719 and soon established himself as an important merchant.[12] By the end of the 1720s he was responsible for about 10 per cent of Stockholm's iron exports. His share continued to increase, culminating in 1750 when he accounted for 38 per cent of exports.[13]

---

[11] Chris Evans and Göran Rydén, 'Iron in Sweden and Britain 1600-1850: interdependence and difference', in Magnusson, *Importance of ironmaking*, I, pp. 408ff.

[12] Jonas Norrby, *Jennings* (Köping, 1991), pp. 6-7.

[13] Stockholms Stads Arkiv [SSA], Tolagsjournaler 1720-54.

Chart: *The Iron exports of Francis Jennings 1720-1754*

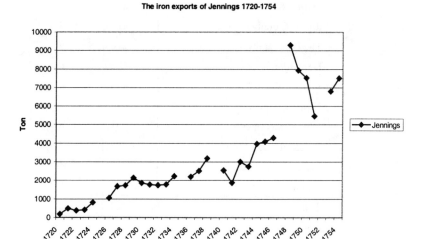

Source: SSA, Tolagsjournaler 1720-1754.

Almost all iron exports at this period were handled by Jennings and a few other large merchant houses, with only a few ironmasters exporting their own iron. Sometimes the merchant houses merely acted as agents, arranging the sale of iron in the name of the ironmaster, but more commonly the merchant houses bought the iron themselves and exported it in their own name.[14] The trade was dominated by Stockholm's largest merchant houses. The ten largest houses accounted for 62 per cent of the iron leaving the port in 1730 and 57 per cent in 1741.

---

[14] Heckscher, *Sveriges ekonomiska historia*, s. 681; Hildebrand, *Fagerstabrukens historia*, pp. 183-84.

Table 1: *Stockholm's leading iron exporters, 1730*

		tons	%
1	Maister & Co	2817	11
2	Robert Campbell	2249	9
3	The Grill family	2200	9
4	Francis Jennings	1860	8
5	Samuel Worster	1488	6
6	Gustaf Kierman	1143	5
7	John Montgomery	912	4
8	Berge-Oloffson-Ström	885	4
9	Johan H. Lefebure	876	4
10	Samuel Wordsworth	860	3
	Total	15291	62

Source: SSA, Tolagsjournaler 1730.

What is more, the major merchant houses exercised an even tighter grip over exports to the critical British market. In 1730, 94 per cent of Stockholm's iron exports to Britain were handled by the ten largest merchant houses.

The role of the great merchant houses was not confined to the handling of exports. Although the social division of labour established within the Swedish iron trade in the seventeenth century insisted upon merchants' exclusion from the actual process of ironmaking, in practice merchants' influence gradually extended backwards into the sphere of production, since the merchant houses often provided the ironworks with credit (*förlag*). Generous credit was essential if ironmasters were to bridge the time-lag between the incurring of running expenses at the *bruk* and the receipt of revenue from iron sales. As a result, merchant houses and the ironworks with which they habitually dealt became bound together. Merchants advanced credit, ironmasters' indebtedness grew, and in time the ironmasters found themselves subordinate to the 'quayside nobility' of Stockholm.[15] This enabled merchants to aggrandise the output of forges that were in their debt, or even to dictate what sorts of bar were made. Ultimately, a merchant might take over a *bruk* that was chronically indebted. The relationship between Francis Jennings and Antoine de Geer, master of the ironworks at Österby and Forsmark,

---

[15] Samuelsson, *De stora köpmanshusen*, pp. 91-95; Hildebrand, *Fagerstabrukens historia*, pp. 183-190; Heckscher, *Sveriges ekonomiska historia*, pp. 505-507.

illustrates the process. Debts mounted to the point where there was no foreseeable way in which they could be redeemed by iron deliveries, so de Geer was forced to sell Forsmark to Jennings.[16]

Jennings, for his part, was implicated in a far wider international network of credit. Much of his trade, as was conventional, was conducted on a commission basis, through a variety of agents who sold iron and other commodities on his behalf in foreign ports – a role which Graffin Prankard performed in Bristol. When Jennings dispatched a cargo of iron, timber or tar to Prankard he drew a bill of exchange on him. In effect, Prankard was advancing credit to Jennings, his principal; credit that would be redeemed through the sale of the commodities belonging to Jennings in local markets. (So, confusingly, Prankard was both an employee of and a creditor of Francis Jennings. It is also worth noting that Prankard often bought iron directly from Jennings, which he sold on his own account, so that Prankard's Bristol warehouse contained iron which was being sold as Jennings' property and iron which was sold as Prankard's.)[17] The transmission of credit across the North Sea was a complex affair, involving a variety of intermediaries. Prankard and Jennings used several bankers and merchants in London, Hamburg, and Amsterdam. The sequence of events was as follows. When Jennings dispatched a shipment to Prankard he drew a bill of exchange upon Skinner, Smith & Co., the Hamburg merchant house with which Prankard traded. Skinner, Smith & Co. would in turn draw upon Thomas Hyam, Prankard's London banker. For his part, Prankard would settle his account with Hyam with cash or bills whenever he visited London. Alternatively, Jennings might draw upon Muilman & Son in Amsterdam, who were either paid directly by Prankard, or who drew upon Thomas Hyam or another London banking house, that of Patrick & Robert Mackey.[18]

The iron whose movement was registered in these transactions was destined for Bristol and Prankard's warehouse. The volume of iron handled by Prankard rose sharply in the late 1720s and by 1730 he was responsible for no less than 53 per cent of the Swedish iron entering Bristol.

By the early 1730s, then, Graffin Prankard was established as the leading importer of Baltic iron in western Britain and Francis Jennings was on the verge of

---

[16] Norrby, *Jennings*, pp. 26-30.

[17] Leos Müller, *The merchant houses of Stockholm, c.1640-1800: a comparative study of early-modern entrepreneurial behaviour* (Uppsala, 1998), pp. 142-43, 156-57; SA [Somerset Archives], DD/DN, 434 and 435.

[18] SA, DD/DN 435 and 442.

becoming Stockholm's most important iron exporter. Their relationship can therefore reveal a great deal about the conduct of trade between Britain and the Baltic. Specifically, an examination of the different grades of iron which Prankard bought through Francis Jennings and their distribution to customers in central and south-western England can offer important insights into the structure of the British iron market.

Table 2: *Importers of Swedish iron in Bristol, 1730*

	tons	%
Graffin Prankard	677.22	53.76
Nehemiah Champion	147.72	11.73
James Day	136.82	10.86
Nathaniel Wraxall	100.17	7.95
Thomas Chamberlayne	58.02	4.61
Robert Smith & Co	31.78	2.52
Jos. Swayne	22.00	1.75
Rob. Rogers	20.21	1.60
John Heylin	20.13	1.60
Daniel Kemble	19.13	1.52
Jacob Elton	14.10	1.12
Jos. Daltera	5.24	0.42
Truman & Charles Harford	3.92	0.31
William Finch	1.49	0.12
Daniel Rogers	1.21	0.10
William Donne junior	0.44	0.03
Total	1259.60	100.03

Source: PRO, E190/1204/1, Bristol Port Books 1730

Graffin Prankard bought a variety of Swedish brands, some for general sale, others for customers who demanded iron with very specific properties. One type of iron, above all others, was of concern to Prankard: the Öregrund iron made at the Walloon ironworks in Uppland. Öregrund was perceived as being the only iron worthy of conversion to steel. It therefore commanded a premium price, more than ten per cent above the market rate for Swedish 'common sorts'. Given that no more than twenty *bruk* made this precious material, it was very much in the interest of a merchant like Prankard to establish some kind of monopoly control over one or another of the Öregrund brands. And since the merchant elite of Stockholm exercised a considerable influence over the Walloon (and other) *bruk* through the *förlag* system, Prankard could hope to achieve near-monopoly conditions by co-operating closely with a leading merchant like Francis Jennings. In Prankard's case he insisted on having first call on the yearly make of the forges at Åkerby and Lövsta in Uppland: 'no other marks will answer here for steel', as he told Jennings.[19] Indeed, through the late 1720s and early 1730s Prankard acted in concert with Samuel Shore (1676-1751), the leading steelmaker in the Sheffield area, in an attempt to tie up the entire British market for these key Öregrund brands.[20] They negotiated year-to-year contracts with Francis Jennings to ensure that they bought up all or nearly all the output from Åkerby and Lövsta. Prankard's share would go to the West Midlands via Bristol, Shore's to south Yorkshire via Hull. Not a single bar was to be released on to the London market for rival merchants to snap up. Prankard and Shore stipulated that any Åkerby or Lövsta bars that were surplus to their own immediate requirements were to be sold on the Dutch market, never in Britain.[21]

Prankard was willing to pay a generous price for Åkerby or Lövsta bars – he could after all pass the costs on – but for the 'common marks' of iron he had to bargain harder. Swedish iron was rated 'tough' in contemporary parlance; that is, it had a hard and durable quality, unlike British-made iron which was generally 'cold-short' or brittle. For some purposes, such as anchor making, the tough qualities of Swedish iron were essential, but 'toughness' had its drawbacks as well. Working with such an unyielding material was a time-consuming and expensive activity. As one English blacksmith told the Swedish traveller Angerstein, 'horseshoes of Swedish iron would be more durable, but less profitable for those who made

---

[19] SA, DD/DN 425, Graffin Prankard (GP) to Francis Jennings (FJ), 16 August 1732. When the Swedish traveller Schröderstierna visited Birmingham in 1750 he reported that Åkerby and Lövsta were the most sought after steel-making brands. See K.C. Barraclough, *Steelmaking before Bessemer. Volume 1: Blister steel, the birth of an industry* (London, 1984), p. 218.

[20] For Shore see David Hey, *The fiery blades of Hallamshire: Sheffield and its neighbourhood, 1660-1740* (Leicester, 1991), pp. 188-91.

[21] See SA, DD/DN 425, GP to Samuel Shore, 9 December 1732, for abortive negotiations for the 1733 season, or GP and Samuel Shore to Messrs Worster, Wordsworth & Jennings, 9 March 1734, for a two-year contract covering 1734-35.

them'.[22] English bar iron might be of poorer quality but smiths found it an easier and more economical material to work with, and for most purposes it was perfectly adequate. For Swedish 'common sorts' to compete effectively on the British market they had to be priced below the rival domestic product. Otherwise, Prankard asserted, 'English [iron] will always sell better than Swedes'.[23]

Importers had also to ensure that the bars they bought were of the dimensions required. (Bar iron was not a homogeneous commodity. It came in a wide variety of shapes and profiles: flats, squares, wides, voyage iron, etc.) Production in Swedish forges had to be adapted to meet the requirements of ironware manufacturers in Britain. Specialist merchants such as Prankard were in a position to do this. Prankard would usually purchase a large proportion of the yearly output of particular forges, if not the entire annual make under a single contract. In such circumstances the importer was able to specify precisely the gauges in which he wanted the bars hammered. In effect, bar iron became a bespoke article. The ability of international merchants of the early modern period to dictate the pattern of production in distant locations is well known, but this ability is usually associated with exotic commodities from beyond Europe, commodities that had to be adjusted to European tastes. The East India companies of both Britain and Holland, for example, intervened directly in production networks in India to ensure that cotton fabrics were woven, printed and coloured in accordance with European fashion. The readiness of merchants to dictate product specifications at long distance for less exalted commodities such as bar iron is more rarely acknowledged, but was nonetheless real. Having bought a large part of the output of Gammelbo forge for the year 1728-29, for example, Prankard told Jennings to 'use thy utmost Endeavour for having as much of it Struck into Narrow flatts as possible the[e] Canst of 60 or 61 to ye Ton full out 15 foott & ½ long & about 1¾ Inch w[ide]'.[24] In this way the changing pulse of demand in the English Midlands could be transmitted to remote *bergslagen* settlements.

But this begs the question of how demand in the British market was structured. Some answers can be had from an analysis of Graffin Prankard's sales of bar iron in the early 1740s. Table 3 provides a regional breakdown of sales for the year April 1741 to March 1742, a year in which Prankard disposed of nearly 400 tons of foreign bar iron, distributed among 58 different customers.

---

[22] Anders Florén and Göran Rydén, 'A journey into the market society: a Swedish pre-industrial spy in the middle of the eighteenth century', in Ragnar Björk and Karl Molin (eds.), *Societies made up of history* (Edsbruk, 1996), p. 277.

[23] SA, DD/DN 424, GP to FJ, 19 December 1728.

[24] SA, DD/DN 424, GP to FJ, 9 June 1729.

Table 3: *The regional distribution of bar iron sales by Graffin Prankard, 1741-42*

Region	tons	%
West Midlands	135.93	34.45
West Country	130.67	33.12
Bristol	60.59	15.36
Re-exports	38.67	9.80
South Wales	14.44	3.66
Unknown	14.21	3.60
Total	**394.51**	**100.00**

Source: Somerset Archives, DD/DN 442.

The West Midlands was Prankard's single most significant market, accounting for more than a third of his sales. Yet its importance must be qualified. Nearly as much iron was sold in the West Country (defined here as the counties of Gloucestershire, Wiltshire, Somerset, Devon, Cornwall and Dorset). Indeed, some of Prankard's best customers were to be found in West Country towns like Tewkesbury, Warminster or Taunton. A further 15 per cent of sales were made in Bristol itself. The final destination of this iron is uncertain. Much of it must have been consumed within the city, but some may have been sold on by Bristol wholesalers to customers further up the Severn valley, whilst other parcels of iron may have been re-exported. A proportion of Prankard's sales – just under 10 per cent – was certainly re-exported: the buyers are identified as shipowners or ships masters. Prankard himself sent small quantities of Swedish bar iron to his trading associates in South Carolina, but most re-exports went to Africa to be exchanged for slaves. Prankard warned Jennings in 1733 that he would not require a large quantity of Swedish 'voyage iron' that year because 'our Guinea Trade is wholly at a Stand', but in more favourable times he sold regular consignments of iron to major Bristol slavers such as Henry Dampier, Isaac Hobhouse, James Laroche and William Jeffreys.[25]

The singularity of the West Midlands lay not so much in the volume of Swedish iron which it absorbed as in the type of buyer. Prankard's customers in the

---

[25] SA, DD/DN 425, GP to FJ, 28 April 1733. See David Richardson (ed.), *Bristol, Africa and the eighteenth-century slave trade to America. Volume 2: The years of ascendancy, 1730-45* (Bristol Records Society, XXXIX, 1987), *passim*, for details of these slave merchants.

Midlands in 1741-42 were few in number (only nine, as opposed to eighteen in the West Country) but they bought in bulk. Buyers in the West Midlands bought on average nearly twice the volume of iron purchased by their West Country counterparts: 15.1 tons against 7.7 tons (or the meagre 1.4 tons taken on average by the ten traders with whom Prankard dealt in the ports of South Wales). Indeed, West Midlands sales were dominated by a handful of customers. Just two of Prankard's 58 buyers - John Kettle of Birmingham and Mary Homfray of Stourbridge - accounted for over a quarter of his total sales. Table 4 lists Prankard's 25 best customers, clearly showing the pre-eminence of these two powerful West Midlands ironmongers.

John Kettle's importance lay not just in the volume of iron he bought, but the type. He was no mere ironmonger, he was a steel manufacturer, one of only a handful in the British Isles, operating a cementation furnace in Birmingham.[26] As such, he was Prankard's main customer for the high-quality bars from Åkerby and Lövsta. Indeed, Kettle constituted a regular and certain market for those Öregrund brands, which explains Prankard's indefatigable efforts to exercise monopoly control over their entry into the British market.[27] Mary Homfray's role was rather different. She too was a buyer of Öregrund brands. Her purchases in 1741-42 were taken entirely from Uppland forges owned by the de Geer family (Åkerby, Strömsberg) or from a source known simply as 'first Oregrounds', and this iron was surely used for steelmaking.[28] Nevertheless, the Homfrays ordinarily bought far more of the common Swedish brands. This was because the Homfray family's principal business lay in supplying nail rods to the West Midlands nail trade, being the proprietors of a slitting mill at Gothersley in the Stour valley. Öregrund iron was wasted in the nail trade; it was far too expensive and difficult to work. The ordinary grades of Swedish iron would do. Indeed, cold-short English iron would serve perfectly well. In recognition of this the Homfrays acquired their own forge at Swindon in Staffordshire, as well as buying in bar iron from some of the major ironmaking partnerships in the Midlands, notably that of the Knight family.[29]

---

[26] Barraclough, *Steelmaking*, p. 95.

[27] Of Kettle's purchases in 1741-42, 61% came from Lövsta and 30% from Åkerby. The source of the remaining 9% is not identified in the accounts.

[28] The Homfrays' involvement in the steel trade in the 1730s and 1740s is not well documented. However, Mary Homfray's youngest son John, who died in 1760, referred in his will to 'my Trade or Business of Converting Steel...' (Public Record Office, PROB 11/855/156), whilst his mother was certainly dealing in imported steel c. 1740: she bought parcels of 'German' (i.e. Styrian) steel from Prankard.

[29] Laurence Ince, *The South Wales iron industry 1750-1885* (Birmingham, 1993), pp. 73-4.

Table 4: *Graffin Prankard's leading buyers of bar iron, 1741-42*

	Name	Location	tons
1	John Kettle	Birmingham	71.30
2	Mary Homfray	Stourbridge	32.08
3	Edward Oliver	Bristol	18.88
4	Thomas Kimmet	Tewkesbury	18.74
5	Ann Kilcott	Warminster	17.42
6	Reynolds & Daniel	Bristol	15.17
7	Joseph Bishop	Truro	14.33
8	William Dyke	Taunton	14.18
9	Cranfield Becher & Co	shipowners	13.09
10	William Jeffreys & Co	shipowners	12.91
11	William Bowyer	Stourbridge	12.53
12	James Laroche & Co	shipowners	11.66
13	Lewes Morgan	Warminster	11.61
14	Joseph Wallis	Lyme	10.85
15	Samuel Cox	Beaminster	9.98
16	William Chilton	Bristol	9.39
17	John Benger	Seaton	8.84
18	Christopher Shallard	Keynsham	7.33
19	Nathaniel Arthur	Bristol	6.93
20	John Roberts	Cirencester	6.57
21	Robert Waylen	Devizes	5.26
22	William Barnsley	Stourbridge	5.01
23	Caleb King	Crewkerne	4.74
24	Rebecca Corson	Wolverhampton	3.97
25	John Jervis	Wolverhampton	3.78

Source: Somerset Archives, DD/DN 442.

If English iron was an ideal material for slitting, would not the same be true of Russian iron, another cold-short bar iron? Prankard was quick to appreciate that it would. He was buying parcels of Russian iron on the Dutch market in the 1720s, and in the early 1730s he began trading directly with St Petersburg.[30] Soon he was importing substantial consignments of iron together with mixed cargoes of hemp and flax.[31]

Table 5: *Graffin Prankard's iron imports by country, 1721-1740*

	Sweden	Russia	'German'	?	Total
1721	4	0	0	0	4
1723	197	0	0	1	198
1726	297	0	95	4	395
1728	772	0	152	9	933
1730	677	20	4	7	708
1731	608	128	16	8	761
1732	481	285	0	3	769
1733	354	433	29	6	822
1734	701	0	0	6	708
1735	933	331	0	6	1271
1740	222	0	0	1	223

Source: PRO, selected Bristol Port Books.

Note. The origin of a few small parcels is not specified. Iron listed as 'German' was probably imported from Rotterdam: the designation is a catch-all term to describe iron brought down the Maas or the Rhine.

Prankard had no difficulty in finding customers among the major Midland ironmongers. He sold 150 tons of Russian iron to Sampson Lloyd of Birmingham in the autumn of 1732 ('a Large Parcel of Muller Fabrick Russia... Deemed ye Mildest Collshire [coldshort] of all...'), and was supplying the Homfrays as well shortly afterwards.[32] The emergence of Russian iron on the British market in the 1720s posed serious questions for both Swedish and British iron producers. English ironmasters had no wish to concede a large part of their domestic market to foreign imports. Because of the organisational peculiarities of

[30] For example, SA, DD/DN 424, GP to Benjohan Furley, 19 May 1729 and 2 August 1729.

[31] SA, DD/DN 425, GP to Messrs Vigor & Davenport, 13 May 1732.

[32] SA, DD/DN 425, GP to Francis Homfray, 14 November 1732. See SA, DD/DN 438 for the 10 tons of Tula bars supplied to Francis Homfray in April 1735.

the British iron trade, with its tendency to vertical integration and horizontal networking, native ironmasters were usually able to collude on pricing policy. Collective assemblies ('quarter days') were convened regularly in most of the major ironmaking districts to consider the level of import penetration and to adjust prices accordingly. In the late 1720s, as Russian imports began to grow in visibility, British ironmasters were already engaged in a struggle to exclude their Swedish rivals as far as possible. They were, Prankard reported, 'Strangely Alarmd at the coming in of so much Swedish Iron'.[33] They began to cut prices accordingly. The 'Ironmasters of ye adjacent Countreys near us dropt ye price last night 20 [shillings] per ton', Prankard told Francis Jennings in July 1728, 'which will inevitably sink the price of Swedes'.[34] Because the local ironmasters had 'taken ye price of English from £18:10 to £17:10 per Ton', Prankard told another correspondent a little later, 'I have been forced to sell best Stockholm for £17 & Gothenburg for £16:5 to £16:10'.[35] In January 1729 the price of English iron in the Severn valley was cut once more, this time to £16.10.0 per ton. And, as Prankard told Jennings, if 'there's any thing of a large Import yᵉ year [the ironmasters] will I believe fall it 10 [shillings] per Ton more which if so I should not be able to Sell any quantity of Common Swedes for more than £15:10'.[36]

The advent of Russian iron sharpened the struggle for hegemony on the British market. Siberian iron, produced amongst virgin forests and exploiting the forced labour of serfs, could be sold in London or Rotterdam at very low prices. In the summer of 1729, when English bar iron was selling at £16.10.0 per ton in Bristol, Russian iron could be bought for £13 in London.[37] On the face of things, Russian iron presented more of a threat to the English product, whose coldshort properties it shared, than the tough Swedish brands. But as has been indicated, coldshort could – if cheap enough – be substituted for tough iron for many purposes, and if English iron was priced at a level below that of Swedish it would be Swedish iron that fell victim to the Russian export drive.[38] Prankard concluded that Russian iron posed more of a menace to Swedish ironmakers

---

[33] SA, DD/DN 424, GP to FJ, 24 August 1728.

[34] SA, DD/DN 424, GP to FJ, 31 July 1728.

[35] SA, DD/DN 424, GP to Abraham Lindenberg, 30 September 1728.

[36] SA, DD/DN 424, GP to FJ, 10 March 1729.

[37] SA, DD/DN 424, GP to Benjohan Furley, 20 August 1729.

[38] As Prankard explained to Jennings in 1733, Government Siberian iron 'comes so Cheap [that it] is applyed to other uses & is Strayned to serve other uses wch otherwise would not be... where [sic] it not on acct of its Cheapness'. SA, DD/DN 425, GP to FJ, 3 March 1733.

than to their British counterparts: 'ye Vast Import of Iron from Russia must & will Disincourage ye Import of so Large a Quantity from Sweden'.[39]

The crisis of British and Swedish ironmaking in the 1740s and 1750s

Despite the vulnerability of Swedish iron producers, the position of British ironmasters was by no means secure. Their policy of restricting imports could hardly be welcome to iron merchants, nor to ironware manufacturers who naturally enough hankered after the widest possible choice of iron. The shape of the British iron market therefore became a matter of political controversy in the second quarter of the eighteenth century. Ironmasters (and landowners who looked to the iron industry as a consumer of their woods) applied to Parliament for increased import duties on Baltic iron. 'Our English Iron makers & Wood Gentlemen', the Birmingham ironmonger Sampson Lloyd reported in 1738, 'are very busy to form a Strong Interest this Sessions to get a further Duty laid on Foreign Iron in order to advance their own'. (He was not impressed: 'it is not for every Man that hath a bad Trade to apply to Parliament to make good the deficiency'.)[40] For their part, merchants and metalware manufacturers pressed for the free importation of iron from the North American colonies. If metalware production (identified as 'ye second trade in the nation' after textiles) was to continue to grow it was necessary for additional sources of bar iron to be found.

Domestic production was manifestly inadequate yet a deepening dependence on Swedish or Russian iron would only aggravate Britain's already negative trade balance with the Baltic. How much better it would be, merchants and manufacturers proclaimed with a flourish of mercantile patriotism, if iron production were to be encouraged in the plantations. The ironmasters maintained otherwise, claiming that American iron was, like the British product, coldshort. There was therefore every danger that American imports would undermine the position of the domestic iron industry without threatening the market position of the tough Swedish brands. Contrariwise, iron merchants sought to demonstrate that the best American irons could be substituted for the Swedish product in the manufacture, for example, of anchors in the royal dockyards. These issues were rehearsed before the House of Commons in 1737-8 and again in 1749-50. On the first of these occasions the ironmasters' lobby

---

[39] SA, DD/DN 425, GP to FJ, 28 February 1733.

[40] Religious Society of Friends Library, TEMP MSS 210/2/42, Sampson Lloyd to Thomas Kirton, 11 February 1738.

successfully rebuffed a petition to Parliament from iron merchants and manufacturers requesting the unrestricted import of colonial bar iron. This was a telling demonstration of the strength of British ironmasters' powers of collective organisation.[41] Yet that collective strength came under mounting pressure as the demand for bar iron within the British economy continued to grow and as domestic iron producers proved unable to respond to that demand. Calls for the importation of colonial iron were renewed and now the common front of ironmasters began to crumble. The corporate strength of the iron trade had always lain in the network linkages that had bound furnace operators, forgemasters, slitters and (often) ironmongers together in capacious partnerships. Yet some of these partners found themselves with torn loyalties. Should the Homfrays identify themselves as forgemasters (hostile to colonial iron) or as slitters-cum-ironmongers (favourable to colonial iron)?

The corporate unity of the iron trade buckled under these strains. Some ironmasters remained committed to a prohibition of American imports, but others were now prepared to contemplate a partial admission of colonial iron, albeit under special conditions. American *pig iron* alone should be allowed into British ports. The forging of those pigs into bar iron would be the province of British forgemasters. In effect, this was an argument for the wholesale reorganisation of bar iron production within Britain's Atlantic empire. Smelting would be transferred to the charcoal-rich colonies, allowing blast furnaces in Britain to be torn down and the woods they had once devoured to be dedicated to the refining of American pig. 'The only thing that seems likely to be of service to this Nation', a Yorkshire ironmaster asserted in 1750, '& Likewise to the plantations, will be to encourage their making pigg Iron so as to Distroy the furnaces in England & consume the wood now used by them at Forges in making american pigg Iron into barr Iron. ...'[42] This, it was hoped, would result in an expansion of British bar iron output ('near double the quantity of Bar Iron') and an opportunity for native ironmasters to drive Baltic iron from the commanding position it enjoyed in the British market.

The 1740s also saw important debates in Sweden about the destiny of the country's most important export industry. The Swedish authorities were well aware of British efforts to stimulate colonial iron imports and, more pressingly, of the growth of Russian exports. Contemporary discussion on what measures

---

[41] Chris Evans, 'The corporate culture of the British iron industry', in Göran Rydén (ed.), *The social organisation of the European iron industry 1600-1900* (Stockholm, 1997), pp. 121-46.

[42] Sheffield Archives, Wharncliffe Muniments, 118/15, John Cockshutt and Joseph Broadbent [unknown], 17 February 1750.

should be taken to eliminate the Russian threat was intense. Should the state offer greater bounties on iron exports? Could the British be persuaded to lower import duties on Swedish iron in recognition of the essential interdependence of the two countries (despite Swedish tariff barriers erected against British textiles and other exports, and despite Sweden's diplomatic alignment with France)? Could the Russians be prevailed upon to cooperate with the Swedes in jointly monopolising the British market (despite the long hostility between the two Baltic powers)?[43]

In fact, the development of the Swedish iron trade took a quite different direction. From the end of the 1740s bar iron output was restricted. Whereas the *number* of ironworks had been limited since the seventeenth century in an effort to conserve natural resources, every ironworks was now assigned a production quota which could not be exceeded. With this, a halt was called to two hundred years of growth. The reasons for this remain controversial. Partly, the new policy reflected a long-standing concern not to over-exploit natural resources. But perhaps other motives were present? Because of Sweden's strong position on the international market, advocates of the restriction policy hoped that capping output would force prices upwards. (The Ironmasters' Association (*Jernkontoret*) was particularly eager to establish a regime of high, stable prices because of its role in arranging preferential loans secured on iron.) Contemporaries were not entirely convinced by this argument, however. There were very reasonable doubts about Sweden's capacity to monopolise the European market, and there were fears that in so far as output restriction would result in higher prices this would merely encourage iron production in other countries.[44]

Was this a mistaken policy? Could it be that the restriction of Swedish output merely paved the way for the great expansion of Russian bar iron making in the second half of the eighteenth century?[45] Perhaps, but it is far more likely that it was the growth of low-cost Russian exports that forced the Swedish authorities to try to limit their own production costs. This was best done by restricting the competition for raw materials, and capping output was an

---

[43] Florén, Rydén *et al*, 'Social organisation', pp. 99-100; Kaplan, *Russian overseas commerce*, p. 21; H.S.K. Kent, *War and trade in northern seas: Anglo-Scandinavian relations in the mid-eighteenth century* (Cambridge, 1973), pp. 61-2.

[44] Heckscher, Sveriges ekonomiska historia, pp. 387-90; K.-G. Hildebrand, *Swedish iron in the seventeenth and eighteenth centuries. Export industry before the industrialization* (Stockholm, 1992), pp. 123-24; Kent, *War and trade*, pp. 70-72.

[45] Hildebrand, *Fagerstabrukens historia*, p. 155.

emphatic way of restricting competition.[46] The supply of charcoal was especially problematic. If the forests attached to a *bruk* were insufficient, additional (and relatively expensive) charcoal had to be bought in on a commercial basis. Any expansion of production would require the share of commercially supplied charcoal to rise in relation to the share of charcoal supplied by peasants under tenancy agreements or in lieu of taxes, thereby precipitating a crisis of profitability for the iron industry.[47] If these considerations weighed upon ironmasters' minds, the position of the peasants who were responsible for charcoal making should also be taken into account. Recent explanations of the restriction policy have focused upon the peasantry and the tension between traditional agriculture and the export-orientated iron industry. The growth of the iron industry could only continue if more and more rural dwellers were mobilised in the cause of charcoal production. But the willingness of the peasantry to make and deliver charcoal could not be guaranteed. Indeed, since sections of the peasantry were politically enfranchised and represented in the *riksdag*, they were in a strong position to thwart further expansion in the iron industry by pressing for policies which kept ironmaking and agrarian production in balance.[48] There was no such difficulty for Russian ironmasters. They could intensify their exploitation of charcoal-producing serfs at will, opening the way for the massive growth of the Urals iron industry in the second half of the eighteenth century.

Conclusion

There is a curious symmetry to developments in the Swedish and British iron industries in the middle of the eighteenth century. Ironmasters and iron merchants in both countries grasped at new patterns of production which would allow them to maintain their position within the international market for bar iron. Swedish ironmasters embraced a policy of restraint in the hope of keeping their energy costs under control and thereby retaining a major share of the British market. The response of British ironmasters to the twin problems of energy shortage and import penetration was more tentative. But the solution which beckoned to some British ironmasters at least – that of concentrating the forge trade in the British Isles and banishing the smelting of iron to the

---

[46] Florén, Rydén *et al*, 'Social organisation', pp. 99-100.

[47] Hildebrand, *Fagerstabrukens historia*, pp. 161-62.

[48] P.-A. Karlsson, *Järnbruken och ståndssamhället. Institutionell och attitydmässig konflikt under Sveriges tidiga industrialisering 1700-1770* (Stockholm, 1990), pp. 13-31, 262-64.

American colonies – echoed the socio-spatial division of labour which the Swedish state had imposed upon its iron industry in the seventeenth century. The British market was a lucrative prize, control over which was exercised by a variety of mercantile groups. The foremost of these was made up of professional ironmasters in Britain who, although they appeared in the guise of industrialists, acted effectively as merchants, buying and selling materials and semi-finished commodities amongst themselves and putting out these materials to contractors at their furnaces, forges or processing mills. They dominated domestic ironmaking. The importation of foreign iron was effected by a rather different set of merchants, those engaged in international trade, like Graffin Prankard. The international merchants should not, however, be seen as absolutely distinct from those engaged in the domestic iron trade. Abraham Spooner, the great Birmingham ironmonger (and bitter rival of Graffin Prankard), was *both* a major importer of iron *and* a member of the ironmaking Knight partnership. Prankard himself, it should not be forgotten, quite apart from being a partner in the famous Coalbrookdale ironworks, was involved in a major industrial complex at Tern in Shropshire (a 'mill for Rowling of Brass Plates and Iron Hoops and slitting of bar iron into Rods for makeing of nails... a wire mill, a forge and a furnace for converting of Iron into Steel...')[49]

The mercantile networks which girded the British iron trade were therefore elastic. They were also potent, for it is quite clear that the British dictated the terms on which international trade took place, even though Swedish merchants sold on a sellers' market and even though the elite merchant houses of Stockholm exercised an extraordinary pre-eminence in the organisation of foreign trade. Almost all Swedish exports to Britain were carried on British ships, notwithstanding the *Produktplakatet* of 1726 (Sweden's equivalent of the Navigation Acts) or the differentiated custom duties which were as much as 70 per cent higher on exports shipped in foreign bottoms. (By contrast, the Dutch and Latin markets were served by Swedish shipping.)[50] Indeed, British merchants were able to decide far in advance upon the particular form which the bar iron was to take, ensuring that Swedish hammermen cut bars into shapes

---

[49] Arthur Raistrick, *Dynasty of iron founders: the Darbys and Coalbrookdale* (2nd edition, 1989), p. 6; Barbara Coulton, 'Tern Hall and the Hill family 1700-75', *Shropshire History and Archaeology*, LXVI (1989), 99-100.

[50] Heckscher, *Sveriges ekonomiska historia*, pp. 670-71; Staffan Högberg, *Utrikeshandel och sjöfart på 1700-talet. Stapelvaror i svensk export och import 1738-1808* (Stockholm, 1969), pp. 19-29; SSA, Tolagsjournaler 1730 and 1741. Note that British ships completely dominated the export from St Petersburg as well: Kaplan, *Russian overseas commerce*, pp. 44-47.

that would trade best on the Guinea coast or that would roll the easier in the mills of the Stour valley.

The diversity of the British market is very evident from Graffin Prankard's accounts and letters. Specific manufacturing processes like steelmaking had very narrowly defined requirements. Similarly, the emergence of specialised metalworking zones around Dudley, Stourbridge and Wolverhampton is clearly registered in Prankard's archive. But the ubiquity of metal manufacturing in western Britain also stands out, revealed in the individually small but cumulatively large quantities of Swedish iron that Prankard sold in the ports and market towns of south-western England. The growth of iron imports in the second half of the eighteenth century was no doubt hastened by the deepening of specialised consumption in the West Midlands or south Yorkshire, but demand for iron was obviously broadly based across the British Isles.

After 1750 the nature of the British market and its relationship to the Baltic began to change. The rapid development of coal technology released the British iron industry from its dependence upon charcoal and opened the way for British ironmasters to control their home market for the first time. In particular, the spread of iron puddling and rolling from the 1780s transformed the prospects for Baltic iron. Swedish exports to Britain fell headlong in the first years of the nineteenth century. Only Öregrund iron held its market position. Russian ironmasters, who had staked everything on the British market, suffered even more grievously.[51]

The balance of power now lay decisively with the British. Swedish travellers had once visited Britain to monitor the all-important market for their iron; now they came to puzzle over the coal-based technologies that had so dramatically ousted all but the best grades of imported bar iron. In the 1820s and the 1830s the recruitment of British technicians became a priority. Swedish industrialists realised that the adaptation of British technologies to Swedish conditions was imperative if their iron trade was to thrive once more.[52] After a lengthy period of

---

[51] Bar iron imports into Britain reached an all-time high of 59,000 tons in 1793 but began to decline thereafter. In the first decade of the nineteenth century imports fell to an annual average of 31,900 tons, the lowest since the 1750s. By the 1820s annual imports averaged just 14,500 tons, the lowest since the seventeenth century. Most of this was Swedish iron destined for the steel centres of south Yorkshire. B.R. Mitchell with P. Deane, *Abstract of British historical statistics* (1962), pp. 140-41.

[52] Chris Evans and Göran Rydén, 'Kinship and the transmission of skill: bar iron making in Britain and Sweden, 1500-1800', in Maxine Berg and Kristine Bruland (eds.), *Technological revolutions in Europe, 1700-1860* (Cheltenham, 1998), pp. 188-206.

experimentation and re-organisation the Swedish iron industry revived, but Swedish iron – still less Russian iron – never recovered the strategic importance it had enjoyed when Graffin Prankard and Francis Jennings were at the height of their powers.

Chapter 9

Ralph Carr: a Newcastle merchant and the Baltic trade in the mid-eighteenth century

Bill Purdue

Ralph Carr was one of the most successful entrepreneurs of eighteenth-century Newcastle. His career demonstrates not only his considerable business acumen and sound judgement, but also the opportunities that were available to a man with such gifts and some capital in the dynamic and socially fluid world of North-East England in that period. He inherited from his father, a merchant and mining agent, a small but pleasant country house and estate together with a few thousand pounds. At the end of his long life the sum of his wealth and possessions was about £200,000. The Baltic trade was crucial to his early success. He built upon Newcastle's long established connections with the Baltic and with Amsterdam, for centuries the entrepot for Baltic exports, as well as the business links established by his father, which he consolidated and expanded by travel as a young man. His career as a merchant casts considerable light upon trading patterns during the mid-eighteenth century.

Even in an age when there was little narrow specialism in the business world, Carr's interests were exceptionally multifarious. He was prepared to deal on his own behalf, to invest, to insure and to lend. His great-grandson Colonel R. E. Carr depicts the width of his many interests as follows:

> It included operations that would now be carried on by shipowners, shipbrokers, underwriters, general merchants, commission agents,

bankers and, we might almost add, marine store dealers. Nothing seems to have been too large or small for him.[1]

In the course of his career he was to arrange finance for the Hanoverian army in Scotland during the '45 rebellion, found the first proper bank outside London or Edinburgh – the 'Old Bank' – farm the tithes owned by Merton College, Oxford and become a considerable landowner.[2]

Although Carr's business interests were varied, they were also linked. If many of them were, in the end, much more rewarding than trade with the Baltic, several of them were much influenced by his involvement in that trade. The Baltic and North Sea trade involved co-operation with Amsterdam merchants and this led to his becoming an international bill-broker and eventually a banker, while it was also a major reason for the extension of his trading activities to the Atlantic. What underpinned all such ventures was a cautious trust. 'Trust', as Francis Fukuyama has demonstrated, is the engine of economic growth.[3] To trust within the confinable limits of blood ties resulted in a degree of certainty but imposed narrow boundaries, while to go beyond this and trust in associates with whom there were no ties of kinship involved more risk but greater possibilities for the expansion of business.

Newcastle's connections with the Baltic go back to at least the thirteenth century when Hanseatic merchants began to supply eastern England with Baltic produce such as timber, herrings, furs and pitch. In the sixteenth and seventeenth centuries the importance of the Baltic trade increased. The Baltic provided the bulk of the materials for the ships of the powers of western Europe, acted as a granary for the continent and supplied copper for the coinage. This trade was, like all trade in or out of the Tyne, controlled in Newcastle by the Merchant Adventurers Company. Formed in the early sixteenth century but probably the successor to the old Gild Merchant, the Merchant Adventurers' Company of Newcastle not only monopolised all import and export, 'foreign bought and foreign sold' trade, but constituted the dominant force in the town's economic, political and social life.[4] The Newcastle Merchant Adventurers' Company had, however, to acknowledge for much of its trade the suzerainty of

---

[1] R.E.Carr, *The History of the Family of Carr* (2 vols., London, 1893-9) vol. I, p. 46.

[2] A.W. Purdue, *Merchants and Gentry in North East England 1650-1830: The Carrs and the Ellisons* (Sunderland, 1999), Ch. 10.

[3] Francis Fukuyama, *Trust* (London, 1995).

[4] See Matt Ridley, *The Merchant Adventurers of Newcastle upon Tyne* (Newcastle upon Tyne, 1998).

the London-based Merchant Adventurers of England, with which body, usually known from the mid-seventeenth century as the Hamburg Company, it retained an uneasy and often quarrelsome relationship. Members of the Newcastle Company who were engaged in Baltic trade were also, usually, members of the Eastland Company, founded by London Merchant Adventurers with the intention of trading through the Sound with countries bordering the Baltic, or of the Russia Company.[5] By the early eighteenth century the control of the London companies over trade with the Baltic was all but finished, while in Newcastle the monopoly of the Merchant Adventurers was beginning to erode as an era of freer trade began.

Ralph's father, John Carr, began his career by serving an apprenticeship as a Merchant Adventurer but, as he became increasingly involved in work as a mining agent or coal factor to landowners, he allowed his membership of the company to lapse. His later involvement in the timber or 'raff' trade with Baltic ports in the 1720s, was in association with Charles Atkinson, a Newcastle hostman or coal-fitter. Outward cargoes in the raff trade usually consisted of coal and sometimes grindstones, which reflected Atkinson's and Carr's other interests. Carr's involvement in this trade was, presumably, technically illegal under the 'foreign bought and foreign sold' regulations of the Merchant Adventurers because of his lapsed membership; but he acted with and behind his partner, Charles Atkinson, who, as well as being a hostman, was indentured as an apprentice to a Merchant Adventurer in 1726. As such Atkinson was not technically authorised to deal on his own account but, to judge by the Newcastle Trinity House Primage Account books, he (and Carr) conducted a steady, if unspectacular trade.[6]

---

[5] There was a clear demarcation between the areas these two companies operated in. The Eastland Company traded with ports from Narva westwards.

[6] Charles Atkinson, like Carr, was a man who found the restrictions of the old monopolistic societies irksome. In 1703 he and six other hostmen were hauled up before the Society charged with 'aideing and assisting gentlemen owners of coles not free of this Society who confederate with the lightermen and buyers of Coles in the Citty of London to the ruin and prejudice of the hoastmen and Cole trade in Newcastle'. Atkinson and other offenders were suspended from their privileges as free hostmen for three months but sought the opinion of the Attorney General, who advised that the Society was not entitled to the sole loading and disposal of coal on the River Tyne. They then issued writs of mandamus against the Hostmen's Company. See F.W. Dendy, 'Extracts from the records of the Company of Hostmen', *The Publications of the Surtees Society*, vol. CV (1901), pp. xxxv-xxxvi and 160. In 1720 a member of the Merchant Adventurers' Company was fined by the Society for allowing Atkinson to retail iron in his name from a cellar in Trinity Chare. See F.W. Dendy, 'Extracts from the Records of the Merchant Adventurers of Newcastle upon Tyne', *The Publications of the Surtees Society*, vol. I of vol. XCIII (1894), p. 252.

By the early eighteenth century, the end of the monopolistic power of the Hostmen and the Merchant Adventurers was in sight but the companies were still strong enough to make membership of them necessary. Since they were ineligible for admission by patrimony, three sons of John Carr were indentured as Merchant Adventurers; the eldest son, another John, died before he could be admitted. The others were Ralph and a younger brother, Benjamin. Ralph was indentured to Matthew Bowes, a Merchant Adventurer and Boothman, in 1728. Apprenticeship usually lasted ten years and Ralph's was not yet complete when he was granted permission to travel overseas. He set out on an extended tour of some of the commercial centres of Europe, which took up the greater part of 1737. The letters he received from his father demonstrate that his travels were occasioned by a serious determination to broaden his horizons and investigate commercial opportunities. Although John Carr was opposed to his son's going abroad on the grounds of his supposed poor health (Ralph had a persistent cough as a young man, even though he was to live to a ripe old age), he quickly appreciated the possibility that the knowledge gained and the contacts made on such travels could help expand his own trade with the Baltic and North Sea ports.

In a period when travel was difficult, arduous and dangerous, Ralph visited Amsterdam, Paris, northern France, Flanders, Holland and the Baltic. His major interest in the Baltic was the newly founded capital of Russia, St Petersburg, the potential of which excited many English merchants at this time. Ralph spent several weeks there and the visit was not without its hazards. The city's wooden houses seem to have constituted a major fire risk and Carr thrice escaped from burning houses. A letter to him from his brother-in-law, John Widdrington, makes clear the interest Newcastle merchants had in this new market for raw materials and semi-manufactured goods:

> I should be glad to make acquaintance with the curiosity of that place and whether you think your stay there will be of any considerable advantage to you with respect to your business.[7]

His father wrote to him after he had left St Petersburg:

> I hope you keep a journal and take notes as much as your time will allow you of everything worth your observation and also the names of the cheap and safe traders and that you be very safe in dealing

---

[7] John Widdrington to Ralph Carr c/o Messrs. Cramond and Timmermann, St. Petersburg, 24 May 1737, Carr-Ellison Papers, Northumberland Record Office (NRO) 855, Box 4.

abroad everywhere because many have been undone by bad correspondents that set out very hopefully and with good stride.

That the Carrs, father and son, did not confine their interests to everyday merchandise is demonstrated by their response to Ralph's enquiry about rhubarb, then a relative newcomer to the British Isles, having been introduced from Russia just over a century before and prized for its medicinal properties rather than its culinary use: 'I enquired ... about the difference of Indian and Russian rhubarb which he makes very little difference in, but saith that from Turkey is accounted the best of them all'.[8] Carr's visit to St Petersburg came shortly after the Anglo-Russian Commercial Treaty of 1737, which greatly improved conditions for British merchants in Russia and led to a sharp increase in Anglo-Russian trade.

On his return to Newcastle, Carr began trading on his own account even before he had finished his apprenticeship. Within a few years he was an established merchant importing and exporting along the coast of Britain and involved in foreign trade with North Sea and Baltic ports. It is clear that a major asset was the close relations he had established with other merchants both at home and abroad. Carr's most important contacts were those with Dutch merchant houses: without them it is unlikely that his Baltic trade would have enjoyed as much success. Holland and Amsterdam in particular had long dominated the Baltic trade with western Europe. Amsterdam continued to be the entrepot for many Baltic exports and, as Carr had journeyed around northern Europe in 1737, it had been Dutch merchants who had given him hospitality and introductions to their kinsmen and friends in other ports. In St Petersburg the house of Cramond and Timmermann had looked after him; they were to remain amongst his most regular correspondents.

Amsterdam was the centre of a vast trading network and the friendly relations Carr established there were not only to further his trade with northern Europe but also to lead to his involvement with trade between Europe and the British North American colonies. His knowledge of the Baltic must have been especially useful because the mid-eighteenth century witnessed an important change in the timber trade. In the first half of the century British merchants dealt preponderantly with Norwegian ports and only after this time did the balance shift to Baltic ports like Riga, Memel and Danzig. In the decade after the completion of his apprenticeship in 1738, Carr had established himself as a trader in general merchandise with ports in the Baltic and the Low Countries.

---

[8] John Carr to Ralph Carr, c/o Messrs. A. Cropps & Co., Amsterdam, 14 Nov. 1737.

He dealt in coal, iron, timber, butter, flax, hemp, tar, grindstones, glass, spirits, wine, salt, whale oil, lead, litharge, alum, copperas, cutlery and sailcloth.

Personal relationships were crucially important to merchants in this period. In the absence of the ability to pay ready cash or specie for goods, there had to be a reliance on credit, even though it was all too easy for a dishonest merchant to pretend that goods had arrived damaged or destroyed, which of course they sometimes did, when in fact they were in reasonable condition. Even within one country the law was an uncertain and tardy ally to the businessman. One had to trust, understand and support one's correspondents. Trust was the basis of eighteenth-century trade and was most easily established between those who shared common standards and similar backgrounds. While certain societies have found it easier to establish trust cultures than others, the merchant involved in trade at a distance did well to be suspicious but in the end was obliged to trust. In early modern societies trust was most easily placed on kinsmen and, indeed, the seventeenth and early eighteenth centuries witnessed British and Dutch merchant families placing family members in foreign ports, thus ensuring they had trustworthy agents. The largest bill-broking houses in the Anglo-Dutch trade, the Cliffords and the Hopes, had family members in both London and Amsterdam, while the Amsterdam firm, Muilman, sent two sons to England. If the advantages of a network of family connections are obvious, there could be disadvantages in the long term. Rather than a means to an end in the efficient exploitation of markets, the family network could predicate the type of business pursued and result in lost opportunities. Leos Müller, in his study of Stockholm merchants, argues that the firm of Carlos and Claes Grill became so dependent on a family network linking Stockholm and Amsterdam that 'Instead of seeking new partners and new business networks on prospective markets, the Grills adopted the traditional, family-business network to new activities.'[9]

It is clear, however, that British and Dutch merchants, in particular but not uniquely, had a similarity of outlook, a common attitude towards business and sufficient social and religious values in common, to create a context for increasing co-operation and business associations that went beyond kinship. Ralph Carr's business success was due in part to his cool judgement of character and an ability to place trust in people to whom he was not related. He also had family loyalties. His business partner for many years was his son-in-law, John Widdrington, in whose probity he had great faith, though he came to distrust his

---

[9] Leos Müller, *The Merchant Houses of Stockholm, c.1640-1800. A Comparative Study of Early-Modern Entrepreneurial Behaviour* (Uppsala, 1998), p. 237. See also Leos Müller's contribution to this volume.

business judgement. His brother-in-law Christopher Scott, one of the principal merchants of Hull, was a kinsman whose business acumen he acknowledged. Hull was a rapidly expanding port and was developing a profitable trade with the Baltic, especially with St Petersburg. Scott was to prove a valuable ally. He and Carr cooperated in the British east coast trade and in many ventures in the Baltic. However, Carr was never circumscribed by family and his most important business relationships were with several Dutch houses in Amsterdam, Rotterdam and along the Baltic coast. His best correspondents were Daniel Crommelin and Anthony Simpson, both based in Amsterdam and Cramond and Timmermann in St Petersburg. Others included the Oodorps of Rotterdam, John Hodgson and John de Neufville of Amsterdam, while a further foreign contact was the Danish house of John and David Brown at Copenhagen.

Such correspondents were people who could be trusted to treat each other honestly in business. They also provided each other with commercial and political intelligence. Thus, when war between Sweden and Russia loomed in 1741, Cramond and Timmermann in St Petersburg wrote to Carr advising him that they had bought flax on his account but warned him of the dangers of war, adding the reassurance that they did not think the Swedes would take British or Dutch ships.[10] Ironically, the ship sent to carry the flax home was lost on its voyage to St Petersburg. It is not known if the loss was due to the war. Cramond and Timermann arranged for another ship to carry the cargo.[11] About the same time, Carr wrote to the Hull merchant Richard Thompson:

> Flax is a scarce article here tho does not advance in proportion to the prices in the Baltic and the difficulty of getting it home. Would be glad to hear what advice you have about the Swedes whether or no they take any of our ships. I hear from Gottenburg that a ship from your place to St Petersburg laden with cloath and lead was taken in there but expected should be released. My last advice from St Petersburg makes no mention of the war or any appearance of it.[12]

Later that month he wrote to another merchant, asking what information he had concerning the war, passing on the news of the ship taken at Gothenburg and adding that insurance in the Baltic had advanced to 10 per cent.[13] Carr was

---

[10] Cramond and Timmermann to Carr, 23 April 1741.

[11] Cramond and Timmermann to Carr, 28 August 1741.

[12] Ralph Carr to Richard Thompson, 5 September 1741. Carr-Ellison Papers, NRO 165 ZCE 10-14.

[13] Ralph Carr to Henry Fraser, September 1741.

reluctant to pay such rates and, writing to Messrs. John and Thomas Simpson, he asked them to insure a ship about to set off from St Petersburg with his flax if this could be done at 5 per cent, adding that, if it was so dangerous as to justify a higher rate, 'I think our friends in St Petersburg will stop the ship from proceeding or the masters themselves will have that prudence.'[14]

Carr's business enterprises fitted neatly together. As a proprietor of the British Linen Company he imported flax on ships he had a part interest in as well as on ships belonging to others.[15] The British linen industry was flourishing although British agriculture produced less flax as 'industrial' crops gave way to food production. Carr imported flax from Holland and Hamburg but increasingly looked to the Baltic and especially Königsberg, where he had good contacts, for further supplies. He was especially active during 1741 because of the opportunities a bad harvest and war in the Baltic gave to a man with inside knowledge.

Carr was particularly involved in buying, selling and transporting corn. During the first part of the eighteenth century, North East England exported considerable quantities of corn, as did Britain as a whole, though there were years of poor harvest when, as in 1740-1, much grain was imported. Among the reasons for this were a stagnant British population between 1720 and 1745, agricultural productivity, a booming continental demand, as the Baltic increasingly failed to maintain its role as the breadbasket of Europe, and government bounties for corn exports. Periodically, Carr also imported corn from the Baltic and brought it in from Scotland. London was the principal wholesale market and Carr maintained close links with London dealers, chiefly, according to one authority, to supply them 'at times when the difference between home and overseas prices did not encourage export'.[16] Carr supplied the London market, exported on his own account and took commissions for overseas buyers from such diverse places as Portugal and the north coast of Africa.

The corn market was gradually monopolised by a small number of substantial players who, supplied with information by agents, were in a position

---

[14] Ralph Carr to Messrs John and Thomas Simpson, 13 September 1741.

[15] In 1741 he imported a considerable quantity of flax: 20 bales on the *Friendship* in January, 40 bales on the *Anna* in May, 40 bales on the *Blagdon* in November and an unspecified amount in the *Anna* in December. Tyne & Wear Archives Service. Newcastle Trinity House Primage Account Books. GU/TH/109/5.

[16] David Ormrod, *English Grain Exports and the Structure of Agrarian Capitalism* (Hull, 1985) p. 40.

to play the market and manipulate prices. The family firm of the Coutts brothers, John in Edinburgh and James in London, were a case in point. They had factors and agents throughout Britain and moved corn between European ports as well as from Ireland to the Baltic. Ralph Carr's association with John Coutts developed from their common involvement in the British Linen Company and they worked closely together. During 1741 when corn was scarce, Carr and Coutts were busy moving grain to the highest-priced markets. Most of the corn Carr imported in the late summer of 1741 came from the Baltic via his correspondents: T. M. Liebenrood and Archibald and Isaac Hope in Rotterdam; Anthony Simpson, Thomas and Adrian Hope, and J. A. Crop in Amsterdam. The Baltic subsequently regained its position as the principal supplier of corn to Britain but, in Carr's time, Baltic grain was usually brought into the Tyne only in years of poor local harvests.

The financial mechanisms of the Baltic trade were complex. Ships' masters rarely carried sufficient cash to pay for the cargo they brought home. These were eventually paid for by bills of exchange drawn upon at Amsterdam or Rotterdam.[17] Carr became very much involved in international bill-broking, not only on his own account but also for other merchants with less capital. He also began to make loans to merchants and gentry in North East England. Thus it was the financial experience gained in the Baltic trade that put him on the path to founding Newcastle's first bank, the 'Old Bank', in 1755. The Baltic trade was financed largely by Dutch money, which was then repaid by British merchants. A direct Russian-British trade, and to some extent a direct Swedish-British trade together with a largely indirect British trade with the rest of the Baltic, was conducted via Amsterdam and Rotterdam where all bills were eventually paid. The principal reason for this was that the Dutch had a favourable trade balance, exporting goods of greater value than those they imported. Their merchants in St Petersburg or Riga had, therefore, cash balances, which they preferred to lend to British merchants than send home as cash. The British who sent mainly ballast cargoes to the Baltic had no such ready cash in Baltic ports.

Jennifer Newman has argued that it was the financial mechanisms of Britain's trade with the Baltic and particularly with Russia that produced the tripartite relationship of American-British-Dutch trade. The need for British merchants to pay off bills in Amsterdam was, she argues, a major cause of the

---

[17] For instance in the spring of 1749 Carr paid two bills, one for £130 drawn in Rotterdam and another issued in Christiania (Norway) and paid at the house of Daniel Crommelin in Amsterdam.

expansion of Dutch trade with the British American colonies via Britain. British merchants could earn the necessary funds to pay off debts incurred in the Baltic trade by shipments of colonial rice, tobacco and other commodities to Amsterdam or Rotterdam. As foreign ships could not trade directly with the British colonies, British merchants assisted Dutch correspondents by loading their goods on British ships in British ports and, after paying duty on them and getting the necessary certificates, shipping them to the colonies. Newman cites Ralph Carr as an example of a merchant engaged in the re-export of Dutch cargoes to the American colonies.[18]

Commission paid by Dutch merchants on cargoes bound for America was certainly useful to Carr in paying for bills cashed in Amsterdam that were largely to pay for goods he had purchased in the Baltic. The Dutch-American trade was not, however, enormously profitable to him. Indeed, an American historian has treated his dealings with the American colonies as a case study in business failure.[19] He probably entered this trade as a favour to Dutch friends but with the near certainty of making a steady if modest profit and in the hope of successfully trading with the colonies on his own account. The ships belonging to his Dutch customers usually traded between Newcastle and New York or New England, rather than the ports of the southern colonies. For a commission, he arranged for all the necessary documentation, a time- consuming and risky business because it is apparent that some of the Amsterdam merchants were evading duties by consigning suspiciously large proportions of their cargoes to intermediate ports like St Thomas in the Virgin Isles. His plans for trans-Atlantic exports and imports on his own account did not come to much, largely because of his reluctance to send goods to American merchants which would be paid for only after being sold on. If Carr could trust when he knew correspondents well, he was not disposed to take risks with those with whom he was not acquainted.

How then did Carr come to do so well? His trade along the British coastline and with North Sea and Baltic ports produced steady but not spectacular profits. Perhaps this was generally true of merchants in North East England. Considered in terms of tonnage, Newcastle's trade was large enough for it to rank as the fourth most important port in Britain but a concentration on tonnage can make

---

[18] J. Newman, 'Anglo-Dutch Commercial Co-operation and the Russian Trade in the Eighteenth Century' in *The Interactions of Amsterdam and Antwerp with the Baltic region 1400-1800* (Leiden: Het Nederlandsch Economisch-historisch Archief, Werken 16, 1983).

[19] William I. Roberts III, 'Ralph Carr: A Newcastle Merchant and the American Colonial Trade', *Business History Review*, Autumn 1968.

the coal ports look more profitable than they really were. In comparison Hull, a port rapidly increasing the amount of trade it did with the Baltic, exported and imported more valuable cargoes. To take one example, the ship *Molly and Jenny* in which Carr had an eighth share was worked hard in 1752. The ship made several voyages to London, as well as Hamburg, Norway, the Baltic and Le Havre for an overall profit of about £120. In 1753 the *Molly and Jenny* lost £3 and, after carrying cargoes to and from Danzig, St Petersburg and Norway, she made only a modest profit in 1754. Carr was a cautious trader content with regular and safe profits. When Daniel Crommelin of Amsterdam and Gulian Verplanck of New York tried to persuade him to take a third interest in a ship dedicated to trading between Amsterdam, Newcastle and New York, he turned them down and his brother-in-law, Christopher Scott of Hull invested with them instead. When his Baltic contact, David Brown of Copenhagen was made Governor General of the Danish settlements in India and held out glittering prospects if Carr lent him a few thousand pounds, Carr was not tempted and refused the loan.

The books of this cautious but successful merchant did not, however, reveal the whole picture. In an undated letter written to his partner, John Widdrington, probably when he was about to retire from active business and, at any rate, later than 1760, he explained his business practices:

> I have often blamed myself that I did not explain to you and the rest in the Counting House my motives which were always justifiable to myself, tho parhaps they might at sometimes not appear entirely so to you for the mode of making out Invoices and Accounts of sales. It is an undoubted fact that every factor acting upon commission business only must soon be undone, if he had no more than 2% commission...

He went on to explain that, as he often had to accept unasked for return cargoes in lieu of payment for goods delivered, he basically added on interest for the time it took to sell cargoes foreign merchants sent to him and then charged more interest for the time he had to wait for payment, while, if he had to retail a cargo, he took the retail profit:

> In all the Counting Houses from Petersbrough down the whole Baltock to Hamburg etc, where I have had admittance and certain information these rules were fully followed, for they like us being obliged to receive whatever their correspondents choose to cram upon them...I have seen all their warehouses filled with numberless

species of goods none of which could be sold until winter set in, and the sledge ways passable over rivers and bogs tho paid for by them six months before that time.[20]

Carr thus ensured that he did well enough from cargoes that he received but only paid for when he sold them, a practice he was not prepared to consider as a supplier to the American colonies. He was probably correct in writing that this was quite a common practice and a necessary one if one was to succeed. Money was not to be made easily. Many drawbacks attended the commission factor as warehouses had to be paid for and there were insurances and taxes to be found and embezzlements to be allowed for 'all to be made good from slender profits'.

By the 1750s Carr was making more money from his bill-broking and the interest he received from loans than from trading on his own account. He was also increasingly conscious of the restraint that shortage of specie and the want of banks placed on trade. A progression to banking was his obvious next step.

Later in life, Carr looked back upon his business career. He did not do so with nostalgia but wrote that '… a merchant has the most anxious time which can never be lessened while he thinks it worth the following'.[21] Trust and caution moderated each other throughout his career. Trustworthy himself, generous and a good judge of character, Carr was all too aware of the dangers present in every transaction. Something of a lone wolf in his business life, he was not circumscribed by being bound to a family network and this perhaps accounts for his ability to switch to new opportunities throughout his career. It was with the Baltic trade, however, that he made his first substantial earnings, established his network of contacts and learned the hard lessons of eighteenth-century business.

---

[20] Ralph Carr to John Widdrington. Undated.

[21] Ralph Carr to his son Ralph Carr, 30 April 1788.

Chapter 10

Migration, civic culture and politics: British middle-class communities in Western Sweden 1730-1900

Martin Åberg

Live free & familiar with the Swedes to outward appearance at least, civil to them I know you will always be, but I would have you also visit them now & then. They are a people that love to be taken notice of and be respected.

Colin Campbell (1686-1757), director of the Swedish East India Company, Göteborg, giving advise to his protégé Charles Irvine on how to befriend the Swedish, 1735.[1]

Cities have in a sense always been 'global' and cross-cultural from an historical point of view. As central nodes in networks of commerce, industry and communications, cities are the places where people from different cultures and nations confront each other – or converge and create the specific, but not easily defined, quality of urban life and culture. This feature is even more striking considering the role of port cities before the advent of modern mass communications, not least so in the case of the cities of the Baltic Sea area. St. Petersburg, Riga, and Danzig (Gdańsk), Stockholm, Bergen, Christiania (Oslo) and Göteborg (Gothenburg), to mention but a few, share a common heritage as

---

[1] Colin Campbell to Charles Irvine, 23 February, 1735. Correspondence, 35-1a, Charles Irvine's Papers. James Ford Bell Library, University of Minnesota.

the urban 'melting pots' of the Baltic, although with very different results from a historical and sociological point of view. Medieval urbanisation patterns and the German expansion into the eastern Baltic excepted, we can see how migration in some cases was seasonal or temporary. In other cases migration resulted in permanent settlements such as the Swedish colony in St. Petersburg from the eighteenth century onwards or the British community in Göteborg during the same period.[2] In some cities ethnic and religious differences led to segregation and stratification; in others, assimilation, integration and eventually a modern civic culture became the result.[3]

British migration to the western Baltic Sea area, however, has not been systematically analysed in previous research on the region. This is the more surprising, considering the geographical proximity of the countries concerned. Although the area has a strong tradition of connections with the German lands from the Hansa period onwards, there have also been intensive contacts between Scandinavia and the British Isles. Whereas it is impossible to establish with any certainty the exact number of individuals and families arriving from England and

---

[2] In general on the Baltic Sea area and the western Baltic (Skagerrak region), cf. David Kirby, *The Baltic World 1772-1993: Europe's northern periphery in an age of change* (London, 1995); Poul Holm, *Kystfolk. Kontakter og sammanhænge over Kattegat og Skagerrak ca. 1550-1914* (Esbjerg, 1991). Specifically on St. Petersburg, see Bengt Jangfeldt, *Svenska vägar till St. Petersburg* (Stockholm, 1998).

[3] For definitions of 'political culture' and 'civic culture' see Gabriel A. Almond & Sidney Verba, *The Civic Culture: Political attitudes and democracy in five nations* (Princeton, 1963), pp. 3-26, although – importantly – from the 1980s the concept has come to imply a more explicit concern with political practice and behaviour, too.

Scotland during different periods,[4] we know that they always constituted a small minority in their new host societies, whether in Bergen, Christiania, or Göteborg. Yet they often came to play an important part in local society and, in the case of Sweden, not just from an economic point of view. As the British adapted to the local environment, they maintained important traits of their original culture, making assimilation incomplete. It is also argued that reinvention of identity was an important aspect of this process and that second and third generation Britons left a permanent mark on the rising Swedish middle class in their respective communities, in part precisely by force of their cultural identity. Furthermore, as assimilation gained impetus, the host society itself created its own image of the newcomers. For reasons to be investigated more closely, not only middle-class life at large but also political culture gradually incorporated 'British' traits in terms of ideologies and civic behaviour. The latter occurred during the nineteenth century – the last phase of migration – i.e. during a period that coincided with industrialisation and the rapid transition of urban governance in Sweden.

Cross-cultural influence, then, worked in both directions. However, as Colin Campbell's remark, quoted above, indicates, all this was far from self-evident when the British started to arrive in western Sweden in somewhat greater numbers in the early eighteenth century. In the following two sections we will first discuss the host cities concerned. Thereafter different waves of migration will be analysed and an assessment will be made of the social composition and characteristics of the migrants.

---

[4] As noted below, most British settled in Göteborg. However, as Bertil Andersson has stressed, no proper registration of immigrants to Göteborg was carried out during the period concerned, immigration of Jews being the sole exception: Bertil Andersson, *Göteborgs historia. Näringsliv och samhällsliv, I, Från fästningsstad till handelsstad 1619-1820* (Stockholm, 1996), p. 139. Swedish church registers for the city during the eighteenth century are incomplete for the purpose of calculating numbers and origins of immigrants. Basically this is the case for the entire period up to the early nineteenth century. The spelling of foreign names has often been corrupted, making it extremely difficult to identify people by name only. In addition to this material there are the church records of the British Factory/English Church in Göteborg. The Swedish authorities formally approved the Anglican Church in 1741, and the British formed their own congregation in 1747. The church was privately financed, although after a while gained financial support from the British government. Church records exist from 1774 in the archive of the British Factory, although only in form of registers of births, deaths, and marriages. This archive also includes minutes and lists of contributions to the British Poor Box, in the latter case from 1733 onwards. However, these fees were levied on British ships entering the port and it is not possible to use the lists to single out local residents exclusively. Another potential source of information are the Swedish pass registers. They cover the years 1758-1760 and the period from 1783 onwards. However, information for example on the pass-holders' occupation is incomplete and, importantly, the registers do not tell us if we are dealing with immigrants proper.

The host cities: Göteborg and Uddevalla

Extensive trade in bulk commodities such as iron, timber, tar and herring traditionally provided Dutch, Flemish and German merchants with ample reason to compete for market shares in Scandinavia. In Sweden the establishment of Swedish East India trade (1731) added to these opportunities. During the same period British and, later, Jewish merchants started to arrive in relatively larger numbers. In the latter case, though, the Swedish authorities opened up immigration only at a late stage, Marstrand becoming the first *porto franco* for Jews in 1775. British migration can be broken down into two major phases. During each phase push and pull factors varied, and as a result the actual role and function the migrants occupied within the economic and institutional framework of society changed. This was eventually to become of crucial importance from the perspective of political culture. The first phase roughly covers the period from the 1730s up to the early 1800s. Migration during this period was part and parcel of the expansion of merchant capitalism as it had evolved and matured in north-western Europe during the previous centuries. The second phase, which continued to the late nineteenth century, was different by nature and is closely connected to the process of Swedish industrialisation. It is during this period that a more profound impact by the British on local political culture can be traced.

To some extent the peak periods and main forces behind migration were the same for the Germans and Dutch as they were for the English and Scots, although certain differences emerge as the groups are compared more closely. In addition, considering the latter two groups, migration from the very outset concentrated on Göteborg and, during the second phase, to a lesser extent Uddevalla. The reasons for this preceded migration proper and were tied to the economic development of Bohuslän from the late sixteenth century onwards, primarily in connection with the decline of herring fishing in the coastal waters of the Skagerrak from the end of the 1580s. Although a new fishing boom occurred in the following century, previously important market places such as Marstrand and other settlements had already dropped permanently behind by the turn of the seventeenth century. Restructuring of the urban network, in turn, was reinforced by the new state policies adopted *vis à vis* the towns on the west coast after the final incorporation of Skåne, Blekinge, Halland and Bohuslän into Sweden in 1658. In effect this meant promoting Göteborg to the position of main port and the major outlet for Swedish trade in western Scandinavia. Smaller towns such as Kungälv and, at least temporarily, Uddevalla were eclipsed as a result of this shifting in priorities (see Map 1).

Map 1: *Host cities in context*

Source: Åberg (1997). Map by Anna-Lena Karlén.

For several reasons, then, Göteborg rapidly became the most important port city on the west coast during the seventeenth century. On the one hand, as the military and commercial priorities of Sweden-Finland were decided on the battlefields to the south and east of the Baltic Sea, the new western provinces often played a lesser part in the geopolitical considerations of the crown. On the other hand, the very same considerations, boosted by mercantilist ideology as well as informed by historical lessons, induced the crown to secure at least one major 'window' on the west. Indeed, building and sustaining a Baltic empire depended on an extensive export trade and free access to western markets. At the same time, however, military experience showed that the western parts of the country would always be extremely vulnerable to surprise attacks from Denmark-Norway.

For centuries the route west to the Skagerrak and the North Sea represented – and not only metaphorically – something of a bottleneck from a Swedish point of view,. Up to 1658 the only free passage was through a small land corridor following the Göta River from Lake Vänern down to the coast where Göteborg had been established in 1619-21, largely according to the designs of Dutch city planners and architects.[5] After 1658 efforts to promote Göteborg as both fortified settlement and trading port continued according to principles laid down by Charles X in a royal memorandum of March 1658 which addressed the problem of the administration of the newly acquired provinces. Although the memorandum focused above all on strategies to integrate the southernmost counties – these being closest to Denmark in terms of language and culture – in principle the same measures were adopted in the case of Bohuslän.[6] Among the older towns in Bohuslän, only Uddevalla could maintain and, indeed, later on increase its relative importance despite the restrictions imposed on trade. During the decades following the loss of the Baltic provinces in the Great Nordic War, including Riga, Uddevalla expanded dramatically. In the late 1740s Uddevalla ranked as the third largest port for foreign trade next to Stockholm and Göteborg.[7] However, at this time Göteborg was not only the key outlet for Swedish timber and iron. The city was also the home port for the profitable Swedish East India trade, and pull factors such as these made Göteborg an even more attractive place for foreign entrepreneurs and merchants. Enter Colin Campbell and the first large wave of British migrants.

Two phases

The 'true' status of the Swedish East India Company has been a topic of some debate, as has the question of its economic contribution to the national economy.[8] What remains a fact, nevertheless, is that not only substantial amounts of investments in the new company came from abroad but also that the personnel of the company were extensively recruited outside Sweden. As Koninckx points out, there were, for instance, close personal connections between the Swedish company and the ill-fated Ostend Company, suspended in 1727 and gradually dismantled from 1731 onwards. Although broker Henrik

---

[5] Cf. Albert Lilienberg, *Stadsbildningar och stadsplaner i Götaälvs mynningsområde* (Göteborg, Skrifter utgivna till Göteborgs stads trehundraårsjubileum genom jubileumsutställningens publikationskommitté VII, 1928).

[6] Åke Holmberg, 'Perioden 1550-1880', in Erik Lönnroth (ed.), *Bohusläns historia* (Göteborg/Stockholm, 1963), pp. 149-364, in particular pp. 191-207.

[7] Sten Kristiansson, *Uddevalla stads historia, II, 1700-1806* (Uddevalla, 1953) pp. 200-1.

[8] The account in this and the following paragraph draws, where no other source is referred to, on Christian Koninckx, *The first and second charters of the Swedish East India Company (1731-1766)* (Kortrijk, 1980).

König of Stockholm stood as the formal applicant to the Board of Trade in 1729, much of the original initiative seems to have been taken by the Scottish merchant Colin Campbell in concert with his Swedish associates Volrath Tham and Niklas Sahlgren. When the first charter was finally granted in 1731, Campbell, Tham and Sahlgren became co-directors with König, and Göteborg was decided as the home port of the company.

Campbell had a long pre-history in East India trade, including as a shareholder in the Ostend Company. Before the Swedish East India Company was eventually dissolved in 1813, numerous Dutch, Flemish, German and not least British officers had served on the Swedish East India vessels as well as becoming directors of the company (after becoming naturalised Swedish subjects), mainly during the first two charters (1731-66). Although the connections with the old Ostend Company should not be exaggerated, its dismantling meant that interests and participants turned elsewhere for investment. At the same time, as the English East India Company was dominated by London interests closely tied to the Bank of England, Scottish merchants in particular looked for alternative enterprises to engage in, the Swedish company being one of them. Indeed, from a Swedish point of view, such input was also necessary as practical experience of East India trade was by and large lacking in the country. Therefore foreigners could quickly obtain key positions in the company as 'tutors', although their relations to their 'disciples' were not entirely without friction. Campbell himself, for example, who joined the very first expedition of the company to Canton in 1732-3, seems to have had little confidence in the capabilities of his Swedish colleagues,[9] a trait perhaps in part accounting for his opinions as later expressed to Charles Irvine. Indeed, befriending the Swedish rather than socialising with them was probably a key characteristic in Swedish-British relations during the initial stage

Most captains during the early period of the company were Swedish. However, the 'second captains' – a category appointed only during the first

---

[9] The journal kept by Campbell during this expedition gives us some illustration of this, although one should also keep in mind the fact that the expedition met with trouble, and that the journal at least in part was constructed in defence of Campbell's own conduct and actions. Cf. Martin Åberg, 'The Swedish East India Company 1731-66. Business strategy and foreign influence in a perspective of change', *Scandinavian Journal of History* 15 (1990), pp. 97-108; The Diary or Journal of Sundry transactions pass'd aboard the ship Friedericus Rex Sueciae 1732-1733 /.../ by Colin Campbell, Svenska ostindiska kompaniets arkiv, H 22:3B, pp. 1-2, 7-8, 16, 23, 24 et passim. Göteborgs universitetsbibliotek. When, for instance, the captain appointed a certain Olof Rudbeck to the position of quartermaster on board, Campbell dryly suggested that Rudbeck was 'no more fit to be a Quartermaster than to be an Admiral' (p. 24).

charter, i.e. up to 1746 – and a large proportion of the remaining officers during both the first and second charters were of foreign extraction. Among a total of 190 officers 26 British were included (13.7 per cent). The case was the same with the officers on board the East India ships, while the sailors usually were recruited locally, primarily from the west coast counties and the Göteborg area. For instance, 13 out of 31 officers were British (the muster rolls included posts from first to fifth officer).[10]

There was Colin Campbell, of course, of the Campbells of Argyll as well as his brothers, but also Charles Irvine, James Maule, and the Pikes, and somewhat later the Erskines and the Chalmers, to give only a few examples. Above all economic considerations served as pull factors to the first British migrants. However, considering the fact that a majority of them came from Scotland – as, indeed, illustrated by the previous examples – political circumstances also stimulated migration in the late 1740s, after Culloden and the defeat of the Jacobites in 1746. France and Sweden had attempted, rather unsuccessfully, to support the rebellion, in part by using the East India Company as an intermediary, and after Culloden several of the Scots who went into exile ended up in Sweden and Göteborg. It is less certain, though, to what extent they settled permanently in the country. In many cases Göteborg only represented a stop on their way to France.[11] The importance of the East India Company as a pull factor probably lessened in the latter part of the eighteenth century. Trade was still profitable, at least throughout the third charter (1766-86), but at that time the organisation of the company had become less transparent and more open to an influx of new participants. For instance, data suggest that the proportion of foreigners in the direct service of the company declined drastically after the second charter as East India trading practices and seamanship had been learnt by the Swedish.[12]

Other opportunities, however, opened up during this latter period, serving as new pull factors. The export trade in iron, timber and herring expanded for most of the century, thus representing profitable alternatives to the merchant houses of Göteborg. As many of the British and their families had settled permanently in the city at this time, it was only natural that they too engaged in this kind of business, and new actors constantly added to the picture. Compared to other

---

[10] Christian Koninckx, *The first and second charters*, pp. 306, 314, 331, 335.

[11] Göran Behre, *Göteborg, Skottland och vackre prinsen* (Göteborg, Göteborgs hembygdsförbunds skriftserie XVI, 1982), pp. 99-118.

[12] Martin Åberg, 'The Swedish East India Company', p. 104.

groups, such as the Germans, though, the British still represented a minority group among the migrants. Of 41 new members accepted by the merchant's guild organisation between 1807 and 1813, 12 originated from Britain, while 24 came from different German lands.[13] This part of migration coincided with one of the most dynamic but also turbulent periods in the history of Göteborg. Although export trade dwindled in the closing years of the eighteenth century and the herring industry once more declined to finally collapse, the Napoleonic wars and the issuing of the Berlin decrees in 1806 meant the beginning of a new, albeit short boom period.

New British firms and families intimately connected to the fate and fortune of the city during the later part of the eighteenth and early years of the nineteenth century were those of John Hall & Co., D. Carnegie & Co., Alex. Barclay & Co., James Dickson & Co. and Gibson & Co.[14] The enterprise of John Hall, for instance, became the major exporter of iron and timber in Göteborg at the turn of the century. In addition, John Hall & Co. owned several industrial establishments in Sweden, including ironworks and sawmills. The firm went bankrupt, however, in 1807[15] and in the profound crisis that struck the European economy after 1815, parts of the established entrepreneurial strata were simply wiped from the commercial map of the city.

In the neighbouring city of Uddevalla a similar situation developed, for similar reasons. While Göteborg remained the major trading port during the period, Uddevalla had nevertheless succeeded in keeping and, indeed, in expanding its position in export trade during the eighteenth century. Competition was always fierce and animosity between the two cities was strong – or at least this was how the situation was interpreted from the point of view of Uddevalla. In reality Uddevalla was always too small and lacked a 'critical mass' in commercial potential to constitute any real threat to the dominance of Göteborg.[16] Though Uddevalla ranked among the larger cities in Sweden at the turn of the eighteenth century the population still numbered only some 4,000 people compared to Göteborg's population of 12,000 inhabitants.[17] As the crisis

---

[13] Bertin Andersson, *Göteborgs historia*, p. 142.

[14] In the case of Alexander Barclay first as partner in Alex. Barclay & Joh. Fischer (1812-1819) and from 1826 in the name of Alex. Barclay & Co.

[15] Artur Attman, 'John Hall & Co:s konkurs', in Hans Andersson (ed.), *Historia kring Göteborg* (Stockholm, 1967), pp. 121-31.

[16] Martin Åberg, *Uddevalla stads historia 1860-1998* (Uddevalla, 1997), p 39.

[17] Lars Nilsson, *Historisk tätortsstatistik, I. Folkmängden i administrativa tätorter 1800-1970* (Stockholm, 1992), Table 1, p. 12.

of the early nineteenth century struck the local economy the effects also seem to have been more far-reaching in Uddevalla than in its neighbouring city. In contrast to Göteborg, however, no British merchant families had settled permanently in Uddevalla before the 1820s. When this happened, it was in connection with yet new changes in the regional flow of export goods and commodities.

In Göteborg relative latecomers such as the Dicksons and the Gibsons managed to survive the economic crisis and added industrial enterprise to their business activities. In a study of 18 large merchant families in Göteborg in 1780, Magnusson concluded that few kinship relations existed between these families and the major merchants and entrepreneurs of fifty years later.[18] However, among the latter group of 15 families, both the Dicksons and the Gibsons were included. The Dicksons, for instance, were heavily engaged in the sawmill industry and timber exports and, from the 1850s onwards, they became famous or – as some would have it – infamous for their business methods when they expanded into the large forest districts in Northern Sweden.[19] The Gibsons, on the other hand, operated on a more local level and became pioneers of the emerging textile industry. Yet other players, such as the Keillers and the Robertsons, arrived in Sweden in the 1820s and became prominent in the engineering industry. Socially and economically, however, the two latter families did not grow to the same stature as the Dicksons and in the case of William Robertson and his descendants, we lose track of the family at the end of the nineteenth century.

As previously emphasised, any accurate estimate of the numbers of migrants as well or the precise size of the local British community is impossible. However, we may consider that the population of Göteborg was some 14,000 persons in 1810, while other estimates for the same year include roughly 1,500 persons as belonging to the merchant strata (families included).[20] Taking this into account it is probably safe to say that the group of British, second and third generation families never exceeded 200-300 persons. Rather, their relative importance originated solely from the commercial success and social performance of a very limited number of top families. This was similar to the case in Uddevalla.

In Uddevalla, British migration comprised only two families after the early nineteenth century crisis, although the Thorburns and the Macfies were already

---

[18] Thomas Magnusson, 'Göteborgskapitalister 1780 och 1830', *Historisk tidskrift* 1, 1989, pp. 46-74.

[19] By which is meant accusations for illegal exploitation of crown forests, viz. 'Baggböleri'.

[20] Lars Nilsson. *Historisk tätortsstatistik*, Table 1, p. 12; Bertil Andersson, *Göteborgs historia*, p. 143.

intermarried when William Thorburn settled down in the city in the early 1820s. Still, in the small town of Uddevalla, including fewer than ten well-to-do merchant families at the turn of the century,[21] the Thorburns came to exercise a profound influence in most areas of the community, primarily from the second generation through the brothers William F. and Robert Macfie Thorburn. At that time the Thorburns of Leith were well established in the Baltic trade. Early activities included an office in St. Petersburg run by James Thorburn who later transferred his business to Göteborg. During the economic crisis after the Napoleonic wars, William Thorburn visited Sweden in 1822 to help James settle his affairs. On the way out he travelled north, through Bohuslän and southern Norway, a journey during which he also visited Uddevalla. Family conflicts back home in Leith seems to have contributed to his decision to settle permanently in Sweden in 1823. There he established a business of his own, focusing on shipping and trade in agricultural products.[22] From the 1840s, the export of oats from the farming districts of western Sweden to England was the backbone of trade, although industrial enterprise also became part of the activities in the same manner as among the British in Göteborg. Typical of these nineteenth century entrepreneurs, such as for instance William F. Thorburn, seems to have been a readiness to engage in almost any new potential area of investment. Writing – in a mix of English and Swedish – in the late 1870s he noted that he ought to

> Buy St. Hasselön & make it a *badort* [seaside resort]. Market Gardening. Railway improving. Lapland iron ores ought to be remembered. Keep a sharp outlook on electrical discoveries and on the *naturkrafter* [forces of nature] which may produce electricity, when the *magasinering* [storing] and sending of it is invented [my italics].[23]

Other British, however, followed in the footsteps of industrialisation. As in the case of the East India trade, foreign competence was badly needed during the first phase of establishing new enterprises. Textile production was the first industrial sector to expand, and many of the foremen in the new companies were of foreign extraction. For instance the first three spinning masters at Kampenhof, the local cotton mill in Uddevalla, were from the same family from

---

[21] Sten Kristiansson, *Uddevalla stads historia, III, 1806-1863* (Uddevalla, 1956), p. 259.

[22] See Bertil Thorburn, *Willm. Thorburns Söner. Ett blad ur den svenska havreexportens historia* (Uddevalla, 1951), especially pp. 81-4.

[23] Undated entry from W. F. Thorburn's diary (although probably no later than June 1879), quoted in Martin Åberg, *Uddevalla stads historia*, p. 46.

Oldfield, the Potters.[24] This meant that the social composition of permanently settled British migrants changed in comparison with the early phase of migration. Compared with the merchants that had arrived in Göteborg during the eighteenth century, lower social strata became more strongly represented among the migrants to both cities.[25] Secondly, different push and pull factors notwithstanding, the major difference between the eighteenth and nineteenth centuries is precisely that migration during the latter phase took place within an entirely different institutional setting. British migration during the nineteenth century became part of the transition from merchant capitalism to industrial capitalism in Sweden.

Entrepreneurial activities and business innovation, or the emergence of 'new combinations' in Schumpeter's sense, occurred under very different conditions during merchant capitalism. Put simply: merchant capitalism meant focusing entrepreneurial activities to control the circulation of commodities, leaving production by and large outside the picture. Industrial entrepreneurial behaviour, on the other hand, implied a more active involvement with the emerging legal, financial and technological framework of industrial society. Indeed, a natural outcome of this often became the need to wield as much political influence and power as possible over the legislature as the institutional foundations of early industrial capitalism were being laid down. During both periods, involvement in the *riksdag* (parliament) and in its committees certainly represented a potential tool for direct manipulation of market conditions in the hands of the business elite. However, when the shift from trade to production is considered specifically from the point of view of migrant groups among the Swedish business community, we see that this change also gave impetus to more vigorous trading activity. As involvement in production increased – hence with increased dependence on the domestic setting as a result – greater stress was placed on integrating with both the national and local institutional context of the host society, including its political dimension. In turn, this option became possible as a result of the first generations of migrants becoming naturalised as Swedish subjects.

From the point of view of the British, then, it may be argued that participation in Swedish East India trade simply meant a grand opportunity to operate under the protective umbrella of royal privileges in a foreign land. Industrial entrepreneurs of British origin a century later were necessarily much

---

[24] Gustaf E. Karlson, *Kampenhofsbolaget kunde dela ut 20 %* (Uddevalla, 1982), pp. 8-9.

[25] As reflected by the data in the marriage registers of the British Factory in Göteborg.

more dependent on the opportunities to take an active part in public affairs in their new home country. Importantly, this process corresponded to changes in the pace and nature of assimilation.

Assimilation and cross-cultural influence

To many foreign visitors Sweden was an awkward country in the late eighteenth century. On the one hand, the country could display a remarkable history of past military and political greatness. On the other hand, Sweden represented a peripheral and poorly developed culture at the very fringe of the modern world. Impressions of the latter kind more often than not were coloured by Enlightenment ideas of Progress but also Romantic ideals about 'Original Man', as with Mary Wollstonecraft who travelled in western Scandinavia in the summer and autumn of 1795. In Sweden she found a peculiar mix of outright barbarism and the kind of simple-minded and admirable honesty she considered typical to man when still in a state of nature. At the same time Wollstonecraft echoed the remarks made by Colin Campbell some 60 years earlier, in particular regarding what could be interpreted as a certain basic insecurity of identity among the Swedish, an insecurity barely disguised by excessive outward politeness and friendliness. The Swedes, she remarked, 'pique themselves on their politeness; but far from being the polish of a cultivated mind, it consists merely of tiresome forms and ceremonies. The sort of superiority which a fortune gives when there is no superiority of education, excepting what consists in the observance of senseless forms, has a contrary effect than what is intended.'[26] And precisely because of such lack of self-confidence they were, to quote Campbell, a 'people that love to be taken notice of and be respected'.[27] When relations with the British became strained, this uncertainty would suddenly erupt into bursts of outright hostility, as when Captain Gustaf Trolle confronted Campbell on his journey to Canton in 1732. In a state of drunkenness, according to Campbell, Trolle suggested that 'the English aboard were a parcel of Strangers that hated the Swedes and had resolv'd to treat them as ill as they could'.[28]

---

[26] Mary Wollstonecraft, *Letters written during a short residence in Sweden, Norway and Denmark*, (1796, reprinted Fontwell, 1970), p. 22.

[27] Cf. footnote 1.

[28] The Diary or Journal of Sundry transactions pass'd aboard the ship Friedericus Rex Sueciae 1732-1733 /.../ by Colin Campbell, Svenska ostindiska kompaniets arkiv, H 22:3B, p. 34. Göteborgs universitetsbibliotek

In considering sentiments of this kind, it becomes a complicated task to assess the pace of integration of the first migrants into Swedish society. Often integration seems to have been more *pro forma*, as in the case of Campbell himself. Consistent with his position as co-director of the East India Company, he rapidly received Swedish citizenship and was raised to the nobility. Yet, at the same time he remained a staunch defender of Scottish interests in Sweden and was behind the foundation of an Anglican Church in Göteborg in 1747.[29] The congregation, in turn, was closely tied to the British Factory in Göteborg, a merchant association which also carried responsibility for keeping a poor box for the British community. Cultural assimilation, although incomplete, came only at later stages, and then mostly in the second generation, such as with the Thorburns in Uddevalla. The first Thorburn in Uddevalla was simply referred to as 'Engelsman på Kasa' ('the Englishman on Kasa', Kasa being dialect for the Kasen mansion where the family had settled).[30]

At the same time the relative lack of cultural identity among the Swedish, as perceived by the British, should not simply be rejected as an example of how national stereotypes colour encounters between cultures. On the contrary, they tell us something substantial about the very conditions in which such encounters take place. Conditions directly linked to the social and cultural make-up of local middle class society in Göteborg and Uddevalla eventually favoured emulation of British culture among the Swedish, rather than the other way around. A useful introduction to this problem is an analysis of the rate and, not least, structure of intermarriage between the British and the Swedish as reconstructed on basis of the marriage registers of the English Church in Göteborg.

Intermarriage between the British and the Swedish or other nationalities was already common during the early part of the first phase of migration, at least as far as the top levels of the East India Company are concerned. Only from the 1770s, however, can we get a clearer picture of such relations, importantly including those British who were not directly connected to the Company. Freedom of religion was granted to members of the Anglican Church in Sweden in 1741, while the local congregation in Göteborg was, as already noted, constituted in 1747. The pattern is similar to that of the establishment of a German congregation in the city in the previous century. The marriage registers of the English Church, however, run only from 1774 to 1896. In addition, the

---

[29] C. Koninckx, *The first and second charters*, pp. 43, 50. See also *Svenskt biografiskt lexikon* (SBL), vol. VII, pp. 264-268. It should be noted that most of the Campbells were not Jacobites, rather they sided with the House of Hanover.

[30] Kristiansson, *Uddevalla stads historia*, p. 161.

material is somewhat ambiguous. We know that some British subjects were also registered in the Swedish parishes of the city, indicating some inconsistency in clerical practice. Secondly, in a limited number of cases, what are clearly non-English and non-Scottish names appear both in the places of the bride and the bridegroom. Although it may be suspected that some of these cases are British widows, previously married to Swedes and retaining their Swedish family names, some room for interpretation is still left open. As a matter of fact, only in a royal decree of 1873 did it become clearly stipulated that mixed marriages between Swedish Lutherans and members of other confessions were the responsibility of the alien congregation.[31]

For such reasons it is possible to make only a simple two-dimensional analysis of the weddings, distinguishing between British-British and British-non-British marriages. As the total number of marriages is quite small, especially for the eighteenth century, it is impossible to cover both phases of migration. The data is representative only for the nineteenth century and the industrialisation phase. For the entire period 1774-1896 – 122 years – a total of only 57 marriages are recorded. Only six of these – of which three were mixed marriages – were registered before 1820. On the other hand, in relation to the problem of assimilation and the hypothesis that industrialisation led to closer adjustment to Swedish society, this process should be reflected not only in differences between the eighteenth and nineteenth centuries but progressively during the nineteenth century as well. Consequently, some difference in the rate of intermarriage should be observable even if we only contrast the pre- and post 1850 periods (see Table 1).

Table 1. *Rate of intermarriage. The English Church in Göteborg, 1774-1896.*

Year		British-British	British-Non British	Total
1774-1849	No	7	12	19
	%	36.8	63.2	100.0
1850-1896	No	8	30	38
	%	21.1	78.9	100.0

Source: Church records, C:1-C.2, E:1. The British Factory, Landsarkivet i Göteborg (GLA).

---

[31] 'Kongl. Maj:ts nådiga förordning angående främmande trosbekännare och deras religionsutövning', 31 October 1873, in *Svensk författningssamling* (SFS), 1873:71.

Between 1774 and 1849 roughly two-thirds of all marriages were mixed marriages, mostly with women as the non-British party, the marriages of Simon Jörgensen and Catherine Archer (1828) and Magnus Prytz and Jemina Carter of Hull (1837) being among the four exceptions.[32] From 1850 onwards, however, mixed marriages became even more common, accounting for four-fifths of all weddings. In addition, during this period marriages between Swedish men and British women became more common when compared to the earlier period (14 out of 38 marriages compared to 4 out of 19 for the pre-1850 period). This pattern would seem to suggest two things.

First, with the general increase in intermarriage, the already close ties between the British and other groups in the local community, most notably the Swedish, gradually became even more extensive. This, in turn, would seem to support the notion that some of the cultural borders separating the British community from the Swedish became more and more blurred. Very much the same pattern holds if we consider the Thorburn and Macfie families in Uddevalla. The first Thorburn in Sweden and his family by and large initially kept to themselves. Indeed, only through the marriages of their children did the family slowly start to assimilate into the local middle-class community of Uddevalla. Whereas one daughter, Jessie (1818-1883), created even tighter bonds to the Macfies through her marriage to William Andrew Macfie, her sister Margaret married a Swede, and so did her brother Robert.[33]

Cultural borders could be blurred in several ways, however. Secondly, therefore, and considering Göteborg specifically, it is important to note the change in structure of intermarriage, i.e. the increase in marriages between Swedish men and British women. Whereas the general increase in intermarriage indicates increased assimilation, the structure of marriage relations suggests that an important addition should be made to this interpretation. Marriage was, indeed, the 'economic and social building block for the middle class'.[34] However, men and women entered marriage on different terms. While women could certainly play an important part in the economic strategies of middle class families,[35] a man marrying into a rich and influential family undoubtedly stood

---

[32] Table 1.

[33] Ättlingar till William Thorburn och hans maka Jessy född Macfie.

[34] Leonore Davidoff & Catherine Hall, *Family Fortunes: Men and women of the English middle class, 1780-1850* (London, 1987), p. 322.

[35] On Sweden, cf. Anita Göransson, 'Kön, släkt och ägande. Borgerliga maktstrategier 1800-1850', *Historisk tidskrift* 4, 1990, pp. 525-44.

in a better position to take an active part in the economic activities of his father-in-law and brothers-in-law. This did of course depend on the family's readiness to accept new in-laws on equal terms. Therefore, rather than suggesting only a one-way process of assimilation, this pattern does also suggest something of the reverse kind: that the Swedes gradually became more socially accepted as suitable spouses among the British themselves. This pattern was presumably closely related to the economic success and prosperity experienced by many British entrepreneurial families in Sweden as well as to certain social and cultural features in Swedish middle class society itself.

Finally, the social position of spouses underwent changes during the period. This part of the pattern becomes more multifaceted and probably reflects a shift in social composition among the migrants. Migration during the eighteenth and the early part of the nineteenth centuries was homogenous in that it mostly included middle class elements. During the nineteenth century, however, working-class and lower middle-class people become more frequent in the material. As indicated this change was related to industrialisation. Similar to our previous example, the Potters in Uddevalla, several of the British migrants to Göteborg were – when such information is submitted to the marriage records – industrial employees. In addition both bride and bridegroom often worked at the same factory. This was the case with James Shaw and Maria Teresia Österberg, married in 1892 and employed as workers at a curtain factory in Mölndal near the city, and Alexander Thomson and Maria Wiesner, married in 1893 and employed at a cotton spinning mill in Göteborg.[36]

Consequently the British no longer constituted a homogeneous social group in their host-cities. Distinctions such as class, status, and ethnicity no longer overlapped within the group. I shall return to the problem of distinctions between the English and the Scots. But in addition to an increasing need for adjustment to Swedish institutional arrangements as a consequence of industrialisation, the fact that the British community was no longer a socially distinctive group in local society may well have furthered the kind of two-way assimilation outlined above, as far as middle class and upper middle class families are considered. In this respect the situation was to some extent similar to relations within the Jewish community in Göteborg during the same period. The first Jewish families arriving in the late eighteenth century were mainly of middle class origin, mostly from Western Europe. With increased migration of less well-to-do Jews from eastern Europe in the nineteenth century, tensions arose in the community, partly for religious and ethnic reasons, but in part as the result of

---

[36] Table 1.

what seemed to have been class-related factors. Middle class Jews simply had more in common with their Swedish business associates, despite occasional anti-semitism among local conservatives, and integrated more closely with the host society, while maintaining their original religious and cultural identity.[37]

Cross-cultural exchange between the Swedish and the British was not only reflected in marriage patterns. The local Swedish middle classes were very much still a class in the making at the turn of the eighteenth century, and the arrival of British and other groups of merchants and entrepreneurs coincided with a critical phase of this process. The fact that the British often represented 'success stories' in local society facilitated cultural emulation among the Swedes, as much as industrialisation made assimilation with Swedish society and its institutions necessary for the British. In addition – although emulation as such is not an entirely uncomplicated concept from a scholarly point of view – one should also bear in mind that middle-class emulation of the aristocracy was probably less characteristic in the western provinces of Sweden than in other parts of the country. Traditionally the nobility was less well represented in the social make-up of this region, leaving the middle classes in the Western cities and towns less hampered by social and cultural constraints. This led contemporary observers and visitors in the nineteenth century to conclude that Göteborg was, indeed, the most *bourgeois* city in Sweden, inhabited by the most hedonistic and economically most prosperous middle-class segments of the country[38] – and with an unmistakable British atmosphere.

The British tended to assimilate with the local environment, and the host society opened up to input from the encounter. Cross-cultural influence of this kind was not unique to British-Swedish relations. In terms of religious behaviour, Herrnhutism, as brought to western Sweden by German immigrants in the late eighteenth century, for a brief period became the religion *à la mode* among upper middle-class circles in Göteborg as well as in Uddevalla. But the main difference between the British and the Germans was precisely the more homogenous social composition of the British migrants up to the nineteenth century and the more prominent economic position they usually came to occupy in local society. German migration to Sweden, on the other hand, was always

---

[37] Cf. Vilhelm Jacobowsky, 'Mosaiska församlingens historia fram till 1955', in *Göteborgs Mosaiska församling 1780-1980. Minnesskrift till Göteborgs Mosaiska församlings 200-årsjubileum* (Göteborg, 1980), pp. 13-32.

[38] Cf. Martin Åberg, *En fråga om klass? Borgarklass och industriellt företagande i Göteborg 1850-1914* (Avhandlingar från Historiska institutionen vid Göteborgs universitet 3, Göteborg, 1991), pp. 91-3, 131-54.

more mixed, comprising people from all social strata and representing a culturally less distinguishable group than the British.

The peculiar mix of Swedish and English written by William F. Thorburn in his private diary has already been noted. But the use of English, for one thing, spread to the non-British as well, not only because the language represented an asset in international business. Textbooks in English were published in Göteborg as early as the 1740s[39] and English was, on certain occasions, also used privately among local Swedish upper middle-class families. For example, a few strategically deployed words of English, or an English phrase conveniently included in correspondence between friends and relations would serve the purpose to underline the message.[40] At an early stage this went hand in hand with an adoption of what were considered truly 'British' habits. The religious and secular associations of the British themselves have already been mentioned. In addition, social life came to incorporate a British style gentleman's club in Göteborg – the Royal Bachelor's Club (1769) – and a Curling club in Uddevalla (1846). Both were the first of their kind in Sweden and both became important for mingling between the British and the Swedish.[41] These and other traits left an undeniable mark on the local environment. When the German poet Ernst Moritz Arndt visited Göteborg in 1804 he made the remark that the city was virtually a piece of 'England set in Sweden ... English taste prevails from the breakfast table until late night ... people drink Porter and Port, one is served Toddy not only before but also while having tea ... dressing habits are the same as those among the modern gentlemen on Pall Mall and in Westminster.'[42]

However, the notion of 'Britishness' does of course pose a problem. The fact that many, if not most, of the British during the eighteenth and early nineteenth centuries were Scottish rather than English, makes relations between these two groups in the host society, and the extent to which the Swedes perceived such differences, an interesting issue. Occasionally a certain awareness of national differences can be detected, although at a late stage and not surprisingly among

---

[39] Göran Behre, *Göteborg, Skottland*, p. 17.

[40] For an example, cf. Martin Åberg, *En fråga om klass?*, p. 137.

[41] In the latter case, however, at first the club met with no success, but it was reinstated again – successfully this time – in 1852.

[42] '... dass Gothenburg Schwedens England ist/.../. England nemlich regiert hier vom ersten Frühstücke bis zum Einkriechen ins Negligé der Mitternacht. /.../ man trinkt Porter und Portwein, man reicht vor und bei dem The Toddy, /.../ man kleidet sich, wie die beaux von Pallmall und Westminster'. Ernst Moritz Arndt, *Reise durch Schweden im Jahr 1804*, vol. 2 (Berlin, 1806), pp. 38-9.

second-generation migrants, i.e. among groups which may have felt more reason than their parents to rediscover, or even reinvent their cultural roots. Robert Macfie Thorburn (b. 1828), for instance, seems to have suggested some kind of difference in temper between the Scottish and other peoples, when he noticed (1893) that '[m]an is not an oister [sic] bound always to remain in the same place. And Scotsmen are known to be the most willing to try new countries and succeed.'[43]

But all in all we know little about the politics and possible internal differences between the English and the Scots, apart from the fact that the Jacobite cause was supported among certain of the Scots in Göteborg during the 1740s. On the other hand, the Scots who arrived during the first phase of migration were certainly not archetypal rank-and-file clansmen dressed in 'highland garb' and ferociously waving a claymore upon landing in Sweden. Rather, in those cases where we may follow the origins of the Scottish migrants, they were urbanised middle-class people from Edinburgh, Glasgow, Leith and Aberdeen. To be sure, opposing loyalties in connection to the rebellion did not follow a clear-cut English-Scottish division and the differences between the Scottish and English migrants at large were probably slight from a cultural point of view. Nationalism as we know it was yet to be invented. According to Colin Campbell, he and the other British were simply referred to by the Swedish as 'the English'. However, these were Campbell's own words when describing the incident with Captain Trolle. Even though Campbell was later to side with the Stuarts, it is possible that this reflected only strictly political motives rather than any distinctive appreciation of his 'Scottishness' as opposed to 'the English', i.e. those people with which he may well have identified himself in other respects.

From a Swedish point of view such differences were if possible even more blurred. In everyday language no distinction was made between the 'Scottish' and the 'English'. Apart from the somewhat ambiguous example of Campbell there are other illustrations of this. As we have seen, the first Thorburn in Uddevalla was nicknamed 'the Englishman on Kasa' by the locals. And the same goes for what eventually came to be the nickname of Göteborg itself. Göteborg has become known as 'Little London' whereas 'Little Edinburgh' would perhaps have been more appropriate. What seems more plausible, therefore, is that the migrants and Swedish alike – in part consciously, in part unconsciously – simply constructed a new middle-class identity and, from the nineteenth century, this was based on perceived differences in national character. For the British this was part and parcel of adjusting to Swedish society and at the same time a way of

---

[43] As quoted in Bertil Thorburn, *Willm. Thorburns Söner*, p. 137.

avoiding complete cultural assimilation. For the Swedish the same logic became a way of coping with and integrating the foreigners with their own culture. Swedish middle class life with a touch of Britain, then, was the result of 'imagining' a community, to quote Benedict Anderson,[44] in the same manner as Swedish national identity, or English and Scottish 'heritage' respectively were invented during the same period. Why 'Britishness', or 'Englishness' rather than 'Scottishness' became a component part of these efforts, except in some cases such as the Thorburns and their curling, is more difficult to say, although early Anglification of the Scottish urban communities could have played a part. It did, however, have implications for local politics.

Local politics: a matter of class or a case of 'institutional channelling'?

The prominent position of the British communities in Göteborg and Uddevalla gave rise to a powerful strand of Anglophilism in dominant circles of society. This is important to stress as Sweden – historically, culturally and linguistically – by tradition had stronger ties to Germany, a trait that was reinforced during the nineteenth century. Middle-class culture as it developed in Göteborg and Uddevalla therefore represented an exception from our point of view and it is from this perspective that the impact on political culture of 'British heritage' should be measured. There are several dimensions to this problem. Contemporary studies suggest the importance of 'institutional channelling', i.e. the influence of host-society institutional structures rather than class and/or ethnicity, as the crucial variable to explain modes of political mobilisation among migrant groups.[45] That is, possibilities and limitations imposed by political institutions ultimately determine choice of strategy. To some extent this holds for the British in Sweden as well, although with some important reservations. According to our hypothesis that changes in push and pull factors related to industrialisation provided the British with stronger motives to adjust to the institutional arrangements in host-society, the 'institutional channelling model' would therefore predict political modes of agency similar to those among the Swedish.

---

[44] Benedict Anderson, *Imagined Communities: Reflections on the origin and spread of nationalism* (London, 1984).

[45] Cf. Patrick R. Ireland, *The Policy Challenge of Ethnic Diversity. Immigrant politics in France and Switzerland* (Cambridge, Mass. 1994).

'Public' and 'private' more often than not tended to coincide in political life, and politics was an integral part of the efforts of many entrepreneurs to advance their business *and* public interests at one and the same time. When the British gradually involved themselves in local politics this became a distinctive feature for them as well. The manner in which the extensive infrastructure projects launched in Sweden from the 1850s onwards were decided upon and implemented became characteristic of entrepreneurial politics. Such projects often included municipal involvement. Two important areas of investment were the construction of national and local railways and, specifically for municipalities, the extension and rebuilding of harbour facilities in connection with increased overseas shipping and trade. Occasionally issues such as these came to overlap. In Uddevalla, for instance, William Thorburn and his son William F. Thorburn became two of the main enthusiasts for integrating the city with the national railway network as rapidly as possible. From the point of view of the entire community, it was argued, the railway would lead to considerably better communications for all parties concerned. From the perspective of family business, however, the railway was also of paramount importance, and especially considering the export of oats from the port at Uddevalla. Although the local railway debate was to drag on for almost two decades, the new railway connection was eventually built in the early 1860s. It connected the harbour facilities in the city directly to the agricultural districts in the interior of the country, i.e. precisely the areas in which the oats were produced. Similar cases of entrepreneurial politics were typical of most municipalities during this period.[46]

However, whereas adjustment to and, indeed, extensive use of established institutions and channels for political pressure was typical of British and Swedish businessmen alike, other factors intervened as well. Ethnicity, let alone religion, was never a problem to the British in Göteborg or Uddevalla. On the other hand class certainly mattered and worked in favour of the established British families. Hence, 'institutional channelling' only provides part of the explanation. Rather, class-related circumstances intervened in two ways. First, as the British mainly represented entrepreneurial success stories and in addition were the subject of cultural emulation among the rest of middle-class society, families such as those previously mentioned were among those often selected to represent the political interests of the municipality. Secondly, as voting regulations were based on income, institutions automatically favoured upper middle-class participation in politics, not least after the legislation on local self-government in 1862. At that

---

[46] M. Åberg, *Uddevalla stads historia*, pp. 49-52; M. Åberg, *Samförståndets tid. Konflikt, samarbete och nätverk i svensk lokalpolitik* (Lund, 1998), Ch. 2.

time the 'old' British families were naturalised as Swedish citizens and thus eligible for public office. Consequently many family members served both as MPs and more frequently as members of their local city council. In Göteborg, five out of 50 members of the first new city council came from British families; or, to be precise, the Dickson family held 4 seats in the assembly and the Gibsons 1 seat.[47] In Uddevalla the Thorburns achieved a similar position, brothers Robert M. and William F. Thorburn serving in the city council for 40 years and 23 years respectively, including periods as chairmen.[48]

Importantly, though, these illustrations tell us nothing about how 'British heritage' also came to permeate local political culture. As was the case with middle-class culture in general, here too we may speak of a two-way process. In this respect, however, other qualities of nineteenth- century political life and its institutions should be considered. Today we live in societies with mature, democratic institutions, although institutions that are slowly readjusting to new conditions resulting from mass migration and globalisation. In nineteenth-century Sweden modern political institutions were still very much in the making. Certainly adjusting to prevalent institutions was part of the picture to the actors, still – in some sense like contemporary post-socialist societies on the eastern rim of the Baltic – the very same institutions were also changing and were not clearly defined. Thus they were also malleable to different pressures, i.e. we have a situation analogous to that of the formation of middle-class identity. This is particularly true when urban governance is specifically considered. When local self-government was introduced, it was in terms of an institutional framework that gave considerable freedom to the municipalities in terms of interpretation. It was this structure that provided a seedbed for different local political cultures. In both Göteborg and Uddevalla 'British heritage' came to be incorporated as a distinctive feature of political culture. As I have stressed elsewhere, influence came about primarily in terms of ideology, as a particularly strong and distinctive commitment to economic and political liberalism.[49]

'Liberalism' did of course precede British migration to Sweden, although the concept referred to almost any kind of idea that could be launched in opposition to the establishment when it began to be used more extensively in public opinion from the 1830s. And although many municipalities were politically conservative

---

[47] Based on the biographical data on city council members, 1863-1962, compiled in Magnus Fahl, *Göteborgs stadsfullmäktige 1863-1962, II. Biografisk matrikel* (Göteborg, 1963).

[48] Oskar Iwar, *Uddevalla fullmäktigeinstitution 125 år* (Uddevalla, 1988), pp. 38-40, 53.

[49] Åberg, *Samförståndets tid*, in particular chapter 2.

rather than liberal, cites other than Göteborg and Uddevalla developed into liberal strongholds as well, such as Jönköping in the interior of the country. What made Göteborg and Uddevalla unique was above all the clear connection between Liberalism and Anglophilism buttressed by a 'British heritage'. Drinking toddy, playing curling, dressing Pall Mall-style, speaking and writing in English, as well as liberal thinking, went hand in hand and formed part of the one and same set of cultural expressions, although certain differences between the cities should be noted. Conservatism on the other hand became more generally associated with the political mobilisation and interests of the lower middle classes, or the 'petty bourgeoisie', occasionally with anti-semitic traits included.

Among local liberals themselves there were substantial differences which came to the fore as industrialisation continued to provoke fundamental changes in the social fabric of society. Issues of municipal interest other than just matters of local infrastructure were hotly debated, not least the problem of poor relief among the working classes. On one hand there were those such as the Social-liberal S.A. Hedlund who argued in favour of more active policies on the part of the state and the municipality in dealing with these problems. On the other hand, extreme liberals such as Charles Dickson defended a perspective which by and large left individual citizens with the responsibility to look after their own well-being. In the long run the latter perspective prevailed, supposedly representing the only valid strategy to educate the common people into becoming responsible citizens. Liberty and equality, although universal in theory, met with practical restrictions. Therefore it was also necessary for middle-class society to set a moral example to the destitute rather than letting them rely on publicly administered and costly means of poor relief. Compassion, however, was also part of the picture and in practical life this meant opting for a wide array of private charities and a system of charitable funds. Individual public-spiritedness embodied in private funding of charitable and other purposes, then, added yet another new trait to politics and became a defining characteristic of middle-class civic culture in Göteborg.[50]

Liberalism, as thus defined, emerged victorious throughout local society for most of the nineteenth century and it accounted for Social Democracy's initial difficulties in taking root among the working classes. To some extent liberalism held its ground, albeit transformed, well into the twentieth century. As the Swedish Liberals split in 1917 – only to reunite again in 1934 – their votes in

---

[50] Cf. Åberg, *Samförståndets tid*, Birgitta Jordansson, *Den goda människan från Göteborg. Genus och fattigvårdspolitik i det borgerliga samhällets framväxt* (Lund, 1998).

both the local and parliament elections dropped. However in Göteborg the Liberals fared better than in most other parts of the country. Strong liberal opinion, informed by pro-British and pro-American sentiments, was also characteristic of Göteborg during the Second World War, not least due to the powerful influence of *Göteborgs Handels och Sjöfartstidning* and its chief editor Torgny Segerstedt.

The picture in Uddevalla is less clear-cut. In this case conservative ideology with a strong religious bias and liberalism more clearly balanced each other during the latter half of the nineteenth century. The majority of the politically influential families in town, though, favoured liberalism, while not only the lower middle classes but also the working classes turned towards conservatism. Not surprisingly, as in Göteborg, the local environment became a critical area for the Social Democrats at the turn of the century, although the underlying reasons differed somewhat. As in Göteborg, liberal opinion developed quite early, at least from the 1840s as reflected in the activities of the local newspaper, *Bohus Läns Tidning*. Yet local liberalism grew stronger and more programmatic only from the mid-century onwards. Interestingly enough this was at a stage when the Thorburn family started to engage more actively in public life. Although we should not ascribe too much to this coincidence, it was during the 1860s and 1870s that the brothers William F. and Robert M. Thorburn succeeded in establishing themselves permanently as two of the most prominent representatives in municipal life. In addition, from the late 1870s, liberal opinion at last also found a powerful – albeit controversial – defender in the press through chief editor Ture Malmgren at the newly founded newspaper *Bohusläningen*.

Opinions about poor relief were in certain respects similar to those in Göteborg. But, due to the prominent part played by orthodox Lutheranism in this part of the country, the kind of paternalism that developed had a slightly different character, blending both liberal and conservative traits in a seemingly contradictory manner.[51] While the liberals stressed equal opportunities and rights – within reasonable limits – of each and all individuals, religious conservatism in Uddevalla stressed the God-given nature of hierarchy in the society. As the upper middle classes often spoke in favour of the former and the lower middle classes and also large proportions of the working classes tended to accept the latter interpretation, opinions did not really meet. While the privileged strove to set a moral example stressing individual achievement, ordinary people were more

---

[51] This and the following paragraph, Martin Åberg, *Uddevalla stads historia*, pp. 147-66.

careful to observe religious orthodoxy even though this also meant accepting an often harsh situation in life.

By way of conclusion, the notion of 'setting an example' as used above is also crucial to our understanding of the role of 'British heritage' in political culture at large, both in Göteborg and in Uddevalla. Political culture on the local level was of course not as such due to the personal influence exercised in practical politics by a few isolated individuals and families. Rather, the importance of the British in our two host cities expressed itself at another level. The economic position of these families in local society, combined with the impression made on their peers by force of their social and cultural habits – albeit habits in part reinvented or imagined – set an example in civic life as well among the middle classes. As modern civic life started to develop, the British served as amplifiers for powerful ideological undercurrents in society and at the same time contributed to the transformation of these into locally specific expressions of political culture.

Conclusion

This paper has analysed the role of British migration to western Sweden, more precisely the cities of Göteborg and Uddevalla between 1730 and 1900. Although numbering only a few people and families, British migrants played an important part in the economic, social and political life of local society. It is argued that British-Swedish relations changed significantly during the later stages of migration, directly as an effect of industrialisation. Industrialisation brought changed conditions of business to the merchants and entrepreneurs making up most of the migrant groups, and this favoured closer adjustment to the institutional framework of the host society, including political life. At the same time, the role the British were to occupy depended to a considerable extent on their success in maintaining, or rather reinventing 'English' or 'British' heritage in Sweden as part of their new identity. By force of cross-cultural exchange this heritage came to permeate local Swedish middle class life as well, including its political culture. These processes left a permanent mark on civic life in the local arena long after the democratic reforms of the early twentieth century.

Part III: 1850-2000

Chapter 11

Coal, chemicals and change: Tyneside's Baltic trade 1861-80

Adrian Osler

Early discussions of the role of shipping in the trades between Britain and the Baltic in the second half of the nineteenth century have, quite properly, concentrated upon the nature and significance of the inward-bound leg of the trading regime, considering the carriage by sea of wood products from the Baltic to the principal British points of demand.[1] Later attention has also turned to the nature and potential profitability of the back-haul (i.e. outward) leg of this trading regime, from Britain towards potential consumers in the Baltic itself. Such a complementary approach raises important supply-side issues, for the economics of the carriage of outward-bound cargoes, principally coal, may well have been critical to the deployment of ships owned in Britain and in other non-Baltic nations to the Baltic in the first place.[2]

Two further factors, one spatial and the other temporal, complicate this important issue of shipping supply. Geographically, there was little coincidence in

---

[1] B. Latham, *Timber, Its Development and Distribution: A Historical Survey* (London, 1957); L.R. Fischer and H.W. Nordvik, 'Shipping and the Baltic Wood Trade to Britain, 1863-1908', in W. Minchinton (ed.), *Britain and the Northern Seas: Some Essays* (Pontefract, 1988).

[2] L.R. Fischer, 'A Flotilla of Wood and Coal: Shipping in Trades between Britain and the Baltic, 1863-1913', in Y. Kaukianen (ed.), *The Baltic as a Trade Road*, VII Baltic Seminar at Kotka, 1989 (Kotka, 1989), pp. 42-44.

the regional siting of the main British ports engaged in the import of wood and the export of coal respectively. Chronologically, during the period under review, the lead shipping engaged in the transport of both commodities was the subject of a technological revolution. This revolution resulted in a rapid and marked change in the composition of each of the major national fleets taking part.

Whereas previous assessments of such matters have – partly as a consequence of lack of detailed evidence – relied heavily upon a 'top down' nationwide approach, the present paper is a determinedly 'bottom up' regional evaluation, and one whose perspective is consciously limited to that of a single port – albeit to that port which has been designated as 'the principal coal exporting port to the Baltic'. On the British side, therefore, analysis is confined solely to shipping arriving into and clearing from the Tyne. In respect of the relevant 'foreign going' areas – those which lay beyond the strait commonly known as the Sound – the use of the term 'Baltic' is restricted in its meaning to comprise the south western flanks of the Baltic Sea itself; the shores of the Gulfs of Riga and Finland; and the southern coast of the Finnish Grand Duchy as far north and west as Åbo (Turku). The Gulf of Bothnia and the ports of the Swedish mainland are thus excluded from consideration.

The first of these two entities, the Tyne, is perhaps the easier of the two to delineate for, despite the fact that the town of Newcastle's hegemony over the navigation and commerce of the river Tyne was eroded as the nineteenth century progressed, the dominance of the 'Port of Newcastle (or, Tyne)' ensured that it remained a readily identifiable unit throughout. The concept of a 'Port of Tyne' also has the advantage that, historically, it may be directly equated with the river's three constituent customs ports (Newcastle, South Shields and North Shields), a grouping which finally acquired a formal designation, the 'Tyne Ports'.[3] Geographically, this last also coincides broadly with the area administered by the Tyne Improvement Commission, established in 1850.

The complementary 'Baltic' entity, however, is more arguable in respect of both location and extent, for, as a geographical descriptor, the term is susceptible to looseness and imprecision of use. Moreover, even the idea of a definite 'Baltic' region (or regions) may be held to result from a peculiarly British approach. In view of such difficulties of context this study confines itself to a more realisable goal, the selection of a recognisable navigational and trading region. It is thus based upon a functional rather than a conceptual 'Baltic' region. Accordingly, some wider considerations have necessarily been set aside in pursuit of this

---

[3]   D.J. Starkey (ed.), *Shipping Movements in the Ports of the United Kingdom, 1871- 1914: A Statistical Profile* (Exeter, 1999), pp. 12-13.

specific aim. The influences of some of the complex political and territorial adjustments which occurred around the Baltic during the third quarter of the nineteenth century, for example, have been eschewed. It should also be emphasized that the author's eventual definition of the 'Baltic' was shaped as much by an assessment of the Tyneside seaman's oft-rehearsed and contemporary, colloquial aphorism, that, 'Rooshia, Prooshia, Memel an' Shiel's' formed the four corners of his globe,[4] as by a close examination of the regular stream of published commercial information available to local shipowners, charterers and exporters through the flourishing medium of Tyneside's late-nineteenth century press.

Chronologically, the boundaries of the study have been set at the years 1850 and 1890. The former may be recognized as marking a literal sea-change in the mood of British trade and shipping consequent upon the repeal of the Navigation Acts, whilst the latter is the date after which it is generally agreed that Britain's overall share of the Baltic carrying trades began to go into a marked decline. Within this overall forty-year period the paper confines its analysis to the twenty-year core, 1860-1880, a period which was of especial economic and technological significance.

Background

From late medieval times onwards, Tyneside's maritime trade was dominated by the shipment of regionally-mined coal, and links to the Baltic were maintained at significant levels throughout much of that time.[5] However, although there was much superficial similarity between Tyneside's coal shipping trade as it was conducted at the end of the eighteenth century and that of the second quarter of the nineteenth century, there was in fact a process of distinct, underlying change. Whereas, formerly, foreign-going (i.e. exported) coal had been a mere ancillary to a market totally dominated by domestic demand – and coastal shipment – by the second quarter of the nineteenth century a significant shift of emphasis towards meeting overseas needs through foreign-going shipments was already in hand.

Stimulated by three favourable reductions in coal export duties during the period 1831-45, the Tyne's foreign-going shipments increased six-fold, reaching a total of one million tons in this latter year. Exports then represented almost a

---

[4]   G. Hodgson, *The Borough of South Shields* (Newcastle upon Tyne, 1903), p. 291.

[5]   R. Davis, *The Rise of the English Shipping Industry* (London, 1962; reprinted 1971), pp. 209-227; A.W. Purdue, 'Ralph Carr: A Newcastle merchant and the Baltic trade in the mid-eighteenth century', in this volume.

third of all shipments and this share continued to rise until the mid-1850s when the export trade and the coastal trade at last reached near-parity. Ten years later, by the mid-1860s, exports of coal finally outstripped stagnating domestic demand and future growth became firmly anchored in the 'Foreign Trades'.[6]

Whilst the shifts and growth of the 1840s had been beneficial to the coal-owners and to the port itself, other events caused apprehension amongst those whose 'interests' lay more in the ownership and operation of ships. The proposed repeal of the Navigation Laws caused vigorous protests amongst the north-east's maritime communities although, it must be said, their Parliamentary representatives exhibited pragmatism rather than conviction prior to the final removal of this national 'protection' in 1850.[7] The real effects of this repeal on the shipping engaged in the region's coal export trades still remain uncertain. Perhaps, in reality, the shock was not too great: the outward trade had never been subject to protection anyway, the reciprocity agreements signed with most northern nations (including those of the Baltic) over the previous twenty-five years had increasingly sanctioned foreign 'competition', and the actual business of coal transport exhibited less distinction between the freight-dependent shipper and the profit-seeking vendor than was found in most other maritime trades. Though hardly a scientific appraisal, local shipping reports suggest no immediate curtailment of Baltic activity: for example, on 1 August 1850, sixty-two 'coal ports' ships passed through The Sound, and thirty of these vessels came from the Tyne alone.[8]

When it did come, the curtailment of this trade originated from two rather different causes. First, it came with the disruption occasioned by the Crimean War (1854-56); secondly it resulted from a prolonged economic depression in the late 1850s that was accompanied by tonnage over-capacity. The former cause was probably not as negative in effect as might at first appear since it was relatively short-lived and, on balance, its effects were probably no more or less than those remarked upon by a naval witness in 1857 that '...in the Colliery Trade I would have thought that the coal sent to the Baltic during the war, for the Navy, would have made up for any loss occasioned by the war...'[9]

---

[6] N.R. Elliot, 'A Geographical Analysis of the Tyne Coal Trade', *Tidschrift voor Econ. en Soc. Geographie* 59 (1968), pp. 82-87.

[7] S. Palmer, *Politics, Shipping and the Repeal of the Navigation Laws* (Manchester, 1990), pp. 24-27, 110-111.

[8] R.E. Keys, *Dictionary of Tyne Sailing Ships* (Newcastle, 1999), p.47.

[9] *Parliamentary Papers*, Report from the Select Committee on Harbours of Refuge, 1857, pp. 64-65.

The same source also, usefully, considered the Baltic Sea as a single geographic trading area and gave contemporary confirmation of Newcastle's primacy as the port of outward trade to the Baltic. Of the 429,000 tons of shipping originating from the three major British participants at that date, Newcastle was accorded no less than a 60 per cent share, followed by Hull with 25 per cent, and Leith with 15 per cent. Indeed, combining such evidence with that gained from the interpretation of data in the various parliamentary annual statements on trade and navigation,[10]10 certainly seems to support the more recent assumption that Newcastle was then 'the principal coal exporting port to the Baltic'.[11] However, this undoubted primacy rested not simply upon the availability of coal, but upon a rather complex structure of extra-national and intra-regional factors.

The principal extra-national factors were undoubtedly those connected with the 'revolutionary changes in the softwood industry'.[12] These revolutionary changes had been brought about by the progressive reduction, equalization and eventual abolition, in 1866, of import duties favouring colonial (i.e. Canadian) timbers over their Baltic counterparts. Baltic timber then penetrated the British market on an unprecedented scale, creating a consequent demand for tonnage which, of whatever nationality, inevitably sought a consistent supply of backhaul cargo to the Baltic – principally coal.[13]

At intra-regional level, concerns centred upon important supply-side issues. In early and mid-century, the River Tyne had been allowed to fall into desuetude, but by the beginning of the 1860s it was undergoing modernisation through a relatively new conservatorship, the Tyne Improvement Commission. Meanwhile, throughout its hinterland an embryonic railway monopoly, the North-eastern Railway, was busily capturing the coal traffic of the larger part of the 'Great Northern Coalfield' and directing it towards the Tyne.[14] Along the riversides, comparatively youthful industries were enhancing a more traditional

---

[10] Starkey, *Shipping Movements*, pp. 7-9.

[11] C. Knick-Harley, 'Coal Exports and British Shipping, 1850-1914', *Explorations in Economic History* 26 (1989), pp. 311-38; Fischer, 'Flotilla of Wood and Coal', p. 48.

[12] Latham, *Timber*, pp. 52-69, 86-105.

[13] W. Minchinton, 'The British Market for Timber from Northern Europe since the 1860s', in Kaukianen (ed.), *The Baltic as a Trade Road*, pp. 83-9.

[14] R.W. Rennison, 'The Development of the North-east Coal Ports, 1815-1914: The Contribution of Engineering (PhD thesis, University of Newcastle upon Tyne, 1987) pp. 225-261.

industrial base, whilst maritime manufacturing technologies were particularly well advanced.[15]

This, then, is the appropriate time to consider a core period in the Port of Tyne's development, 1860 -1880, and to provide a quantitative appraisal of the port's outward Baltic Trade, its ships and its carriers. That such a historical appraisal is possible results in large part from the unique way in which the Newcastle Customs Office collated and published their shipping statistics, for the Port of Newcastle's published Bills of Entry were – in perverse 'Geordie' fashion – really bills of clearance.[16]

Outward trade and shipping in 1861

Data from the first year represented by the Bills of Entry, 1861 (Table 1), confirms that coal dominated the outward trade to the area of the Baltic under consideration, making up a remarkable 94 per cent, by tonnage, of all bulk cargo shipments. Furthermore, the combined coal products exports, 315,000 tons, indicate an important sectoral market for the port, representing 16 per cent of all Tyneside's foreign-going coal. Prussian and Russian demand was near-balanced, with each taking around 43 per cent of the Baltic total, whilst the German Confederation's Baltic states accounted for barely 13 per cent between them. Concentration of exports was such that only a dozen Baltic ports, out of the three dozen actively engaged, accounted for some nine-tenths of all the coal products received. Significantly, just three ports helped shape the equality of demand between Russia and Prussia: Cronstadt (serving the Russian capital), which took an outstanding one-third of all Baltic-bound shipments; and the linked Prussian ports of Swinemünde and Stettin which together took around a quarter.

Initially, the role of chemicals in the Baltic export regime might appear rather insignificant, for chemicals composed just 2.5 per cent of all bulk products shipped. But, examined more closely, chemical exports are seen to have been an important and high value item in their own right with, surprisingly, an estimated commodity value approaching half that of coal. Tyneside was at that time Britain's largest chemical manufacturing area.[17] Some 8,800 tons of chemicals – principally alkalis and soda – sent to the Baltic in 1861 represented not only 30

---

[15] J. Clarke, *Building Ships on the North-east Coast, Part 1 c. 1640-1914* (Newcastle, 1997); N.R. Elliot, 'Tyneside: a study in the development of an industrial seaport', Part III, in *Tidschrift voor Econ. en. Soc. Geographie* 53 (1962), pp. 263-268.

[16] Newcastle Bills of Entry and Shipping List, 1861-1880.

[17] W. Campbell, *The Chemical Industry* (London, 1971).

per cent of Tyneside manufacturers' foreign-going chemicals trade, but almost 8 per cent of their total annual production. St. Petersburg was by far the most important Baltic consumer, taking a 44 per cent share, whilst the developing Prussian port towns of Stettin and Danzig were next in rank. Nationally, Russia absorbed just over a half of the Tyne's Baltic-bound chemicals and Prussia a third, with the remainder destined for the German states.

Other hinterland products which figured as consistent (if low-level) exports were: lead and iron (in both refined and processed forms); millstones and grindstones; cement; glass; earthenware; and a variety of fire-clay products. These last are worthy of note, for they came from a relatively recent and specialist local industry, and one which was expanding rapidly in sympathy with urban and industrial needs – producing firebricks for domestic and industrial hearths, glazed pipes for sewers, and high-temperature retorts for gas-making.[18] The major port cities of the Baltic, such as Riga, were a natural market for such items since they faced urban expansion and emergence from a proto-industrial condition.[19]

Table 1. *Bulk Product Exports (tons), 1861*

Coal Products	Chemicals	Earth Products	Iron and Lead
314696	8811	7001	5269

Compiled from *Newcastle Bill of Entry and Shipping List*, 1861, 'Exports' (note - Earth Products include grindstones, millstones, clay, fire-clay, bricks, firebricks and cement)

Surprisingly, perhaps, Tyneside's exports of engineering manufactures in 1861 were modest in quantity, but they were of technological significance, including, for example, agricultural implements, heavy metalworking machinery, steam launches and no fewer than fourteen complete locomotives and tenders destined for the British-financed, Riga-to-Dünanberg railway (new-built ships might also be added but, since these were exported on their own 'bottoms', they have been omitted from the present study). In the British context the relatively isolated geographical position of the Tyne meant that – unlike, say, the Humber – its opportunities to participate in transhipment were limited, although some sizeable parcels of cotton (received before the American blockade set in) and tinplate featured amongst them in 1861.

---

[18] J. Cowen, 'On the Manufacture of Fire-Clay Goods', in *The Industrial Resources of the Tyne, Wear and Tees* (London, 1864), pp. 207-212.

[19] D. Kirby, *The Baltic World, 1772-1993* (London and New York, 1995), pp. 164-6.

It must be emphasized that this entire Tyne-based, Baltic-going trade of 1861 was carried by an exclusively sail-powered transport regime, and that the composition and nature of the shipping engaged in this carrying work indicates that it was a regime which was entirely north European in character and enterprise too (Table 2). The fleets of just three of the participating national groups formed a first tier of carriers, comprising vessels from England, the states of the German Confederation (both its Baltic and the North Sea coasts) and Prussia. These three national fleets together made up 80 per cent of the total tonnage capacity employed. Below these, a second tier of providers originated from Scotland, the Dutch Republic, Denmark and Russia, and these in combination accounted for a further 16 per cent of the tonnage employed. Of the remaining half-dozen nationalities Norway headed the list, but its individual contribution was barely 1 per cent.

Table 2. *Shipping Cleared Outwards by Place of Origin (register tons), 1861*

England	German Con.	Prussia	Scotland	Dutch Rep.	Denmark	Russia	Others
80229	69364	30013	11864	11537	8099	5465	6953

Compiled from *Newcastle Bill of Entry and Shipping List*, 1861, vessels 'Entered Outwards'

In general, the proportion of sailings, i.e. clearances, made by ships of each nationality closely matched that nation's own proportion of tonnage, but there was one notable exception, that of the English fleet. Although accounting for only a quarter of all clearances, it provided something over a third of the total tonnage employed. This was a direct result of the relatively large size of individual English ships, which were mainly concentrated in the 200 to 300-ton range (by comparison, though the fleet of the German states was numerically much larger, its total tonnage was considerably less, for its ships were much smaller, mostly of 50 to 200 tons).

No less than 92 per cent of the English-owned tonnage deployed from the Tyne was registered in ports on the east coast, and this figure rises to a remarkable 97 per cent if London is included. Ships from the north-east's own 'coal ports' were by far the largest component in this English mercantile fleet, contributing nearly two-thirds of its tonnage capacity. Theirs was an amazingly parochial contribution too, for nearly 90 per cent of the 'coal port' tonnage originated from the Tyne's own ports of registry (Newcastle, South Shields and North Shields), whilst vessels from its nearby competitors, the rivers Wear and Tees, barely figured at all.

Although the deployment of particular ships within the various national carrying fleets may now appear a randomly complex matter – as a consequence of the hundreds of vessels and dozens of destinations involved – upon analysis it becomes clear that there was an underlying rationale for, in terms of the routes they served, individual ships can be seen to have behaved much in accordance with their territorial origins. Put simply, English shipping concentrated on the important Russian coal route to Cronstadt and, to a lesser extent, onwards to St. Petersburg itself (indeed, English-owned ships only rarely involved themselves with other areas, Russian or non-Russian). Prussian ships, meanwhile, acted almost without exception as general 'national carriers', restricting their trading activities largely to their own Prussian ports, whilst the ships of the (much smaller) Russian fleet exhibited near-exclusive national tendencies too. Conversely, the Danes, Scots and Dutch were trading to regions out-with their own territories and thus, not surprisingly, acted far more independently of national bias, taking up established roles in a variety of generalist or specialist 'cross trades'. For example, Dutch ships (which mostly looked to freight timber home) were prominent in the specialist carriage of chemicals outward from Tyneside to Russia.

However, irrespective of size, character and origin, no carrier could ignore the immutable logic of the Baltic's climate. The trade was a rigorously confined seasonal business, and one of unpredictable annual variations too. Generally, ships might leave the Tyne in early March and then the trade would continue through (if desired) until mid-autumn when, to avoid the risk of costly over-wintering, British vessels made sure that they left the upper Gulf ports before the ice set in there or in The Sound; few British masters would risk reaching the Kattegat after mid-December.

Such seasonality did not, however, result in a single cycle of supply and demand (see Table 7 below). Instead, activities were phased, with tonnage leaving the Tyne for the Baltic in three distinct waves: the first commencing in early March and peaking in April, the second reaching its climacteric in July, whilst the third (and least prominent) emerged in October. In the intervening periods, from May to June and August to September, there was a considerable reduction in sailings - probably because the greater part of the available tonnage was already deployed. Naturally, coal exports themselves reflected this tonnage commitment pattern, but coal volumes fell more steeply in the troughs of the cycles when, broadly speaking, it seems that shipments of goods other than coal helped occupy cargo space.

Although it is a commonplace to speak of all the above as the 'Baltic Trade', it seems that for the individual ship operator it was not regarded as a dedicated trade as such, but only as one component within a much broader annual pattern. The intermittent character of such engagements is supported by a close analysis of the outward Baltic sailings (1,350) from the Tyne in 1861. Considerably less than one in ten of the ships engaged could be considered as 'constant traders', whilst less than two in ten of those employed by the major fleets made even two outward sailings. Overall, some two-thirds of all sailings from the Tyne to the Baltic were undertaken by ships that made only a single outward trip during the year. This last fact, the general singularity of participation, highlights the question that has been raised as to whether such outward, coal-carrying trips were profitable ones.

In the absence of contemporary voyage accounts, analysis of the Bills of Entry can at least help provide a guide as to the balance of probabilities. There is little or no evidence for the mere ballasting or part-loading of outward bound ships: full (or even excessive) loading was the norm. This would seem suggestive of anticipated profits through either sales or freight, or by a combination of both. The stowage factors routinely achieved in practice were some 6 per cent above those cited in contemporary manuals such as Stephens,[20] and this seems to have offered opportunities to enhance revenue earning. Indeed, if the relatively small ships of the non-English fleets (which totaled by far the greatest number of ships engaged) considered the outward trip worthwhile, then surely their larger and more efficient English competitors will have done so too? Economies of scale alone dictated that a 250-ton English ship carried two and a half times as much coal per man as did its well-run 100-ton Dutch counterpart.

Analysis of data, on a port-by-port and month-by-month basis of actual exports achieved and freight rates offered (Table 3), also makes it possible to estimate the earnings opportunities offered by the major ports within the Baltic, and the results thus obtained probably help explain, for instance, the strong attraction of Cronstadt for English shipping.

Table 3: *Earnings Opportunities for Coal Shipment to the Five Highest Ranking Ports, 1861*

	Exports (Keels)	% of Total Exported	Freight Value (£)	% of Freights Earned
Cronstadt	4891	44%	65349	53%
Stettin	1876	17%	20072	16%
Swinemünde	2002	18%	18534	15%
Kiel	591	5%	6107	5%
Riga	705	6%	5066	4%

Calculated from *Newcastle Bill of Entry and Shipping List*, 1861, 'Exports', together with monthly sampling of freight rates quoted in *Newcastle Daily Journal*, 1861 (note - 1 Keel equals 21.2 tons)

---

[20] R.W. Stephens, *On the Stowage of Ships and their Cargoes* (London, 1863).

Similarly, it has been possible to use these actual export figures and the freights on local offer to calculate a destination-weighted, pan-Baltic mean freight rate, which, at 9.7 shillings per ton, correlates closely with Fischer's more theoretically derived series giving 10.4 shillings per ton – a level at which his calculations suggested that in 1863 British sailing vessels would have returned an acceptable 6 per cent excess of revenue over marginal costs.[21] But only twenty years later, by 1880, the comfortable situation which had obtained for British sailing vessels within the Baltic had completely disappeared.

Outward Trade and Shipping in 1880

By 1880, the Tyne's exports of coal products to the Baltic stood at some 899,000 tons, a near three-fold increase over the figure of 1861. Naturally, the river's gross foreign-going trade had grown correspondingly too, but the Baltic's share of this had also increased, standing at 20 per cent compared with the 15-17 per cent of twenty years before. Such figures of course represent secular growths rather than a single smoothly progressive change. Russia now accounted for 68 per cent (as against 43 per cent formerly) of the Baltic's total coal imports, and this import activity had become ever more concentrated, for just seven ports now absorbed nine-tenths of all Baltic-bound coal. Cronstadt had enhanced its previously dominant position even further, its share having risen from a third to almost a half, and it received ten times more (industrially-important) coke than any other port. Similarly, Swinemünde, was still the second ranking port – continuing to realise a near 15 per cent share – whilst a group of third-rank ports comprising Riga, Stettin (town), and Newfairwater with Danzig, accounted for 5 per cent to 7 per cent each. But these latter were now joined by a new entrant at this level, Reval (Tallinn).

Even more striking than the expansion in coal had been that in chemicals for, with the Tyne's chemical exports to the Baltic standing at over 36,500 tons in 1880 (and even 41,000 tons in 1879), this branch of trade had seen a greater than four-fold growth since 1861. However, the Baltic's take-up of the Tyne's global chemical exports had remained static, at approximately 30 per cent, whilst Russia's share of intra-Baltic demand had fallen by over 10 per cent. This relative decline resulted from the fact that – as with coal – there had been a significant change of import destination, but with the shift in chemicals taking place westwards rather than eastwards. Stettin, and not St. Petersburg, now dominated the chemicals market, taking some 13,500 tons (37 per cent of

---

[21] Fischer, 'Flotilla of Wood and Coal', pp. 52-5.

imports), an amount which totaled more than twice that of the new second and third-ranking chemical ports, Danzig and Riga. St. Petersburg and Cronstadt now accounted for only some 5,500 tons between them whilst, further westward, Königsberg and Reval had each risen to positions where they sustained 3,000-ton import levels.

Apart from coal and chemicals, as Table 4 shows, there was a marked continuity in the other principal commodities exported, although with considerable expansion in volume.

Table 4: *Bulk Product Exports (tons), 1880*

Coal Products	Chemicals	Fertilizers	Earth Products	Iron, Lead, & Copper
889000	36641	4014	24496	36816

Compiled from *Newcastle Bill of Entry and Shipping List*, 1880, 'Exports' (note - Fertilizers comprise manure and superphosphate)

However, if such re-orientations indicated a marked change in trade since 1861, then the degree of change in shipping had been even greater. Of course, neither change occurred independently of the other – and the exact interplay of cause and effect still remains for discussion – but the most significant, and inescapable, factor by 1880 was the translation of the major part of the Baltic's carrying trade out of sail and into the holds of purpose-built steam ships. Although, at some 800 sailings each, the clearances from the Tyne to the Baltic by ships under sail and those propelled by steam were more or less equal in number, this superficial similarity belied a great disparity in effective capacity, for the resultant aggregate tonnage of steam far outweighed that of sail. In fact, rather than a directly proportional half, steamships actually contributed just over three-quarters of the total carrying capacity employed.

Most remarkably, British shipping operators effectively defined the composition of the whole 'fleet' of 1880, for British vessels contributed some three-fifths (59 per cent) of the entire total of 700,700 register tons engaged (Table 5). Most significantly, this British dominance had resulted from the overwhelming adoption of steam (and not from increased efficiencies in the use of sail) for only 3 per cent of this British operational total constituted sailing tonnage. By comparison, the new state of Germany – now the second rank nation – contributed almost a further fifth (19 per cent) of the entire Baltic-bound tonnage, although this German fleet was still heavily weighted towards sail, supplying some 12 per cent through sail and only 7 per cent through steam. Norway's rise up the national rankings to fourth place, clearly also relied upon the strength of its sailing fleet, which totaled over 5 per cent of the entire Baltic-bound fleet's tonnage (its steam contribution was less than 1 per cent). The

Swedes, however, had swung firmly towards steam, whilst the remaining minor participants, the Dutch and Russians, retained broadly two-thirds of their tonnage in sail.

Table 5: *Shipping Cleared Outwards by Place of Origin and Ship type (register tons), 1880*

	U. K.	Germany	Denmark	Norway	Russia	Sweden	Holland
steam	412057	54529	35515	6949	5901	13771	3936
sail	17007	78955	14424	27070	15226	6457	8909
total	429064	133484	49939	34019	21127	20288	12845

Compiled from *Newcastle Bill of Entry and Shipping List*, 1880, vessels 'Entered Outwards'

The great differential between the British and 'the rest' was also apparent in the size of the individual steamship units they employed. For the most part British ships were concentrated in a distinct 400 to 800 tons (register) band, extending upwards to include a significant group of 800 to 1000-tonners, and a scattering even at 1200 to 1400 tons. The bulk of non-British steamers, however, lay within a more diffuse band with a much lower initial starting size (around 200 tons) and ships of over 800 tons were rare.

Given that Tyneside-registered ships had held the leading regional position in the English Baltic-going fleet in the sailing era, it might have been anticipated that, as acknowledged pioneers in the building of coal-carrying, iron screw steamers, such a regional advantage might have been accelerated or at least maintained.[22] It is not clear, however, that any such technological advantages had positive economic consequences for the north-east by 1880 in respect of the Baltic trade. Shipping owned in Hull and London had come to command that trade, for these two ports each deployed something like a quarter of the tonnage engaged. The ships of the other north-east 'coal ports' had also broken the old-established parochial pattern. West Hartlepool, with a tonnage share amounting to one-eighth, now lay in third ranking place, and was positioned above the Tyne's own fleet, whilst the newer, east coast Scottish ports, had also strengthened their standings.

---

[22] C.M. Palmer, 'On the construction of iron ships and the progress of iron shipbuilding', *The Industrial Resources of the Tyne, Wear and Tees* (London, 1864); R. Craig, *The Ship: Steam Tramps and Cargo Liners, 1850-1950* (London, 1980), pp. 5-17.

The failure of the Tyne's ship operators to respond to the Baltic opportunities generated in their own port during the 1860s and 1870s as yet remains unexplained, but may well have had much to do with the following factors: the difficulties of disposing of large numbers of ageing sailing vessels; an inability to realize more modern ownership patterns;[23] an unwillingness to raise new capital for shipping; and lastly, and more indefinably, the diversion of individual enterprise and capital into other entrepreneurial activities. Certainly the new breed of individualistic, larger-scale, north-eastern shipowners who began their rise to prominence in the late 1880s rapidly extended their horizons – both literally and metaphorically – to regions beyond the confines of the Baltic and its, perhaps, rather pedestrian financial returns and old-established operational ways.[24]

Change: 1861 to 1880

Having considered the marked differences in trade and shipping exhibited by the years 1861 and 1880, we now turn to the nature, emphasis and timing of the changes that had taken place over the intervening years. The Baltic element of the Tyne's coal export trade had generally followed the gross, global export trends of the port during the twenty or so years under discussion and, in sectoral terms, there had been a distinct rise in Baltic demand during the latter part of the 1870s. However, as a consequence of its unusual geographical and political environment, it is evident that the Baltic often proved a volatile marketplace, susceptible to factors that rapidly translated themselves into fluctuations against the secular trend. In this context exports to an important market division, 'Russia's Northern [principally Baltic] Ports', as defined in official annual statements, can act as a useful indicator in following and outlining change.

For example, on the political front, events surrounding Prussia's moves to annex Schleswig Holstein clearly halted growth in the years 1863-5, whilst trade was similarly stultified in the same manner in the late 1870s when the closure of the Black Sea during the Russo-Turkish war led Tyneside's shippers to fear that a blockade – and British naval action – might ensue within the Baltic itself.

---

[23] S.P.Ville, 'Patterns of Shipping Investment in the Port of Newcastle upon Tyne, 1750-1850', *Northern History* 25 (1989).

[24] G. Boyce, *Information, Mediation and Institutional Development: The Rise of Large-Scale Enterprise in British Shipping, 1870-1919* (Manchester, 1995); pp. 26-43; N.J. Robinson, *Stag Line and Joseph Robinson and Sons* (Kendal, 1984), pp. 5-7; W. Runciman, *Before the Mast and After* (London, 1924).

Commercially, there is some indication that macro-economic factors also triggered exaggerated swings in the Baltic trades as, for instance, in 1872-73 when the onset of the so-called 'Great Depression' was marked by a particularly severe contraction of Baltic demand.

This last event, occurring as it did in the early 1870s, is of particular interest for, paradoxically, it seems to have coincided with a major transformation in the technology of the Baltic carrying trades – the penultimate shift from sail to steam. Although as a trading area the Baltic had initially been unattractive to British steam shipping, it has been well demonstrated by Pearsall that the region was in fact subjected to a lengthy exposure to its potential.[25] By the late 1840s, regular paddle steamer services were in place from London and Hull to the (then) only commercially viable destination, St. Petersburg. Though curbed briefly by the 'Crimean War'- whose urgent transport needs actually helped confirm the efficacy of steam in Baltic waters - and Hull's competitive and individualistic shipowners subsequently renewed their penetration of the Baltic with a new technology: the iron screw steamer.

Such expansion, though, barely touched the Tyne. Of the 173 arrivals of British steamers at Cronstadt and St. Petersburg in 1861 only seven originated from the Tyne, and these represented the total scheduled sailings of two new 750-ton Sunderland-owned steamers, the *Deptford* and the *Southwick*, carrying heavy machinery, cotton, general goods and – probably uneconomically – coal. Seemingly, the Baltic venture was not successful, for this local 'Diamond Line' did not re-appear in the following year and its constituent ships were routed elsewhere. Although a few Baltic-bound steamers did continue to call into the Tyne, the river's main Baltic trade remained firmly in sail until 1865, in which year steam had still grown to little more than 4,000 tons out of a total of some 91,000 tons dispatched to Russia's Baltic ports.

However, 1865 did prove to be a turning point, for steam growth accelerated over the next three years, reaching nearly 50,000 tons in 1868. Then, early in 1869, two major steam shipping companies operating from Hull – Bailey & Leethams and Wilsons – entered the Tyne with aggressively-promoted scheduled sailings which, it seems, had the capture of the Stettin trade as their primary objective.[26] The immediate outcome seems to have been decided in Wilsons'

[25] A. Pearsall, 'British Steamships in the Baltic, 1820-1870', in Kaukianen (ed.), *The Baltic as a Trade Road*, pp. 136-56; D.J. Starkey, 'Ownership Structures in the British Shipping Industry: The Case of Hull, 1820-1916', *International Journal of Maritime History* 8 (1996), pp. 83-86.

[26] A. Credland and R. Greenwood, *Bailey and Leetham* (forthcoming); J. Harrower, *Wilson Line* (Gravesend, 1998).

favour, for Baileys withdrew their advertising within a few months, although they continued to retain a significant operational agency in Newcastle. Interestingly, this external competition was of no immediate benefit to the port of Tyne, for its steam clearances actually fell in 1869, although they recovered thereafter.

Indeed, as demonstrated by Pearsall, there was now something of a hiatus in steam cargo carriage to the Baltic, and this seems to have been especially true for the carriage from the Tyne. There, sampling suggests, the proportion of steam tonnage rose by only a meagre amount before the early 1870s, and the indications are that as a provider it lagged behind the main trends in Baltic-bound steam tonnage.

Table 6: *The Introduction of Steam-Powered Shipping into the Trade from the Tyne to 'Russia's Northern (Baltic) Ports', 1865-1880*

Sample Year	1865	1868	1869	1870	1871	1873	1876	1878	1880
Steam tonnage	4155	49648	32709	94063	111797	79349	215815	221232	354628
Total tonnage	90983	179610	179501	256063	281269	182894	334122	346883	481344
% in steam	5%	28%	18%	37%	40%	43%	65%	64%	74%

Compiled from: *Annual Statement of Trade and Navigation*, 1865-1870; Annual Statement of Trade of the United Kingdom, 1871-1875; *Annual Statement of Navigation and Shipping*, 1876-1880. Supplemented by sampling from *Newcastle Bill of Entry and Shipping List*, 1865-1880, vessels 'Entered Outwards'.

Depressed trading conditions may explain this lethargy in part, but the full picture is not yet clear, and such a lack-lustre period makes the rapid expansion of steam over the ensuing few years seem even more remarkable. Undoubtedly the arrival of dedicated 'tramp' steamers and short sea traders, with their much superior compound engines, improved hatches, more accessible holds, provisions for deck stowage, and faster cargo handling, then played a significant part.[27] But, even so, it is not altogether certain whether it was such new-built tonnage, rather than older (if upgraded) vessels, which actually drove the expansion that led to British shipping's dominance in the Baltic in the early 1880s. Further analysis will certainly be required in order to ascertain what exactly was the case in respect of the Tyne's own outgoing Baltic trade.

One thing, however, can be said with certainty about the introduction of the purpose-built, cargo-carrying steam ship into the Baltic. It was the tool which

---

[27] J.A. MacRae and C.V. Waine, *The Steam Collier Fleets* (Wolverhampton, 1990), pp. 124-128.

was successfully used to break the multi-cyclical seasonal supply chain, a feature of the Baltic trades which had bedeviled outward traffic throughout the era of sail.

Table 7: *Tonnage Supply Comparisons, 1861 and 1880: totals (register tons) and seasonal patterns*

	Jan	Feb	Mar	Apr	May	Jun	Jul	Aug	Sep	Oct	Nov	Dec
1861 (tons)	816	3282	13439	34040	26323	26312	42348	19559	20066	28377	7946	1016
% per month	0%	1%	6%	15%	12%	12%	19%	9%	9%	13%	4%	0%
1880 (tons)	6103	6102	48270	69878	96066	112103	115410	88680	80265	48311	22615	9715
% per month	1%	1%	7%	10%	14%	16%	16%	13%	11%	7%	3%	1%

Compiled from *Newcastle Bill of Entry and Shipping List*, 1880, vessels 'Entered Outwards'.

Similarly, in the Baltic trades as elsewhere, such steamers were the vessels which introduced the concept of the scheduled general imports carrier, the 'liner', as distinct from the more occasionally chartered carrier of general import goods. In this last respect, though, it must be recognised that the sailing ships of the non-British nations continued to provide an essential, parallel niche service well into the era of dominance by steam, providing a complementary – if not always competitive – role and function.[28]

Conclusion

This paper represents work in progress, but it does seem possible to answer at least some of the questions addressed above. Although necessarily limited to a regional context, it is hoped that the findings outlined may contribute towards the overall study of shipping and trade between Britain and the Baltic. Quantitative determinations made from primary sources uphold the prior, qualitative impression that the area of the Baltic previously delineated (from Kiel to Åbo) formed a coherent trading region in the late nineteenth century. This

---

[28] Y. Kaukianen, 'The Profitability of Sail and Steam in the Baltic: Finland', in Kaukianen (ed.), *The Baltic as a Trade Road*, pp. 167-203.

trading region was both recognizable at the time and, in the historical context, can be seen to have enjoyed sectoral importance within the development of the Tyne's foreign-going coal trade.

A detailed, port-by-port, analysis suggests that British sailing ships deployed from the Tyne in 1861 were anticipating significant revenues on the outward (coal-laden) as well as the inward (timber-carrying) legs of their voyages, thus supporting Fischer's contention that engagement in the Baltic trades represented a genuine 'joint producer' activity for the shipowners concerned. However, an equivalent regional analysis has yet to be performed for the steamship era.

Upon close examination it is clear that although coal did indeed dominate the Tyne's Baltic-bound exports throughout the period under review, the resultant export pattern was not as monolithic and undifferentiated as has been previously represented, for it also comprised identifiable sub-trades which were exploited to the benefit of both trading partners. Even during the early part of the era, when sail was still ascendant, the ready availability of outward-bound shipping can be held to have encouraged the consignment of products which Tyneside's own industries were uniquely positioned to supply. Such products had values, end-user functions and growth potential which stimulated demand outside the framework of coal and which provided, in due course, a core of general traffic upon which steam cargo-liner operations might gain momentum.

That the Port of Tyne's apparently well-placed, long-established maritime 'interests' do not themselves appear to have participated more fully in this later, steamship-based period of expansion of trade with the Baltic is one of the more surprising results of the present study, and it is certainly a feature which merits further investigation. Indeed, such a Baltic-focused investigation would help to illuminate the broader patterns of change which were then occurring in local ship ownership and deployment.

Chapter 12

Great Britain and the Baltic 1890-1914

Andrew Lambert

This chapter will consider the role of the Baltic in British security policy between 1890 and 1914, with particular emphasis on the period 1904-1906. It will contend that the offensive strategic opportunities offered by the Baltic were the key to British attempts to maintain the peace and stability of Europe down to 1914. British deterrence of Germany, based on the threat to her Baltic trade, bases and coast, was the key to maintaining the European status quo.

World power

Between 1815 and 1914 the security policy of the British Empire was based on deterrence. Deterrence is an attempt to manipulate behaviour through the threat of harm.[1] While it is a relatively crude form of politics, and relies on those who are to be deterred acting rationally, it has been a major tool for national security policy since the formation of states. As a unique, satiated, global trading empire Britain desired nothing more than to be left in peace to expand her commercial opportunities. Having no significant territorial ambitions, she preferred to rely on her overwhelmingly powerful fleet to secure her role in world politics. The fleet controlled access to the extra-European world, and posed a series of strategic problems for every other major power that made it the most important power-political instrument of the age. The basis of British deterrence was accurate

---

[1] See: P. Morgan, *Deterrence: A Conceptual Analysis.* (London, 1977) esp. pp. 9-10.

signalling of political intent, clear demonstrations that the body politic was united and the mobilisation of the fleet. The threat posed was not the mutual annihilation of the modern age, but the inevitability of defeat, after a long drawn out war of economic attrition and limited direct contact in a war that only Britain could win. Furthermore, any state that went to war with Britain had to recognise that her other rivals would soon exploit the opportunity to secure political or territorial concessions. France was relatively easily deterred between 1840 and 1898, by the twin threat of a British fleet and a German army. Russia and the United States, for all their continental mass, and internal self-sufficiency, were also unwilling to take the risk. Russia learnt the hard way in 1854-6, the United States was wiser in 1861.

British policy towards Europe was dominated by a reluctance to enter into binding political commitments. By maintaining her 'free hand' Britain could use her influence to sustain the balance and avert war. The key to this semi-detached role was unquestioned naval mastery, which required a fleet equal to the next two powers. Powers that wished to exert influence over Britain attempted to restrict her naval pre-eminence, through sustained battleship building programmes. However, the British response was invariably to meet and overwhelm the rival fleet with a sustained arms race, as an alternative to war.

British security architecture was based on the experience of the Revolutionary and Napoleonic Wars, as developed in the light of recent experience, new technology and the shifting balances of European politics. Its success must be judged by results. Between 1815 and 1914 Britain went to war with a major power on only one occasion, and that was an aberration. Throughout the century she secured her aims by deterrence, arms races and skilful diplomacy. In this context the role of particular regions could rise and fall, as old enemies faded away, and new combinations arose, but the one theatre that remained of vital concern throughout the nineteenth century was the Baltic. Unlike other major powers Britain had the strategic flexibility to apply her power where her rivals were most vulnerable, rather than trying to meet them at their chosen point of attack.

The Baltic in British strategy

The Baltic was of critical importance to Britain as a strategic theatre for naval operations between 1815 and 1890.[2] While the likely enemy was Russia, and the

---

[2] Lambert, A.D. 'Part of a long line of Circumvallation to confine the future expansion of Russia: Great Britain and the Baltic, 1809-1890' in G. Rystad, H. Böhme and W. Carlgren (eds.), *In Quest of Trade and Security: The Baltic in Power Politics, 1500-1900* (Lund, 1994), pp. 297-334.

Scandinavian powers remained neutral, there was no reason why the British could not take control of the sea, impose a blockade, and develop offensive plans. The theatre was given added importance by the lack of alternatives: quite simply, Britain could not reach Russia's vitals anywhere else, making operations in the Gulf of Finland the inevitable response to Russian action in Central Asia, the Balkans or the Far East. Although British statesmen and army commanders tended to talk down the chances of success in this theatre, and naval officers rarely discussed the offensive element in British naval policy, there could be no other explanation for the maintenance of an overwhelming naval force, which was largely configured for offensive operations in coastal waters. If the policy makers between 1865 and 1890 did not think such operations were likely, then their procurement policy, the acid test of strategy, was simply incredible.

Most commentators argue that the ability of the Royal Navy to take the offensive between 1890 and 1905 was compromised by the general rise of naval force around the world, and in particular by the rapid reconstruction of the Russian fleet, as an ally of France from 1894. In fact an early assault on French naval bases, both metropolitan and colonial, remained central to British naval planning down to the entente of 1904. Russian bases were harder to reach, and would have had to wait until the French fleet had been destroyed. There would be little need to plan for Baltic operations in this scenario, as they depended on the successful outcome of the first offensive against France. Even so, Tsar Nicholas II recognised the danger and between 1903 and 1908, with German support, repeatedly attempted to close the Baltic to British warships. That support reflected deep-rooted German fears for their Baltic coast and trade.[3]

The events of 1904-5 returned the Baltic to the forefront of British strategy. For the first time since 1894 it appeared probable that the Baltic would be the theatre for large-scale operations against the leading European power at the outbreak of war. This paper will assess the importance of the Baltic in British thinking during the First Moroccan Crisis. It will argue that the Baltic was a vital strategic theatre, providing the only realistic opportunity to deter a German attack on France, within the context of the wider British policy of resisting German hegemonic ambitions. In order to reach a balanced appreciation of the place of the Baltic in British policy it will be necessary to assess the German perception. For too long historians have uncritically accepted the view of the British Army given at the Committee of Imperial Defence in August 1911. It must be recalled that when the Chief of the Imperial General Staff dismissed the

---

[3] Norman Rich, *Friedrich von Holstein: Politics and Diplomacy in the Era of Bismarck and Wilhelm II*, (2 vols., Cambridge, 1965), vol. II, p. 679 for 1903.

possibility of combined operations on the German coast, and called the naval plans 'madness', he was fighting the Admiralty for an increased share of the defence budget and claiming that the army was now the first service in British defence policy.[4] The Army was hardly disinterested, and its analysis was dominated by the fear of being placed under the Admiralty, an inevitable consequence of the large-scale amphibious operations in a maritime context that the Navy was proposing. For the Army, subordination to the French Army was preferable to falling under naval control.

The German challenge

British interest in the Baltic was revived by the need to counter the increasingly ambitious policy of Imperial Germany, and given a particular focus by the German decision to build a large battlefleet-based Navy. From 1897 Tirpitz made it clear that the new fleet was being built up as a direct challenge to Britain's freedom of action in European politics. Tirpitz wanted to create a battlefleet of such strength that it would hold the balance between Britain and the Franco-Russian alliance, depriving Britain of her 'free hand' in Europe, the position she had used to thwart the Kaiser's blustering efforts to secure Germany's 'place in the sun'. The Germans presumed that long- running colonial rivalries between Britain and the Franco-Russian alliance would preclude any meaningful rapprochement. On this basis they calculated on bargaining their way to an empire. However, the Tirpitz plan drew attention to Germany's ultimate ambition, in a manner guaranteed to annoy Britain.[5]

The ambitious Tirpitz plan required a complete change of German naval thinking, for the original impulse for a German fleet had been defensive. While the Kiel Canal had enhanced the ability of the fleet to conduct this defensive role, the Baltic coast and shipping remained a glaring weakness, and only escaped a serious attack in 1870 because the German army was able to destroy Imperial France in little more than a month. In 1900 the Imperial Navy war game culminated in a British assault on the fleet at Cuxhaven. The German fleet was annihilated.[6] This result, repeated in 1903[7], would have a powerful impact on German thinking.

---

[4] 114th Meeting of the CID, 23 August 1911, CAB/2, Public Record Office, London (PRO). All subsequent archival references are to materials from the PRO.

[5] Paul M. Kennedy, *The Rise of the Anglo-German Antagonism 1860-1914* (London, 1980), p. 266.

[6] Ivo N. Lambi, *The Navy and German Power Politics 1862-1914* (London, 1984), esp. p. 215.

[7] Report on German naval manoeuvres, February 1904, No. 719 ADM 231/40.

The British response

By early 1904 many in Britain recognised the threat posed by the German fleet, notably Lord Selborne, First Lord of the Admiralty.[8] Others were seeking defence economies through improved relations with France, and possibly Russia.[9] These two strands of policy were harmonised by Selborne's appointment of Admiral Sir John Fisher as First Sea Lord in October 1904. Fisher would oversee the effective British response to the German Navy. Appointed to increase efficiency, save money and improve Britain's naval position, Fisher would ultimately harness every aspect of his programme to defeat the German challenge, without recourse to war. However, the basic aim had been to improve the Royal Navy against all comers, Germany happened to be the only nation to challenge Britain at sea. The Conservative Government had begun the process with the Anglo-Japanese Alliance of 1902, which reduced the need for naval forces in the Far East, and focused on the threat of France and Russia. Subsequently this movement was described by Kipling, in typically Edwardian Imperial hyperbole, as a response to the 'barbarians thundering at the gates', leaving no doubt that the 'barbarians' in question were 'Huns'. The allusion was clear to Tirpitz.[10]

In July 1904, three months before he took office, Fisher outlined his integrated reform package, 'the scheme', under a typically biblical motto:

ORGANISATION FOR WAR;
IF THE TRUMPET SHALL GIVE AN UNCERTAIN SOUND,
WHO SHALL PREPARE HIMSELF TO THE BATTLE.[11]

His aim was to produce a more powerful Royal Navy without increased expenditure. This would secure British interests, primarily peace and stability in Europe. In the event Fisher's strategic redistribution took place after the diplomatic pattern of the European state system had been transformed by the signing of the Anglo-French Entente of April 1904. The Conservative ministers recognised that they had to settle their colonial differences with France, and

---

[8] Admiral Sir G.A. Willes to Selborne, 27 December 1903, and Selborne Cabinet Memorandum 26 February 1904, in D.G. Boyce (ed.), *The Crisis of British Power: The Imperial and Naval papers of the 2nd Earl of Selborne* (London, 1990) pp. 166, 170-2.

[9] Kennedy, *Anglo-German Antagonism*, p. 266.

[10] A. von Tirpitz, *My Memories* (2 vols., London, 1919), vol. I, pp. 186-7. 'The Rowers' evidently got under the Grand Admiral's skin.

[11] R.F. Mackay, *Fisher of Kilverstone* (Oxford, 1973), pp. 310-11.

possibly Russia, in order to support the Dual Alliance against the fundamental threat of German hegemony. It should be emphasised that the Entente was a temporary alignment, to prop up the Franco-Russian bloc, which was temporarily weakened by the war in the Far East. Unless Britain intervened there was a real danger that France would be bullied by Germany, removing the last check on the Kaiser's ambition.

Copenhagen revisited

In order to support her new entente partner, Britain needed a strategy that could hurt Germany. This strategy would have to build on Britain's command of the sea, the basis of her own security policy, and enable her to uphold the European balance against potential hegemonic states. The preferred British policy was to secure these aims through the possession of a powerful deterrent. For this role the Royal Navy needed to be reinforced by the 'projectile' of an amphibious army.[12] To be an effective deterrent the Royal Navy had to be overwhelmingly superior to any conceivable enemy, and possess the capability to inflict unacceptable damage. To be a credible deterrent the Navy needed an offensive strategy that was taken seriously by Germany.

In his discussions with the German delegates at the Hague Peace Conference in 1899 Fisher noted their concern for the Baltic coasts and trade. To exploit this concern he developed his concept that the Army should become an amphibious force to threaten the naval bases and coasts of hostile states. While the point was universally applicable, it was of particular importance against Germany, as Britain had no alternative means of exerting influence. Fisher's Baltic, 'Copenhagen' and amphibious plans were all variations on the theme of finding the most vulnerable point and applying superior force as the basis of deterrence.[13] To support his programme he would reform the Navy, and take control of the Army. The Army would be cut to provide the defence economies the politicians required, and transformed into an amphibious auxiliary for the Fleet.[14] Initially Fisher's work was directed against the Franco-Russian alliance,

---

[12] Fisher's attempts to get the Army to sea for joint exercises in 1903-04, while C-in-C Portsmouth, were consistently vetoed by the Army Council, which was terrified that his ideas would be taken up after their Indian frontier and invasion bogeys had been exploded. See Lord Fisher, *Memories* (London, 1919), pp. 166-8.

[13] Mackay, *Fisher*, pp. 216-224.

[14] See Fisher to Lord Esher 19 November 1903: Fisher, *Memories*, pp. 166-8, at p.167.

and the first base he thought of 'Copenhagening' was Toulon, using submarines to 'ferret' the French ships out of harbour for the Royal Navy to destroy.[15]

Once in office Fisher used a combination of naval activity, calculated newspaper bluster and careful development to gain maximum advantage from German fears that Britain would launch a pre-emptive strike, and wipe out their fleet.[16] He quickly persuaded Lord Selborne, who told the Prime Minister on 26 December 1904: 'It is no use of paradox, nor said to shock. He meant it'.[17] However, given his underlying objectives, it may be that Fisher intended his King and the politicians to take him seriously – in order that they might convey this threat to the Germans with complete conviction. Effective deterrence requires a credible threat.

The Russo-Japanese War 1904-05

The Kaiser had hoped the Russo-Japanese War of 1904-05 would bring Russia into alliance with Germany, expecting that France would tamely follow her ally to create a continental anti-British alliance. Ironically, after Berlin had ruined French attempts at mediation, the war proved to be a disaster for German policy. The architects of *Weltpolitik*, Wilhelm, Chancellor Bülow, and Holstein overreached themselves.[18] In pushing their agenda the German leadership suffered a severe defeat in Europe, and did not obtain any of the colonial compensations that had been a key element in the domestic propaganda of *Weltpolitik*. This lesson would be brought home with a vengeance in the First Moroccan crisis.[19]

The Russo-Japanese war transformed the strategic landscape for Britain. It removed the visionary threat to India, which the Army had talked up for years.[20] It also improved the naval balance in Europe, wiping out the Russian Navy and covering the return of British battleships to home waters to facilitate Fisher's

---

[15] Mackay, *Fisher*, pp. 302-3, 314.

[16] He told the journalist J.A. Spender about his 'Copenhagen conversation with the King in late 1904: A.J. Marder (ed.), *Fear God and Dread Nought: The Correspondence of Admiral of the Fleet Lord Fisher of Kilverstone* (London, 1956), p. 20.

[17] Mackay, *Fisher*, p.319.

[18] Jonathan Steinberg, 'The Copenhagen Complex', *Journal of Contemporary History* 1 (1966), pp. 23-46 (p. 31).

[19] Rich, *Holstein* II, p. 682; Kennedy, *Anglo-German Antagonism*, p. 269.

[20] A. Friedberg, *The Weary Titan: Britain and the Experience of Relative Decline, 1895-1905* (Princeton, 1988), p.260, for Fisher's dismissal of the threat to India.

'Strategic redistribution' and 'nucleus crew' system. These two measures provided Fisher with a large number of modern warships in Home Ports, almost all of which were either in full commission, or manned by the essential core of officers and ratings, and therefore capable of being filled up from the naval barracks and proceeding to sea quickly.[21] This policy enabled Fisher to mobilise a fleet superior to the German Navy to meet the next crisis, and to do so quickly, without causing undue commotion in the dockyards. He was convinced that the first blow would be decisive, and was anxious that Britain should seize the initiative at sea. The first trial mobilisation occurred in January 1905, using men brought home from overseas stations when many old and weak ships were paid off.[22] The reserve ships joined the Channel Fleet immediately, and took a full part in exercises. The value of the nucleus crew system was driven home by the Civil Lord of the Admiralty, Arthur Lee. In a speech delivered on 3 February 1905 Lee spoke of the Royal Navy getting its blow in first, a scarcely veiled hint to Germany that the fleet at sea was ready, and that recent experience at Port Arthur showed that such operations were well within the bounds of practical politics. Fisher always intended to attack at the outbreak of war, with the available forces, to secure maximum surprise.[23] Little wonder that the Kaiser exploded, demanding a public apology from the British ambassador.[24] However, as the Director of Naval Intelligence (DNI) minuted in early June 1905, British policy was to support France, without threatening Germany, and prepare for war quietly.[25]

Within three weeks the DNI had outlined the strategy for a war with Germany: blockade, coastal offensive operations and the movement of a fleet into the Baltic. He did not raise the specific issue of the Swedish iron ore trade, which would shortly become the target of British thinking. Admiral Sir Arthur Wilson, commanding the Channel Fleet, considered that only an amphibious operation in the Schleswig region, aimed at the German fleet, would create an adequate diversion of German forces from the French frontier.[26] In fact the German strategic situation in the event of a war with France and Britain was weaker than Wilson suspected.

---

[21] Marder, *Fear God and Dread* Nought, pp. 36-8.

[22] Mackay, *Fisher*, p.316.

[23] Ibid., p.320.

[24] Steinberg, 'Copenhagen Complex', esp. p.39.

[25] Marder *The Anatomy of British Sea Power: A History of British Naval Policy in the pre-Dreadnought era, 1880-1905* (London, 1964), pp. 499-500

[26] Ibid., pp. 500-506.

Germany deterred

Despite the early success of Tirpitz's naval policy, using colonial tensions to push through successive Naval Laws that increased the fleet, the Germans were convinced that they would have to traverse a 'danger period' in which Britain might use her superiority to wipe out their fledgling fleet. That the Germans should have thought in these crude, power-political terms when other navies had risen and fallen without the Royal Navy interfering, said more about the deep seated anxieties of the Wilhelmine Empire than about practical naval planning. German fears of a pre-emptive strike featured in their war plan of 1897, and several annual exercises thereafter.[27] In 1902 the German Navy League seized on rumours that such an attack was mooted in England to launch an major pamphlet offensive in Germany, which boosted League membership.[28] However, the scare-mongering became self-fulfilling. When war with Britain became a possibility, in 1904-05, the alarmism of the previous decade led to a genuine war scare, and exposed the deepest fears of the German Navy. In truth German policy-makers were guilty of 'mirror-imaging'. They contemplated 'Copenhagening' military rivals under similar circumstances,[29] and recognised the threat posed by their naval build up. They were also guilty of a poor historical understanding, for Germany, unlike weak, neutral Denmark in 1807, stood on the threshold of continental hegemony.[30] The prospect of German hegemony in Europe would force Britain to fight, because it would enable her to threaten British command of the sea.[31]

In October 1904 Fisher exploited the infamous 'Dogger Bank' incident to push through key elements of his 'scheme' under the cover of preparing for war with Russia. Moreover, he was not alone in placing the blame on the Kaiser. The German reaction to the incident was one of profound panic. If war broke out Germany, with no effective allies, had to expect British attacks on her trade, shipping, colonies and coasts.[32] Chancellor Bülow hurriedly prepared a German-Russian treaty for mutual defence. The Tsar, shaken by the speed and strength of the British response, kept the option open while there remained a danger that

---

[27] Steinberg, 'Copenhagen Complex', p. 28.

[28] P. Hislam, *The Admiralty of the Atlantic* (London, 1908), pp. 23-4.

[29] Kennedy, *Anglo-German Antagonism*, p. 275.

[30] Steinberg, 'Copenhagen Complex', pp. 43-5.

[31] Sir Edward Grey at the 11th Meeting of the CID, 26 May 1911, CAB/2.

[32] Kennedy, *Anglo-German Antagonism*, pp. 271-2.

the incident would result in war. Thereafter he insisted on telling France before he would sign, which Germany refused to allow.[33]

The 'Copenhagen' complex of October 1904 reflected real fears, and real activity on the other side of the North Sea. Not only was the annual German naval war-game a British attack, but the Germans then discovered the British were also war-gaming the scenario. The Kaiser was convinced, telling his Chancellor 'The preparations for mobilisation are going forward at high pressure, and the possibility of being attacked by an overwhelmingly superior force is imminent'. Bülow agreed that war with England was possible, and that such a conflict would allow Britain to destroy the German fleet, seize her colonies and ruin her trade. Germany could only strike back through Russia, and Russia showed little interest in any such plans.[34] The Kaiser responded by discussing the possibility of overrunning Denmark by land, to close the Baltic narrows. Under an Imperial order of 3 December 1904 work began on a new operations plan, but in February 1905 the Chief of the Great German General Staff, Graf von Schlieffen, reported that the army could not spare six divisions from the war plan.[35] The German Navy was forced to admit that it was utterly defenceless in the face of the determined British attack that was widely expected.[36] In consequence Germany was painfully aware of her weakness in this key sector even before the Moroccan crisis broke. This understanding would have a profound influence on the events of the summer of 1905, and explains the relatively low profile deterrent performance of the Royal Navy. In the interval German concern was sustained by alarming rhetoric and the movement of ships and squadrons. Britain had between two and three times the naval strength of Germany, even without the French fleet. While these figures demonstrate the massive British advantage, they do not adequately convey the superiority of individual British ships over their German contemporaries, which were smaller and less heavily armed; or the immense weight of tradition that bore down on any fleet that had to contemplate action with the Royal Navy. In alliance with France the advantage was simply overwhelming. To suggest that such a force would have been impotent to enter and control the Baltic, with Russian bases at hand, *and* keep the Heligoland Bight under control defies logic.

---

[33] Rich, *Holstein* II, p. 689.

[34] Ibid., pp. 689-90; quotation from Kaiser to Bülow, 29 November 1904, at p. 689.

[35] Kennedy, *Anglo-German Antagonism*, p. 274.

[36] Steinberg, 'Copenhagen Complex', pp. 32-7.

The First Moroccan Crisis, 1905

Significantly the first test of the new Entente system was generated by those sections of the German elite that were not intimately concerned with naval policy. German policy makers attacked one aspect of the entente, the settlement of Morocco, to attempt to divide the new partners, at a time when Russia was engaged in the Far East. From June 1904 Germany refused to accept that Morocco would fall to France, a programme that culminated with the blatant gesture of landing the Kaiser at Tangier in March 1905, where he offered his support to the Sultan, as an 'independent' sovereign. The object was to use this colonial issue to show France that Britain would not stand by her, just as Russia had failed her in 1898. At this stage Germany possessed significant military advantages over France, and Russia was effectively disabled by the war with Japan. Now, if ever, was the time to 'Copenhagen' the French army.[37] It is clear that Foreign Ministry Counsellor Holstein and Schlieffen were thinking about such a war.[38]

German pressure on France resulted in the removal of the French architect of the entente, Foreign Minister Delcassé, but British support for the French position in Morocco, although short of an alliance, was made clear to the Germans. Consequently Germany obtained no tangible reward. German power was countered with British power, and this proved highly effective, building on German concerns. Throughout the crisis the German Chancellor, Bülow, and his foreign policy adviser Holstein, complained that the British were preparing to attack them. Foreign Secretary Lord Lansdowne observed many years later that there was much 'loose talk in naval circles' but this was not serious.[39] Either Lansdowne had forgotten the events of 1904, or he was being deliberately disingenuous. In fact Fisher had written to Lansdowne in late April, urging him to recognise that he had a 'golden opportunity to fight the Germans in alliance with the French, so I earnestly hope you may be able to bring this about'. He went on to boast, 'We could have the German fleet, the Kiel Canal, and Schleswig-Holstein within a fortnight.[40] However, what Fisher did not discuss with his political masters, or his naval subordinates, was his conviction that the

---

[37] Rich, *Holstein* II, p. 696.

[38] Ibid., p. 697.

[39] G.P. Gooch & H. Temperley (eds.), *British Documents on the Origins of the War* vol. III (London, 1928), pp. 53-87, esp. pp. 56, 58, 73-8, 81, 87.

[40] Fisher to Lansdowne, 22 April 1905, in Marder, *Fear God and Dread Nought*, p.55.

Baltic was the key to deterring Germany. Threatening to send a fleet into the Baltic would play on deep- rooted fears.

Consequently Fisher used a planned summer cruise of the Channel Fleet into the Baltic to make his point in Berlin and Kiel. Leaving Spithead in mid-August 1905 the fleet called at Ymuiden in Holland, and then anchored in the Graa Diep off Esbjerg, a valuable anchorage for operations in the Heligoland Bight, and one eminently capable of being developed and secured. Admiral Wilson was instructed to be ready for a descent on the German Coast.[41] At the same time Fisher mobilised his newspaper allies, who produced a barrage of bellicose anti-German rhetoric. By playing on the 'Copenhagen Complex' of the German Navy he created a powerful diplomatic lever to restore the balance in Europe at a time when France stood almost alone, and key German decision-makers were seriously thinking about engineering a war. However, the gesture only worked because the Germans feared British operations in the Baltic. The key to successful deterrence is to build on the fears of the enemy. In large measure German ambitions in 1904-05 were defeated by British sea-based deterrence. Deterrence worked because it was built on real capabilities, and attacked known German fears. In this Fisher exploited his genius for public relations, making him the most efficient, as well as the most effective, First Sea Lord of the modern era.

Having failed to break the entente in 1905 Germany pinned her hopes on the Algeciras Conference, where Bülow sought a tangible reward for German acceptance of French control in Morocco. However, the Conference met in early 1906 under the guns of the combined British Mediterranean and Atlantic fleets, and resulted in the first major diplomatic defeat suffered by Imperial Germany. The new Liberal Foreign Secretary, Sir Edward Grey, saw the entente as the backbone of British security policy, and upheld it with vigour.[42] German policy failed because it had been inconsistent, opportunistic and ill co-ordinated. While the Germans had not sought a preventive war, they had risked one over an issue of minor importance to Berlin;[43] consequently they had been overpowered by the British, for whom the issues at stake were far more important.

Fritz Fischer argued that the German climbdown in 1905 was largely due to the reluctance of Tirpitz to risk the Navy.[44] After the crisis Tirpitz, who had

---

[41] E.E. Bradford, *Admiral of the Fleet Sir A.K. Wilson* (London, 1923), pp.199-201.

[42] Kennedy, *Anglo-German Antagonism*, p. 283.

[43] Rich, *Holstein* II, p. 745.

[44] Fritz Fischer, *War of Illusions: German Policies from 1911 to 1914.* (London, 1975) p. 56.

always opposed the use of naval resources for coast defence, reluctantly accepted the need to divert a large proportion of the naval budget to this area.[45] While the resulting improvements would make British offensive operations more difficult in the future, they also demonstrated how far German vulnerability had influenced the decisions of 1905. Tirpitz had been so alarmed that he did not dare use the events of 1904-05 to support his call for an enlarged battlefleet:

> such a shift in the *real power factors* that even a calm and rational English government *must* come to the decision to crush such an opponent before he had reached the military strength so dangerous for England's world position.[46]

There could be no clearer demonstration of the value of British naval deterrence. Fisher had quite literally stopped Tirpitz in his tracks with a succession of measures, culminating in the *Dreadnought*, that would have persuaded any rational regime to back down. Unfortunately Tirpitz and his Imperial master required a further demonstration of British power and political resolve.

Norway, the Baltic and British strategy

Mutual fear of British naval operations in the Baltic had already brought Russia and Germany to the brink of a new alliance in December 1903, when Germany offered Denmark a Russo-German guarantee of support in the event of a Russo-British war. This reflected German naval concerns.[47] The break up of the Union of Sweden and Norway in June 1905 brought the question of access to the Baltic to the top of the diplomatic agenda.[48] This issue reminded British diplomats that free access to the Baltic in time of war was of paramount importance for deterrence and war-fighting. The new King of Norway, Haakon VII, was Edward VII's son-in-law, and British influence was heavily used to further his candidacy. This alarmed the Kaiser, who saw malice in his uncle's every act. Wilhelm was convinced that Britain would secure dominant influence in Norway and use it to damage Germany, most obviously by securing an advanced

---

[45] Lambi, *Navy and German Power Politics*, p. 334.

[46] Kennedy, *Anglo-German Antagonism*, p. 286.

[47] Folke Lindberg, *Scandinavia in Great Power Politics, 1905-1908* (Stockholm, 1958), pp. 5-7. Rich, Holstein II, p. 679.

[48] Patrick Salmon, '"Between the Sea Power and the Land Power": Scandinavia and the Coming of the First World War', *Transactions of the Royal Historical Society, 6th Series*, 3 (1993), pp. 23-49, esp. pp. 28-33.

base for Baltic operations. The direct result of Wilhelm's alarm was impulsive personal diplomatic offensive that culminated in the Treaty of Björko, signed with the Tsar on board the Imperial yacht on 24 July 1905.

British influence in Norway was the key argument used to persuade the Tsar to enter an alliance the main purpose of which was to exclude British warships from the Baltic. In his dreams Wilhelm saw the new grouping attracting the support of all the minor powers of Scandinavia and Northern Europe. However, when Wilhelm moved to close the Baltic, by bringing Denmark into the partnership, he discovered that Danish opinion was hostile, while the British were already aware of his scheme. On 2 August he had to tell the Tsar that he could not press the case in Copenhagen.[49] Chancellor Bülow was not displeased: his Imperial Master had foolishly restricted the application of the treaty to Europe, leaving Germany exposed to British global power without being able to call on Russian resources in Asia. Bülow's insistence on re-negotiating the Treaty ended what little hope there had ever been of seeing it come into effect.[50]

In this first round of the struggle for access to the Baltic the British had won, and won relatively easily. The 'Copenhagen Complex' had been decisive, for the German fleet could not hope to resist a British attack, and their potential Russian allies did not have a fleet. British policy would uphold unrestricted access to the Baltic, and keep the Scandinavian nations from falling under the domination of Germany or Russia.

Fisher reminded the Germans of British naval power, and the speed with which his fleet could be mobilised, just as the Norwegian question came to the boil. A typical Fisher-inspired article in the *Fortnightly Review* of September 1905 drew attention to events of the summer in a way that could not be misinterpreted.[51] One of Fisher's tame publicists trumpeted:

> This huge assembly of fighting vessels completely demonstrated that the whole fighting force of the country is now ready to *strike at a moment's notice*, with its whole strength, officers and crew being familiar with their ships. The manoeuvres revealed that for the first time in the history of the British Navy the fleet had been organised so as to enable it, in case of war, *to strike first*, and to strike with all its power. The strength of a fleet consists not in the number of ships,

[49] Lindberg, *Scandinavia*, pp. 35-7.

[50] Rich, *Holstein* II, pp. 718, 728.

[51] P. Kemp (ed.), *The Fisher Papers* vol. II (London, 1964), pp. 301-14.

but in readiness to proceed to sea immediately, and fight instantly, on the declaration of war, *or before*. Only by these means can England be sure that she can act upon her traditional policy of making her enemy's shores her frontier, and thus crushing her foe, or foes, without interfering with the ordinary life of these islands, and the progress of commercial and industrial activity.

The new Channel fleet would 'cruise more frequently in the North Sea, and repeated incursions into Scandinavian waters will be made'. These would support British interests in the Baltic, sending an unequivocal, if unwelcome, signal to Germany.[52] This was the public face of deterrence; raw power touching a raw nerve.

The status of Norway remained an issue for the next three years, with the Foreign Secretary taking care that the final settlement, a four-power guarantee, did not affect the status of the Great Belt. When he reported his work to the Committee of Imperial Defence the DNI, in the absence of the First Lord and the First Sea Lord, asked for the issue to be held over. He did not want to see the neutrality and integrity of Norway guaranteed, because that would leave British strategy 'seriously handicapped'. His reasoning was clear: 'If the Germans occupied the Danish islands, it might be necessary for us to seize a Norwegian Port – say Christiansand.'[53] In March 1907 Fisher explained the rationale behind his strategy to Nansen, the Norwegian minister, while walking down Whitehall. If Germany occupied Denmark, as most people presumed she would, Britain would seize a Norwegian port, probably Christiansand, as a forward base to open the Baltic narrows. Nansen was not surprised by the tone and content of the conversation. When he asked if the Royal Navy could force the Great Belt, especially in the face of mines, Fisher observed that it was absolutely essential.[54] To guarantee the neutrality of Norway would give the other signatories of the Treaty *casus belli* if Britain acted in this way.

The following week Fisher accepted the Foreign Office position, but the Foreign Secretary, Sir Edward Grey, went on to stress that he preferred to uphold the integrity of Norway, not her neutrality.[55] Integrity would allow Britain to use a

---

[52] 'British Naval Policy and German Aspirations', *The Fortnightly Review*, September 1905, in Kemp, *Fisher Papers* II, pp. 301-10.

[53] 95th Meeting of the CID, 21 February 1907, CAB/2.

[54] Lindberg, *Scandinavia*, pp. 65-6 et seq.

[55] 96th and 97th Meetings 28 February, 25 April 1907, CAB/2.

Norwegian port without complications with the other Great Powers. British newspapers, which were all linked to Fisher, kept up the pressure to resist Russo-German Baltic plans, and a Scandinavian bloc. Grey used Treaty commitments from 1855 and 1856 and British trade interests to break up all attempts by Russia and Germany to exclude the Royal Navy from the Baltic. Although the diplomacy was tortuous, the Foreign Office maintained the basic aim of ensuring British access. German plans to close the Baltic to the warships of non-riparian powers were still being discussed with the Russians at Swinemünde in August 1907. However, the two Emperors did not dare to take such an overtly anti-British step, and by November the initiative had finally collapsed. Russian resistance crumbled after the Anglo-Russian entente of 1907 was concluded, and France was drawn into the question by Britain. In March 1908 the question was effectively settled.[56]

Baltic war plans

On coming to office Fisher had moved quickly to prepare the fleet for war. He wanted to seize the initiative at the outset with a full-scale offensive, to inflict the type of 'knock-out-blow' that dominated the thinking of contemporary strategists. These preparations did not need to be specific: they could be used against France, although she was already an entente partner, Russia, or most likely Germany. In late 1904 and 1905 Fisher began to work out the detail of his war plans, using the Director of Naval Intelligence and other picked officers to study particular aspects, from the use of hulks to block the German North Sea rivers to the impact of mines. These built on recent work in the DNI's department.[57] In 1906 Fisher directed a detailed investigation of the strategic issues involved in forcing the Baltic and wiping out the German fleet, leaving the execution of the work to his brightest thinkers, Captain George Ballard, Captain Edmond Slade, Captain Maurice Hankey RM and Julian Corbett. Their work appeared as the Admiralty War Plans of 1907. These were perfectly coherent and eminently practical, being based on the lessons of the Russo-Japanese War, about which the Royal Navy knew far more than the Germans.[58]

The Ballard plans set up a blockade, based on the Channel and the North Sea, and concentrated the modern battlefleet in the Humber. The war opened

---

[56] Lindberg, *Scandinavia*, pp. 67-275, for an excellent study of this process.

[57] Naval War College Strategical War Games, 1902-03: NID no.675, vol. 36, ADM 231/37.

[58] P. Towle, 'The Evaluation of the Experience of the Russo-Japanese War' in B.M. Ranft (ed.), *Technological Change and British Naval Policy, 1860-1939* (London, 1977), pp. 65-79.

with the large-scale use of old ships to block up the German rivers on the North Sea coast, at identified points at least ten miles from the shore. They then deployed the older battleships to seize the island of Borkum, as an advanced destroyer base to keep the Germans pinned into their harbours. This would allow the main fleet to sortie into the Baltic, complete the commercial blockade and attack the German ports. It was expected that the German fleet could be drawn out from Kiel to give battle. If not it would be attacked where it lay.[59] The 1908 War Plans included amphibious operations to secure Denmark, and attack the Kiel Canal.[60]

The key test of British war planning would be its value as a deterrent. In mid-1906, after the final failure of Germany's policy over Morocco at the Algeciras Conference, the British naval attaché collected and analysed the opinions of German newspapers on the role of their fleet in war. The consensus was that they should stand on the defensive, giving priority to closing the Baltic against the British. However, if the British entered Baltic their fleet would be 'as good as lost – at any rate helpless in Kiel'.[61] Another newspaper reasoned that the Royal Navy possessed superior numbers, organisation, position and command of cable communications and would open any war with a surprise attack, as Japan had in 1904. The strategic redistribution was seen to be aimed directly at Germany, while the scale and purpose of the latest British manoeuvres was unmistakable. The DNI minuted:

> This paper shows a very just appreciation ... of the true meaning of the recent reorganisation of the navy, and of the danger Germany will incur if she ever ventures to dispute the command of the sea with us.[62]

Although he had developed effective war plans against Germany, and used them to secure a major diplomatic success, Fisher's attempts to continue his strategic planning, and introduce a Naval Staff, were consistently thwarted by

---

[59] The 1907 War Plans are in Kemp, *Fisher Papers* II, pp. 316-468. Kemp is unduly reliant on hindsight in his criticism of these plans. At the time they were drawn up they were realistic, and reflected the lessons of the Russo-Japanese war. Admiralty interest in this war had far more to do with mines, torpedoes and offensive operations against fortified bases than long-range gun fire. The 1907 plans are also in ADM 116/1043B.

[60] ADM 116/1043B: see W3 Part One and Two. I am indebted to Shawn Grimes for the benefit of his advice and expertise on this subject.

[61] Report by Captain P. Dumas, 28 July 1906, in Kemp, *Fisher Papers* II, pp. 296-7.

[62] 'English War Manoeuvres in German Commercial Seas', *Dresdner Nachrichten* 5 February 1906, in Kemp, *Fisher Papers* II, pp. 297-301.

the attacks of Lord Charles Beresford, the Army and many in the Liberal Government that had come into office at the end of 1905. His maritime strategy was summarily rejected by the War Office and the General Staff, which concluded that Baltic operations had had no effect on the 'Crimean War'.[63] The adoption of a 'Continental Commitment', which gave the Army an elevated role in national policy, was the minimum level of military power that Britain could promise to secure the Entente, and with it the Anglo-Russian Entente of 1907. While these diplomatic relationships were the basis of British security policy, they could never be a realistic peacetime strategy to secure British interests.[64]

Economic warfare

The refusal of the Army to take part in maritime planning after 1905 forced the Navy to create a naval deterrent strategy. Fisher based this planning around the blockade as the one strategy that would bring the Germans to give battle. By 1908 the Admiralty Trade Division was satisfied that a blockade would have an intolerable effect on the German economy.[65] The DNI presented these conclusions to the First Lord as a paraphrase of Mahan's first *Seapower* volume. Where the American declared that Cromwell's battlefleet had, 'caused the grass to grow in the streets of Amsterdam', Vice-Admiral Charles Ottley the Director of Naval Intelligence, claimed, 'grass would sooner or later grow in the streets of Hamburg'.[66] Work on economic warfare had already informed the War Plans of 1906-7, while the Secretary of the Ballard Committee, Maurice Hankey, was convinced the blockade was a decisive strategy.[67]

A rigorous blockade of Germany would require the Royal Navy to operate in the Baltic, where it could cut German iron ore and food supplies from Sweden. The threat of such action would, if anything could, force the German fleet to come out and give battle.[68] Fisher understood that decisive battle could only be secured under favourable conditions by forcing the enemy to fight. Julian

---

[63] Donald Schurman, *Julian S. Corbett*, 1854-1922 (London, 1981), pp. 42-3; Lambert, 'Great Britain and the Baltic', pp. 346-7.

[64] Kennedy, *Anglo-German Antagonism*, p.280.

[65] Avner Offer, *The First World War: An Agrarian Interpretation* (Oxford, 1989), pp. 230-2.

[66] A.T. Mahan, *The Influence of Seapower upon History 1660 - 1783* (London, 1890), p.133; Ottley to McKenna, 5 December 1908, quoted in Offer, *First World War*, p. 232.

[67] Kemp, *Fisher Papers* II, pp. 316-7.

[68] Offer, *First World War*, pp. 250-51.

Corbett's studies demonstrated that this could be achieved by cutting the enemy's vital trade routes.[69] For Germany the only vital sea trade route was the supply of iron ore from Sweden across the Baltic. Unless this route could be threatened or cut there would be no decisive battle.

After Fisher left the Admiralty, in January 1910, his work on economic warfare and Baltic operations was ignored by his successor, Admiral Wilson. The Admiralty had a chance to put a blockade strategy into the heart of British policy at the August 1911 CID meeting, but Wilson wasted the opportunity. Because he did not believe in the blockade his August 1911 presentation to the CID lacked any intellectual rationale. His plans to attack Borkum, or Heligoland, were simple operational matters that ignored the softer, and more significant, target offered by the annual movement of 4.5 million tons of Swedish iron ore to Germany's Baltic ports. It was little wonder they were dismissed, along with their author.

Consequently work on economic warfare shifted to the Committee of Imperial Defence (CID), where it was directed by Hankey, with the support of Lord Esher. However, the value of blockade in wartime was far from clear. The 1909 Declaration of London, following the Declaration of Paris of 1856, made 'free ships – free goods' the basis of International Law.[70] The London Declaration provoked such an outcry that it was never ratified. Fisher, McKenna and Hankey saw blockade as a vital weapon for Britain and considered the Declaration a reckless weakening of this critical strategic instrument, but Fisher was confident the agreement, even if signed, would fail at the outbreak of war.[71] Hankey and Esher placed stringent economic warfare in the War Book in 1912.[72] By this time British naval power had once again been the key to deterring German aggression.

Agadir 1911

Germany exploited the Agadir Crisis to attack the political cohesion of the Triple Entente. However, Lloyd George exploited his Mansion House Speech to

---

[69] Schurman, *Corbett*, p. 67, referring to correspondence of March 1907 between Fisher and Corbett, resulting in the pamphlet Some Principles of Naval Warfare: ADM 116/1043B; Julian S. Corbett, *Some Principles of Maritime Strategy* (London 1911) (1988 edition, ed. E. Grove), p. xxiv; Kemp, *Fisher Papers* II, pp. 318-345. See more generally Schurman, *Corbett*, Chs. 3- 5.

[70] Bertrand Semmel, *Liberalism and Naval Strategy* (London, 1986).

[71] Ibid., pp. 118-9; Offer, *First World War*, pp. 270-84.

[72] Ibid., pp. 253-7.

give Germany a clear warning that Britain would not stand by and see France beaten. Tirpitz, with no viable operational plans against Britain, the Kiel Canal far from complete, way behind in the Dreadnought race and insecure even in the Heligoland Bight was easily deterred. He and his Imperial master 'yielded to the British threat'.[73] In December 1912 the German Government elected to prepare for war, but agreed to postpone the event for 12 to 18 months, so that Tirpitz could increase his defensive forces and complete the Kiel Canal. As the Chief of the General Staff, Moltke the Younger, quipped, the navy would never be ready.[74]

The Canal was vital to German strategy: until it was capable of carrying Dreadnoughts between the two German seas Berlin did not dare to launch a war. As soon as it was ready the First World War broke out. The two events were inextricably connected. Fisher understood this point, and made it the basis of his war planning. Consequently the Baltic remained the key to any serious offensive against the one sea route that was vital to Germany down to 1914, and Fisher still believed it could be used to force the High Seas Fleet to give battle. It has been customary to dismiss him as an outdated crank, and his schemes as impracticable, but Fisher knew what he was attempting, and unlike so many smaller men, was prepared to follow his ideas. For him the Baltic remained the decisive point for the application of British naval pressure on Germany.[75]

In view of the immense superiority of the Royal Navy in 1905 the only limits on offensive operations in the Baltic were coastal artillery, mines and torpedo craft: Germany had no submarines. The artillery could be avoided, unless Denmark fell into German hands, an act which would have been pregnant with wider diplomatic problems for Berlin. Torpedo craft would be neutralised by stronger British flotilla and cruiser forces, while the torpedo was still far from perfect. In the Russo-Japanese war, about which the Royal Navy was better informed than any other force, torpedoes had only hit stationary or crippled ships at short range, and even than had trouble sinking ancient Russian cruisers. Mines were the greatest danger, but Fisher saw them as the key to his offensive plans. In early 1905 DNI Charles Ottley proposed an offensive minefield to cover the Elbe, Weser and Jade to pin the Germans in their North Sea ports while the main British fleet pushed into the Baltic, and forced them to give

---

[73] Fischer, *War of Illusions*, p. 80.

[74] Ibid., p. 163, Lambi, *Navy and German Power Politics*, p. 383.

[75] His *Records* and *Memories*, along with Admiral Bacon's *Life* provide ample evidence of his continuing concern. The Admiralty file ADM 116/3454, concerned with his resignation, has yet more of his vigorously expressed views.

battle there in defence of their vital trade routes.[76] German mines would be cleared, as the Royal Navy was the world leader in mine counter-measures.

Fisher wanted to change the strategic position by adopting new weapons.[77] The purpose of Fisher's reforms was to release significant heavy forces for offensive operations against European rivals, initially France and subsequently Germany. He recognised that the widespread use of mines would turn the North Sea into a strategic dead zone, occupied only by submarines and flotilla craft, he and his successors failed to provide the mines, or suitable minelayers, deliberately removing both from pre-war estimates.[78] Plans for large-scale offensive minelaying were submitted in 1913, but Churchill, the only enthusiast, balked at the cost of 50,000 mines.[79] This was a missed opportunity, especially after Corbett's history of the Russo-Japanese War had demonstrated the strategic value of minefields.[80] The failure to invest in minelaying suggests that deterrence had a higher priority than the war-fighting capability on which it was based in pre-war policy. Although the two roles were closely connected, their relative priority affected procurement.

Conclusion

In assessing the relevance and value of the Baltic in British policy it is important to understand that Fisher's failure to match concepts to procurement reflected the fact that he was not seeking war, not the weakness of the concepts. Fisher, like all rational British policy-makers in the era, wanted to avoid war through the effective application of British power to support the status quo. His particular contribution was a unique insight into the mechanisms of deterrence, as part of his overall policy objective of securing the maximum value from a limited budget. His reforms produced a more efficient, effective and war-like fleet, one

---

[76] Submarine Automatic Mines: Naval Staff memo. by Ottley, DNI, 12 February 1905: ADM 116/866B.

[77] N. Lambert, 'Admiral Sir John Fisher and the concept of Flotilla Defence, 1904-1909' *Journal of Military History* (1995), pp. 639-60. N. Lambert, 'British Naval Policy, 1913-1914: Financial Limitation and Strategic Revolution', *Journal of Modern History* 67 (1995), pp. 595-626.

[78] Mackay, *Fisher*, pp. 374-8.

[79] A. Day, *The Admiralty Hydrographic Service: 1795 – 1919* (London, 1967), pp. 266-9, 326. A.J. Marder, *From the Dreadnought to Scapa Flow: The Royal Navy in the Fisher Era*, vol. 1, *The Road to War 1904 - 1914* (Oxford, 1961). p. 328.

[80] J.S. Corbett, *Maritime Operations in the Russo-Japanese War 1904 - 1905* (Restricted: vol. 1 printed 1914, vol. 2 1915; published 1995, Annapolis and Newport RI).

that had the capability to take the initiative at the outbreak of war, and impose itself on any enemy. Recognising that the Germans were very nervous about their Baltic coast and trade he ensured that his planning reflected this, and reinforced their concern with his alarming, apparently loose, talk about 'Copenhagen', and getting in the first blow.

In 1912 Fisher, now in retirement, explained his methods to Churchill, re-using the motto of the 1904 reforms. 'Don't imagine I'm warlike', he began, advocating the maintenance of a clearly superior fleet. 'So I do earnestly pray that the Government will not allow the Navy trumpet to give an uncertain sound, and the German then will not prepare himself for the battle'.[81] Unfortunately Churchill did not follow his advice; the Royal Navy played no part the diplomacy of July-August 1914. This failure to follow the usual pattern allowed the Kaiser to delude himself into thinking that Britain would not act.

In 1905 and 1911 the threat of British naval action in the Baltic had stabilised the European balance, avoiding the twin dangers of war and a hostile German-led Continental bloc that would destroy the Empire. The Baltic played a critical role in Fisher's naval policy, while his 'Copenhagen' and Baltic ideas were realistic, effective options which he deployed to preserve peace and defeat the naval challenge of Germany. These were the victories he sought. The efficacy of his strategic thinking in war is an altogether different question, although it is one on which there remains room for further study.

---

[81] Fisher to Churchill, 5 March 1912, in Marder, *Fear God and Dread Nought* II, p. 436.

Chapter 13

Baltic Lutheran and Anglican Dialogue 1900-50

Nicholas Hope

I wish to speak about what historians might consider an inconsequential subject: the steps taken towards Christian unity between the established Nordic Lutheran churches and the Anglican church in the first half of the twentieth century. A Lutheran German contribution was almost absent. A major reason, so some argued at the first 'Faith and Order' world conference held at Lausanne in August 1927, lay in weak Lutheran doctrinal teaching on the 'Church'; that since the Enlightenment especially, Lutheran German theology had concentrated on the abstract 'nature' (*Wesen*) of Christianity at the expense of the church universal.[1] After 1918, other reasons included an obsession amongst Lutheran German churchmen at international gatherings of colleagues with rectifying German war guilt, and the destruction of liberal by dialectical theology. However, what is both ironic and extraordinary, is precisely the rediscovery of Christian universality by representatives of the Anglican and Nordic Lutheran established churches in an ultra-nationalistic European half-century dominated by endemic social crisis and two world wars.

Hesitant exploratory talks between individual churchmen led to serious official dialogue and, in the interwar period, the establishment of a fragile framework of intercommunion which included two new Lutheran Latvian and

---

[1] J.F. Laun, *Die Konferenz von Lausanne: Berichte, Ergebnisse, Aufgaben* (Gotha, 1928), pp. 1-6.

Estonian republics. This rediscovery of the 'Church' was, however, accompanied by a massive setback. The new total states, atheist Soviet Russia and racialist Nazi Germany, almost destroyed it. Denmark and Norway were occupied by Nazi Germany (1940-5); Finland barely survived Soviet Russian occupation in 1939-40 and an ambiguous relationship with Nazi Germany thereafter; Latvia and Estonia experienced the brutal wartime occupation by both regimes and re-incorporation in Soviet Russia in 1945. Hence this paper's concentration on the interwar period. The landmarks, apart from intercommunion, were the Stockholm conference of 1925 on the urgent postwar issue of Christian 'Life and Work' convened almost single-handedly by the Swedish archbishop, Nathan Söderblom (1914-31), and the Anglican Oxford conference of 1937 on 'Church, Community, and State' which confronted, as the official report put it, the fundamental religious problem 'of the relation of the Church to the all-embracing claims of a communal life' made by new total states.[2] Progress between Stockholm and Oxford, put crudely, was from one led by bishops to one which included the voice of a modest sprinkling of lay experts, and from lofty postwar clerical ideals to a new professionalism in a bleak landscape of unemployment, social deprivation and belligerence suggesting a new war which many churchmen felt might annihilate western Christian civilisation.

The background to this new initiative was a deep sense of endangered church establishment. Rapid change since 1870, determined by the values of free enterprise and the urban-industrial community, questioned the validity of Anglican and Lutheran establishment, both as acceptable church order and as relevant moral teaching. If religion was considered at best a private matter by a new industrial working class and an entrepreneurial middle class, how did Protestant churchmen break out of such new enforced isolation at home? The Christian social Gospel might have to be thought out afresh. Questions of Christian faith and order and Christian life and work were the same coin.

Anglo-American initiatives

These were determined by the challenge of empire and Christian mission, meaning confrontation with a plural Afro-Asian world of churches and religions, and Christian youth fellowship visible as the spectacular growth of the YMCA and the SCM (Student Christian Movement). All of the first generation of English and Nordic ecumenists came from this background. Also, special to

---

[2]   J.H. Oldham (ed.), *The Churches survey their Task: The Report of the Conference at Oxford, July 1937: Church, Community, and State 8* (London, 1937), p. 9.

England and the Nordic countries around 1900, was the rapid advance, in a new urban-industrial landscape dominated by major free church, temperance, and labour popular movements, of Protestant associational churchmanship, expressed in the involvement of parishioners in parish meetings, parish outings, and social initiatives. Liberal individualism as a Protestant ideal was replaced by a new gathered, collective ideal, and by 'Christian Socialism' and practical theology active in new suburban parishes. On the other hand, there was inward renewal in these established churches, visible as a revival of institutional religion. Tradition in church order and in the liturgy became interesting. In England, the Anglo-Catholic revival, and in Sweden, what can best be described as a national high-church ecclesiology, peaked in the interwar period. Their singular contribution to 'Catholicity', or the church universal, was the rediscovery of episcopacy as an essential element in church order.[3] The Lambeth conference (1888) thus listed in four articles (the 'Quadrilateral') the essential requirements for intercommunion: the Bible 'containing all things necessary to salvation' as the rule and ultimate standard of faith; the Apostles' Creed as the Baptismal Symbol, and the Nicene Creed as the sufficient statement of the Christian faith; the two Christian sacraments, Baptism and the Eucharist; and the Historic Episcopate 'locally adapted in the methods of its administration to the varying needs of the nations and peoples'.

To turn this into reality was far from easy before the First World War made Christian dialogue a dire necessity. These established Reformation churches were very isolated. Local etiquette and procedures reinforced aloofness. The Nordic churches, in Sweden especially, were also closer to German culture and Protestant German university theology, and German rather than English was the preferred language. Randall Davidson's visit as Dean of Windsor to Sweden and Denmark during August and September 1889 to find out whether both churches fulfilled Lambeth's requirements, illustrated the restrictions imposed by etiquette and language.[4] Davidson's notebooks point to a real conflict between his sincere vision of Christian unity – he schooled his chaplain, George Bell (1914-24), well for the diplomacy of postwar Christian reunion – and his aristocratic Midlothian and Windsor ways (he loved Tweedside fishing and shooting). Davidson never forgave, it seems, archbishop Sundberg for not being at home in Uppsala to receive him. It may even account later for Davidson's wariness towards

---

[3] G.H. Tavard, *The Quest for Catholicity: a Study in Anglicanism* (London, 1963), pp. 38-9; see bishop Headlam's preface (1924) to Y. Brilioth, *The Anglican Revival: Studies in the Oxford Movement* (London, 1925), pp. viii-ix.

[4] Davidson was Archbishop of Canterbury from 1903 to 1928.

Söderblom's vital ecumenism.[5] Even if Davidson approved of Sweden's Apostolic succession and her main Sunday service with communion – in particular the charming custom at Leksand where boats carried Sunday communicants across sunlit and calm Lake Siljan – he was horrified by an apparent ignorance amongst senior Swedish clergy of the Anglican church. Leksand's rector had never heard of an archbishop of York, or of a dean, and considered Anglo-Swedish intercommunion something entirely alien. Things did not improve much in Copenhagen, though Davidson enjoyed lunch with king Christian IX, and czar Alexander III who seemed determined in his broken French to sound him out on the possibilities of railway-building in northern Sweden. More positive conversations with the Danish primate, Bruun Juul Fog (1819-96), whom Davidson noted down as a grand old man of similar speech and mannerisms to his predecessor archbishop Tait (1868-82) and one who knew something of English culture, were cooled nevertheless by Fog's overt satisfaction in Denmark's abolition of bishops at the Reformation, his overdrawn 'Evangelical Alliance' view of Newman as a born papist, and his approval of Spurgeon's strong Calvinist view of papal advance in the late Victorian Anglican church. Any accommodation with Anglican ordination procedure would split, it seemed to Fog, the Danish People's Church of 1849 into further church parties. Davidson's brief encounter with Fog was in fact symptomatic of an outcome which would favour Swedish initiatives in future. If Anglican clergy found their Danish counterparts more congenial and Anglophile than their Swedish colleagues, any positive dialogue always foundered on an evangelical Danish ecclesiology. Apostolic succession was considered an evil thing, and Anglo-Catholicism as a form of Roman advance: hence Danish objections to intercommunion which might disunite their national Church. Much later, Headlam, bishop of Gloucester (1923-45), a keen advocate of Christian reunion, noticed this during his Danish visit in the spring of 1927 as the real sticking-point amongst his Danish friends.

Swedish rediscovery of the 'Church'

Here dialogue might well have rested. In Sweden, Finland, Denmark, and Norway, the mood at this time was to increase national and ecclesiastical

---

[5] Y. Brilioth, 'Ärkebiskop Davidson's Svenska Resa', *Från skilda Tider. Studier tillägn Hjalmar Holmquist* (Stockholm, 1938), pp. 86-103. Davidson's two diaries have not survived since Brilioth made a typescript in 1935-36: Davidson Papers, 522, ff.186-226po, Lambeth Palace. I thank Miss Melanie Barber for this information. More positive on Sundberg: L. Österlin, *Churches of Northern Europe in Profile* (Norwich, 1995), pp. 213-19.

differentiation at the expense of a shared Lutheran Reformation. And yet youth, particularly in Sweden, would not have political inwardness. A new cohort of liberal and socially committed ordinands at Uppsala University warmed to the Anglo-American SCM and, as a 'Young Church Movement' inspired by contemporary urban German practical theology, went on crusade in nearby industrial Stockholm, Gävle, and the new timber industry towns. All of a sudden, around 1900, the urban-gathered parish congregation, community, social engagement, the workplace and its social ethics, entering into dialogue with socialists – all these became priorities. This was accompanied by a new sense of spiritual roots, the home parish, and of Sweden's historic Reformation as a source of Christian renewal in a national sense: expressed at the time of Sweden's separation from Norway (1905) by Manfred Björkquist's classic Young Church slogan, 'The Swedish People - A People of God' (1908).[6] The overall effect, however, was a rediscovery of the Christian Church, first as a vibrant Peoples' Church (*folkkyrkan*) – meaning a return to Early Christian fellowship, the Church instituted by the Gospel and the sacraments of Baptism and the Eucharist in an all-inclusive home parish congregation contrasted with an evangelical view of the congregation as one united by personal conversion – and, second, as a modern Swedish practical theology freed from the old German connection.

Three future Swedish bishops led the way. Einar Billing (1871-1939), bishop of Västerås (1920), and Gustaf Aulén (1879-1977), bishop of Strängnäs (1933-52), personified this new Swedish national interest in the 'Church', and an appropriate Swedish theology; Nathan Söderblom supplied the international aspect through his prewar work for the SCM, where he made contact with eastern Orthodoxy, and via his involvement in modern French and German comparative religion at Paris and Leipzig. Hence Söderblom's religion of revelation: the Christian faith revealed prophetically by Jesus and rediscovered by Luther, which coexisted with a modern pseudo-religion of culture serving the values of the modern nation-state.[7] Here there was room for the 'holy', or 'sacred'. Söderblom's 'Evangelical Catholicity' thus meant the church universal – no doubt with Protestant overtones, which made no distinction between visible and invisible, personal and institutional religion. Modern national churches remained simply provinces of the church universal. Therefore the Lutheran

---

[6] A. Tergel, *Ungkyrkomännen, Arbetarfrågan och Nationalismen 1901-1911* (Uppsala, 1969), p. 145.

[7] *Uppenbarelsereligion. Några synpunkter i anledning af Babel-Bibel-diskussionen* (Uppsala, 1903); also, *Svenska Kyrkans Kropp och Själ* (Stockholm, 1916).

Augsburg Confession of faith could coexist with the Anglican Thirty-Nine Articles; bishops and the Apostolic succession in England and Sweden were essential safeguards in modern national churches.

Swedish-Anglican Initiatives

Progress between the Lambeth 1908 conference, which looked into Sweden's historic episcopate, ministry, and confirmation rite, the first official Anglican visit to Uppsala in September 1909, and the Lambeth 1920 conference's official recommendation of Anglican and Swedish intercommunion, was thus driven to a large extent by Söderblom's vision. Söderblom kept dialogue alive in wartime; Davidson shied away, thinking even in November 1918 that international church conferences were premature.[8] But the times were more urgent for Söderblom, given the Russian October revolution's proximity, Finland's declaration of republican independence in December 1917, and the imminent likelihood of new Estonian and Latvian republics. Söderblom thus sketched out already during 1917 the broad outlines of Stockholm (1925): a lasting peace, the duty of all Christians to work for reconciliation, the expansion of ecumenical dialogue, and a new international legal framework which could prevent future war. But the peace was inauspicious. Sweden's prewar liberal political environment evaporated. The first labour government in Europe came to power in March 1920, and it included in its programme, church disestablishment and disendowment.

A historian could afford to be negative about the effectiveness of postwar dialogue. Little had changed prewar standards of etiquette and procedure amongst established churchmen. Allegiance to national church order seemed preferable to an international Christian life and work cause. This was the tenor of bishop Hensley Henson's very funny account of his assisting – with Woods, bishop of Peterborough – Söderblom in the consecration of the bishops of Västerås (Einar Billing) and Skara at Uppsala cathedral in September 1920. Söderblom's adroitness collapsed, so Henson wrote in his diary,

> by having to deal at one and the same time with two, and they conflicting, exponents of Anglicanism. When he placates Peterborough, he alienates Durham; when Durham smiles approval, Peterborough frowns discontent. Mainly, he exhibits the conventional forms of what is called ecclesiastical liberalism. He

---

[8] To Söderblom, 15 Nov. 1918: G.K.A. Bell, *Randall Davidson, Archbishop of Canterbury* (2 vols., Oxford, 1935), vol. ii, p. 941.

plays with socialism; affects a mighty concern for democracy; and proclaims his scorn for clericalism. But he is ambitious and fond of power. He likes to play the part of a great prelate, and has many of the attractive qualities which mark the character of our own Archbishop (Davidson)! The two men are in fact very similar.

Thus, Henson concluded, 'does ecclesiastical isolation matter to the spiritual Christian to whom the politics of churches and hierarchies are properly indifferent'.[9] Indeed, given episcopal reservations on both sides, only unofficial Anglo-Swedish intercommunion followed in 1922. Sweden's bishops considered it more important to know whether the Anglican Church was sound on Scripture 'as *norma normans* both with regard to life and doctrine, and the building of our salvation on God's grace alone received by faith'. The Anglicans, given their traditional reserve towards detailed doctrinal definition, were satisfied at once about the Swedish church holding all the essentials of the Christian faith. Their sticking point, however, was Apostolic succession, since the Swedish church was in full communion with the Norwegian, Danish, Icelandic, and Finnish churches which had lost such continuity.[10] Evangelical Catholicity for this reason was not for irenic Anglican leaders like Davidson or Temple. Neither attended the Stockholm conference. 'They preferred their own Liberal Catholicism, which to them was better theology and better English.'[11] Even Söderblom, when it came to it, was patriotic and fussy about traditional church order. He stated openly in his correspondence after his consecration of the first Estonian and Latvian Lutheran bishops at Tallinn in June 1921 and Riga in May 1922, of this as 'reinforcing the Lutheran ring established round the Baltic, *mare Lutheranum*', and of Riga as 'the Evangelical centre of Eastern Europe'.[12] Söderblom was also angered by the new Estonian bishop's unilateral initiative in declaring Tallinn cathedral an historic episcopal church (since 1240) against the vocal opposition of its German congregation which considered it to be in the

---

[9] H.H. Henson, *Retrospect of an Unimportant Life* (2 vols., Oxford, 1943), vol. ii, pp. 38 (17 Sept.1920), 46 (26 Sept.1920).

[10] G.K.A. Bell, *Documents on Christian Unity: A Selection from the First and Second Series 1920-30* (Oxford, 1955), p. 77; R. Rouse & S. Neill (eds.), *A History of the Ecumenical Movement 1517-1948* (2 vols., London, 1967), vol. i, pp. 471-2.

[11] B. Sundkler, *Nathan Söderblom: His Life and Work* (Uppsala, 1968), p. 323; 'Liberal' and 'Evangelical' Catholicism: S.E. Brodd, *Evangelisk Katolicitet* (Uppsala, 1982), pp. 169-81; see Bell's amusing account of Davidson's stalling tactics during Söderblom's visit in May 1921: Bell, *Davidson*, vol. ii, pp.1048-51.

[12] Sundkler, *Söderblom*, p. 277.

hand of the *Ritterschaft*. It seems that Söderblom feared the Estonians might remove the old portraits and epitaphs including those of the old Swedish families.[13]

Interwar revival of Church Authority and the Church Spiritual

A new interest in the Church managing its own affairs and in the history and shape of the Christian liturgy, coloured Anglo-Catholic in England and 'high-church' in Sweden, was a significant trend in the interwar period. The friendship and shared interwar ecumenical work between Yngve Brilioth (1891-1959), Söderblom's polyglot secretary and son-in-law, eventually bishop of Växjö (1937) and archbishop (1950), and Headlam, bishop of Gloucester, is an illustration. Brilioth, who worried like Söderblom about Sweden's new socialist direction, took a keen interest in possible postwar Anglican disestablishment suggested by William Temple's 'Life and Liberty Movement' calling for a degree of autonomy in the Church of England; by the Enabling Act of 1919, which gave the Church of England a general power subject to parliamentary control to legislate for itself; and by the infelicitous outcome of the revised prayer book controversy in 1928. But Brilioth also liked, as archbishop Ramsey put it succinctly later in his study of pre-1914 and interwar Anglican theology, the Anglican permanent characteristics consisting of 'an appeal to Scripture, and the Fathers, the fondness for Nicene categories, the union of doctrine and liturgy, the isolation from continental influences'.[14] Brilioth thus published major books aimed at the English educated public on the Victorian Oxford Movement and the post-1918 revival of eucharistic faith and piety.[15] Anglo-Catholic sacramental piety centred on the celebration of Holy Communion was an ecumenical way forward in markedly secular times. Anglo-Catholic tradition based on Newman's Anglican early church also modified considerably, so Brilioth thought, the influence of modern Protestant German theology's Bible criticism and Life of Jesus research, and its over-intellectual emphasis on great Protestant German theologians and their schools of thought. Headlam took a similar-minded

---

[13] W. Kahle, *Lutherische Begegnung im Ostseeraum* (Gütersloh, 1982), pp.141-2. In 1927, the Estonian state declared the cathedral state property, and put it under the Estonian consistory.

[14] A.M. Ramsey, From Gore to Temple: *The Development of Anglican Theology between Lux Mundi and the Second World War 1889-1939* (London, 1960), p. viii.

[15] *The Anglican Revival* (1925), see footnote 3; *Eucharistic Faith & Practice Evangelical & Catholic* (London, 1930), repr.1934, 1939, preface by the Anglo-Catholic liturgist A.G. Hebert.

mission to the Lutheran Baltic after his first visit to Denmark, Sweden, and Finland in 1927. It was modestly successful. He brought Finland eventually in June 1935 into line with Anglo-Swedish intercommunion, and Estonia and Latvia in June 1938, after much nail-biting controversy in both Houses of Convocation at Canterbury. Reading between the lines of the reports of the official discussions, one can see how much it mattered to the Latvian and Estonian bishops. They saw their membership of an episcopal framework as a means to throw off German church order and theology, and begin afresh in a 'universal Church'. But this was already almost too late and too controversial. Headlam could do no more than confide to a friend: 'Uniting Christendom demands great endurance, unlimited patience, and a digestion to suit all emergencies.'[16]

A return to Anglo-American initiatives

On the other hand, it has to be said that the more worldly side of this dialogue on the place of the Church in interwar social crisis, summarised by the Stockholm conference slogan 'doctrine divides while service unites', was remarkably successful in furthering Anglican and Baltic Lutheran relations. It built the foundations of the first modern political platform of the church universal at the World Council of Churches at Amsterdam in 1948. The Birmingham conference on Politics, Economics, and Citizenship convened by Temple in April 1924, which Söderblom addressed, included many of the churchmen and new professional experts present both at Stockholm in August 1925 and at its continuation conference at Oxford in July 1937.[17] The Anglican input became a considerable one. A younger generation of Anglican bishops really took over Söderblom's role after his premature death in 1931: notably Bell as bishop of Chichester (1929-58), who edited the Stockholm report, chaired its 'Life and Work' Council (1932-34) and its administrative committee (1934-38), and Temple, who continued the work of COPEC both at Oxford and at wartime Malvern in January 1941. These bishops listened to the experts. The universal church had indeed a say in modern public affairs. Bell and Temple penned this down for a far wider public than dreamt of ever before in best-selling wartime Penguin Specials of 1940 and 1942 which have still great

---

[16] *Lambeth Occasional Reports 1931-8*, pp. 218-47. Headlam to Miss P.L. Wingfield, 26-7 June 1938, R. Jasper, *Arthur Cayley Headlam: Life and Letters of a Bishop* (London, 1960), p. 264.

[17] Söderblom and COPEC: Sundkler, *Söderblom*, pp. 350-3. Between 1929 and 1939, ten of Sweden's twelve dioceses were filled with socially committed bishops.

relevance today.[18] One could say very crudely, therefore, that the 1930s and 1940s were Anglican in contrast to the Lutheran Swedish 1910s and 1920s.

What made the Oxford theme 'Church, Community, and State' so very urgent in July 1937, one too which aimed to unite the parallel ecumenical themes of the Stockholm 'Life and Work' and the subsequent Lausanne 'Faith and Order' conference (continuation at Edinburgh in August 1937), was the reality of dictatorship, whether Communist, Nazi, or Fascist, which aimed at controlling society and its value system as such. Christian civilisation was at stake. Hitler's Germany after 1934 showed, too, that there was no united Protestant German church, but merely powerful factions consisting of the Nazi '*Reichskirche*' and 'German Christians', the Confessing Church, and what was left of the old state churches known as the 'intact' *Landeskirchen*. Much, therefore, revolved around finding an appropriate language to express the values of the church universal. In particular, the word 'community' revealed quite distinct approaches to a common subject of great concern. Community as the German '*Volk*' jostled with the French '*Nation*' and American 'Society'. What Oxford did show, however, was a clear Anglo-American voice, given the absence of official Roman Catholic and German delegates. Three hundred of the 425 present representing 120 communions in forty countries (including all the Baltic nations) came from the British Empire and the United States. However, the course of the conference demonstrated something far more difficult to put into historical prose. Joseph Oldham (1874-1969), the elder statesman of the early Ecumenical Movement, and Bell's successor as chairman of the 'Life and Work' Council, who prepared the Oxford Conference, summed up Oxford's value thus: 'In the periods of silence there was often an overpowering sense that things were happening in the spiritual world [in a] mixed gathering of this kind sharing in the characteristic forms of worship of some of the great classical traditions of Christendom'.[19] This gave hope at a time, Oldham felt, when 'the real crisis of the Church relates not to its social programme but to its faith'.[20]

The conference made far clearer to a far wider of churchmen and laity for the first time, the very necessary modern distinctions between the Church of faith and the Church as an institution, between the worshipping congregation and the life of the world, between the individual and collective action whether of church

---

[18] Bell, *Christianity and World Order* (1940); Temple, *Christianity and Social Order* (1942), repr. May and August 1942, 150,000 copies.

[19] Oldham (ed.), *The Churches survey their Task*, pp. 18, 20.

[20] W.A. Visser T. Hooft & J.H. Oldham, *The Church and its Function in Society: Church, Community, and State* 1 (London, 1937), p. 105.

authorities or of laypersons; or as Sir Ernest Barker argued, between '*Volk*' as 'a unitary word' and 'community' in the English sense, which is 'essentially multiform ... not readily definable by any objective criteria of blood or speech or creed or culture'.[21] Temple continued this argument as archbishop in wartime (1942-44) in his *Christianity and Social Order*. Temple saw as basic a respect for every person simply as a person, the family as the primary social unit of responsible Christian citizenship, or in Temple's diction, the service of the 'person-in-community'. So strong was Temple's conviction that he almost erased the words 'individual' and 'individualism' from the Christian vocabulary! 'Best' and 'worst' Christian standards, Temple felt, prevented an all too easy lapse into a pagan idolatry of state and nation.[22]

One might conclude with the remark that the value of Anglican and Baltic-Lutheran dialogue in the first fifty years of the twentieth century lay really in the spirit and not so much in measurable benefit. As Bell put it much later in 1954,

> Public meetings at the time, resolutions or messages adopted by a world conference, have their uses. But it is the encounter of delegate with delegate, or of individual churchman with individual churchman, that matters most; together with the general kindling of the spirit which is so clearly perceptible at a conference that has been wisely planned. Conferences, therefore, are a means to an end, not an end in themselves.[23]

---

[21] *Church in Community: Church, Community, and State 5* (London, 1938), p. 25.

[22] A.M. Suggate, *William Temple and Christian Social Ethics Today* (Edinburgh, 1987), pp. 65-71, 171-2. Temple's Anglican incarnational theology and its similarities to Söderblom's theology of Revelation: Ramsey, *From Gore to Temple*, chapter 10.

[23] G.K.A. Bell, *The Kingship of Christ: The Story of the World Council of Churches* (London, 1954), p. 29.

Chapter 14

The Memel Question in British foreign policy 1919-24

Lutz Oberdörfer

The sudden collapse of four great empires at the end of the First World War and the more or less uncontrolled emergence (and disappearance) of successor states confronted the policy makers of the victorious nations with many interconnected and intractable problems. The peacemakers had to deal not only with problems that were common to all, but also with the particular and often conflicting interests of each power. They also met against the background of revolution, famine and economic and political chaos. In contrast to their predecessors at the Congress of Vienna, Wilson, Lloyd George, Clemenceau and Orlando could not ignore the new strength of nationalism. They were, as Anthony Adamthwaite has written, 'presented with a fait accompli – self determination in central and eastern Europe was a reality'.[1] But how could stable nation states be built in a balanced political and economic environment and how could the creation of mini Alsace-Lorraines be avoided? The Allies had no clear solutions to these problems, no common strategy and perhaps lacked the power to resolve them. When their experts were asked about these faraway and unknown regions, the politicians discovered that the ethnic map of Eastern Europe 'presented such a patchwork quilt of nationalities...as to preclude the formation of relatively "pure"

---

[1] Anthony Adamthwaite, *The Lost Peace: International Relations in Europe 1918-1939* (London, 1980), p. 2.

nation states without wholesale and forcible population movements'.[2] It soon it become obvious that the new states had not only territorial claims, but also many other longstanding grievances against one another.

Compared with western Europe, the Mediterranean or the Far East, the region south of the Baltic Sea was not an area of traditional British interest or concern. On the other hand the United Kingdom could not – for well-founded reasons – ignore the problems of this part of Europe. Great Britain's main interests in the region were to create and preserve a workable balance of power, to further peaceful conditions through the peace treaties and the League of Nations and, most important, to eliminate the dangers of small conflicts getting out of hand and spreading to the whole continent. A final aim was to promote favourable conditions for British trade and commerce.[3] The traditionally dominant great powers in the Baltic region, Germany and Russia, had been greatly weakened by war and social unrest. But they had the potential to recover – as the British Foreign Office was fully aware.[4] In the longer term it was in Britain's interest to counter both their potential threats and France's hegemonic ambitions. And what if a revived Germany and a resurrected Russia were some day to combine against the postwar order they had been compelled to swallow in their hour of defeat? A further danger was that Poland, the main pillar of the new *cordon sanitaire* but also surrounded by enemies because of her expansionist, sabre-rattling policy (strongly criticised in London), would seize as much territory outside 'ethnographic' Poland as she could.[5]

There were many, often interconnected, problems south of the Baltic to deal with: problems which, if not resolved, could get out of hand and, if the worst came to the worst, could play the role of a second Sarajevo. The points where potentially dangerous tensions eventually developed were Danzig (Gdańsk), Vilna (Vilnius), Memel (Klaipeda) and – a little further south – Teschen. I will concentrate on the Memel problem – one described by Jürgen Heideking as the

---

[2] Philip Longworth, *The Making of Eastern Europe* (Basingstoke, 1992), p. 68.

[3] G.H. Bennett, *British Foreign Policy during the Curzon Period, 1919-24* (Basingstoke, 1995), p. 43; in a broader perspective, see P. Salmon, 'British Security Interests in Scandinavia and the Baltic', in John Hiden and Aleksander Loit (eds.), *The Baltic in International Relations between the Two World Wars* (Uppsala, 1988), pp. 113 f.

[4] Harold I. Nelson, *Land and Power: British and Allied policy on Germany's frontiers, 1916-1919* (London, 1963), p. 98.

[5] Martin Gilbert, *Sir Horace Rumbold: Portrait of a Diplomat 1869-1941* (London, 1973), pp. 182 f.; M.L. Dockrill and J.D. Goold, *Peace without Promise: Britain and the Peace Conferences 1919-23* (London, 1981), pp. 113 f.

'Gordian knot' of the peace settlement in north-east Europe – and how British diplomacy handled it.[6]

At Versailles and in the pre-conference preparations following the armistice, the destiny of the German port of Memel and its hinterland was only of minor concern for Great Britain.[7] There was little reliable knowledge of this corner of Europe, as members of the Foreign Office complained.[8] However, Memel was strongly linked to the future of Polish-Lithuanian relations. The governments in Warsaw, Paris and Washington favoured a federal union between Poland and Lithuania, which would then acquire Memel from Germany as a vital port. In this way Poland would be further strengthened and Russia cut off from direct territorial access to Germany.[9] In particular the Poles were opposed to an independent Lithuania which they could see only as a constant menace and potentially an open corridor between their great enemies Russia and Germany.[10] Such an argument was also taken seriously in London, since it was expected that Russia would one day re-absorb at least Estonia and Latvia.[11] Nevertheless, for the present the Foreign Office was sceptical about a new Polish-Lithuanian union. Instead, Balfour suggested a federation of Estonia, Latvia and Lithuania with Finland and perhaps Scandinavian states.[12] With the aim of giving Lithuania free access to the sea, the pre-conference paper of the Foreign Office on German Territorial Questions argued as follows: 'There is a small district in the extreme north of Prussia, including the town of Memel, to which a claim might possibly be put forward by the new Lithuanian state.'[13] Added to this was a suggestion that there should be some consultation with the inhabitants of the area concerning the frontier.

During the Peace Conference itself, Lithuania and Memel were low on the agenda. The Lithuanians themselves spared no effort to achieve recognition as an

---

[6] J. Heideking, *Areopag der Diplomaten. Die Pariser Botschafterkonferenz der alliierten Hauptmächte und die Probleme der europäischen Politik 1920-1931* (Hamburg, 1979), *p. 113.*

[7] On Versailles, see Alan Sharp, *The Versailles Settlement: Peacemaking in Paris, 1919* (Basingstoke, 1991) and K. Schwabe (ed.), *Quellen zum Friedensschluß von Versailles* (Darmstadt, 1997).

[8] Public Record Office London, FO 608/198.

[9] Nelson, *Land and Power*, pp. 119 f.

[10] FO 371/5374, N 794/5/59.

[11] FO 371/6803, N 9045/44/55.

[12] Nelson, *Land and Power*, p. 64. On Balfour's foreign policy in general, see Jason Tomes, *Balfour and Foreign Policy: The International Thought of a Conservative Statesman* (Cambridge, 1997).

[13] FO 371/9266, N 8177/173/59.

independent state by the Western Powers and intensified their claims for as much territory as possible, territories often well outside their existing 'ethnic border'. Their demands included not only the Protestant Memel territory but also the port of Libau, as well as extensive territories on the west bank of the Niemen (Nemunas or Memel) river up to the Pregel river, but not including Königsberg, and territories in the south up to Brest-Litovsk and in the north east up to the River Düna or Zapadnaja Dvina.[14] The British were very sceptical towards these demands. The Lithuanian appeal to history was seen as a double-edged weapon and the Foreign Office remarked that 'their imperialism makes the Poles look almost moderate'.[15]

The Americans, Poles and French, already in favour of a Polish-Lithuanian union, were ready to give Lithuania considerable parts of East Prussian territory on the west bank of the Niemen. Eventually that scheme was rejected – no Lithuanian representative took part in the relevant discussions of the Polish Commission – and the British position more or less prevailed. It was recommended that the Memel river (the lower Niemen) should form the new frontier of Germany, a proposal which affected 945 square miles and nearly 150,000 people. Two main justifications were given for this transfer of territory and population: the Niemen was recognised as the 'ethnic frontier' between Germans and Lithuanians and Memel harbour as the natural sea outlet for Lithuania. But because the future status of Lithuania had not been determined, it was decided that the cession of the Memelland should be made in 'favour of the Allied and Associated Governments'. Such a solution had the 'advantage of not prejudicing the future and of leaving' to the Allies 'greater liberty of action' as the French Foreign Minister remarked.[16]

The German government protested against the decision on 25 May 1919, declaring that the inhabitants 'including the minority speaking Lithuanian as their mother-tongue have never desired separation from Germany' and that the town of Memel, founded by Germans in 1252, had never belonged to Poland or to Lithuania. Simultaneously the Berlin government offered Poland the establishment of free ports at Danzig, Königsberg and Memel.[17] With strong Polish backing, the Allies declined to admit that the transfer of Memel conflicted

---

[14] FO 371/3937, 9266 and FO 608/198.

[15] FO 608/198, N 7994.

[16] *Papers Relating to the Foreign Relations of the United States. The Paris Peace Conference* [hereafter, FRUS], vol. VIII (Washington, 1946), p. 809.

[17] FRUS, vol. VI (Washington 1947), pp. 837 f.

with the principle of self-determination. Later, in an often-criticized view, they erroneously stated that 'the district has always been Lithuanian' and again they underlined that Lithuania needed Memel as an outlet to the sea.[18] Under the Treaty of Versailles Germany had finally to renounce all rights over the Memel territory in favour of the Allies. For the time being the area was placed under a French High Commissioner who represented the Allied Powers.[19]

After Versailles, British policy south of the Baltic Sea was much influenced by escalating military conflicts in the region, where the Poles soon were involved in bitter border conflicts. The British government was especially worried about the possible consequences for the stability of north-east Europe as well as the international prestige of the League of Nations. But the United Kingdom – which had so many problems around the globe to manage – possessed neither the means nor the will to pursue a vigorous policy in the Baltic backed, if necessary, by force. On the other hand Poland was supported by France and Britain could not allow Poland, the most important buffer between defeated Germany and Soviet Russia, to be overwhelmed or even weakened.[20] All this had, of course, repercussions for the handling of the still undecided Memel question. At the beginning of 1920 a Foreign Office memorandum stated that there were still no arrangements concerning the ultimate fate of the Memelland: whether it would remain German, or become Lithuanian or be granted a plebiscite.[21] Shortly afterwards a discussion about the best possible solution for the Memel question took place which showed two different opinions in the Foreign Office. One view preferred to hand over Memel as quickly as possible to the Lithuanians, whatever the fate of their state. Others believed that a decision should be taken only after very careful consideration of the broader consequences and that it seemed, in the end, that it was better 'that the port should go back to Germany'.[22] For the present the first opinion more or less prevailed for two interconnected reasons: in the Foreign Office there was a growing irritation at, and distrust of, the behaviour of France and her Polish client, seeming to strive for supremacy in the whole region. To further British interests and to balance the French, a British vice-consul was appointed to Memel in April 1920.[23]

---

[18] FO 371/9266, N 8177/173/59; FRUS, VI, pp. 926 f.

[19] FO 371/17183, N 8703/541/59; FRUS, XIII (Washington, 1947), p. 237.

[20] Gilbert, *Sir Horace Rumbold*, pp. 182 f.; Bennett, *British Foreign Policy*, pp. 41 f.

[21] FO 371/3625, No. 168481.

[22] Ibid., No. 187793.

[23] Ibid., Nos. 184235 and 193611.

Furthermore, the Lithuanians did much to promote their aims in the United Kingdom.

In May 1920 British diplomacy became active in the Memel question, aiming to resolve a still undecided issue which might easily become a danger in an unstable balance of power. The Foreign Office tried to come to agreement with Paris to allocate Memel to Lithuania and Lord Derby was instructed to propose such a measure to the Conference of Ambassadors.[24] But the French were not ready to deal with Memel until there was a decision on the *de jure* recognition of Lithuania. As a result of the French 'delaying tactics', as Lord Curzon called them, the British agreed with Derby that the best course open would be to postpone a settlement of the Memel question 'until some decision had been taken' on the *de jure* recognition of Lithuania.[25] For those reasons Memel was not put on the agenda of the Conference of Ambassadors. Meanwhile, however, with the increasing ferocity of the fighting between Poland and Soviet Russia overshadowing all other events, Polish-Lithuanian animosities (which the Allies had allowed to drift[26]) reached a new and dangerous dimension. In defiance of Allied warnings, on 9 October 1920 Polish troops under General Zeligowski forced the Lithuanians to evacuate the mainly Jewish- and Polish-inhabited city of Vilna, the historical capital of Lithuania.[27]

At the time of the Zeligowski raid into Vilna the Allied powers were still discussing the eastern frontiers of Poland. The 'aggression of the Poles' confronted the League of Nations with a fait accompli which also 'grievously flouted' the prestige of Great Britain.[28] But the British government felt weak in the region and was unable and unwilling to do anything of real importance without, let alone against, Poland's protector, France.[29] Furthermore, Great Britain was unwilling to risk an open breach with an uncompromising and exultant Poland: in the end this could have much more damaging consequences for the post-war order in an unstable eastern Europe. For those reasons London was disposed to accept the status quo after the Polish occupation of Vilna and as Poland's superior forces were threatening to overrun the whole of Lithuania. By February 1920 the best solution for east European stability was seen in a Polish-

---

[24] Ibid., Nos. 208775 and 200346.

[25] FO 371/5379, N 2020/1949/59.

[26] FO 371/5374, N 794/5/59.

[27] The most powerful supporter in the background was Jozef Pilsudski.

[28] FO 371/5374, N 1355/5/59.

[29] FO 371/5400, N 102/272/55; Bennett, *British Foreign Policy*, pp. 49 f.

Lithuanian union and British diplomacy should intensify its efforts to bring this about. Lithuania, it was argued, had in the end no other alternative but to 'choose between being reabsorbed by a reconstituted Russia and federation with Poland or with the Baltic States and Poland'. And, as long as there was a risk of Lithuania falling back into Russian hands the Western Powers should not allow either Vilna or Memel to be incorporated into Lithuanian territory.[30]

In November 1920 Lord Curzon informed the British embassy in France that the Memel problem 'can best be dealt with, when we see how the Polish-Lithuanian dispute is settled' and that 'if a Polish-Lithuanian Confederation is brought into being ... then Memel could be settled at the same time.'[31] Only in that case could Memel go to Lithuania.[32] On the other hand, as the British knew, relations between Poles and Lithuanians were so embittered and so stalled that there was no real chance for a union based on the will of both peoples, in particular that of the Lithuanians, who feared the ultimate ruin of their nationality in any combination with the much stronger Poles.[33] But such a situation, of course, did not mean that a federation was excluded as the 'only and effective solution' and there was hope that – while both parties renounced the use of force – a union might eventually come about as a 'natural consequence' of events and interests.[34] Memel was seen primarily as 'a bribe' to influence the Kovno government.[35] The head of the Northern Department of the Foreign Office, J. D. Gregory, put pressure on the Lithuanians by stressing the German character of Memel to make it clear that 'it was not as clear as daylight that it should without any question' be considered as 'belonging in the natural order of things to Lithuania.' But, Gregory believed, if it was possible to accomplish a general settlement of all the east European problems which needed a Polish-Lithuanian rapprochement, it was 'more than probable' that Memel would fall to Lithuania.[36]

---

[30] FO 371/5401, N 541/272/55.

[31] FO 371/5379, N 2020/1949/59.

[32] FO 371/6803, N 9046/44/55.

[33] FO 371/6798, N 4471/44/55.

[34] FO 371/6274, N 2078/359/59.

[35] FO 371/6726, N 5324/553/59.

[36] Ibid., N 2686/553/59. There was always the danger that a Polish-Lithuanian conflict could lead to a new Russo-Polish war and in the result to disastrous consequences, perhaps not only for East Europe.

Initiated by the British consul in Danzig, Fry, a discussion started in 1921 about the possibility of Memel becoming a Free City or Free State under the protection of the League of Nations. This was a solution which a majority of the Memellanders themselves seemed to prefer and which supporters in Britain assessed as the most likely to solve the problem most rapidly and with the greatest advantage for Britain's long-term interests.[37] There was a growing sympathy for such a solution in the Foreign Office, but the view still persisted that Memel should eventually go to Lithuania as compensation for her loss of Vilna and with secure rights of transit for Poland.[38] The British government should, however, take no initiative in the matter. At the end of 1921, the discussions on Memel were given a fresh impetus by the French, when Jules Cambon proposed the establishment of Memel as a Free City on the lines of Danzig.[39] Again there was a strong connection with Polish-Lithuanian relations which were showing no signs of improvement: Poland was threatening to wipe Lithuania off the map, despite all the Allied efforts to work for moderation. More and more, both Western Powers realised that the Kovno government must be cajoled or forced into accepting the loss of Vilna and its surrounding region. There was still some hope in London that withholding *de jure* recognition of Lithuania might influence the Kovno government to swallow the bitter pill of giving up its popular and much publicized claim for the Vilna district. This at once raised the issue of Memel and the Lithuanians placed a very high priority on its possession.

The French government, supported by Lord Hardinge, wanted now to settle the *de jure* recognition of Lithuania and the Memel question simultaneously. The latter should be established as a Free State under French protection. Both Poland and Lithuania would receive guarantees that they could use the Niemen River and the outlet to the sea at Memel. Baltic and British diplomats supposed, however, that Paris above all wanted to strengthen the French position in the Baltic by obtaining control of two strategic points – Memel and Vilna – in cooperation with its Polish partner.[40] The British government disapproved of settling the questions of *de jure* recognition of Lithuania and of Memel simultaneously. Memel was now seen as a useful pawn to be held in reserve for negotiations with both Kovno and Warsaw, and its future should remain

---

[37] Ibid., N 5324/553/59.

[38] FO 371/6733, N 14247/4165/59.

[39] Ibid.

[40] FO 371/8062 and 8063.

dependent on a final settlement of the Vilna problem. From Lord Curzon's point of view, the time had not yet come to raise the Memel question.[41] In the Foreign Office the balance of argument was in favour of Memel going finally to Lithuania. But this should take place only gradually. Certain safeguards should include a large measure of local autonomy as well as the right of transit to Poland.[42] Most important from British viewpoint was to prevent Memel and its relatively ice-free harbour from falling into Russian hands if the latter at any time absorbed Lithuania.[43]

In the summer of 1922 the French government, backed by Warsaw, confirmed that it would make Memel a Free State, but was now ready to deal the question with separately from *de jure* recognition of Lithuania.[44] At the same time a change of opinion took place in the Foreign Office, as the Free State idea gained a growing number of supporters in Britain. The Foreign Office also stressed that the tradition and civilisation of Memel were German, that the Memel district was commercially and culturally far ahead of Lithuania and that the overwhelming majority of the population, traditionally friendly towards Britain, utterly rejected union with Lithuania. After listening to these arguments Curzon wrote to Hardinge in September 1922 that 'the best solution would be one which would enable Memel eventually to become part of a more enlightened Lithuania and that nothing should now be done which would permanently exclude the possibility of such a solution'. On the other hand, Curzon considered that 'a considerable interval should be provided for, in which Memel will have time to develop her own strength and prosperity and – here we have a new train of thought – to take her own decision with regard to her future destiny.'[45]

In December 1922, Great Britain, France and Italy agreed to the establishment of a Free State of Memel under the League of Nations for a limited period 'at the end of which the position would be examined afresh'. The only question left open was the possibility of 'some sort of recognition of the nominal sovereignty of Lithuania' over the planned Free State. The Poles always feared that Lithuania wanted to use Memel as a natural outlet for its eastern

[41] Ibid., N 3451/343/59.

[42] FO 371/8058, N 7503/39/59.

[43] FO 371/8062, N 4382/343/59.

[44] Ibid., N 6346/343/59.

[45] Ibid., N 7503/343/59.

territories and strongly objected to this.[46] The Polish government, supported by France, also stressed again the necessity of an alternative route to Danzig. It was clear that a Free State under the League of Nations represented, in all likelihood, by a French High Commissioner at Memel would give Poland the security it wanted of using Memel as an alternative outlet as well as an inlet to Danzig in case of emergency.[47] It is not clear how far Polish opinion influenced the Memel Committee of the Conference of Ambassadors around the turn of the year to give up the idea of recognising the nominal sovereignty of Lithuania.[48] It is clear, however, that they wanted the Soviet Union to have no influence in the matter. Soviet wishes in that direction as well as a threat not to recognise a one-sided Western solution of the Memel (or the Vilna) question were, at least officially, totally ignored.[49]

The main reason given for a Free State of Memel was the city's role as a natural sea outlet not only for the Lithuanian state – recognised *de jure* in December 1922 – but also for eastern Poland. And to give Memel a large hinterland was valued in London as being in the best interests of British trade.[50] The uncertainty over Lithuania's future status played a very important role, as well as the expectation that 'the absorption of an unwilling Memel into Lithuania would be a source of constant irritation' and friction which, as soon as Germany recovered from defeat, could have dangerous consequences for peace in the region. For the Foreign Office, which entirely agreed with the paper of the Memel Committee, pacification in Northern Europe remained the paramount aim.[51] And for that reason the most satisfactory solution of the Memel question would be – regardless of the fine detail – the one that best served stability in the Baltic. To further such a development Great Britain pursued classical realpolitik.[52] In Whitehall the conviction was still strong that, behind the problem of Memel and her relations with Lithuania, lay the ambitions of Poland

---

[46] FO 371/8063, N 10788/343/59.

[47] FO 371/6800, N6196/44/55; FO 371/9256, N 334/173/59.

[48] FO 371/9255, N 195/170/59.

[49] FO 371/8059, N 11211/39/59.

[50] FO 371/9258, N 948/173/59.

[51] FO 371/9256, N 334/173/59; FO 371/8062, N 4382/343/59.

[52] As Foreign Secretary Lord Curzon stressed in March 1922, in a minute discussing a Lithuanian memorandum on the Memel question. FO 371/8058, N 2195/39/59.

and the policy of France, the possible reaction of a recovered Germany and the unknown quantity of Russia.[53]

Before the view of the Western Powers was made public, the Lithuanian government, getting wind of the impending decision, tried to forestall such an adverse development by use of force. In January 1923, in the shadow of the Ruhr occupation and the Turkish crisis, and in defiance of Allied warnings, Lithuanian soldiers and irregulars invaded Memel, protected as it was only by a weak French force.[54] Britain and France were taken by surprise. The Lithuanian occupation, imitating successful Polish examples, was a heavy blow to the authority of the unprepared Allies. Britain and France protested against this act of aggression, tried to exert commercial pressure on Lithuania, sent naval forces to Memel and threatened Kovno with severe consequences. Not for the first time since the Paris Peace Conference, the Western Powers issued warnings that possessions gained by use of force would prejudice the claims of those who resorted to such means. To be effective such warnings must be backed by a credible threat. *The Times* warned on 23 January 1923:

> The Memel affair may appear to some as of minor importance. But it has a far wider significance than the mere allocation of the district to this country or that. The reputation of the Powers is at stake, and at no moment since the war it has been more imperative that the authority of those responsible for the resettlement of Europe should be respected. Europe is on the verge of several possible disturbances, for some of its more importunate States are very quick to detect any relaxation of the moral control which alone keeps unsatisfied aspirations in check.

Two days earlier the British ambassador in Warsaw telegraphed that he and his French and Italian colleagues saw the only 'safe solution' as being the expulsion of the invaders and the reestablishment of Allied authority at Memel. Otherwise the prestige of the Western Powers and of the Treaty of Versailles would 'suffer an irreparable blow'.[55] But the argument that it was important to

---

[53] FO 371/8059, N 11074/39/59.

[54] The forces under Budrys took action with the avowed object of putting down riots in the Memelland. Following the Zeligowski example the Lithuanian government disowned the 'spontaneous' action. Shortly before the Lithuanian invasion of Memel the Foreign Secretary as well as the Prime Minister of the country promised 'that under no circumstances' would Lithuanian troops enter the Memel territory. FO 371/9256, N 438/173/59.

[55] Ibid., N 527/173/59. The governments in Riga and Reval, fearing a conflagration in northeastern Europe, reacted with dismay to the Lithuanian action.

avoid disastrous consequences for east European stability was outweighed by arguments that Britain and France did not have the means to fight the Lithuanians, who might also be supported by Soviet Russia

In January 1923 the internal British position towards the behaviour and demands of the Kovno government, which was busy fostering a chauvinistic and 'even bellicose' language in the whole Lithuanian press quickly softened.[56] Contrary to the original object – emphasized immediately after the Lithuanian invasion – of seeking a 'permanent peaceable solution in consonance with the wishes of the inhabitants of Memel and district' and despite warnings from the British representative at Warsaw, Max Müller, who preferred to use force against the invaders at Memel as the lesser evil and despite the recommendation of the Allied Memel Commission for a plebiscite, London chose a policy of concessions towards the aggressor.[57] To eliminate a troublesome problem on the basis of a compromise with Lithuania seemed more important than the political and economic wishes and interests of the Memellanders.[58] At the end of January the Allies refused to demand a plebiscite. Gregory, head of the Northern Department of the Foreign Office, summarized the dominant opinion thus: 'We have to come to the conclusion that we must have peace and that we only can get it by accepting facts.'[59]

The French position developed in similar fashion. Paris urged the importance of re-establishing the full authority and sovereignty of the Allies at Memel.[60] On 29 January 1923 Poincaré – speaking to Lord Balfour – complained about the abominable behaviour of the Lithuanians which 'had put the allies in an embarrassing and indeed humilating position'. But considerable forces were necessary to restore and then hold the situation, resources which France – at least for the moment – could not made available.[61] On 2 February the Foreign Office criticized the 'slowness of the French to forget their national

---

[56] FO 371/9260, N 1435 and 1437/173/59.

[57] FO 371/9257, N 611/173/59 and N 633/173/59 and FO 371/9258, N1937/173/59. On 28 January 1923 the Foreign Office was informed by Consul Fry that an overwhelming majority of the Memellanders would vote in favour of a Free State: FO 371/9258, N864 and 866. Again the British minister in Riga, Vaughan, argued against a Free State of Memel which would give France a footing in the Baltic and the possibility for an air and/or naval base there: FO 371/9260, N 1006, 1437, 1439/173/59.

[58] FO 371/9258, N 925/173/59 and FO 371/9260, N 1257/173/59.

[59] FO 371/9258, N 948/173/59.

[60] FO 371/9256, N 424/173/59.

[61] FO 371/9259, N 973/173/59.

annoyance' and accept the facts. But only six days later Lord Crewe declared that the Paris government 'appear to be so convinced now that the Memel question must be get rid of at any cost'.[62]

On 16 February 1923 the Conference of Ambassadors passed 'their final decision' with regard to the transfer of Memel to Lithuania.[63] But there still remained the difficult task of negotiating a settlement with the Kovno government. The Western Powers were ready to compromise and to give up the idea of 'absolute autonomy' as the most reasonable solution. But they were not willing to accept an unconditional settlement. For both Britain and France it was indispensable to save face and to vest the surrender of the Memel territory with an appearance of legality. As far as possible, they wanted to obtain safeguards in respect of the local administration and the Polish interest in using the Niemen river and the port of Memel, both significant for the economically backward north east of the country.[64] It was of the greatest importance for the British that any settlement must have real safeguards to prevent Memel ever going to Russia.[65] While Germany was seen as having 'now largely lost its importance' in the Baltic the Allies felt bound to take Polish interests and ambitions very seriously indeed.[66]

Commenting on early information about Lithuanian preparations to raid Memel, Lord Crewe stressed the serious political repercussions of any such attempt: 'The Polish government, who are much interested in Memel, might ... retaliate by declaring war on Lithuania,' a real danger also seen by the Foreign Office.[67] The Warsaw government at once protested against the invasion of the

---

[62] FO 371/9260, N 1257/173/59.

[63] Ibid., N 1528 and 1539/173/59.

[64] Timber was the by far most important produce of the region and, with coal, by far the most important export item of the Republic of Poland. See J. Pagel, 'Der polnisch-litauische Streit um Wilna und die Haltung der Sowjetunion 1918-1938', in *Jahrbücher für Geschichte Osteuropas*, neue Folge, 40 (1992), p. 50.

[65] FO 371/9261, N 1898/173/59; FO 371/9262, N 2949/173/59.

[66] The Berlin government protested in strong terms against the Lithuanian invasion and mobilised some forces in the Tilsit region. But despite this, as Vaughan reported in January, 'Lithuania seems to be on good relations with Germany' (FO 371/9257, N 614/173/59) – and the Kovno government 'in general have all along shown confidence that Germany would not move against them': FO 371/9258/173/59. Surveying 1923, the British representative summed up: 'In spite of the seizure of Memel by Lithuanians and their subsequent "persecution" of the German element there, the two governments have remained on good terms, probably owing to the fact that it appeared to be in their common interest to remain so.' FO 371/10376, N 1782/1782/59.

[67] FO 371/9255, N 9684/173/59.

Memel district and expressed its confidence in the determination and ability of the Western Powers 'to repulse the invaders from territory transferred to them by Treaty of Versailles, to impose such a settlement of its status as they think fit and to enforce respect of treaty by Lithuanian government.'[68] Otherwise – as the Polish Foreign Secretary Count Skrzynski commented to Max Müller – 'the situation may have disastrous consequences for Eastern Europe generally'.[69] To protect her interests Poland was also ready to run the risk of a new war with Moscow, should Soviet Russia go to the assistance of Lithuania.[70] The Poles – gathering troops for this purpose – also offered the Allies military help under French command to turn the Lithuanian forces out of Memel.[71] The Western Powers considered the offer but thought it impossible to accept.[72] Britain was very sceptical about the real ambitions of the Polish government, distrusted the Poles and feared the possible consequences for European stability.[73] Count Skrzynski again pressed for a speedy solution to the Memel incident, based on throwing out the invaders, but on 21 January 1923 Curzon ordered Max Müller to make it plain in Warsaw that Memel was not their affair. During his conversation with the British ambassador on 20 January, the Polish foreign minister, partly under public pressure, indicated a readiness to link up Vilna with Memel.[74] On the same day Lord Crewe telegraphed the intention of the French government that the Council of the League 'should be invited at its forthcoming meeting to hand over the settlement of the Vilna question to the Allied governments in order to enable the latter do deal with it, if necessary, simultaneously with that of Memel'.[75] Forty-eight hours later the French ambassador in London formally requested the British government to associate itself with the French proposal.[76] The hint of the Polish foreign minister and the suggestion of the French government led to an intensive discussion about the British position in the Foreign Office. Realpolitik was the guiding principle.

---

[68] FO 371/9256, N 388, 389, 393/173/59.

[69] FO 371/9257, 502/173/59.

[70] FO 371/9258, N 865/173/59; FO 371/9259, N 1037/173/59.

[71] FO 371/9255, N 318/173/59; FO 371/9256, N 389, 516, 540/173/59.

[72] Heideking, *Areopag*, p. 117.

[73] FO 371/9257, N 581, 630/173/59.

[74] Ibid., N 630, 636/173/59.

[75] Ibid., N 640/173/59.

[76] Ibid., N 830/173/59.

Because 'not all the King's horses or the King's men will reinstate' the Allies at Memel or the Lithuanians at Vilna, Great Britain should support the proposed 'double outrage', Lord Curzon wrote. And Gregory noted: 'There is of course a prima face immorality in the suggested compromise of condoning both the Vilna and Memel seizures, but ... that is the only means of securing a permanent peace between Poland and Lithuania and the alternative is to prolong a state of disturbance which may sooner or later lead to a general conflagration in the whole of the East of Europe'. Lindsay too could see no other possibility, but had misgivings about the ultimate wisdom of such a policy. On 25 January 1923 Curzon instructed Crewe to support the now 'inevitable' course of settling the Polish-Lithuanian trouble by giving Vilna to Poland and Memel to Lithuania, with conditions securing the commercial interests of Poland and some degree of autonomy to the Memellanders. At the same time Britain and France ignored a new Soviet note claiming the right to be consulted in the affair.[77]

It soon became obvious that it would be very difficult to translate the Memel-Vilna deal into practical policy. The Lithuanians showed no readiness to accept the loss of Vilna, or the demands of the Allies over Memel. The Warsaw government, on the other hand, refused to sacrifice any interest at Memel. The Polish foreign minister simultaneously condemned the 'outstanding clemency' with which the Allies treated the Lithuanian coup at Memel and stressed that the situation would have been much better and easier if Allied or Polish troops had used force immediately after the Lithuanian invasion.[78] At the same time there were threats of war, many rumours and indications about forthcoming military adventures and French as well as British diplomats spoke about the real danger of war. On 14 February Müller noted that Allied ministers were 'very apprehensive of hostilities between Lithuania and Poland' and Vaughan wrote four days later from Kovno: 'Both sides seem to be calling for war.'[79]

The French wanted to break the growing incalculable deadlock at a time of dangerous international tensions and to foster the aims and wishes of their main partner in Eastern Europe.[80] In the second half of February 1923 the French advocated final recognition of the existing eastern frontier of Poland, established after the Treaty of Riga, and a fixing of the Polish-Lithuanian frontier in such a way as to give the entire Vilna region to Poland. On 26 February Lord Curzon

---

[77] Ibid., N 640/173/59; FO 371/9258, N 879/173/59.

[78] FO 371/9259, N 1037/173/59; FO 371/9315/306/55.

[79] FO 371/9315, N 1485, 1638/306/55.

[80] During the Ruhr crisis France in particular needed support from Poland.

cabled acceptance of a course of action which London had till now always declined to follow.[81] During the following days it became obvious that both Western Powers now wanted to settle the Polish eastern and north-eastern borders question independently of Memel. Lord Crewe's objection that the planned new negotiations with Lithuania 'are less likely to be successful if before they begin or during their course' the Allies 'formally recognize the unconditional sovereignty of Poland over Vilna and transfer the sovereignty of East Galicia to Poland subject to safeguards far less onerous and definite than those required of the Lithuanian government in respect of Memel' could not produce a change of mind in London.[82] The main reason was that a delay in the settlement of the Polish frontier question 'may prove embarrassing'.[83] And because a very early settlement was seen as 'imperative' not only for Polish but also for British interests, the decision on Polish frontiers 'should not be postponed pending the deliberations with the Lithuanians and not be made in any way dependent on those deliberations'.[84] At the same time the whole Polish press abandoned Memel and concentrated its firepower on an immediate positive decision with regard to Poland's frontiers in the east and north east.[85] The Polish foreign minister repeated, during an interview with Max Müller, his threat 'that in certain eventualities' the Polish army would advance on Kovno and 'wipe Lithuania off the map'.[86] British and French diplomats, very dissatisfied with the course of events, heavily criticized the 'stubborn obstinacy' of the 'intractable' Lithuanians who 'have put themselves out of court altogether by their impossible behaviour'.[87] On 23 February Gregory noted that the Lithuanians 'have defied us pretty successfully for a month now' and that perhaps a definite settlement of the frontier question would be 'a salutary lesson' to Kovno with the effect of also stopping them 'from pursuing a mad policy of adventure against the Poles'.[88] The British representative in Lithuania wrote on 22 February to Lord Curzon: 'the Lithuanian government argue, and not

---

[81] FO 371/9315, N 1729/306/55.

[82] FO 371/9316, N 22211/306/55.

[83] Ibid., N 2129/306/55.

[84] Ibid.

[85] Ibid., N 2095/306/55.

[86] Ibid., N 2003/306/55.

[87] FO 371/9261, N 2063/306/55; FO 371/9315, N 2729/306/55; FO 371/9316, N 1799/306/55.

[88] FO 371/9315, N 1729/306/55.

without reason, that to acknowledge Polish sovereignty over Vilna would be compound an act of treachery. I cannot blind myself to the justice of the Lithuanian cause, and it is the impossibility of reconciling justice with expediency that renders a solution of the question so difficult.'[89]

Without consulting Russia and in defiance of strong Soviet warnings, on 15 March 1923 the Polish frontiers agreement, based on the de facto situation, was signed by the Conference of Ambassadors.[90] The decision was received with great enthusiasm by the whole Polish nation and strongly condemned as an act of injustice in Lithuania. Kovno as well as Moscow, which supported the Lithuanian position, declined to accept the verdict as binding or permanent. Lithuania would never give up her claim to Vilna.[91]

As was foreseen by insiders, the Vilna decision made the Lithuanians still more defiant on the difficult issue of Memel. Immediately after 15 March Poland again concentrated on the unresolved Memel problem. Supported by France, Warsaw tried to use the transfer of sovereignty of Memel district to Lithuania as a lever to influence Kovno in favour of Polish aspirations. The most important points of controversy continued to be the Polish claim for Lithuanian recognition of the Polish possession of Vilna and demands for a settlement which would guarantee Poland the use of the Niemen river and the port of Memel as an outlet for her commerce and produce. The Foreign Office still held the view that any convention 'would be worthless' if 'Lithuania is to continue to deprive Poland of all access to Memel'.[92] At the same time, against the background of the Ruhr crisis, the London government aimed to avoid giving the French any grounds to accuse Britain of weakening the common front that was so necessary to keep Lithuanian ambitions in check.[93] But soon the British, facing so many pressing problems, softened their approach. In June 1923 the Foreign Office no longer saw any advantage 'in plunging into the perpetual quarrel' between Poland and Lithuania. A memorandum noted: 'We want to get the Memel question settled. It is quite complicated enough. When it is settled the improvement of Polono-Lithuanian relations must be left to the two

---

[89] FO 371/9316, N 2003/306/55.

[90] FO 371/9317, N 2633/306/55.

[91] Heideking, *Areopag*, p. 121; FO 371/9317, N 2632, 2633, 2804, 2868/306/55; Pagel, 'Der polnisch-litauische Streit', pp. 41 f.

[92] FO 371/9264, N 6454/173/59.

[93] Britain and France had many differences over dealing with the Ruhr conflict. At the same time, the Paris government felt obliged to support her main ally in eastern Europe.

countries concerned. It seems impossible to exaggerate the hatred that exists.'[94] British diplomacy had to realise that the Kovno government was in effective possession of Memel and that the Lithuanians felt under no immediate pressure to give way to Allied demands over the planned convention and her much criticized behaviour in the Memelland, formally still under Allied sovereignty.[95] But since the Lithuanians were in possession of the district, and since none of the powers 'were prepared to turn them out by force' the British saw no other way than 'to appeal to their sense of reason and justice'.[96]

Finally, after protracted and from a British point of view unsatisfactory negotiations, a compromise was found in a convention110 which disappointed the Warsaw government and dashed the hopes of a great majority of the Memellanders.[97] The Memel Treaty which established an autonomous regime for the district under Lithuanian sovereignty was signed in May 1924 and entered into force for all parties on 25 August 1925. Again - as in the cases of Vilna or East Galicia - it had become obvious that the use of force, the resolute producing of *faits accomplis*, could be of great advantage in enforcing national aspirations. And the impotence of British power - at least in the Baltic region - had been amply demonstrated anew.

---

[94] FO 371/9319, N 4623/306/55. In the Foreign Office it was agreed 'that the state of affairs in Eastern Europe is so uncertain and unstable that no useful purpose would be served by attempting to forecast what might happen in certain hypothetical cases.' FO 371/9273, N 2071/8312/59.

[95] There was no readiness at all to open the Memel river for Poland as long as the Poles were in possession of Vilna.

[96] FO 371/10360, N 483/107/59.

[97] For the text of the Memel convention, see FO 371/10365, N6600/196/59. Despite this the German government did not formally protest: Heideking, *Areopag*, p. 124.

Chapter 15

The Baltic States and Great Britain during the Second World War

Antonijs Zunda

In the inter-war period the Western democracies, and Great Britain in particular, played an important role in the establishment and continued existence of the Baltic States. Latvia saw Great Britain as one of its main allies and the guarantor of its independence. Throughout this period, intensive economic and political relations existed between Great Britain and the Baltic States. With the outbreak of the Second World War, the existence of these relations was threatened and following the occupation of the Baltic States in 1940 they ceased altogether.

The incorporation of Latvia, Lithuania and Estonia into the Soviet Union in the summer of 1940 did not come as a surprise to Great Britain. It recognised these acts by the Soviet Union *de facto*, but not *de jure*. Winston Churchill considered that the question of the lawfulness of territorial changes in Eastern Europe and the Baltic should be decided at the post-war peace conference. In the winter of 1942, with negotiations for a treaty of alliance between Britain and the Soviet Union, British policy towards the Baltic States became unfavourable. The Foreign Secretary, Anthony Eden, advocated concessions to the Soviet Union and the rapid recognition of the incorporation of the Baltic States. However, no official steps were taken by the British government. At the end of the Second World War the British position had not changed. Nevertheless, a request submitted by the envoys of the Baltic States in London during the Potsdam conference in July 1945, that Great Britain support the claims of the people of Latvia, Lithuania and Estonia for freedom and independence, was ignored.

Relations between Great Britain and the Baltic States at the beginning of World War II (1939-1940)

With the outbreak of the Second World War, relations between Britain and the Baltic States faced a series of new problems. The traditional inter-state mechanisms, which had existed for years were seriously threatened. The Baltic States had become internationally isolated, with little room for manoeuvre. In 1938, following the lead of the Scandinavian countries, Latvia, Lithuania and Estonia had declared absolute neutrality. In the summer of the following year, they had rejected guarantees from Great Britain, France and the USSR, as well as proposals for non-aggression pacts with Germany. Their only international protection came from the League of Nations and the Baltic Entente of 1934. However, the mutual differences between the states of the Entente were so great that this union gave no practical benefits. The situation was further complicated by the Molotov-Ribbentrop Pact and subsequent agreements between the USSR and Germany, which meant that at the outbreak of war the Baltic States were in fact within the military and political sphere of influence of the USSR, even though they preserved economic and diplomatic ties with Britain and other Western countries.

Following Germany's invasion of Poland, the Polish government requested that Great Britain render all possible assistance in accordance with the agreement of 25 August 1939 between the two countries. On 3 September, Great Britain and France declared war on Germany. According to the British historian John Hiden, this indicated that Britain also had strategic interests in the Baltic region.[1] Another British historian, Patrick Salmon, emphasises the opposite, that by the autumn of 1939 Great Britain had abandoned its strategic interests in the Baltic.[2] It has to be admitted that most historians of foreign policy in Latvia believe that the Polish-British treaty did not change British strategy in the Baltic. Great Britain, at the beginning of the war, did not wish to undertake any political or military commitments in respect of guaranteeing the security of the Baltic States. Moreover, the British

---

[1] John Hiden, 'On the Edge of Diplomacy? Britain, the Baltic and East-West Relations between the Wars', in John Hiden and Aleksander Loit (eds.), *Contact or isolation? Soviet-Western relations in the interwar period* (Stockholm, 1991), p. 318.

[2] Patrick Salmon, 'British Security Interests in Scandinavia and the Baltic 1918-1939, in John Hiden and Aleksander Loit (eds.), *The Baltic in International Relations between the Two World Wars* (Stockholm, 1988), p. 125.

government believed that the situation in the Baltic region would not appreciably influence its own security.[3]

The British position on the Baltic issue at the end of 1939 was one of serious concern about trade between the Baltic States and Germany. Britain did not want to see strategic goods, e.g. timber, bacon, butter being supplied to Germany. This problem featured repeatedly in the negotiations between Great Britain, Latvia, and the other Baltic States in 1939-40. There is no reason to think that Great Britain was seriously concerned at this stage about the possible incorporation of the Baltic States into the USSR. Churchill, above all, believed that the Soviet Union should be masters of the eastern Baltic.[4]

Following the defeat of Poland at the end of September 1939, it became even clearer to the Baltic States that they must abandon any illusions regarding possible assistance from Britain and France. The Western powers were now fully occupied with the war against Germany. In such a situation, the Baltic States attempted to implement a careful and balanced policy in relations to both Germany and the USSR. Latvia and Estonia proclaimed their neutrality, hoping thereby to avoid being drawn into the conflict.

On 2 September 1939 the Latvian neutrality declaration was published in the press. Its text was co-ordinated with Estonia. Lithuania had already notified its decision regarding neutrality on 1 September. The Latvian government adopted a law regarding territorial waters (4 miles from the coast), as well as regarding the air space above these waters.[5] Some states protested against these measures. The British embassy in Riga disputed Latvia's rights to a 4-mile territorial waters zone on 27 October and 1 November 1939. However, notwithstanding these protests, the Latvian government stood its ground. In a reply of 3 January 1940, the Latvian Ministry of Foreign Affairs declared that Latvia would hold to the proclaimed 4-mile zone. However, such a stand had no practical meaning because, from 5 October, Soviet military bases had been located in Latvia. Consequently, Great Britain could not ignore the fact that Latvia's territorial waters had in fact become also the territorial waters of the Soviet Union.

---

[3] I. Feldmanis, A. Stranga and M. Virsis, *Latvijas Ārpolitika un starptautiskais stāvoklis. 30.gadu otrā puse* (Riga, 1993), pp. 333-38.

[4] Winston S. Churchill, *The Second World War*, vol. I, *The Gathering Storm*, (London, 1948), p. 285.

[5] 'Deklarâcija par Latvijas neitralitâti', *Brivâ Zeme*, 1939.g. 2.sept.

Great Britain generally valued Latvian neutrality. The British envoy to Latvia, Charles Orde, reported on 1 January that Latvia had attempted to observe properly its self-proclaimed neutrality, though he noted that certain problems were caused for Latvia by the activities of the USSR and Germany.[6]

However, neutrality did not save the Baltic States and on 24 September 1939, following a request from the USSR, negotiations were begun for a mutual assistance agreement, which after a few days, ended with the establishment of Soviet military bases in Estonia. A similar fate befell Latvia. On 5 October, it was forced to sign an analogous agreement and to let Soviet military forces into its territory. During the negotiations, the Soviet Foreign Minister, Vyacheslav Molotov, openly notified the Baltic States that to hope for the support of Great Britain was unreal, as Britain at that time was already at war with Germany. The Baltic States were forced to capitulate in the face of overwhelming force.[7]

In the early stages of the war, the British government observed the actions of the USSR in the Baltic States with a certain reserve, attempting not to take a clear stand or become involved in some way in these events. However, the growing pessimism regarding their future was reflected in the British press. On 23 October 1939, the *Daily Telegraph* ran an article called 'Nordic Neutrality'. It emphasised that Finland felt threatened by Moscow and was ready to fight for her independence, while Estonia, Latvia and Lithuania by their actions (here was meant the establishment of USSR military bases), had put their independence at great risk.[8] Material of a similar nature appeared elsewhere in the British press over the next few days. In response to these articles, the Latvian envoy in London, Kârlis Zariðð, sent a protest note to the Foreign Office in which he pointed out that 'notwithstanding the traditional friendly relations which exist between states, the tone of the British press in recent times has not been particularly friendly towards Latvia.' Zariðð quoted some of the more colourful epithets used by the British press in respect of the Baltic States. They were called Russia's vassals and jerry-built republics.[9]

The British consul in Estonia, Wilfred Galliene, felt that the new Estonian cabinet, which was formed following the concluding of the bases agreement

---

[6] Public Record Office, London (PRO). FO 371/24759, N383/383/59. All documents cited subsequently are from the PRO unless otherwise stated.

[7] Edgars Andersons, *Latvijas vēsture. Ârpolitika II*, 1920-1940 (Stockholm, 1984), p. 206.

[8] 'Nordic Neutrality', *Daily Telegraph*, 21 October 1939.

[9] FO 371/23606, N7202/8511/59.

with the Soviet Union, would not last long. Galliene in his dispatches from Tallinn to London emphasised that the new Estonian government was similar to the Kerensky-led provisional government in Russia in 1917. He thought that the new Estonian government would soon be replaced with a communist government completely loyal to Moscow.[10]

The change in British policy towards the Baltic States in the autumn of 1939 manifested itself in concrete forms. This is best shown over the issue of the sale of British weapons. The British government, for no apparent reason, refused to sell Estonia the 12 Spitfires for which an agreement had been signed in 1938. The British Foreign Office justified this decision on the basis of new circumstances and new allies such as had been formed at the end of 1939.[11] Latvia did not fare any better. During the visit of the Latvian Foreign Minister, Vilhelms Munters, to England in December 1938, agreement had been reached for the sale of weapons and ammunition to Latvia. However, in the autumn of the following year when the Second World War had already begun, Great Britain took a negative stand on this issue. On 30 September 1939, the British War Ministry recommended that the supply of ordered military materials to Latvia be halted. Daniel Lascelles of the Foreign Office indicated, when writing to the War Ministry, that in the circumstances, it was no longer necessary for Britain to strengthen the defence capabilities of the Baltic States. Following the establishment of Soviet military bases in the Baltic States, it would be foolish to supply these states with weapons as they would, sooner or later, fall into the hands of the USSR. In explaining the new British attitude towards the Baltic States, Lascelles at the same time indicated that military assistance should continue for Finland since it was ready to fight for its independence.[12]

Zariòð, the Latvian minister, tried to bring about a change of policy. He referred to the fact that the money for the weapons had already been paid to London banks and that the Vickers Armstrong factory was ready to fulfil the Latvian order. On 27 October 1939 he tried to extract from the British nine 75mm Vickers cannons, 250 machine guns, artillery ammunition, reserve parts for aeroplane engines and other necessary military equipment.[13] However, his activities produced no concrete results: Great Britain did not sell

---

[10] Ibid., N5483/564/59.

[11] FO 371/23605, N3166/381/59.

[12] Ibid., N4937/381/59.

[13] Ibid., N5724/381/59.

any weapons to Latvia. The reasons emerge clearly from the Foreign Office archives. A War Ministry official commented on one occasion: 'Latvia will probably be occupied completely in a few weeks. We have to do everything to avoid implementing the order. That will only assist Russia.'[14]

On 12 September 1939, Churchill proposed a plan called 'Operation Catherine'. It envisaged denying Germany complete control of the Baltic Sea and cutting its supplies of iron ore from Sweden. Nothing was said in the plan regarding operations of the British fleet in the territorial waters of Latvia and the other Baltic States.[15] Churchill planned to utilise two or three 29,000 tonne Royal Sovereign type ships built during World War I, three 10,000 tonne cruisers, and as other fleet auxiliaries. However, the British Admiralty realised that this operation would be successful only if co-operation with the Soviet Union was obtained. A very important factor in carrying out the plan was also the position of Norway and Sweden. Without their support, any success by the British fleet in the Baltic Sea was doubtful. However, as has been noted previously, the Scandinavian countries had proclaimed their neutrality.

On 21 September 1939 the leadership of 'Catherine' was entrusted to Admiral Boyle. Under his leadership the rebuilding and strengthening of the ships, so that they would not be easy targets for German bombers, was begun. However, as the shipyards were heavily overworked due to the war, preparations for the operation could only really begin in the spring of 1940. Even then, 'Catherine' was not implemented, mainly because of the opposition it aroused within the Admiralty.[16] It should be noted that the possibility that the Baltic States would receive assistance with 'Operation Catherine' was insignificant. In this case, one has to agree with the British historians John Hiden and Patrick Salmon, that Great Britain never promised direct military support to the Baltic States.[17]

In the early stages of the war, Great Britain was interested in trade relations with the Baltic States and wanted to continue at pre-war levels.

---

[14] Ibid., N5724/381/59.

[15] K. Lautenschlager, 'Plan "Catherine". The British Baltic Operation, 1940', *Journal of Baltic Studies* 5 (1974), pp. 213-14.

[16] See Arthur J. Marder, '"Winston is Back": Churchill at the Admiralty 1939-1940', in Arthur J. Marder, *From the Dardanelles to Oran: Studies of the Royal Navy in War and Peace* (London, 1974), pp.105-78.

[17] John Hiden and Patrick Salmon, *The Baltic Nations and Europe: Estonia, Latvia and Lithuania in the Twentieth Century* (London and New York, 1991), p. 104.

However, that was no longer possible as Germany blockaded the Baltic Sea. The British government was also worried about its enemy, Germany, actively trading with the Baltic States. On 9 September 1939, the British envoy in the Baltic States, Charles Orde, following instructions from the Foreign Office, suggested to the Baltic States that they organise wartime trade with Britain through Sweden and Norway. Great Britain suggested that they should first send their goods by ship to the Swedish port of Sundsvall and thence by railway to the Norwegian port of Trondheim, and from there by ship to Britain. Orde promised the Baltic States all possible support, in order that strategic war goods did not fall into the hands of Germany.[18] The British consul, Thomas Preston, in his despatches from Kaunas also wrote that the creation of conditions in which Latvian and Lithuanian goods could be sent to Britain would be of great moral and material support to these states in wartime. However, there was no such support from the British side.

In time of war, Latvia was in much need of the traditional British exports – coal, coke, oil, and cotton. She was nevertheless unable to organise trade with Britain at the levels of the previous year. The most serious obstacle, as noted earlier, was the Baltic Sea blockade. Germany attempted to sink or capture all Latvian ships heading for Great Britain. The Latvian government was also afraid that Germany would interpret this as a violation of the neutrality policy, and would not like the maintenance of trading relations with Great Britain.

Latvia's agricultural attaché in London, Emils Zolmanis, informed the government that Britain refused to give Latvian ships protection and in this way was discouraging trade between the two countries. The British side also refused to assist in resolving the problem of insuring commercial shipping. In time of war, this was very high – up to £200,000 per ship.[19] Within a few months of the beginning of the war low prices, the high cost of insurance and transport, and fear of Germany had reduced mutual trade between Great Britain and the Baltic States to a minimum. The situation was made even worse when, at the end of 1939, Latvia refused even to send a trade delegation to London to discuss and resolve the problems created.

At the same time Latvia, looking for a way out of the situation which had been created, concluded trade agreements with the Soviet Union (18 October 1939) and Germany (15 December 1939). During the negotiations, Germany

---

[18] FO 371/23609, N4193/4193/59.

[19] Latvijas Valsts Vēstures arhivs (LVVA)-2574.f., 4.apr., 7352.l., pp. 61-2.

officially requested that Latvia not engage in trade with Great Britain. Latvia rejected this request. A similar request was made by Germany to Lithuania in December.[20]

At the beginning of 1940, Great Britain did still try to save the collapsing trade with the Baltic States. The British government issued an invitation to the Latvian government to discuss the problems of wartime economic relations between the two countries. This time the Latvians agreed to send a delegation to London and talks commenced on 26 February. From the British side, two requests were advanced: an increase in Latvian exports to Great Britain, and a reduction in trade with Germany. However, in practice, Britain could do nothing to revitalise trade between the two countries. The head of the Baltic section in the Latvian Ministry of Foreign Affairs when evaluating these talks recognised that Latvia had nothing to hope for from them, and that its participation in them was merely a demonstration of Latvia's good will.[21]

At the end of 1939, Great Britain was somewhat indifferent to the military, political and economic strengthening of the Soviet Union in the Baltic States, considering that this was mainly to the detriment of Germany. The aim of British foreign policy was not to allow the USSR and Germany to draw closer together, and not to allow any deterioration in relations between the USSR and Britain. Soviet pressure on the Baltic States fitted into British strategy. This was confirmed by Churchill's remarks, reported in *The Times*, where he declared that the increase in the influence of the USSR in the Baltic States would strengthen its front against Germany and bring closer confrontation between them.[22] Churchill considered that the USSR in particular should be the dominating force on the eastern shore of the Baltic Sea and was delighted that Latvia, Lithuania and Estonia were included in the Soviet Union's, not Germany's sphere of influence. It was not in Britain's interests, he said, to protest against Soviet military bases in the Baltic States. Churchill considered that these bases would serve only for a war against Germany and therefore should not be a cause for British dissatisfaction. The Russian fleet in the Baltic Sea was not a threat to Britain's strategic interests. Only the presence of Germany there was dangerous because she was Britain's enemy.

---

[20] FO 371/24759, N172/172/59.

[21] LVVA-2574.f. 3.apr. 3291.l., p.194.

[22] *The Times*, 2 October 1939.

In wartime, Great Britain was more concerned with how to make the USSR an ally, rather than the legality of Soviet actions in the Baltic States from the point of view of international law. By the beginning of 1940, any illusions the Baltic States may have had regarding some kind of British military support had to be abandoned. This is confirmed by a report from Orde in Riga of 1 January 1940 which noted that Latvia was looking with concern at London's recent policies towards the Baltic States. The public in these states was concerned about the readiness of the Western democracies to sell their independence cheaply. Orde concluded that the establishment of Soviet military bases was the prelude to the complete annihilation of Baltic independence. In signing the base agreements, the Baltic States had in fact signed the death warrants for their own sovereignty. The peculiarity of the new situation was that the Baltic States had in fact become a protectorate of the Soviet Union. Orde was convinced that the Soviet Union would allow the Baltic States to maintain their languages and cultural autonomy. He also recognised that the Western democracies could not counter Soviet actions in the Baltic. The fate of eastern Europe and the Baltic States had been decided by the results of the Nazi-Soviet agreements. Orde believed that they now had reason to regret the policy of absolute neutrality to which they had adhered so strictly during the three-power talks in Moscow during the summer of 1939. The Baltic States had then refused the guarantees offered to them by Great Britain, France and the USSR. Because of this Britain did not have a legal basis to interfere in their affairs.[23]

At the end of January 1940, Zariòð had a long discussion with the director of the Northern Department of the Foreign Office, Laurence Collier. In his report of the discussion Collier wrote, that possibly, in the not too distant future, the British government would have to examine the issue of the Soviet Union's policies in the Baltic. Whether Britain recognised Soviet actions in the Baltic States would depend, to a large extent, on whether the Soviet Union supported the British Empire in its conflict with Germany. Collier considered that in principle, this would be an amoral deal on the part of Great Britain, but it was however dictated by the needs of the situation.[24]

The British *chargé d'affaires* in Tallinn, Wilfred Galliene, in a report of 17 February 1940, also noted the specific situation of the Baltic States. He considered that, after the Nazi-Soviet Pact, Latvia, Lithuania and Estonia had

---

[23] FO 371/24759, N383/383/59.

[24] FO 371/24761, N5833/224/59.

become totally isolated internationally. If Russia or Germany so wished, they could annex these states at any time. As both Russia and Germany were ancient enemies of the Baltic States, only their defeat would ensure the renewal of the independence and existence of these states.[25] A disturbance in Anglo-Latvian relations was caused by a speech in February 1940 on Latvian radio by the President, Kârlis Ulmanis. On 12 February, the speech was also published in the Latvian press. The next day, the *Daily Express* published a front-page article with an account of the Ulmanis speech together with commentary. Ulmanis emphasised that Stalin would in the near future put new demands to the Baltic States. The newspaper especially emphasised that this time the Baltic States would not surrender and were ready to fight. The *Daily Express* drew attention to the section of Ulmanis's speech, which stated that Latvia must be ready for great sacrifices in the near future. Everyone must be ready. Each family would have to give one man in uniform. The situation was serious and the country had to think about extraordinary measures.[26]

In addition, on 15 February the *Daily Express* published a similar article with the headline, 'Red Danger in the Baltic Increases'. In it was emphasised that Estonia and Latvia had already received new demands from the USSR regarding increases in the Soviet military contingent: the terrorisation of the Baltic States had begun. However, Latvia, Lithuania and Estonia were ready to fight and had requested weapons and other forms of assistance from the Western allies.[27]

After these articles in the British press, the *chargé d'affaires* at the Latvian embassy in London, Teodots Ozoliòð, turned for assistance to his Foreign Minister, Vilhelms Munters. He wrote that Latvia and Estonia had become better known to the British public as a result of these publications. He also drew attention to the statement in the *Daily Express* that Zariòð would be hastily recalled to Riga to assist in the preparation of an appeal to the Western allies. The basic idea of the appeal was to be – give us weapons! At the end of his telegram, Ozoliòð wrote that he thought that this was just a press rumour. However, the *chargé d'affaires* requested that the Ministry of Foreign Affairs in Riga clarify the position of the Latvian government.[28] From Tallinn, Galliene reported the echoes of the Latvian President's speech in Estonia. Some

---

[25] FO 371/24765, N2484/2484/59.

[26] *Daily Express*, 13 February 1940.

[27] *Daily Express*, 15 February 1940.

[28] LVVA-1313.f., 1.apr., 153.l., pp. 10-11.

believed that it was associated with new demands by the USSR in relation to the Baltic States. Others felt that the Baltic States, utilising the Finnish-Soviet War, were trying in this way to free themselves from the influence and the military bases of the USSR.[29] Orde, from Riga, drew attention to the activation of mutual military contacts among the Baltic States. He reported the visit of the commander of the Latvian Army, Kriðjânis Beríis, to Tallinn and his talks with General Johan Laidoner and also about Beríis' visit to Lithuania and his contacts with their military leaders.[30]

According to the Latvian historian, Edgars Andersons, the Ulmanis speech had no serious political meaning. It had no connection with the Finnish-Soviet War (the Winter War) or the vague promises by the Western states to support Finland. Andersons considers that Latvia, in the winter of 1940, had no real capability of its own to free itself from the Soviet military bases. Latvian army reserves were minimal and they were not prepared for a long military operation.[31] Ulmanis's speech did, however, create a general focus of attention. This was accentuated by the presence in Riga at the same time of a delegation of British businessmen. The press attempted to link the Finnish-Soviet War, the Ulmanis speech and the Latvian government's talks with the British business delegation and to explain them as a fundamental turning point in Latvian policy. Documents in the archives of Latvia and Great Britain do not confirm such a hypothesis. Britain, as has been noted earlier, was indifferent to the security problems of Latvia. In February-March 1940, Great Britain had no intention of being on Latvia's side or of assisting her to squeeze out the Soviet military bases.

A new phase in the relations between Great Britain and the Baltic States began in April 1940 following the German invasion of Denmark and Norway. At this time, Britain took a decision to convert the British consulates in Lithuania and Estonia into separate legations. Up to the beginning of the war, Great Britain had only one legation in the Baltic States, located in Riga. In the circumstances of war, permanent British legations were opened in Kaunas and Tallinn. The governments of Estonia and Lithuania welcomed this step. Nevertheless, it did not presage any real changes in Britain's strategy in relation to the Baltic States. Their role and meaning in Britain's policies were not increased even though Lithuania and Estonia interpreted this step as

---

[29] FO 371/24765, N2484/2484/59.

[30] Ibid., N2518/2518/59.

[31] Andersons, *Latvijas Vēsture*, pp. 364-5.

providing the basis for the activation of Great Britain's policy in the Baltic States.[32]

However, this was fated not to happen, as in June 1940, the USSR utilised the conditions of the Molotov-Ribbentrop pact and began openly to put pressure on the Baltic States. On 15 June they received Soviet ultimatums regarding the entry of unlimited numbers of forces into their territories, as well as demands to change their lawful governments.[33] On 17 June, Zariòð received a telegram from Munters which stated that Soviet forces had entered Latvia in uncontrolled numbers and were taking possession of important State institutions. Zariòð understood that in such a situation, the extraordinary powers granted to him previously by the Latvian government had come into effect. He utilised these powers all through the Second World War and also in the post-war period, in order to defend the interests of Latvia and its citizens.

The sovietisation of the Baltic did not come as a surprise to Britain. Foreign Office officials were calculating whether it was possible to force some concession from the USSR by recognition or non-recognition of the occupation of these states. Britain was at this time in an unenviable situation. She was almost alone in the war against Germany. In the summer of 1940, there was a real threat of a German invasion of the British Isles and every possibility of support was important.

On 16 July 1940, Zariòð, had a discussion with Collier. Disclosing an understanding of the events in Latvia, Collier, in his report on this meeting, wrote: 'We do not have to hurry with either recognition or condemnation of the Soviet actions in the Baltic; the stronger position we take, the greater the possibility that the policies of the USSR will change in a direction which is to our benefit.'[34]

The British Foreign Secretary, Lord Halifax, did indeed agree that the processes which had occurred in the Baltic States were not lawful. Halifax thought that it was enough that Britain did not recognise the actions of the USSR in the Baltic. He was more concerned about the fate of British property than about the loss of independence of the Baltic States.[35] London at this time was thinking more about effective counter-measures exactly in this direction. At this time almost half of Latvia's gold reserves were in England's banks –

---

[32] FO 371/24765, N3686/3686/59.

[33] Ibid., N5824/5824/59.

[34] Ibid., N6085/5917/59.

[35] Ibid., N6025/5917/59.

worth some 31.4m lats. Ships of the Baltic States were impounded, as was even the account of the Latvian minister.[36]

The Soviet ambassador, Ivan Maiskii, actively demanded the transfer of the gold and other property of the Republic of Latvia. In discussions with the Foreign Secretary, he repeatedly requested that the issue be settled. Halifax explained that there were two problems. The first was associated with the fact that the USSR had nationalised all British property in the Baltic. The second problem was of a political nature, namely, that Britain considered the actions of the Soviet Union in the Baltic States to be unlawful. Therefore, the British government did not recognise the new governments of the Baltic Soviet republics or their rights to any property.

In turn, Maiskii tried to prove that the Baltic Soviet republics had voluntarily joined the USSR, without forced sovietisation. Therefore, according to Maiskii, in the new situation the USSR was the legal successor to the property of these states. He demanded that the Baltic States' gold and hard currency in British banks, ships and other property be transferred to the Soviet Union. By impounding the property of the Baltic States Britain was infringing the sovereignty of the USSR and its lawful rights. Halifax declared that this was only the version of events as described by the Soviet ambassador.[37] The British ambassador in Moscow, Sir Stafford Cripps, had other views. He defended the view that the British Government should show a readiness to recognise the actions of the USSR in the Baltic States as lawful, if the Soviet Union was ready to co-operate with Great Britain against Germany.[38]

With the beginning of discussions between Britain and the Soviet Union regarding the fate of the property of the Baltic States, the Foreign Office requested detailed information regarding British property in the Baltic from its legations in Riga, Tallinn and Kaunas. For example, Douglas MacKillop from Riga wrote that British investments in Latvia at the beginning of 1940 were some 34.7 million lats. Summarising the information, the British Treasury determined that the value of British property losses were £1.7m in Latvia, £600,000 in Lithuania and £1.5m in Estonia.[39] The Foreign Office

---

[36] Ibid., N6024/5918/59.

[37] FO 371/24763, N6042/2039/59.

[38] Gabriel Gorodetsky, *Stafford Cripps's Mission to Moscow, 1940-1942* (Cambridge, 1984), pp. 63-73, 79, 94.

[39] FO 371/24763, N6177/2039/59.

also received claims from British firms regarding losses of property in the Baltic States. For example, on 12 August 1940 a telegram arrived in London containing information regarding British losses in the Riga wood-processing enterprise J. Potempa, to the value of 720,000 lats. Claims were also lodged by the British bank Lazard Brothers to the value of £759,000 and British Shell – £140,000.[40]

On 14 August 1940, the fate of British property in the Baltic States was debated in parliament. The Deputy Foreign Secretary, R. A. Butler, explained that the government would consider the claims of the various firms, banks and private persons. Butler also emphasised that the government was paying sufficient attention to the matter and it was working to recover British property. The issue was not without hope as the values of the impounded property and the nationalised property were nearly equal.[41] Halifax also defended the principle of mutual compensation: losses for both sides were approximately equal and therefore could be written off. During the war, the British government had requisitioned those Baltic ships which were in British ports, in total some 20 ships amounting to 37, 641 tonnes.[42] The USSR also advanced a claim for this property. The British government took an unyielding position.

By the end of the summer of 1940, the British government's policy towards the annexation of the Baltic States had in principle crystallised. The annexation of the Baltic States was to be recognised *de facto* but not *de jure.* The issue of the lawfulness of territorial changes was to be left to the post-war Peace Conference. This approach was confirmed by Winston Churchill on 5 September 1940. Speaking in parliament, he declared that Great Britain did not recognise as lawful territorial changes, which have occurred in wartime. The lawfulness of new borders in Europe would be approved by means of international agreements.[43]

The British legations in the Baltic States ceased operations on 5 September 1940. However, by the end of the year the British government concluded that in relation to the issue of the Baltic States, it should accept the US formulation, i.e. not to recognise forced changes in the Baltic. Nevertheless, it is true that the British position on this issue was never as strong as that of the

---

[40] FO 371/24764, N6417/2039/59.

[41] FO 371/24763, N6249/2039/59.

[42] FO 371/24764, N6979/2039/59.

[43] FO 371/24765, N7562/2039/59.

United States of America. This could be explained by the complicated situation in which Great Britain found herself. During this period she was not only at war with Germany, but also was trying to prevent the establishment of a Soviet-German alliance.

Great Britain and the problem of the Baltic States (1941-1945)

New problems for the diplomats of the Baltic States in London arose after 22 June 1941, when the Soviet Union came into conflict with Germany. Britain and the Soviet Union had now become official allies. Soviet diplomats tried to take advantage of this and again raised questions regarding recognition of the incorporation of the Baltic States, new borders, and the regulation of property relations. The British government was forced to take a conciliatory stance, one facilitated to some degree by the attitude of the Foreign Secretary, Anthony Eden. He openly expressed the view that the involvement of the USSR as a stable British ally was more important than the problem of the Baltic States. That this was not a very moral view is acknowledged by the British historian, David Kirby. However, war is war and any state in a similar situation must first of all consider its own security interests.[44]

Kirby, when comparing the attitudes of the USA and Great Britain regarding the Baltic States, writes that the former was governed in its policies more by moral principles, while for Great Britain, elements of political calculation were more characteristic. This has been confirmed by several British Foreign Office documents. An analysis of them shows that the stance of the US State Department on the Baltic States issue created a certain amount of alarm in the Foreign Office. The Latvian envoy in Washington, Alfręds Bilmanis, had submitted a request at the beginning of 1942 to allow his state to join the Atlantic Charter, which was directed against the Axis states. As the US State Department discussed this possibility, a member of the Northern Department of the Foreign Office, A. Warner, noted: 'I very much hope that the USA will not go further than its current support for the Baltic States. The State Department knows about our talks with Moscow and any new steps from the US side may make our positions very difficult.'[45]

---

[44] David Kirby, 'The Baltic States, 1940-1950', in M. McCauley (ed.), *Communist Power in Europe 1944 -1949* (London, 1977), p. 24.

[45] FO 371/32735, N1040/347/59.

At the end of 1941, the British Foreign Office took a decision which weakened the status of the diplomats of the Baltic States based in London states. From now on they could communicate only through the Northern Department, and they were prohibited from approaching any other official British institutions. Such a decision without a doubt restricted the activities of the Baltic diplomats. Further steps followed. The Baltic legations in London received official Notes in which was emphasised that Baltic diplomats were in future prohibited from making statements regarding political issues. A little later came an instruction that contacts with the British Foreign Office should only be in the form of letters.

This notably unfriendly unfavourable policy was defended by the British ambassador in Moscow, Stafford Cripps. He bombarded the Foreign Office with reports in which he recommended the acceptance without delay of all Soviet demands in respect of the Baltic States. Cripps recommended that the Baltic gold held in London banks should be transferred to the Soviet Union without delay. He was also in favour of handing over the requisitioned ships of the Baltic States and their crews to the Soviet Union.[46] Eden took a very similar position. He recommended in December 1941 that the new borders of the USSR be recognised, including the legality of the annexation of the Baltic States.

On 16 February 1942, the Latvian minister, Kârlis Zariòð, submitted a long memorandum to the Northern Department regarding the situation in Latvia. In the introduction, he wrote that the Latvian envoy in Stockholm, Voldemârs Salnais, had good contacts with Latvia and objective information regarding what was happening there. The memorandum described the atrocities committed by Soviet and German occupation regimes during 1940-1941 against civilians. Zariòð informed the British government of the mass deportations of the inhabitants of Latvia to Siberia, the nationalisation of property and other persecutions. He also drew attention to the fact that Moscow had commenced regular radio broadcasts in Latvian, in order to persuade the Latvian public of the legitimacy of the Soviet regime.

As shown in Foreign Office documents, Britain was not particularly worried by the policies of either the Soviet or the German regimes in the Baltic States. A minute by Warner on the Zariòð memorandum read: 'We are

---

[46] FO 371/24763, N6257/2039/59.

only seriously interested in the property policies of the German regime in Latvia.'[47]

At the beginning of 1942, the Royal Institute of International Affairs submitted to the British Foreign Office an extensive investigation entitled 'The Future of the Baltic States'. After an exposition of Latvian, Lithuanian and Estonian history and an evaluation of the German regime, it concluded that, after the defeat of Germany, Great Britain would not be able to fundamentally influence the policies of the Soviet Union in the Baltic. 'Whether we want it or not, the USSR will dominate the Baltic Sea region.'[48] The British War Cabinet's secret instructions on propaganda work against the USSR in wartime contained similar views. 'Russia after the war will attempt to strengthen its influence in Europe. Firstly, it is in their interests to have a strategically safe border established in the East. Especially, they want inclusion of the Baltic States, the Eastern parts of Poland, Bessarabia and Bukovina in their territory. We have to be ready for this.'[49] Eden, who was conducting intensive negotiations with the Soviet Union for a treaty of alliance between the two countries, supported this approach, which was also reflected in the position taken by the Northern Department. Warner wrote: 'We, together with the USA, should not give Russia a free hand in Eastern Europe with the exception perhaps of the Baltic States.'[50]

The calculations in British policy in relation to the Baltic States are even more clearly revealed in a special report prepared for Eden by the Northern Department. The introduction declared that the Baltic States had always been in either the German or the Russian sphere of influence. The notion of their independence and neutrality was an illusion, and this had been proved by the events of 1939, when they had lost their independence and had again been included in Russia's sphere of influence. Russia's interest in these states was firstly, strategic. If the Baltic States remained as part of the German Reich, their future existence would be even more complicated. The Soviet system would, however, provide the best possibility for self-preservation, even though in the end everything would be decided by Moscow.

The report emphasised that after the war Great Britain would not be able to have any concrete involvement in Eastern Europe. 'We can agree or also

---

[47] FO 371/32730, N348/4/59.

[48] Ibid., N1377/4/59.

[49] CAB 119/47, paper N66.

[50] FO 371/32740, N611/611/59.

disagree with the Russian claims, but in fact we will only be able to refer to the Russian undertaking to observe the principles of the Atlantic Charter. If we are in opposition to Russian policies in Eastern Europe after the war, in this way we will quickly reconstruct the Russian-German union. That could happen in reality if we do not allow Russia to determine the fate of Eastern Europe.'[51] The authors of the document repeatedly asked what was advantageous for Britain? To make strong demands on the Soviet Union to renew pre-war conditions in eastern Europe, including the Baltic States? Or to maintain the balance of power in Europe in the post-war period and not allow either Russia or Germany to dominate? In the end, the conclusion was reached that Britain had better take into account Russia's strategic interests, and that the implementation of the principles of the Atlantic Charter in different regions of the world should be approached differently.

In his comments on this report on 29 January 1942, Eden stated that it was doubtful whether even such a formulation would fully satisfy Stalin. Eden was worried that Russia might not like the British reference to the Atlantic Charter and the implementation of its principles – even if differentiated – in territory controlled by them after the war. It was possible, Eden believed, that Stalin would hold to the formula that the Baltic States had, in the summer of 1940, voluntarily joined the USSR and therefore would not accept any references to this question. Eden was also worried about the possible reaction of the USA: 'I'm afraid that it will be hard for us to persuade the USA that our approach will give Eastern Europe more real security and that it conforms to the principles of the Atlantic Charter.'[52]

However, not everyone in Great Britain at this time thought the same as the civil servants in the Foreign Office. On 1 April 1942, the Dean of Chichester sent a letter to the Foreign Office in which he asked the British government to take the side of the Baltic States more actively. He also wrote that the British government should not recognise the incorporation of the Baltic States into the USSR as lawful. At the end of the letter, the Dean also referred to the Atlantic Charter, which he believed placed certain obligations upon the government.[53] Orme Sargent of the Foreign Office noted cynically: 'Typical church position.'

---

[51] Ibid., N611/611/59.

[52] Ibid., 611/59

[53] FO 371/32740, N2449/611/59.

In 1942, the policy of Great Britain towards the Baltic States became even cooler. In March, Cripps stated openly in an interview in *The Times* that it was in Britain's strategic interests to recognise the incorporation of the Baltic States quickly.[54] This interview caused a large amount of activity on the part of the Baltic States diplomats in London. Protest notes were sent to the Foreign Office and *The Times* received long letters from the Baltic diplomats. At the same time Orme Sargent, in one of the meetings on the Baltic States issue, emphasised, 'I understand that we want the agreement with Russia to have included the notion of some sort of autonomous element for the Baltic States. However, it seems that at the moment if we approached Russia with this, it would appear to be a bad joke. It is obviously impossible. Only, if the atmosphere at the time of the signing of the agreement was favourable, we could perhaps convince Stalin to publicly make a statement regarding the regime which would await the Baltic States in the USSR after the war.'[55]

At a meeting on 18 April 1942, Foreign Office officials already believed that it not be correct to ask the Soviet Union for such a one-sided declaration. The interests of the Baltic States would be sufficiently well protected by the constitution of the Soviet Union, in which there were articles in respect of the rights of republics, up to and including the right to secede from the union. It is true that the participants recognised that such articles were declaratory and that such rights existed only on paper.[56]

The final stage of negotiations for the Anglo-Soviet treaty in the winter and spring of 1942 showed that Eden, Cripps, Sargent and Warner were ready to make concessions to the Soviet Union, i.e., to satisfy its demands in the Baltic. As recompense for this, Britain would receive the consent of the Soviet Union to sign the long awaited treaty between the two states. In the event, Great Britain was somewhat surprised that the Soviet Union agreed not to include in the agreement a demand regarding the recognition of new borders.[57] On 26 May 1942, the co-operation agreement between the Soviet Union and Great Britain was signed. Even though during the preparation of the agreement the British side had, in principle, agreed to the recognition of the incorporation of the Baltic States, this was not written into the official text of the agreement. The people of the Baltic could breath a little easier.

---

[54] FO 371/32735, N1773/347/59.

[55] Ibid., 612/59.

[56] Ibid., 612/59

[57] Hiden and Salmon, *Baltic Nations*, p. 122.

Most of the credit for this should probably should go to the American government. As is shown by British Foreign Office materials, it kept up pressure on Britain not to accept the Soviet demands.[58] The Soviet Union had also, at the last moment, changed its tactics and no longer insisted that its Western border be fixed in the agreement. Stalin began to believe that this could tie his hands in the post-war period.

At the end of June 1942, under the influence of Soviet pressure (the Soviet ambassador, Maiskii, was particularly active), Anthony Eden took the decision to exclude the ministers of the Baltic States from the Diplomatic Corps list. Ministers from the Baltic and other occupied states were included in a separate annex to the Diplomatic Corps list.[59] This made the position of the diplomats of the Baltic States even more problematical. It is interesting to note Anthony Eden's own memorandum, 'Representatives of the Baltic States' which he submitted for approval by the British Cabinet. Eden stated that as a result of sustained pressure by the USSR the British Foreign Office had taken a decision to change the status of the three ministers of the Baltic States. ' One must hope that this step will fully satisfy the government of the Soviet Union, and at the same time not take away diplomatic immunity from the envoys of the Baltic States. I cannot answer as to how the Court shall react to this. I believe that no concrete steps will follow.'[60]

Nevertheless, Eden had made a mistake. Concrete reactions to this official change in policy by important British institutions soon followed. Zariðð wrote an official letter of protest to the Foreign Office drawing attention to the fact that the *Who's Who* had published maps in which the Baltic States were already shown as part of the Soviet Union.[61] A similar protest was sent by the Estonian legation in relation to an analogous publication by the Royal Institute of International Affairs.[62]

The leading newspapers in Great Britain also reacted to the changes in the government's policy. On 19 December 1942, an article appeared in *The Times* in which the Baltic States were classified as part of the group of Axis states and described as German satellites. Once again, Zariðð sent a protest note. Warner

---

[58] FO 371/32735, N1040/347/59.

[59] Ibid., N3497/2453/59.

[60] Ibid., N3447/347/59.

[61] Ibid., N3869/347/59.

[62] Ibid., N4196/337/59.

in his reply suggested that Zariòð turn to the editors of *The Times* with this protest and demand a retraction of the publication.[63]

The Latvian legation in Washington also tried to stop unfavourable changes in British policy towards the Baltic States. At the beginning of 1943, a voluminous document on the inter-war history of the Baltic States was sent to the Foreign Office. It emphasised that the twenty years of independence would be erased from the hearts of the people of the Baltic States. The choice of the people of the Baltic States to live independently and separately from Russia was final. In the document it was indicated that after victory over the Axis powers, the people of the Baltic States definitely wished to renew their statehood and to be included in the post-war renewed Europe. As their security guarantee, they envisaged a collective system of security of European states, without any foreign military bases on their territories. Thus, the strategic interests and security of the Soviet Union would not be threatened.[64]

Unfortunately, such memorandums from Latvian legations were ignored in London. Only the position of the United States worried the British government to any extent. Sargent considered that the State Department would not worry too much if Russia again occupied the Baltic States. The Americans knew that such actions would not cause the least counter-pressure from the British government, or from parliamentary circles. Great Britain would accept it as a self-evident fact.[65]

This British diplomatic view was close to reality. Indeed, neither mighty America, nor Great Britain was prepared to go to war with the Soviet Union for the sake of eastern Europe or the Baltic States. For both Western great powers Baltic interests were subordinated to the greater priority of good relations with Joseph Stalin. That was cynical, as the British ambassador in Washington Lord Halifax acknowledged, but it was a fact in itself. The US Under-Secretary of State, Sumner Welles, had a different point of view, but that was only his personal view and nothing more.

In the autumn of 1943, Maiskii continued to put pressure on the Foreign Office over the future of the Baltic States. Thus, for example, on 10 September he stated that he thought that the Baltic problem was, at the moment, more of a priority for Great Britain and the Soviet Union than for the USA. Maiskii thought that it would be better if, in the post-war period,

---

[63] FO 371/32735, N6540/347/59.

[64] FO 371/36779, N5389/5389/59.

[65] Ibid., N5455/5389/59.

America withdrew from active interference in the resolution of Europe's problems. By attempting to drive a wedge between the United States and Great Britain over the Baltic problem, Maiskii hoped to make Britain even more prone to making concessions. Maiskii also openly hinted that in the next four or five months Soviet forces would again be in the Baltic States. Britain without a doubt would have to accept this. In case Great Britain thought otherwise, then the agreement of 26 May 1942 on post-war co-operation between the USSR and Great Britain would be seriously threatened.[66]

Without a doubt, and forced by the circumstances of war, Great Britain took heed of such hints by the Soviet Union. At the same time, the British effectively ignored proposals from the representatives of the Baltic States that the future of their states should be resolved after the war in accordance with the principles of the Atlantic Charter. Kârlis Zariòð, Jûlijs Feldmanis, Latvia's representative at the League of Nations, and the Latvian envoy to Belgium Miíelis Valters all submitted such proposals to Churchill.[67] With the end of the war approaching, the British government understood that, in the near future, they would have to clarify their position in respect of the post-war order in Europe, including the Baltic. The issues of post-war borders and the recognition or non-recognition of the incorporation of the Baltic States were still in the foreground. In January 1944, the Foreign Office received instructions from the Prime Minister to clarify the British government's position on both these issues.[68]

Warner of the Northern Department prepared a special memorandum in which it was emphasised that Great Britain could, in principle, agree to the territorial demands of the Soviet Union as far as they corresponded to the western borders of former Tsarist Russia. However, it should be explained to the Soviet Union that such discussions of detail should be better left until after the final defeat of Hitler. Warner also recommended that there should be no hurry to give official recognition to the incorporation of the Baltic States during wartime, even though the Soviet Union had repeatedly demanded it. Warner thought that this would cause the government additional problems in parliament, as well as in its relations with the United States. He considered that it should be explained to Stalin that the British government would face real difficulties which the British government if it suddenly made a new public

---

[66] FO 371/36779, N5455/5389/59.

[67] Ibid., N6272/5389/59.

[68] FO 371/43052, N506/506/59.

announcement regarding the borders issue.[69] In reminding Stalin that the resolution of territorial problems should be left to the post-war Peace Conference, Warner also wanted to emphasise that the British government did not wish to dispute the claims of the Soviet Union to Bessarabia, Bukovina and the Baltic States. He acknowledged that Russia would, in the near future, acquire the territories and it was quite clear that Great Britain could not in any way delay this happening.[70]

Zariòð, as if suspecting new activities in the Foreign Office over the issue of the Baltic States, sent them his own memorandum on 1 February 1944. He wrote: 'Reports from the battlefield indicate that the Russian army is again close to the borders of Latvia and the other Baltic States. The leaders of the Soviet Union and the press are intensively propagandising the view that the Baltic States are a lawful part of the Soviet Union. I wish to remind you that the actions of the Soviet Union in the Baltic States in 1940 have not been internationally recognised. The lawful international status of the Republic of Latvia has not changed.'[71]

The British press at this time reflected the problem of the Baltic States. On 7 February 1944, a letter from the commander of the Soviet army's Lithuanian division, Vladsa Karveïa, and the chief of staff of the Estonian corps, Johanes Lukas appeared in *The Times*. They wrote: 'In 1940, the people of the Baltic made their choice. That was a free, unforced choice by ballot for the commencement of a new, socialistic way of life for Lithuania, Latvia and Estonia.' The appearance of such materials in the British press indicated that, at the beginning of 1944, the Soviet Union had begun a campaign for the faster recognition of the incorporation of the Baltic States. It should be pointed out, that the timing of this campaign coincided with discussion of the Baltic issue in the Foreign Office.

The legations of the Baltic States reacted sharply to the press campaign. An official letter of protest was sent to *The Times*: diplomats from Estonia, Lithuania and Latvia – E. Sapera, V. Balicks and T. Ozoliòð – wrote, 'The attacks on the legitimate governments of the Baltic States and their representatives by your newspapers are Soviet propaganda which, in such a manner, is trying to falsely inform your readers.' However, the Soviet campaign in the British press was not finished. On 24 March 1944, the

---

[69] Ibid., N555/506/59.

[70] Ibid., N665/506/59.

[71] FO 371/43052, N671/506/59.

Manchester Guardian published a letter from three representatives of the Soviet Baltic republics' intelligentsia – Jânis Sudrabkalns, Lindas Giras and Hans Kruus: 'We, the representatives of the intelligentsia of the Baltic States, highly value the assistance which our people, by freeing them from fascism, have received from the Soviet Union and its Red army. The Baltic States will go down the path which they began in June 1940.'[72]

The Archbishop of Canterbury, on the other hand, asked Eden to support the peoples of the Baltic. In his reply Eden wrote: 'I sympathise with you regarding the Baltic States, but I'm afraid that this time is not the most favourable to approach the Soviet Union with any requests. The USSR is always very sensitive to our every action regarding the issue of the Baltic States.'[73] A well-known friend of the Baltic States, the British MP Alfred Bossom, also tried to intervene in these events. On 29 September 1944, he wrote to Eden: 'The attitude of Russia towards the Baltic States is clear. However, when the time comes, I hope that you will do all that is in your power to force Russia not to be too harsh towards these three small nations, whose freedom in their time was welcomed by both America and Britain.'[74] However, the official position of the British government at the end of 1944 was given in a reply by the Foreign Secretary to a question from H. Williams, MP. It was very brief, 'Her Majesty's Government has not recognised any other governments in Lithuania, Latvia and Estonia other than those which existed up to June 1940.'[75]

Even at the end of 1944 the British government did not recognise the incorporation of the Baltic States into the Soviet Union as lawful. This position did not correspond to the line which was being taken by British diplomats in secret talks in Moscow. Even Churchill was ready at the end of 1944 to achieve agreement with Stalin regarding the division of Eastern Europe into spheres of influence. At the beginning of 1945 and the Yalta conference Great Britain, and to a certain extent the USA, demonstrated a willingness to write off Bulgaria, Rumania, Poland, Czechoslovakia, Hungary and Yugoslavia to the Soviet Union's sphere of influence. The claims of

---

[72] *Manchester Guardian*, 24 March 1944.

[73] FO 371/43052, N4300/506/59.

[74] Ibid., N6160/506/59.

[75] FO 371/43052, N8102/506/59.

Estonia, Latvia and Lithuania to have their independence renewed were nearly always ignored.[76]

In 1945, as the war neared its end, the British Foreign Office returned to the issue of the Baltic States once and for all. At a meeting held on 27 February, it was determined that the changes in the Baltic had already been recognised *de facto* by the British government in July 1940. On concluding the alliance with the USSR in May 1942, Great Britain had been prepared to promise that it would not object to the incorporation of the Baltic States into the Soviet Union. At the last moment, this agreement had not been included in the text of the treaty, but the USSR had afterwards always considered that there were no differences on this issue between the two countries. Nevertheless, in January 1945, the Foreign Office decided that Britain had not recognised *de jure* the incorporation of the Baltic States and that the last word regarding the fate of these states would come at the international Peace Conference.[77]

On 3 July 1945, prior to the meeting of the three Allied great powers in Potsdam, the envoys of Lithuania, Latvia and Estonia in London sent a message to the Foreign Office in which they emphasised that the Baltic States had been occupied three times in the last war, and requested that the British government support the claims of these people and their longing for freedom and independence.[78] Unfortunately, the government of Great Britain again gave preference not to moral principles, but to political expediency. The appeal was not heard and these states were incorporated into the USSR for nearly fifty years.

Conclusion

The Second World War caused shocks on a global scale. Under its influence the international order established in the 1920s and 1930s collapsed. These processes directly affected relations between the Baltic States and Great Britain. The Baltic States were incorporated into the Soviet Union and Great Britain quietly accepted such a policy. The British Foreign Secretary Lord Halifax emphasised that the processes occurring in the Baltic States were not lawful, but made no official protest to the Soviet Union.

---

[76] Hiden and Salmon, *Baltic Nations*, pp. 123-4.

[77] FO 371/47042, N2355/719/59.

[78] Ibid., N8160/719/59.

Forced by war, Great Britain thought more about strengthening her position in the war against Nazi Germany than about observing the principles of justice and legality. The Baltic States were in an unenviable situation. They were ground between the millstones of the Soviet Union and Nazi Germany. The Soviet Union did all that it could to persuade Great Britain to recognise Soviet policy in the Baltic *de facto* and *de jure*, and Great Britain nearly succumbed to such pressure. Nevertheless, in the last resort Britain adopted the US formula which provided that the issue of the legality of the territorial changes in Eastern Europe and the Baltic States should be discussed and decided at the post-war Peace Conference – a Peace Conference that was, however, never held.

Chapter 16

Always the buffer? Poland as NATO's new eastern frontier

Kaare Dahl Martinsen

Poland's quest for NATO membership can best be explained by the fear that Poland would once more be a buffer state between East and West. How to overcome this predicament remained a central concern for changing Polish governments. The outcome as it gradually emerged was conditioned partly by domestic factors and partly by external changes either in neighbouring countries or in NATO.

From the early 1990s, achieving NATO membership was a top priority for all the major political parties in Poland. But this consensus did not prevail when a strategy on how to achieve it was deliberated. Conflicts arose over matters not directly linked to the quest for membership. These concerned three separate issues: parliamentary attempts to control the armed forces and military intelligence, economic cooperation and trade with the eastern neighbours, and Russia's role in the region.[1] Especially the design and implementation of a Polish eastern policy had wider implications for Poland's position within the Alliance once membership was granted. Membership was not regarded as a final target, but rather as a platform for the conduct of a more active foreign and security policy.

---

[1] J. Stefanowicz, 'Central Europe between Russia and Germany', *Security Dialogue* 26 (1995), pp. 55-71.

The role NATO played in the internal Polish debate until the country became a full member in 1999 is what will be discussed here. This implies a shift from most writing on NATO expansion where attention has centred on the debate within the Alliance, the pros and cons of accepting new members. Often this was discussed in the light of anticipated Russian reactions and how these would affect NATO negatively.[2] Eastward expansion has been expected to aggravate the divisions within NATO and impede the ability to act jointly and swiftly. Moreover, the issue of costs, i.e. the price tag for accepting new, militarily weaker members is not set, nor is the question of who will cover it. This may well prove to be a catalyst for internal conflicts in the Alliance. One need only to recall President Chirac's assertion made during the 1997 Madrid NATO summit that France would not pay a centime of the costs for NATO expansion.[3]

Useful as this focus may be, questions pertaining to the new member states' reasons for applying, and how membership may affect both their internal political developments and positions on NATO policies and in particular NATO's relations with the former Soviet republics to the east of Poland, have remained largely unaddressed.

Polish NATO membership is still very new. The concluding discussion on whether NATO can accommodate Polish priorities, and what the potential consequences on Alliance cohesiveness may be, is unavoidably somewhat tentative. Although this may appear as a return to the start, progressing from NATO's impact on Polish politics to Poland's influence on NATO's eastern policy, it seems the only logical route to take if the relevance of domestic factors is to be assessed.

The relevance of domestic factors

Politicians in applicant countries have repeatedly made the link between NATO and domestic factors by claiming that preparing for membership is an important push towards democracy. A counter-argument might be that other organisations than NATO seem more suited to assist the democratisation process in the applicant countries than NATO. That might well be true, but even when including the EU, no other organisation seems to be as attractive as NATO. This in itself gives NATO considerable leverage in setting criteria for domestic

---

[2]   E.g. M. E. Brown, 'The Flawed Logic of NATO Enlargement', *Survival* 37 (1995), pp. 34-52.

[3]   *Le Figaro*, 10 July 1997.

change in the applicant states. The desire to use NATO to influence domestic politics was openly admitted, for example, by the Clinton administration.[4]

The relevance of domestic factors in influencing national policies on security issues has more often than not been given scant attention. This is probably due to the predominant view in much academic writing on European security up to 1989 where the bipolar balance of power was regarded as the primary determinant of national security policies. An increase in power for one party meant a relative loss to the other. The problem was that the understanding of security was equated with power, and whereas security understood solely in terms of military power may be a zero-sum game, security more broadly understood is not. Restricting analytical focus to power precludes the ability to look at the non-zero-sum nature of security. With the disappearance of bipolarity in Europe, the explanatory value of power has not been forfeited, but it has lost its solitary position. This has two clear implications for security studies, first the need to start out with domestic formulation of national interests, secondly looking at how these are implemented. Security theorists have traditionally focused on the fact that state actions may reduce the security of others, forgetting to incorporate into their analysis the possibility that they may not do so. Indeed two other options, i.e. that a state's decision on security matters may be either irrelevant, or that it may enhance the position of its neighbours, must also be considered. In fact, all of these possibilities can be found when examining the response of Poland's neighbours to NATO's enlargement.

Analysts often regard foreign policy formulation as a rational and pragmatic process, based on geopolitical realities and national interests.[5] In the case of Poland, the geopolitical realities changed radically with the demise of Soviet hegemony and Soviet-style society. Radical changes like these occur rarely. But when they do, they necessitate a redrawing of both domestic and foreign policy. Since the two processes concur in a context where national priorities are not yet fixed, the interdependence and interplay between them will be more intense than in a stable and predictable setting.

In Poland, the change of political leadership and with it foreign policy priorities took place within a relatively short time. Domestic concerns and reforms ranked top of the agenda. Planning and one-party rule had to be

---

[4] S. Talbott, 'Why NATO Should Grow', *New York Review of Books*, 10 August 1995.

[5] E.g. I. Prizel, *National Identity and Foreign Policy: Nationalism and Leadership in Poland, Russia and Ukraine* (Cambridge, 1998).

eliminated, galloping inflation and increasing unemployment combated. In foreign policy, the main priority was to develop cooperation with the West. Yet how this could be done without neglecting Poland's eastern neighbours was far from clear. Quite soon, the need to balance the two, and make Polish eastern policy complementary to and not independent of its Western policy became a recurring problem.

The need to cooperate as closely as possible with the West, while at the same time developing a relationship with its eastern neighbours, has been promoted by the political leadership irrespective of party colour. However, this consistency in priorities did not mean that the conduct of foreign policy was unperturbed by internal political changes. President Walesa attempted to use foreign policy issues to bolster his own position, even if this meant prolonged conflict with government and parliament. Another difference, far more important and difficult than presidential style, concerns popular perceptions of the neighbouring countries. These originated in historical events and developments that had to be addressed before the political dialogue could unblock. Prominent here was Soviet, and later Russian reluctance to acknowledge culpability for the Katyn massacre. But also pre-war conflicts over Cieszyn with Czechoslovakia, Vilnius with Lithuania, war-time massacres and deportations of the Polish population in Belarus and Ukraine, post-war resettlements of the Ukrainian and Belorussian minorities in Poland, were some of the unsolved issues that could be exploited by politicians to oppose government foreign policy initiatives.

German unification combined with close political cooperation between the Soviet Union and Germany seemed to reintroduce the buffer status from the inter-war years.[6] In the Polish context, the most feasible worst-case scenario was not a Russian attack, but rather that Russia would extract promises from NATO or Germany, precluding Polish membership in the Alliance. Membership obviously made that impossible, but it also means that closer contacts between Russia and the West would be less likely to evoke Polish fears.

Initial reorientation of Polish security policy

The Polish government had played an instrumental part in ending Soviet hegemony over Central and Eastern Europe. However, once completed, the initial official policy lacked coherence and direction. In 1990, Foreign Minister

---

[6] Poland's geo-strategic position as a buffer was highlighted after the Duma elections in December · 1993 when the newly elected nationalist politician Vladimir Zhirinovsky showed a map where Poland once more was divided between Russia and Germany.

Krzysztof Skubiszewski declared he preferred a united Germany inside NATO. Yet at the same time, Prime Minister Tadeuz Mazowiecki stated that the best interim solution would be to retain Warsaw Pact troops in the former GDR pending the creation of an all-European security system.[7] A year later, Deputy Minister of Defence Janusz Onyszkiewicz declared that his government had no plans of joining NATO at all.[8] Yet the government's views were changed in 1991. This was due less to public debate than to the brutal Soviet attempts to oppress Baltic independence by military means in January that year. The Central European governments were prompted into action. At a joint meeting in Budapest, the Polish, Czechoslovak and Hungarian foreign ministers demanded the termination of the Warsaw Pact's military cooperation.

The impression of Central European unity was further strengthened soon after when the heads of state of the three countries met in the spring of 1991 in the Hungarian town Visegrád. But the joint declaration issued was rather tame. Despite the efforts made by the Polish Foreign Minister Skubiszewski to expand cooperation to cover defence and security, only trade and economic development were singled out as top priorities.[9] Soon after in Prague in July 1991, at a meeting of the Political Consultative Committee, the only remnant of Warsaw Pact, the Pact was formally dissolved. The Soviet representatives recommended supplanting the Pact with a system of bilateral security treaties. This idea was not immediately rejected by the Central European countries. Yet when the Soviet side insisted that these treaties should include an article prohibiting the signatories from joining an alliance aimed at the other, it was interpreted as little more than a continuation of Soviet hegemony over Central Europe. Not surprisingly, it was rejected by the Hungarian, Czechoslovak and Polish representatives.[10]

---

[7] B. Donovan, 'Eastern Europe and German Unity', *Report on Eastern Europe*, 2 March 1990, pp. 48-51 (p. 51).

[8] V. Kusin, 'Security Concerns in Central Europe', *Report on Eastern Europe*, 8 March 1991, pp. 25-40 (p. 35).

[9] J. Weydenthal, 'Building a National Security System', *Report on Eastern Europe*, 14 June 1991, pp. 12-16 (p. 14).

[10] Only the Romanian government accepted, yet parliament managed to delay ratification. After the Soviet coup attempt, the Romanian government withdrew its acceptance.

NATO as the sole option

The attempted coup in Moscow in August 1991 had strong reverberations in Central Europe. The Polish, Czechoslovak and Hungarian presidents gathered for emergency talks. In a joint declaration issued in Cracow, the need for regular consultations on security issues with NATO was underlined. This was obviously only intended as an interim solution. The declaration concluded: 'there is a need to create conditions for the direct inclusion of Poland, Czechoslovakia and Hungary in the activities of the Alliance.'[11] Some foreign observers interpreted this as the beginning of Central European coordination on security matters. Yet the efforts stranded on the Czech Prime Minister Václav Klaus' opposition to any kind of institutionalised Central European network outside NATO and the EU.[12] Believing that the Czech Republic ranked first, he claimed that any group creation would only postpone the date of membership.

The new leadership of Czechoslovakia and especially President Havel attempted, admittedly very briefly, to launch CSCE as an alternative option to NATO. This possibility never received any noticeable attention in Poland, probably because a strengthening of the then CSCE and later OSCE was identical to the plans for an all-European security system launched by the Soviet and later Russian leadership at the beginning of the decade. A few articles were written exploring the possibility of a non-aligned Poland, but as a rule they concluded that this would mean a return to the buffer predicament of the inter-war years.[13] One of those opposing NATO membership, Professor Marcin Król, argued that since NATO had lost a clear mandate with the fall of the Warsaw Pact, it was in a state of chaos and disarray. Polish foreign policy autonomy would be constrained, and Polish mediation in East European conflicts would be close to impossible.[14] But Professor Król remained a solitary exception.

None of the regional organisations that emerged after 1989, e.g. the Visegrád Triangle, later to be called the Quadrangle, the Pentagonale Group and the Central-European Free Trade Association (CEFTA), have frequently been mentioned as organisations with a potential to meet the security problems of the regions. Yet none has played any significant role in developing cooperation so far. Visegrád have not moved beyond the level of discussion forum. CEFTA has

---

[11] *Gazeta Wyborcza*, 7 October 1991.

[12] V. Klaus, ' Změny v Praze a evropské souvislosti', in *Česká cesta* (Prague, 1994), pp. 131-137.

[13] S. Szafarz, 'Neutralna Polska', *Przegląd Tygodniowy*, 23 January 1994.

[14] M. Król, 'Co możemy i na co nas stać' *Życie Warszawy*, 20 September 1994.

made some progress easing trade barriers between the countries, but the EU is of course overshadowing the organisation completely in the economic field.

The attention given to these organisations in Western articles is somewhat puzzling. It seems to imply an unwillingness to address hard-core security politics, i.e. the need to create an arrangement that may function as a safeguard against external threats. The fact that these organisations hardly ever emerge in the security debate in the Central European countries does not imply less scholarly sophistication, but a keener perception of what these organisations are capable of delivering. Similarly, the wars in Yugoslavia showed that the efforts to create a system of interlocking, cooperating European preventing armed conflicts were insufficient. Judging from contemporary Polish press reports on the war in Bosnia, NATO was regarded as the only organisation capable of ensuring safety against military aggression.[15]

Yet despite the overwhelmingly positive view of NATO, Poland as well as the other Central European countries failed to engage the Clinton administration in a dialogue on the region's security problems. This was worrying, not least since concurrent developments in Russian politics were interpreted as being heavily Soviet in style and contents. International politics were still perceived as dominated by two opposing blocks. The concept of a 'near abroad' embracing the former Soviet Union republics as well as the insistence on a *droit de régard* over Central European security matters, became pronounced in the course of 1993. These ideas enjoyed the support of all the factions in the Russian Duma. Unperturbed by these developments, the West continued to perceive President Yeltsin as guardian of stability and reforms. In particular Strobe Talbott, U.S. Deputy-Secretary of State, was regarded in Central Europe as an advocate for a 'Russia-first-and-only-Russia' policy. The security concerns of Poland and the other Central European countries received scant attention. This was perhaps due to Washington's calculations that the eastward expansion of the EU would occur within the near future. A larger EU was not opposed by Moscow and would therefore not affect the relationship between Russia and the USA.

The Clinton administration would have preferred a tandem expansion, preferably with the EU paving the way. But as Madeleine Albright later explained: 'the security NATO provides should not have to wait until tomato

---

[15] R. Kuźniar, 'Polish Foreign Policy – an Attempt at an Overview', *Yearbook of Polish Foreign Policy 1993/1994* (Warsaw, 1994), pp. 9-20 (p. 9).

farmers in Central Europe start using the right kind of pesticides.'[16] Only with the launching of Partnership for Peace (PfP) in October 1993 was a framework for contacts with NATO created. PfP was not membership. Initially, it was not a foregone conclusion that it would lead to it either. PfP was sometimes referred to as 'Partnership for Appeasement'. The official Polish attitude expressed by President Walesa was that PfP ran the danger of being a permanent waiting room. Yet despite contemporary misgivings, the importance of PfP can hardly be overestimated.[17] PfP enabled the partnership countries to set individual targets for the transition of their military forces and politics in agreement with NATO. The collaboration was reciprocal; it provided the Alliance with a testing ground for cooperating with non-members with security problems very different from those traditionally handled.

Under the auspices of PfP, each country could enter an Individual Partnership Programme with a set of targets worked out with NATO to ease military cooperation. The partnership country would subsequently implement the targets, and finally invite NATO to verify them before moving onto new, and more complicated projects. To oversee this process and advise the government on how to proceed, a retired German general was appointed. This was a clear signal not only to the foreign audience that Poland wanted to overcome historical animosities, but also to the domestic audience that NATO meant new patterns of cooperation. The more projects the partnership country managed to sign with NATO, the closer the cooperative relationship. By the end of 1997, the number of Polish PfP projects was 450, more than any other PfP country.[18] This gave Poland a considerable advantage compared to the two other new members where the political will to fund the requirements agreed with NATO has been doubted.[19]

---

[16] S. Winter, 'NATO/EU: Expansion of NATO hopes to expand EU eastward', *RFE/RL Newsline*, 7 May 1997, http://www.rferl.org/nca/features/1997/05/F.RU.970507141653.html.

[17] F. Nietz, 'W przedpokoju NATO', *Gazeta Wyborcza*, 14 January 1994.

[18] *Development of Poland's Political and Military Relations with NATO*, Warsaw: Armed Forces of the Republic of Poland, 1999, http://www.wp.mil.pl/integra2.html.

[19] The Czech Republic has been openly criticised by NATO for its lack of efforts, see M. Mocek, 'Pozvání NATO je výzva k činu', *Mladá fronta Dnes*, 9 July 1997. In Hungary, the plans for buying new fighter planes were suddenly postponed until after 2003, see *RFE/RL NewsLine*, 24 August 1998, http://www.rferl.org/newsline/1998/08/240898.html.

Secrecy and democracy

Despite the increasing number of projects, one of the most complex issues concerned the introduction of parliamentary control over defence and security matters. This was one of the original requirements listed for every PfP country to fulfil. In Poland, this turned out to be extraordinarily difficult not only due to the problems of removing the remnants of one-party rule, but because it became intertwined with President Walesa's conflict with parliament over the extent of presidential power.[20] Walesa tried to exploit the strong support NATO enjoyed to increase his own influence over politics. Before 1989, security and defence matters had been decided in the National Defence Committee. Walesa preferred to retain this arrangement. Not only would it exclude politicians from influencing policy formulation but it would secure his authority and control. The Sejm objected to this arrangement. In March 1990, two prominent Solidarity members were made vice-ministers of defence with the mandate of introducing democratic control. This failed to solve the issue. In 1994 tensions increased further when military intelligence was transferred from the Ministry of Defence to the General Staff.

Dissatisfaction with Walesa's authoritarian style contributed to his defeat in the presidential elections in November 1995. With Kwasniewski as the new president, the Union of the Democratic Left controlled both government and president. Compared to Walesa, President Kwasniewski was far more restrained. This provided the government with the necessary scope for the conduct of foreign policy. Parliamentary control of the armed forces was implemented, thus fulfilling NATO priorities. Thus, NATO proved to be a tool that could be used to widen democratic control. This linkage must be taken into account to understand both Polish support for membership and further NATO expansion.

Polish eastern policy

Popular perceptions of the neighbouring eastern countries complicated the government's ability to build a cooperative relationship with the new, democratically elected governments in Vilnius, Minsk and Kiev. The on-going conflict between president and government over the responsibility for foreign policy was a further constraining factor. President Walesa's desire to retain

---

[20] A detailed study of this conflict is provided by D. R. Herspring, 'Civil-military relations in post-communist Poland: problems in the transition to a democratic polity', *Communist and Post-Communist Studies* 33 (2000), pp. 71-100.

responsibility for foreign and security issues had a historical parallel in the pre-war leadership of Marshall Jozef Pilsudski. The fact that Walesa often declared Pilsudski to be his ideal hardly improved Poland's image in the east.[21] Pilsudski's leadership in the war against Soviet Russia in 1920 with the subsequent incorporation of vast tracts of land with a predominantly non-Polish population, and the occupation of Vilnius, evoked negative memories in Russia, Lithuania, Belarus and Ukraine.

On the issue of how an active eastern policy could be combined with the NATO and EU membership aspirations, Walesa was clear. He did not want to create the impression that both 'directions', East and West, were given the same weight. The main emphasis was put on creating a dialogue with NATO and the EU. An increasing number of politicians and commentators accused the government of neglecting the eastern dimension. The editor of the influential Paris-based journal *Kultura,* Jerzy Giedroyc, claimed that the political elite completely lacked a concept of what Poland's role in the regions should be.[22] By focusing exclusively on the West, Poland failed to take advantage of the opportunities to establish strong relations with those eastern neighbours desperately looking for closer contacts with the West. To them Poland constituted both a model of how transition could be implemented as well as a bridge further West.

Giedroyc's criticism evoked debate, not least since the foreign policy during the early 1990s seemed to yield few tangible results. Until the launching of PfP in 1993, Polish foreign policy had concentrated on the West with little success. NATO's main concern was to develop a dialogue with Moscow. The EU maintained a political dialogue with the Central European countries. At the same time, it protected its markets from any unwelcome competition frequently initiating anti-dumping measures which hurt the transitional economies gravely.[23] Relations with the East were in limbo. The end of Soviet rule over the Baltic states, Belarus and Ukraine was regarded with sympathy. But apart from official expressions of support and approval from parliament and government, little was done.

The apparent impotence was not only due to scarce resources. The political leadership could not assume that the strong support for closer ties with the West

---

[21] W. Wladyka, *Fortidens skygger i polsk politikk, reformprosessens utfordringer etter valget,* (Oslo: IFS Info, no. 4, 1993).

[22] Ibid., p.11

[23] See U. Moebius, *Antidumpingpolitik der Europäischen Union* (Berlin, 1996).

would apply if a similar strategy were applied to the eastern neighbours. The unsettled historical questions as well as the situation for the Polish minorities opened up a set of difficult issues affecting popular opinion far more than NATO and EU did. Moreover, the problems varied depending on the neighbouring country, and the political leadership might have feared that once they were introduced into the political agenda, other issues would lose interest. Moreover, an active Polish policy towards Lithuania, Belarus or Ukraine, could not avoid affecting Polish-Russian relations. These remained of prime importance to Poland, not least since NATO would hardly consider Poland's application for membership if relations between Moscow and Warsaw were characterised by strong animosity. In a parliamentary debate on Polish eastern policy, foreign minister Skubiszewski advocated a neutral position for Poland, stating that 'Russia has remained a major power, despite its current limitations and problems, and it is going to reinforce this position. ... Poland does not want to side with either party in the conflict.'[24]

The decisive change appeared after the launching of PfP in October 1993. Although it fell short of full membership, it provided Poland with institutionalised channels for dialogue with NATO and its members. But most important, it meant that the Polish government could involve NATO through consultations. Particular problems could also be presented and discussed in the North Atlantic Cooperation Council where all PfP countries were members. Polish-Russian relations had lost their exclusive bilateral character. PfP and the growing willingness of NATO to consider expansion seriously provided another impetus for change. President Clinton emphasised that NATO required that applicant countries settle historical grievances with their neighbours. This compelled the Polish leadership to turn its attention eastwards to improve relations and increase cooperation.

No grand designs or initiatives materialised. Political changes in the neighbouring countries forced Poland to differentiate and adjust according to the political status in each country. Belarus and Slovakia constituted difficult challenges. Both had initially started out as pro-Western countries dedicated to continued democratisation and market reforms. Yet in the early 1990s, this changed gradually in both countries. Both the Belarusian and Slovak governments increased cooperation with Russia in defence and security matters in the course of 1993 and 1994. In the case of Slovakia, this period lasted until 1998 when the pro-Russian government of Vladimir Meciar lost the elections.

---

[24] *Polityka*, 17 October 1993.

In Belarus, the authoritarian dictatorship of Alyaksandar Lukashenka was strengthened, in no small amount due to economic and political assistance from Russia.[25] The importance of Belarus for Russian security may also be deduced from the new Russian Military Doctrine approved by the Security Council.[26] Two important changes from the previous doctrine dating from 1994 underline Belarus's value. The 1994 version had started with a preamble stating that ideological confrontation was waning as the result of varied efforts made to increase international cooperation and reduce risks. This was apparently intended to enable a distinction to be made between threats and dangers to Russia's security, and permit a concentration of efforts on countering the latter. In the current version, both the preamble and this distinction are removed. Instead, the necessity of increasing military and security cooperation with Russia's allies is emphasised. In the case of Europe, this narrows down to Belarus. Furthermore, Belarus location lends itself to the fulfilment of another target, namely exerting influence on developments in Eastern and Central Europe. Russian military constructions in Belarus show this. Current works includes the building of an anti-missile station in Baranivichi and a radar station in Vileyka. Recently, the two countries have signed an agreement merging the air commands of the two countries. This leaves Poland in a quandary since an increased Russian military presence in Belarus will have a clear impact on Poland's position within NATO. NATO may become reluctant in its allocation of manpower and resources to Poland if this is seen as likely to trigger an escalation on the Belarusian/Russian side.

After Lukashenka dissolved Parliament in 1996, the presidents of Poland, Lithuania and Ukraine issued a joint protest. Yet this was a unique example of trilateral unanimity, the three countries have later adapted policies towards Belarus reflecting their rather different relationship with the West and Russia. Poland and Lithuania have become host countries to a growing community of Belarusian dissidents. In addition the drop in living standards has led to an influx of illegal immigrant workers, as well as Belarusian citizens crossing the border to sell their goods in neighbouring Polish cities. Parallel to this has been an increase in smuggling and prostitution apparently controlled by Belarusian/Russian gangs.

---

[25] For an analysis of this relationship, see M. Balmaceda, 'Myth and Reality in the Belarusian-Russian Relationship – What the West Must Know', *Problems of Post-Communism* 46 (1999), pp. 3-14.

[26] 'Konseptsia natsionalnoi bezopasnosti Rossiiskoi Federatsii', *Rossiskaya gazeta*, 10 January 2000.

Poland does not recognise the current Belarusian parliament as legally elected, and has therefore refused to develop the bilateral relationship in any way beyond the level of diplomatic presence. Although this policy was implemented gradually after 1996, i.e. in the wake of Lukashenka's dissolution of Parliament, relegating official contacts would have little impact on Poland. Trade with Belarus is marginal. It was regarded as highly unlikely that Belarusian authorities would stop the transit of goods en route to Poland from Russia. That would have meant bringing Russia into the conflict and a considerable loss of income both to Russia and Belarus. Yet no signs have appeared that the Polish government will revise their policy towards Belarus.

Lukashenka's illegitimate rule combined with his frequent anti-Polish rhetoric, effectively limit the scope of Polish policy towards that country. Relations with Ukraine are very different. From the outset, it was obvious that developments there, and in particular the relationship between Kiev and Moscow would have a far greater impact on Poland than any political debacle in Belarus. Yet Ukraine represented a set of very different problems. This was not only due to the sheer size of the country or its population, but also to the unsettled relationship between Kiev and Moscow, as well as the historical antagonism between Poles and Ukrainians. Polish parliamentarians had met with the leadership of the Ukrainian democratic movement Rukh early in 1990. The meeting ended with a joint declaration emphasising the need for cooperation overcoming mutual fear and animosity. This hope was more than polite phrases; according to a survey published in 1992, independent Ukraine was regarded as the greatest threat to Polish statehood, a position traditionally allotted to Germany.[27] These factors explain why the official Polish reactions to the Ukrainian declaration of independence in July 1990 were muted compared to the enthusiasm displayed when the Lithuanian Parliament had done the same only a few months earlier.

In the relationship with Kiev, the need to proceed carefully was necessitated by the Ukrainian government's attempts to engage Poland in a close relationship. The Polish government had presumably nothing against functioning as a bridge to NATO and the EU since this only enhanced the influence of Poland in regional politics. Yet the Ukrainian strategy was disconcerting since it envisioned using the relationship withs Poland as a tool to

---

[27] J. Kloczkowski, 'Mity i rzeczywistość. Uwagi o polityce III Rzeczypospolitej wobec Ukrainy', in J. Kloczkowski (ed.), *Od komunizmu do...? Dokąd zmierza III Rzeczpospolita?*, Cracow, 1999), pp. 119-127.

distance itself from Russia. This could easily result in a strained relationship between Warsaw asnd Moscow.

Democracy and stability in Ukraine mean reduced exposure for Poland. However, the Polish government knew from its recent past, that transition to democracy and market economy was not necessarily conducive to stability in the short term. Economic recession in Ukraine had meant an influx of cheap labour to Poland as well as open-air markets and bazaars in most Polish towns. This was at a level Polish border authorities could barely handle. If recession continued and internal sstrife between ethnic groupings broke out, Polish authorities feared an influx of refugees. To counteract this, Ukraine needed investment and political cooperation above the level Poland could meet. Poland therefore, welcomed the Stability Pact agreed between NATO and Ukraine in 1997, and hoped that this would promote western investments in the Ukrainian economy. The EU's lack of interest in Ukrainian developments, perhaps best expressed in the pressure exerted on Poland and other Central European applicants to introduce a strict visa regime on Ukrainian tourists, has evoked strong criticism in Poland.

Political support was given to the independence movement in Lithuania in 1990-91. Yet the relationship with Lithuania was marred by the lack of support for Lithuanian independence displayed by the Polish minority in the Vilnius region. Poles numbering close to 260,000, or 7 per cent of Lithuania's population, feared that independence from Moscow would pave the way for anti-Polish sentiments. Thus, until 1994, virtually no progress was made in the relationship between Poland and Lithuania. An inter-state treaty was not signed before spring 1994, making Lithuania into the last of Poland's neighbours to do so. In 1997, the relationship was upgraded and called a 'strategic partnership', and expanded to include a joint Parliamentary Assembly, the Consultative Committee of Presidents, and the Council for Inter-Governmental Cooperation. Political and economic cooperation progress relatively smoothly. Nevertheless, the number of joint armed forces projects is quite impressive when taking into account both the scarcity of resources of both countries and the brief period since cross-border contacts were close to none.[28]

Both Poland and Lithuania have been concerned about developments in the Kaliningrad enclave. Both fear an increased Russian military presence. Such plans surfaced in 1994 when Pavel Grachev, the Russian Minister of Defence claimed to have received both the funding and political backing from President

---

[28] The issue of *Polska Zbrojna* from 19 May 2000, provides a detailed listing of ongoing projects.

Yeltsin for the construction of new military installations there.[29] So far, there are no indications that military presence has been enhanced as a counter-measure against Polish NATO membership. Yet the enclave has remained a reason for concern, not only because of the falling standards of living and rising unemployment, but because the Russian leadership has not made its intentions in the region clear.[30] Both Poland and Lithuania have attempted to attract the attention of the EU to the dismal conditions of the Russian population, so far to no avail.

The civilian authorities in Kaliningrad have voiced an interest in continued economic cooperation with Poland. However, these efforts have been frustrated by lack of support from Moscow. Polish interests in maintaining good relations with Kaliningrad were initially based on the need to keep pace with the growing German attention for the region during the first half of this decade. In particular the Russian plan for a Via Baltica highway connecting St. Petersburg with Berlin across Kaliningrad attracted Polish attention, but outright opposition was only voiced in connection with the short-lived plans envisaging a re-settling of ethnic Germans from Kazakhstan and the Volga region.

The relationship with Russia remains influential. However, the ability to conduct a dialogue and proceed with economic and political cooperation with Russia has been obstructed by historical issues, unsettled debts and, not least, the lack of a consistent Russian position on NATO expansion. When visiting Warsaw on a tour of Central Europe in August 1993, Yeltsin stated that he had no objections to Polish NATO membership. Travelling on to Prague, he repeated that Russia had 'no right' to prevent the Czech Republic from joining any organisation.[31] His entourage, claiming he had been misunderstood and misquoted, subsequently denied this. Yet the prevailing sentiment in Poland, and presumably in the other Central European states as well, was that Russia's policy towards the region lacked clarity and direction.

This became particularly acute during the centre-left government of Waldemar Pawlak lasting from 1993 to 1995. In 1994, representatives of the government coalition parties recommended that Poland should accept a Russian zone of influence including the Baltic states, Belarus and Ukraine. In particular, the minister of foreign economic relations Leslaw Podkanski recommended a

---

[29] W. Luczak, 'Gra pancerną kurą - co kryje sie za ideą tworzenia 'specjalnej strefy obronnej' Rosji w Kaliningradzie', *Żolnierz Polski*, no. 6,1994, p. 14.

[30] T. Wrobel, 'Kaliningrad, Wielka niewiadoma', *Polska Zbrojna*, 6 February 2000, p. 37.

[31] *RFE/RL Daily Report*, 27 August 1993.

reversal of the priorities of the Ministry for Foreign Affairs to accommodate this stance. The political opposition, and in particular the then chairman of the Sejm's foreign policy committee Bronislaw Geremek accused the centre-left Pawlak government of harbouring Russophile sentiments. Geremek declared that any 'emphasis on privileged Polish Russian dialogue may be viewed with alarm. ... This is disturbing and can amount to a violation of the principle of consensus over Polish foreign policy.'[32] Geremek feared that a closer Polish-Russian political relationship would conflict with US policies, and therefore be detrimental to NATO membership possibilities.

The Polish perception of Russian developments was throughout the 1990s markedly less optimistic than the views held in the West. The Polish political leadership, irrespective of party affiliation, never disregarded the possibility of an anti-democratic backlash in Russia. In general, Polish politicians were in favour of the Russian-NATO Basic Treaty signed in May 1997. Yet at the same time they were wary that the Treaty might grant Russia a *droit de régard* in NATO affairs.[33] This interpretation, at the time prevalent in Moscow, would have weakened Poland's position whether inside or outside NATO and consolidated its buffer status. The practicalities of Russian-NATO relations had hardly been put on the agenda before NATO's bombing of Yugoslavia. Russia responded by freezing all contacts. Poland was, like all the other Alliance members, affected. Yet this did not prevent Polish politicians from voicing harsh criticism of the Russian war in Chechnya. Polish representatives were actively supporting the move by the Parliamentary Assembly of the European Council to suspend Russian membership due to the war. Chechen exiles have established an information office in Warsaw.[34]

Trade and security

In the efforts made to improve relations with the eastern neighbours, economic considerations played a major part. The collapse in trade with the former planned economies happened almost parallel to a rapid growth in trade with the West. Nevertheless, the redirection of trade did not mean a redirection of

---

[32] Ibid., footnote 12.

[33] I. Kobrinskaja, *Długi koniec zimnej wojny* (Warsaw, 1998), in particular chapter 5, 'Europa Środkowo-Wschodnia w rosyjskiej strategii polityki zagranicznej', pp. 99-118.

[34] During the first Chechen-Russian War (1995-96), a similar office was established in Cracow. The current one is located in the Palace of Science and Culture, a Soviet 'gift' to Poland built in the 1950s.

commodities. Goods traded with other planned economies were difficult to market in the West. Thus, by 1993-4, the Ministry for Foreign Trade started to push for a stronger political emphasis on economic cooperation with the other transitional economies. This created tensions not only with the then right-wing opposition in parliament, but also in the relationship with the president. According to the so-called 'Small Constitution' lasting from 1992 to 1997, the responsibility for foreign policy was vested with the president. Narrowly defined, this meant that foreign trade was outside the presidential portfolio. However, since this reorientation of foreign trade policy could be interpreted as undermining the overall foreign policy priorities, the president and the right-wing opposition immediately accused the government of endangering integration with the West.

The conflict became particularly acute in the case of Ukraine. Foreign minister Andrzej Olechowski tried to negotiate a so-called 'strategic partnership' with Ukraine in May 1994. Political relations made progress, but the lack of economic reforms in Ukraine impeded trade and undermined the efforts of creating an economic pillar supporting the partnership. The massive needs for investments by far surpassed what Poland could, and indeed would be willing to pay.

During the debate on how to increase trade, the political and economic changes in Russia came to play an unexpected role. Instead of concentrating on market possibilities for Polish goods, the negative effects of economic cooperation with Russia received most of the attention. Jaros•aw Mulewicz, Chairman of the World Centre for Trade and Finance with the East, warned that trade could mean a halt to restructuring of the Polish economy. Cooperating with enterprises operating according to state planning principles would not provide their Polish partners with incentives to continue adapting to the market. On the contrary, this would lead to the 'Russification of Poland's economy'.[35]

Mulewicz's opinions were uttered at a point when disagreements over Poland's reform strategy had not subsided. Critics both in the West and within the government parties advocated a more gradual approach to the reforms in Poland, permitting the state to retain a controlling stake in the larger enterprises. This would slow down restructuring and, if not reduce, then at least even out the upsurge in unemployment resulting from the waves of bankruptcies following a

---

[35] J. M. Calka, 'Poland's Eastern Policy in 1994', *Yearbook of Polish Foreign Policy 1995* (Warsaw, 1995), pp. 49-56, footnote 10.

quick withdrawal of state ownership. In short, they advocated that Poland should copy Russia's reform strategy.

At the beginning of the 1990s, the total dependence on Soviet and later Russian natural gas supplies was regarded as a potential security risk. Economic blackmail was mentioned as a threat to national security in the Polish military doctrine published in July 1992. This threat materialised, albeit briefly, in the winter of both 1992 and the following year when gas deliveries suddenly and without warning dropped. It turned out that the reason was not Russian political pressure against Poland, but rather reduced Russian deliveries to Ukraine due to payment problems. The Ukrainian response was simply to siphon off the gas quantities required. Polish authorities tried to reduce this risk by engaging Western countries in the construction of pipelines connecting the Polish grid to North Sea Gas. The costs are regarded as prohibitive, and so far these attempts have only received a tepid response in the West.

The Ukrainian behaviour was not only a problem for Poland, but also for Russia. Plans to construct a pipeline through Belarus, thus circumventing Ukraine, were launched in 1992. An agreement on the construction was signed a year later.[36] If implemented, this will mean an increased mutual dependence. It is expected that trade and industrial cooperation between Poland and Russia will grow especially during the construction phase. The regular contacts needed to keep the gas flowing, and export incomes as well, will mean that Russian-Polish relations have two legs, a political and an economic. This gives Poland an advantage when compared to Hungary and the Czech Republic, both having struggled to retain Russian interest in continued energy trade. This will also to a certain degree compensate for the lack of official contacts and dialogue between the two. Despite the fact that the two countries signed a Partnership Agreement in 1993, Poland has found it difficult to improve relations. At the moment of signing, the Agreement was proclaimed as a breakthrough paving the way for political contacts. Yet in retrospect the Agreement seems to have lost all relevance. Political cooperation between the two did not increase, and minor practical problems impeding trade (customs delays, import taxes, payments) have remained unsolved. Not surprisingly, Moscow refuses to discuss major issues like

---

[36] The signing of the gas agreement with Russia cannot be attributed to the efforts of the Ministry for Foreign Trade, but rather to mutual Russian-Polish interests in exploiting what might be a very profitable deal for both. Russian industrialists and politicians followed the Polish debate with great interest, and interpreted this as enabling a revival of coproduction of military hardware (sic). This side effect has failed to materialise. See Calka, 'Poland's Eastern Policy', footnote 9.

the Kaliningrad enclave and the increasing military cooperation between Belarus and Russia with Poland.

Poland's effects on NATO

Until membership was a fact, Polish foreign policy was influenced by the differing and contradictory signals coming from NATO countries when expansion was addressed. When the issue of costs and military preparedness arose, the Polish government realised that this could be a powerful argument against expansion, or relegate Poland to a secondary status within the Alliance.[37] The Polish response was to constantly assure NATO of Polish willingness to share responsibilities and burdens.

Polish politicians were aware that a secondary status, real or imagined, would limit Polish influence in NATO and undermine Alliance unity. They followed the debate in the West closely, and with growing apprehension. Among the European Alliance members, a pattern emerged where Germany and Denmark favoured enlargement, whereas the Mediterranean countries, led by France, were clearly reluctant. The problem for Poland, as well as the other applicants, was the entanglement of enlargement with the debate on NATO's role after the demise of the Soviet threat. The two issues were inter-linked, but the debate concerning expansion could more easily be reduced to a 'for' and 'against' issue and therefore lend itself to political debate more easily. Those doubting that the Alliance had any future saw no reason why it should expand. Yet some among those who favoured retaining NATO as a military factor feared that expansion would mean accepting members without significant military capacity.

A new turn was made in March 1996 when the US Congress's Budgetary Office presented a cost assessment.[38] In August the same year, detailed cost scenarios were compiled by researchers at the Rand Corporation.[39] In the following year, yet another estimate with widely different conclusions was made

---

[37] E. Cziomer, 'Polen und die NATO-Beitrittskosten', in A. Pradetto and F. Melanie Alamir (eds.) *Die Debatte über die Kosten der NATO-Osterweiterung* (Baden-Baden, 1998), pp. 151-160.

[38] *The Costs of Expanding the NATO Alliance*, Congressional Budget Office, Washington D.C., March 1996.

[39] Later reprinted as R. D. Asmus, R. L. Kugler and F. St. Larrabee, 'The Costs of NATO Enlargement', in P.H. Gordon (ed.), *NATO's Transformation: The Changing Shape of the Atlantic Alliance* (Lanham, 1997), pp. 177-203.

public.[40] All agreed that the final sum largely depended on the new members' military hardware and political will to finance an upgrading. This led to worries in the West that once membership was achieved, the political will to finance the upgrading would wane. In the case of the Czech Republic, this assumption has proved true. In 1996, the Czech Prime Minister Václav Klaus referred to the importance of the material status of the Czech armed forces as 'really secondary' since joining NATO was a political question.[41] Only the Polish government presented a reply correcting some of the data, but also, more convincingly, adding a detailed modernisation plan with a scheme for how this should be financed.[42] Despite this, the plans have at best been only partially implemented.[43] Lack of capital is only one part of the explanation; lack of clarity concerning the future role for Poland's domestic armaments production is another.[44]

Choosing sides

Poland differs from the two other new members in that it 'is the only one that has unambiguously demonstrated its potential of becoming not only a consumer but also a provider of security'.[45] Releasing this potential depends not only on Polish diplomacy and developments in neighbouring countries, but also to what extent the rest of NATO is willing to let Poland pursue its ambitions. Polish ambitions to increase cooperation with her Eastern neighbours both bilaterally and through NATO, will mean an increase in the number of problems that will have to be addressed by the Alliance. Mediterranean members' reluctance to get involved in any eastern policy not primarily centred on Russia may result in a regionalisation of NATO, whereby a cluster of countries plays a particular regional role. This is less of a novelty than it sounds. Yet until now the USA has

---

[40] *Report to the Congress on the Enlargement of the North Atlantic Treaty Organization: Rationale, Benefits, Costs and Implications*, Bureau of European and Canadian Affairs, U.S. Department of State, Washington D.C., 24 February 1997.

[41] V. Mastny, *Reassuring NATO: Eastern Europe, Russia and the Western Alliance* (Oslo: IFS, Forsvarsstudier no.5, 1997), p. 80.

[42] J. Urbanowicz, J. 'A Question of Billions', *The Warsaw Voice*, 2 February 1997.

[43] See W. Stepek, 'Siły Zbrojne RP a interoperacyjność ze strukturami Sojuszu Północnoatlantyckiego', in E. Cziomer (ed.), *NATO w systemie bezpieczeństwa europejskiego* (Cracow, 1999), pp. 37-46.

[44] W. Stankiewicz, *Konwersja zbrojeń. Oczekiwania i fakty* (Warsaw, 1999).

[45] Mastny, *Reassuring NATO*, p. 88.

always been part of such clusters. With an increased Europeanisation of NATO, the future role of the Americans seems less predictable.

Poland's choice of Alliance partners within NATO will have a clear impact on this process. To Poland, the prime objective has been to escape from the role as buffer state. This is the reason why Polish politicians regarded the close relationship between Moscow and Bonn with apprehension. Chancellor Kohl was aware of this, and initiated a pattern of cooperation at different levels between Germany and Poland to reduce the reasons for concern. Moreover, the German government played an active role advocating Polish membership in NATO.[46]

The Polish governments have striven for close cooperation with both the USA and Germany. Yet in the event of a conflict between the two over the future of NATO, the position of Poland will be impaired because it would have to choose. Until now, Germany and the USA have shared the same views on European security and NATO strategies. Nevertheless, German and US perceptions on the economic reform process within Russia as well as the future of the Baltic Sea Region differ. Representatives of the Clinton administration were far more vociferous in their criticism of Russian politics and lack of reforms than Germany has been. So far, Poland has been staunchly pro-American in its foreign and security policy. This is also clearly reflected in the number of military cooperation projects between Poland and NATO members. In 1997, Germany ranked as number one with 238 projects, followed by the US with 172. France comes third with 103 projects, most covering the exchange of officers and language training. Denmark comes as number four with 76 projects.[47] Yet the sheer numbers hide the scope of the different projects. Applying measures based on cost, time and number of men involved, the US would rank first. The issue that may well turn out to be the reason for more open disagreement between Poland and Germany concerns future membership for the Baltic countries. The Polish government favours Baltic NATO membership, the German government does not.[48] The Clinton administration

---

[46] In 1994, the German Minister of Defence Volker Rühe was censured by Foreign Minister Klaus Kinkel for pursuing a too active policy of eastward expansion. For a dismayed Polish comment, see W. Kostyrko, 'Niemcy zdyscyplinowani', *Gazeta Wyborcza*, 10 January 1994.

[47] *Defence Cooperation with NATO Member States*, Warsaw: Armed Forces of the Republic of Poland, 1999, http://www.wp.mil.pl/integra3.html.

[48] A. Krohn, 'Security Cooperation in the Baltic Sea Region: Germany as a Transatlantic and European Actor', in G. Artéus and A. Lejiņš (eds.), *Baltic Security: Looking Towards the 21st Century* (Riga,1997), pp.111-125.

was against excluding anybody from future membership. Poland shares this view. Yet one issue that may turn out to be very difficult for Poland, the USA and NATO concerns the ongoing process within the EU to provide the Union with a military dimension to bolster its 'Common Foreign and Security Policy' (hence CFSP).

A characteristic feature of the debate on NATO in Poland, was the clear-cut distinction between NATO and other international organisations when it came to security matters. The security dimension of the EU in particular, especially the efforts to devise CFSP as well as the potential usage of WEU, has rarely been debated. The reason may well be ascribed to the general confusion and lack of clarity surrounding the CFSP for most of the past decade. But from a Polish perspective, the numerous negative events marring cooperation between Warsaw and Brussels must be included to understand the lack of enthusiasm for the Union. Poland was the first country to initiate counter-measures against the EU, when the unilateral import restrictions were briefly introduced against Union agricultural products in 1993. From an early stage, the EU was considered as a reluctant partner preferring to give aid instead of facilitating trade and political integration.[49] NATO rapidly came forward with workable interim solutions. The EU has failed to do so. Moreover, NATO has expanded whereas EU enlargement is continuously being postponed due to the lack of internal reforms. Furthermore, Polish observers have interpreted the increasing number of new requirements the applicant countries have to fulfil, as resulting from lack of strategy on the part of the EU. This was clearly expressed in the controversy following the European Commission's proposed Partnership for Accession launched in March 1998.[50] EU's failure to explain the need for this institutional innovation strengthened the impression that the Commission was merely postponing expansion.

Attempts to create a more distinct European component within NATO, or giving the WEU an independent role in European security politics have caught the attention of the Polish media only very recently.[51] A few observers have questioned Poland's pro-American policy. Claims that Poland runs the danger of being identified as 'the Trojan horse of the Americans' have been voiced in the

---

[49] R. Soltyk, 'L'opinion polonaise hesite', *Le Monde Diplomatique*, February 1999, p.8.

[50] M. Popowski, 'Poland's Relations with the European Union', *Yearbook of Polish Foreign Policy 1998* (Warsaw, 1998), pp. 68-75, p. 74.

[51] R. Kupiecki, 'Europejska tożsamość i amerykańskie przywództwo', in Czaputowicz, J. (ed) *Integracja europejska. Implikacje dla polski* (Cracow, 1999), pp. 405-438.

press.[52] This may make cooperation with the other NATO partners difficult, in particular with France. The risk of alienating France will probably not deter Poland from pursuing an active policy in the Baltic region. A negative German reaction will have greater consequences. So far, there have been no cases where the two countries have conflicted openly. Such an occasion may emerge with Polish advocacy of Lithuanian NATO membership, or if German economic and political presence in the Kaliningrad region were to increase.

Polish scepticism towards French European policy is not only based on French anti-Americanism; the French position on EU expansion plays a significant role. In 1993, EU declared that associate countries (i.e. Central Europe) could become members once specific economic and institutional conditions had been met. However, the French prime minister Balladur came up with additional criteria on democratisation, human rights, minority protection, under the heading Stability Pact. Although this was claimed by some to be motivated by the need to address the security problems in Central Europe prior to accepting new Union members, the reception in the applicant countries was characterised by bewilderment because the OSCE and the European Council had already listed the same criteria.[53]

The apprehensive Polish attitude towards a stronger role for the EU, let alone France, in European security matters, is not difficult to understand. France's earlier advocacy of a stronger role for Europe within NATO, or the more recent endeavours to vest the EU with a defence component, have been associated with French political ambitions aimed at weakening US presence.[54] The French government, fearing German dominance in Poland, played a leading role in the establishment of the so-called Weimar triangle between France, Poland and Germany in 1991. But practical cooperation involving joint military exercises, language training, exchange of officers and security experts, developed rapidly between Germany and Poland. So far, the Weimar triangle has not developed beyond the level of a discussion club.

---

[52] A. Krzemiński, 'NATO to nie tylko Ameryka, Rzeczpospolita Europa', *Polityka*, no. 12, 1999, pp. 40-41, p. 40. Zbigniew Brzezinski repudiated this claim as meaningless, yet at the same time asserted that Poland should play an active role. Maria Wągrowska et al. 'Sojusznik to nie satelita, rozmowa z prof. Zbigniew Brzeziński', *Polska Zbrojna* 31 March 2000, pp. 5-6.

[53] M. Sæter, 'Stabilitetspakt for Europa: EUs sikkerhetspolitiske profilering i det større Europa', *Internasjonal politikk* 52 (1994), pp. 199-214.

[54] See P. Winand, *Eisenhower, Kennedy, and the United States of Europe* (Basingstoke, 1993), and G. B. Solomon, *The NATO Enlargement Debate 1990-1997: Blessings of Liberty* (Westport, 1997).

Lately, the intensive contacts between Germany and Poland have waned.[55] Cooperation still takes place, also in security matters, but the prevailing perception among Polish politicians and security experts is that Schröder's government is far more preoccupied with EU reforms and the relationship with France, than with Central and Eastern Europe. Early in 1999, a headline in the Warsaw newspaper *Życie* ran: 'Germany is turning away from Poland'.[56] If German policy does not change, Poland will be forced to rely on countries displaying greater interest and involvement. In the case of NATO, this will mean the USA.

Germany's lack of interest means that Poland, and the other applicants in the region, have been deprived of their most efficient channel for information in the EU system. Moreover, without active German support, the larger Mediterranean countries constituting the so-called 'olive alliance' will influence EU enlargement. The Nordic members Denmark, Sweden and Finland could be a potential counterweight provided they coordinate their policies. There have been no traces of that so far.

French fears over a German dominated Central European cluster are therefore probably unfounded, but not only because of German inertia. The two other Central European members, Hungary and the Czech Republic, have very different security perceptions. In the case of the Czech Republic, a dependency on Polish diplomatic efforts in attracting the attention of Germany was more or less openly admitted.[57] This has now ended. The belief that NATO expansion would create a more German-dominated NATO where the three new members would tail German NATO positions seems unlikely. Not only because Poland has other views of security in the Baltic region and what role NATO should play, but also because the security need of the two other new members are very different. Upon signing, the Czech Ambassador to NATO Karel Kovanda underlined that for the Czech, Hungarian and Poles were only two allies among 18, and that joint admission did not mean joint positions.[58] Yet they have one thing in common: they all agree on the need not to preclude future expansion.

---

[55] R. Freudenstein and H. Tewes, 'Stimmungstief zwischen Deutschland und Polen', *Internationale Politik*, no. 2, 2000, pp. 49-56.

[56] M. A. Cichocki, 'Niemcy odwracali się od Polski', *Życie*, 28 January 1999.

[57] M. Szymanowski and P. Zidek, 'Husité na Baltu, Česká armáda a diplomacie objevily důle itost Polska', *Respekt*, no. 40, 1995, p. 2.

[58] *CTK News Summary*, 15 March 1999.

A Baltic NATO?

The Baltic region is a prime example of a constricted geographical area containing a number of states with different perceptions and accordingly different ambitions. This has been clearly expressed in their views on NATO, and in particular the US presence. Whereas Poland, Lithuania, Latvia and Estonia have strongly supported every effort aimed at engaging the Alliance in the region, other countries like Belarus and Russia have been adamantly against any such development. For a long time, the Clinton administration was very reluctant to make it known that it would prefer to see other Western powers play the leading role in the region. This turned out to be very difficult. The perceptions of Germany and Denmark on how to increase security for the smaller countries have little in common with that of Sweden. Finland has been more concerned about creating close relations with Estonia, and has so far attempted to give the EU a more pronounced role through the so-called Northern Dimension.[59] So far, this has failed to yield any tangible results beyond a series of conferences and seminars.

To increase cooperation, the Baltic Sea Council was established in 1992. Apart from providing the setting for discussions and rudimentary cooperation, it has achieved very little. Judging from press reports, attracting the interest of politicians in the proceedings of the Council seems increasingly difficult. In particular Russian officials decline to attend meetings. One may be tempted to ask whether the removal of hard-core security issues from the agenda explains the lack of interest displayed by prominent politicians in the member countries, but above all in Russia.[60]

The efforts displayed by neighbouring western states to engage the Baltic states in political cooperation failed for two reasons. One was that only soft-core security issues like political and economic reforms, and minority issues, were involved. All of these were already on the agenda in the OSCE, the European Council, and the EU. Hard-core security was not on the list and therefore fell short of what the political leadership in the Baltic states had declared to be their prime ambition. Secondly, leaving the task to the western countries initially produced little more than rivalry between Sweden and Denmark. The Baltic presidents published a joint response in late November 1996 accusing NATO of

---

[59] P. Lipponen, opening address at the seminar 'The Euro-Arctic Barents Region – Dreams and Realities', Rovaniemi, September 1997.

[60] J. Dragsdahl, 'Dødvande i Østersøen', *Weekendavisen*, 2 October 1997.

having 'an obscure perspective of the Baltic states'.[61] The inertia displayed by the surrounding states, with the notable but rather inefficient exceptions of Denmark and Poland, increased pressure on the US. In January 1998, a US-Baltic Charter was signed. Although it provides the framework for increased cooperation in a number of fields, including security and defence, it contains no promise of NATO-membership.

Concluding remarks

A central issue in much of the literature on international cooperation is how organisations like NATO reduce uncertainty.[62] Yet the focus has usually been confined to cooperation within an organisation: the relationship between members and non-members has rarely been analysed. NATO is a tricky organisation on this point, because the borderline separating PfP countries from full members is not always easy to draw. The close relationship that developed between Germany and Poland before NATO expanded showed this. This sets NATO apart from the EU where the separating line is much more identifiable. The EU lends itself more easily to analysis, a reason for the imbalance in theoretical attention between the two organisations. NATO has proved itself more flexible and prone to change after the end of the Cold War than initially expected. If the progress in membership negotiations between the two may be taken as a yardstick, the difference is clear.

European NATO members have more or less openly preferred to delegate the responsibility for drawing up an eastern policy to the EU in the belief that economic crisis and stagnating political reforms could best be addressed by the Union. The reasoning was simple and in accordance with what was perceived by the population in the region as the greatest danger.[63] The choice of the EU would have been irreproachable had the Union designed an efficient aid policy towards the region, which would have led to greater political integration. Based on its own experiences, Poland knows the limitations and pitfalls of the EU

---

[61] *Joint Declaration of the President of the Republic of Latvia, the President of the Republic of Estonia and the President of the Republic of Lithuania*, Riga, 21. November 1996, quoted by P. Dunay et al., *The Effects of Enlargement on Bilateral Relations in Central and Eastern Europe* (Paris, 1997), p. 30.

[62] C. A. Wallander, 'International Institutions and Modern Security Strategies', *Problems of Communism*, January-April, 1992, pp. 44-62 (p. 51).

[63] R. Smoke (ed.), *Perceptions of Security: Public opinion and expert assessment in Europe's new democracies* (Manchester, 1996).

strategy, in particular the failure of the EU to create functioning interim solutions comparable to the PfP.

The debate within NATO and in current security politics may be summed up in the question: what next? This is perhaps a bit premature; the integration of the new member countries is far from finished, and the direction of NATO-Russian cooperation remains open. Yet the question seems above all to concern the relationship between the Alliance and the states-in-between. Some of them, especially the Baltic states, find themselves in a situation not very different from Poland's at the beginning of the 1990s. NATO will have to come up with solutions short of membership to address their concerns. Polish experiences are valuable when the eastern policy of the Alliance is re-assessed in the light of the recent expansion. Accepting new members into NATO is nothing new. But in contrast to previous expansion rounds, the role and purpose of the Alliance are now changing radically. What is relevant in the case of Poland is that the opportunity to influence the political agenda is much greater in a context where routines are being changed. It is also easier because many of the domestic conflicts outlined here, now seem to be solved. This is not least due to President Kwaśniewski's more conciliatory approach when compared to Walesa.

Returning to the title question whether Poland still is a buffer state, it is possible to answer in the negative. Poland is unlikely to become a buffer state within NATO if this is understood in the political sense as the impotent member whose interests are easily discarded when it suits the strategies of greater powers. Poland's ability to avoid this fate rests on NATO's will to conduct an active Eastern policy irrespective of whether this means new members in the foreseeable future, but also on the ability of Polish politicians to bring clear priorities into the Alliance. To do that, a broad domestic debate is a precondition. Without a broad political support at home, it is unlikely that the other NATO countries will consider policies and initiatives presented by Polish representatives in Brussels. Since Poland has gained considerable experience both as a PfP country, and in the bilateral relations with her eastern neighbours, that would undoubtedly be a loss to NATO.

It is perhaps a paradox, that Poland's ability to do away with its political buffer status as a NATO member rests upon its geographical location as exactly that. This is not as fanciful as it may sound: Western European states with a geographical location spelling vulnerability (e.g. Belgium, Denmark, Norway) have overcome this through cooperation. 'The notion that security is invariably and for all time predetermined by geography has been one of the more durable fallacies promoted by theories of international relations.'[64] In this perspective, Polish security politics fits into a larger European pattern. What is different for Poland now is not so much that it is the border country of NATO, but that this position is being turned into a valuable asset.

---

[64] Mastny, *Reassuring NATO*, p. 13.

Chapter 17

Diplomatic eyes on the North: writings by British ambassadors on Danish Society

Jørgen Sevaldsen

The reflections offered in this paper on national stereotyping and Anglo-Nordic cultural and ideological encounters take as their point of departure a small number of texts of a particular local genre, i.e. books on Denmark by former British ambassadors to that country. These works are not travel literature or travel descriptions in the ordinary sense. They may be described, rather, as reflections or observations on Danish society by professional British diplomats, aimed in some cases at British audiences, in others at Danish ones.

In 1992, the year of the Maastricht referendum in Denmark, no fewer than two such works were published. One, *Signposts to Denmark*, was written by Dame Anne Warburton, the British ambassador from 1976 to 1983.[1] The other, *Og gamle Danmark....En beskrivelse af Danmark i det herrens år 1992*, by Sir James Mellon, the ambassador from 1983 to 1986.[2] Both works refer in turn to the most famous British description of Denmark of all times, Robert Molesworth's *An Account of Denmark as it was in the Year 1692*, published in

---

[1] Anne Warburton, *Signposts to Denmark. A Personal View* (Copenhagen, 1992).

[2] James Mellon, *Og gamle Danmark...En beskrivelse af Danmark i det Herrens år 1992* [And Ancient Denmark...An Account of Denmark in the Year of Our Lord 1992] (Aarhus, 1992).

London in 1694.[3] Warburton notes in her foreword that she always felt well received and happy in Denmark and adds that 'no doubt that largely accounts for the difference in tone from the account of "Denmark 1692", written by the British minister who fell foul of King Frederik III' (The king in question was in fact Christian V, but never mind). Similarly, the subtitle of Mellon's book: 'An Account of Denmark in the Year of Our Lord 1992', clearly establishes the link with Molesworth – and a 300th anniversary at that!

In this paper I propose to concentrate on the works by Molesworth and Mellon – the two works that have proved particularly influential in a Danish context. Three aspects in particular of their works will be dealt with: First, the way in which they illustrate the general point that descriptions of foreign societies often tell us as much about the author's views of his own country as about the 'other' society. Secondly, as examples of reactions by liberal Britons – we cannot say 'Englishmen' as Molesworth was born in Ireland and Mellon is Scottish – to what they perceived as societies marked by unhealthy conformity – in Molesworth's case the oppressive conformity of absolute monarchy; in Mellon's case the less openly oppressive, but still uncomfortable uniformity imposed by heavy taxation, a comprehensive welfare state and a tradition in politics that celebrates consensus and compromise rather than the establishment of strong executives. Thirdly, local reactions to them. The interesting thing is that their works still live in the Danish discourse on national characteristics. Quotations from Molesworth are offered to demonstrate that dullness and the cultivation of mediocrity were already part of the Danish national character in the seventeenth century; and Mellon's suggestion that the Danes are not really a nation but a tribe is quite often referred to in contemporary discussions about Danish national identity in the present world. It would be an exaggeration to say that Molesworth has ever been a popular figure in Denmark, but both Warburton's and Mellon's 1992 books were received with friendly appreciation. This, together with the fact that there are no contemporary equivalents from other great-power diplomats, prompts a final question: what is it about Anglo-Danish relations that suggested to two recent British ambassadors that there was a market for books on Danish society written from a British point of view?

---

[3]   Robert Molesworth, *An Account of Denmark as it was in the Year 1692*. (London, 1694; reprinted, Copenhagen, 1976). A Danish translation with an introduction to Molesworth and his mission in Denmark by Erik Kjersgaard is available in Robert Molesworth, *En beskrivelse af Danmark som det var i 1692* (Højbjerg, 1978).

Robert Molesworth and Danish absolutism

Robert Molesworth (1656-1725) wrote his *Account of Denmark...* after having spent a period of time as British envoy to Denmark from 1689 to 1693. There is no time here to tell the fascinating story of his stay in Copenhagen in any detail, nor to discuss his work in the context of seventeenth-century travel writings and dystopias. Molesworth, a member of the Protestant Irish gentry, is now known to historians of the early modern period as a member of a group of early radical Whigs called the 'Commonwealth men'.[4] He was sent to Denmark by William of Orange to negotiate the hiring out of a part of the Danish army to help the new king defend his position vis-à-vis the Stuarts, and also to try to counteract French influence in the Danish court at a time when France and Britain were fighting each other on all fronts in Northern Europe. The army side of his mission was a success – a part of the army of the Danish king fought with William at the Battle of the Boyne in 1690; the rest of the mission was less successful, so Molesworth was recalled in 1693. On his way home he wrote the *Account* which was published in London, anonymously at first, in 1694.

In the preface to his book he makes some interesting observations on the role of travel literature in furthering consciousness about political liberty: a plea, as it were, for the importance of comparative constitutional studies based on personal observation. He defends the publication of a book on a lesser known country in the North by suggesting that Northern countries suffering under the yoke of absolutism are particularly well suited as examples, because the many pleasures of life in Southern Europe might detract visitors from seeing clearly the oppressive nature of the constitutional systems there:

> An *English-man* should be shewn the misery of the enslaved Parts of the World, to make him in love with the happiness of his own Country; as the *Spartans* exposed their drunken Servants to their children, to make them in love with Sobriety.

---

[4] Molesworth, his circle and his works including *An Account of Denmark* are discussed in Caroline Robbins, *The Eighteenth-Century Commonwealthman: Studies in the Transmission, Development and Circumstance of English Liberal Thought from the Restoration of Charles II until the War with the Thirteen colonies* (Cambridge, Mass., 1961). A forthcoming PhD thesis, 'Robert Molesworth's "Account of Denmark" – its roots and its impact', by Hugh Mayo at the Department of History at Odense University, Denmark, promises a rehabilitation of Molesworth from the treatment given to him by Danish historians.

But the more polished and delicious countries of *France, Spain,* or *Italy,* are not the places where this observation may be made to greatest advantage; the manner of Living, goodness of the Air and Diet, the magnificence of the Buildings, pleasantness of the Gardens, pompous Equipage of some great Persons, dazzle the Eyes of most Travellers, and cast a disguise upon the Slavery of those Parts; and as they render this Evil more supportable to the Natives, so they almost quite hide it from the view of a Cursory Traveller, amusing him too much from considering the Calamities which accompany so much Splendour, and so many natural Blessings: or from reflecting how much more happy the conditions of the People would be with better usage. But in the *Northern Kingdoms* and *Provinces* there appears little or nothing to divert the Mind from contemplating Slavery in its own colours, without any of its Ornaments. And since, for that reason, few of our Gentlemen find temptation enough to Travel into those Parts, and we have hardly any tolerable Relation of them extant, though we have frequent occasions to being concerned with them, I thought it might be of use to publish the following *Account of Denmark* which I took care to be informed of upon the place with the greatest exactness possible, and have related fairly and impartially, which may save the Curious the labour and expence of that *Voyage.*

In 1660, Denmark had moved from what Molesworth and other radicals at the time termed a 'gothic', mixed constitution to absolute monarchy, much to the worry of British Whigs ('Gothic' referring here to seventeenth-century ideas that the Baltic Goths had been ancestors of the Saxons and blessed with elective forms of kingship). Molesworth analysed the causes of the turn to absolutism in Denmark and found them in the Danish nobility's failure to live up to its duty to uphold the mixed constitution, and in the fact that the king could dispose of a large army at the time of his coup. Further, he described the unhappy consequences of the royal take-over: lack of public debate, uniformity, and oppressive taxes that were used not least to uphold large standing armies. The large number of foreigners at the court and in the administration, used by the monarch to bolster his control of the state, was also noted. There were important lessons for Whigs in Britain in this, and it is obvious that most of the points Molesworth makes about the unfortunate state of affairs in Denmark have clear references to the debates about the constitutional balance in Britain, about standing armies and about the presence of Dutchmen at the court of William III.

An Account of Denmark became a great publishing success in Britain. It was widely discussed, it made an impression on John Locke, was referred to in Parliament on several occasions during the eighteenth century, and was read by the fathers of the American Constitution. In Denmark, government circles were, not surprisingly, concerned about the bad image given to the Danish monarchy abroad. The book, certainly, also found its way into Denmark and became a point of reference for the domestic opposition to absolutism. Today, Molesworth's book is best known for the passage in which he sums up his impressions of Danish society:

> ... To conclude; I never knew any Country where the Minds of the People were more of one *calibre* and pitch than here; you shall meet with none of extraordinary Parts or Qualifications, or excellent in particular Studies and Trades; you see no Enthusiasts, Mad-men, Natural Fools, or fanciful Folks, but a certain equality of Understanding reigns among them: every one keeps the ordinary beaten road of Sence, which in this Country is neither the fairest nor the foulest, without deviating to the right or left: yet I will add this one Remark to their praise, that the Common People do generally write and read.

This passage is now probably the most quoted foreign comment on Danish society: a must in anthologies on Danish identity, frequently quoted by journalists and a regular feature as light relief in after-dinner speeches in Anglo-Danish gatherings.

Molesworth's political writings have not been much discussed in British historical literature, except for the treatment of his life and ideas given in Caroline Robbins's work on the Commonwealthmen[5]. Danish historians have appreciated *An Account* as an interesting source for social conditions and court politics in the early 1690s, but his very negative assessments of things Danish are often partly ascribed to character flaws in Molesworth himself – to vanity, arrogance and bad-temperedness. First and foremost his anti-Danishness tends to be explained by the assertion that he was not really writing about Danish politics, but making a contribution to the constitutional debate in Britain. In our context the interesting thing is to see how Molesworth's comments on Danish national characteristics in the age of Absolutism are now fitted in with comments on the mental consequences of the contemporary tax-financed Scandinavian welfare model. So it is time to turn to the recent books by Dame Anne Warburton and in particular to James Mellon's *Og gamle Danmark*.

Published in 1992, the two books are very different. *Signposts to Denmark* is an affectionate introduction to Danish institutions, regions, manners and

---

[5] Robbins, *Eighteenth-Century Commonwealthman*.

values, written for the benefit of English-speaking visitors and residents of the same class and background as Dame Anne herself. There are few politically controversial points in it. Denmark is pictured not quite as a utopia, but as a well-functioning and attractive society with fairy-tale features, but a slight tendency to public overspending. Mellon, too, is a diplomat with a long and happy relationship with Denmark, known in Denmark not only for this book, but also for a charming book on biblical motives from medieval frescos in Danish village churches. *Og gamle Danmark,* however, goes way beyond the genre of polite introduction to a foreign culture.

James Mellon and Danish tribalism

Og gamle Danmark is, in fact, an ambitious analysis of the nature of Danish society and politics. It discusses the points where Denmark might provide lessons – of a positive or negative kind – for the rest of Europe, and it extends a fair amount of friendly advice for Danes on how to preserve the best parts of their social life in the Europe of the Single Market. As mentioned, the subtitle of the book refers to Molesworth's earlier *Account of Denmark*. The main title itself is even more loaded with meaning. The words *Og gamle Danmark* ('And Ancient Denmark') come from the Danish national anthem, and the anthem itself continues something like this: 'And Ancient Denmark shall last as long as the beech tree is mirrored in the blue sea'. In other words, the book addresses the basic question of the chance of survival of a small country and culture like Denmark as an individual entity in the new Europe.

The first thing to note is that the book only exists in Danish. It was, however, originally written in English, offered to British publishers but not accepted by any of them, and then translated into Danish and published for Danish readers in 1992. A second thing to note is that Mellon writes from a Scottish perspective. Not a nationalist one, however; he himself is clearly a person who regards the United Kingdom as a viable and sensible thing, and is also a pro-European in favour of the European Single Market. The pro-union attitude is clearly behind the first element of his analysis of Danish society. The Danes, he claims, do not constitute a *nation*, but a *tribe*. Whereas in a nation, coherence is provided by reaching a synthesis of diverse elements, by a weaving together of various threads, tribal coherence has its source in a tribal feeling celebrating uniformity as an important goal. In a nation, differences are not rejected, if they can at all be fitted into the whole. This is why in proper nations such as the USA and the UK you can easily combine being 'American' or 'British' with other identities of a hyphenated variety – you can be Spanish-American or Scots-British. In a tribe, cultural identity is defined through a common language. Furthermore, the tribe demands loyalty from its members in return for providing the framework for the majority of social functions and duties. The tribe takes it upon itself to make sure that membership is beneficial to all, not just some, of its members. Decisions taken apply to all – spectacular exceptions from the rules are not accepted.

Mellon's discovery of the tribal nature of Danish society came to him, he writes, after his experiences in Africa:

> In 1983 I arrived in Denmark after five years in Africa, which opened my eyes to the similarities between Danish society and African tribes. My description of Danish society might just as well have been a description of an African tribe like the Ashantis.[6]

Throughout the book he returns to this notion while insisting that the particular tribal history of the Danes has 'given them a racial and cultural homogeneity which is unique in a European context'.[7] He finds the ramifications of this situation especially interesting in two areas: politics and the welfare state.

Tribalism explains much of the character of Danish politics, which Mellon finds fanatically devoted to the notion of consensus. Government politicians do not really see it as their task to lead, but to put into law what a majority of the population can agree on through their elected MPs. In Mellon's view, consensus politics have attractive sides: it creates a greater harmony between people and politicians than you find in most other countries. Yet the costs are also obvious. The search for consensus makes for dull proceedings in the Danish parliament; there is a lack of politicians willing and able to lead, and inside the European Union Denmark constantly creates problems and delays because other members have to wait while the Danes try to establish a consensus among themselves on the important issues. His advice to the Danes therefore is that they change their political system to make it possible for governments to lead effectively, not least in relation to European questions.

As for the welfare system, the Danish model is largely tax-financed as becomes a tribal society, and aims not only at saving people from poverty and hardship, but at creating a large degree of equality of condition in society. These ambitions on the part of the state apparatus will, Mellon thinks, have to be modified if the Danish economy is to remain healthy in the Single Market. The high taxes and high social benefits will have to come down, otherwise foreign investors will stay away and Denmark will have difficulties in staying competitive. At the same time some activities and functions will have to be

---

[6] Mellon, *Og gamle Danmark*, p. 18. My translation.

[7] Ibid., p. 19.

moved from the public to the private sector to prevent public finances from breaking down.[8]

From this brief and simplified summary of major points of the book it will already be clear how British Mellon's perspective is, and how much it depends on the political culture in which he is anchored. First, of course, the definition of a 'nation' is clearly grounded in a strong Anglo-American tradition of seeing a nation as the organisation within a given territory of several cultural and ethnic groupings. Mellon refers to the tradition that anyone born in Britain becomes a British citizen. The same is not true in Denmark, where in true tribal tradition you have to be received into the nation and where belonging to the nation is defined more in terms of shared values and shared language. This last factor is something that Mellon refers to again and again: the strikingly intimate relationship between Danishness and the Danish language. His insistence on this point is, certainly, curious to a Danish reader; but becomes more understandable as he reminds us of the situation of writers from non-English communities in the English-speaking world:

> ...The key to the Danes' ability to retain their cultural independence, the most important weapon in their fight to retain Danish national identity, is of course their language. The fact that Danish literature is written in Danish makes it a representative of Danish identity. Authors in other countries, for instance the USA or for that matter Scotland, Wales or Ireland, write their works in English, yet are conscious of being Americans, Scots, Welsh or Irish. Not so much, that is, because of the language they use, but because of the themes they deal with. Irish books are about the Irish and their problems, but are only rarely written in Irish. Danish authors write with double effect: they write in Danish, and they write about Danes. ... The distinctiveness and independence which the language gives to the Danes, their ability to isolate themselves and communicate with each other in an almost secret code, is of great importance for their attitude to their own language and sense of being Danish.[9]

The background in a Scottish experience is clear enough here. Non-British readers of Mellon's book may, however, be tempted to consider how exceptional the Danes really are in this respect. Would the French, Germans,

---

[8]   Ibid., pp 169-173.

[9]   Ibid., p. 43.

Norwegians, Swedes, Poles or Latvians feel less inclined than the Danes to regard their language as central to the national identity of the inhabitants of their state? And in connection with Mellon's general definition of a 'nation', it scarcely needs mentioning that competing definitions have come very much to the fore in recent years in the UK, not least in Scotland itself. When Scottish nationalists describe Scotland as a 'stateless nation', they explicitly reserve the term 'nation' for the constituent parts of the Union. The United Kingdom is, in this view, a *state*, not a nation.[10]

Mellon's comments on political life and the nature of Danish consensus politics, too, are clearly grounded in his British background. He sees how the Danish electoral system of proportional representation creates a multi-party situation where coalition governments are the order of the day, and you sometimes have even minority coalition governments depending for their survival on constant coalition-building with parties outside the government. This, he says, simply is *not* parliamentarism. True parliamentarism works by facilitating the emergence of a government capable of governing. 'A parliamentary system is based on the notion of "we" and "the others". "We" are in power, "the others" are in opposition'.[11] As mentioned before, Mellon sees some commendable consequences of the Danish cult of consensus, but clearly prefers electoral systems that produce a clear, confrontational situation between Government and Opposition. Here again, one might note that a few years are a long time in constitutional history in Britain nowadays. Tony Blair has called for an end to 'tribalism' (!) in British politics and a move towards a culture of political co-operation. Following the election of a Scottish parliament in May 1999, coalition politics on a regular basis has become a reality on British soil.

In some respects Mellon follows straight in the footsteps of the traditional criticism of the tax-financed, Nordic welfare state by economists and journalists reared in an Anglo-American 'economic man' view of society. From such a perspective it sounds incomprehensible that a large number of citizens are willing to pay very high taxes to finance a welfare state that not only promises to provide a basic safety net, but also aims at redistributing wealth and quality of life in society. The particular Nordic traditions here are often explained by factors such as the strength of Labour movements, the particular class constellations in Scandinavian politics, particular collectivist

---

[10] See e.g. David McCrone, *Understanding Scotland. The Sociology of a Stateless Nation* (London, 1992), pp 16-33.

[11] Mellon, *Og gamle Danmark*, p. 79 ff.

experiences connected with the co-operative movements, the democratic influences of Folk High Schools, etc.[12] A frequent liberalistic reaction to this type of welfare state is that it must inevitably lead to strained public finances, a stifling of enterprise, and societies characterised by dull uniformity and cultivation of mediocrity.

Mellon, however, takes the analysis further. He notes the relative cohesion and lack of open conflict in Danish politics and society, and the homogeneity and social peace that most often prevails in the labour market. However, he locates the sources of cohesion not in historical traditions connected with mass movements or ideologies, or in some kind of rational choice by Danish voters, but more mystically in tribal urges to protect and secure the welfare of all members of the group. Where economic and political theory fails to explain a phenomenon, anthropology steps in, and in that respect Mellon's book might be said to be part of a current trend. Mellon's belief in the permanence of the tribal element in Danish society also allows him to end his analysis on an optimistic note. True, some adjustments will be needed in the political system and in welfare organisation, but Danes have been clever in adapting to changing circumstances, and their social cohesion and the support provided by their unique language will carry them through. Mellon even asks the rest of Europe to pay attention to the Danish experience: it might provide a clue to how to preserve national identity and social cohesion in a world of global competition and monetary union. So in the end the question implicit in the title of the book: Will Ancient Denmark continue to exist as a separate entity in the future? is answered with a 'yes, probably'.

Has Mellon's book then acquired the status of a modern Molesworth? Certainly not in Britain, for the simple reason that it has never been published in English. Yet the book was first intended for the British market as a contribution to the discussion on the future of the welfare state, using Denmark as an example.[13] One may wonder what this lack of interest in the UK illustrates. That Denmark was a more important player on the European scene in the seventeenth century than it is now? That the mental horizons of the British reading public are less European now than they were in the days of John Locke? The answer, if I were to hazard a guess, lies more in the mixed nature of Mellon's message, at least as presented in the version that became the Danish book. What lesson could British readers really draw from it? That

---

[12] See e.g. David Arter, *Scandinavian Politics Today* (Manchester, 1999), part IV, for an up-to-date survey on the literature on the 'Nordic model' and the 'Nordic Welfare State'.

[13] Information kindly supplied by Sir James Mellon to the author.

Britain had a bright future in EU because (a) its political system allowed its leaders to take firm decisions on their behalf in Brussels (b) its low taxes and no-egalitarian-nonsense social security system gave the British economy a competitive advantage in Europe, and (c) the structure of the British 'nation' as a multi-ethnic unity was more in tune with the shape of the future Europe than that of a homogeneous 'tribal' society like the Danish? Or would they conclude that British identity would in fact slowly disintegrate in the new Europe because the British lacked the tribal feeling as a nation in Mellon's sense, necessary to maintain a sense of community in a Europe of the single market, not to mention the single currency? One might also imagine that a publisher would like to see a more unambiguous warning set up to make an interesting book – on the lines, fore example, of Roland Huntford's *The New Totalitarians* (1971), the classic modern attack on the Scandinavian welfare model from a liberal British point of view. There are a few elements of that type in Mellon's book; but on the whole it is too balanced and ambiguous to satisfy requirements for a dystopia on Molesworthian or Huntfordian lines. In contrast, the Danish edition was well received by half-intrigued and half-flattered Danish reviewers, and for a time the notion of Danes as a tribe became part of the local discourse on identity and European integration.

Mellon and the general image of Scandinavia in Britain

In many ways Mellon's points fit in well with some types of contemporary British comments on contemporary Scandinavia, but there are, of course, other views – stereotypes, clichés or whatever you would call them – that it might be interesting to discuss. The basic point is that for most people in Britain, Scandinavia is a peripheral part of the world. It is perceived to be more distant than, say, the Low Countries, and has a low profile in the media. If you look for stereotypes you will find them on a scale from the very positive to the very negative. On the positive side you find notions of the Nordic countries as civilised, egalitarian, well-ordered, prosperous places; even egalitarian utopias. Thus when the prominent Scottish author Alasdair Gray recently argued that his countrymen might look across the North Sea for partners for an independent Scotland, he evoked a picture of 'countries whose small local money markets support national communities without huge class differences, countries where public services are still efficient, crime and destitution are not taken for granted, national pride is shown without military display or pompous ceremonial. I mean the Scandinavian countries.'[14] On the other side you find more negative notions of grey dullness and parochialism, of regulated uniformity and state-controlled dystopias.[15] Some years ago *The Times'* correspondent in Copenhagen explained to his readers how foreigners living in Denmark 'often complain that the place is little more than a tiny Lutheran backwater and a provincial, boring if perfectionist, Noddyland with nine months of winter and 12 months of high taxation'.[16] Not long ago David Mellor, commenting on the Chelsea footballer Brian Laudrup's homesickness, asked him in the *Evening Standard* why he wanted to go home to live in 'one of the most boring countries on God's earth'.[17] It is interesting to see that Denmark in particular seems to be used as a warning example of the kind of society Britain could become if the process of 'decline' continued and Britain lost its global influence. As 'another Denmark', Britain would still be a civilised society, but an inward-looking and unglamorous one without a sense of mission in the world. A few years ago a journalist reported how a Conservative backbencher thought there was 'something of the Danish' about John Major's election as Prime Minister. 'What my friend was hinting at was that he thought the election of Mr Major to the Tory leadership...had somehow reduced Britain's status in the world to that of a bland Scandinavian country'.[18] I suppose that the farming image and smallness of Denmark compared to other Scandinavian countries makes it the preferred choice in this respect.

---

[14] Alasdair Gray, *Why Scots Should Rule Scotland.* (Edinburgh, 1997), p. 108.

[15] References to the literature on Anglo-Danish stereotypes can be found in J. Sevaldsen, 'Britain's Role in Danish Life in the Post-War World' in J. Sevaldsen & O. Vadmand, *Contemporary British Society* (Copenhagen, 1998), p. 281ff.

[16] Christopher Follett, *The Times*, 17 September 1986.

[17] David Mellor, *London Evening Standard*, 30 October 1998.

[18] Nicholas Wapshott in *The Observer*, 6 January 1991. In the BBC' s 'Any Questions' programme on 29 May 1987, Roy Hattersley tried to argue that if countries such as Germany, Holland, Belgium and Denmark did not need an independent nuclear deterrent in NATO, Britain did not need one either. The economist Mary Goldring countered that she worried about 'this country's place in the world' and did not 'want to be counted with Denmark. I reckon that we have a little more to contribute to the world than that...' Last year, the *New Statesman* argued that Rupert Murdoch was not, in fact, an enemy of British soccer, but had injected money in the game that had kept British players at home and attracted top performers from abroad: 'Without Mr Murdoch, British football might now be a backwater, like the Danish or Greek leagues.' *New Statesman*, 11 September, 1998, p. 4.

Mellon and an Anglo-Danish 'special relationship'?

A final point might be made about the genre of ex-ambassadorial portraits of Denmark which has, in modern times, been cultivated only by British ex-ambassadors. British authors and their publishers rightly think that they can count on reader interest in Denmark for books mixing, impressions, analysis and 'friendly advice' by British observers. I doubt whether, for example, French, German or even Swedish ex-ambassadors would feel tempted to try their hand in this genre, or that the reviewers would take advice from such sources as seriously as they did in these cases. Why is that? An answer would involve a long survey of Anglo-Danish – or Anglo-Nordic relations – for which there is no space here. A few key elements might, however, be suggested.

As a whole, Britain has for most of the nineteenth and twentieth centuries been seen in Denmark as the 'friendly local great power'. There have been periods of trade conflicts between the two countries, disagreements about fishing rights and the division of oil-bearing seabeds, but Britain has not been seen as a threat to the territorial integrity of Denmark or to the maintenance of the democratic structures of society. The contrast with relations with Germany and the Soviet Union is obvious. The sense of having special ties with Britain was dramatically strengthened by the experience of the Second World War. Britain became the main source of support – material and moral – for the resistance against the German occupying forces, and the fact that it was British troops who liberated the country in May 1945 became deeply ingrained in the minds of a whole generation of Danes. In the late 1940s and early '50s London became the 'window to the world' for Danish politicians, and in some respects a gateway to the USA as Britain and Denmark became members of NATO in 1949. This feeling of Britain as Denmark's special contact among the great powers faded away during the '50s as the United States came to dominate the military scene, and as both Britain and Denmark started on the road to the European Common Markets. Cooperation was close in both fora, but the idea of a special relationship between Britain and the Nordic countries became difficult to keep alive. The EFTA experience in the 1960s was not an entirely happy one in this respect. In fact, I think that the event that finally persuaded the Danish economic and political elite that there was no 'special relationship', and that no forms of exclusive British-Nordic cooperation could be alternatives to the EC, was Harold Wilson's imposition of the 10 per cent import surcharge in 1964 without consultation with Britain's EFTA partners. In Denmark, the British embassy and the Danish business community were just then preparing a series of trade fairs to promote Anglo-Danish trade, and the bitterness over what was seen as insensitivity to the EFTA partners was enormous.

One sees the same pattern in Anglo-Danish relations within the EC, later the EU. On the one hand there has been a sense of a common experience: accession at the same time, many common interests and values, including widespread Euro-scepticism – but also conflicting interests in some areas, and above all an understanding that relations with France and Germany are the key relationships for both countries. Danish priorities and attitudes are, I think, summed up nicely in an interview with a Danish government official working in Brussels in a newspaper some years ago. Asked about his balancing between British and German points of views within his particular policy area, he answered: 'When I attend negotiations in Brussels, I normally have a beer with the British representative in the bar after the meeting. At the meeting itself, however, I find myself in agreement with the German in nine out of ten cases.'[19] The feeling that in spite of occasional disagreements and divergences of interest there are cultural affinities between the British and the Nordics that make dialogue useful and close relations natural is still there, and no doubt accounts for the readiness of Danes – in our own time, at least – to listen with interest to what British commentators have to say about their society.

Competing models?

In the past, Scandinavia has provided utopias as well as dystopias for British observers. Utopias for Britons of a social-democratic frame of mind, and dystopias connected with images of bureaucratic terrorism, dull uniformity and parochialism. The latter picture is, of course, not one which is exclusive for British observers – Scandinavian critics of the particular Nordic versions of corporatism, egalitarianism and welfare thinking have also warned against the stifling effects on individual freedom of these phenomena.[20] Which of the images a particular writer chose to subscribe to will, no doubt, depend a good deal on his or her general political persuasions and social ideals.

It might be tempting to predict that books of the kind that Mellon wrote may be a thing of the past. Yet the interest in national approaches to social issues seems to be very much alive. In fact, friendly competition among governments in western and northern Europe these days seems to take the form of PR exercises claiming that one's own particular approach to economic

---

[19] Lars Olsen. 'Dans mellem venner', *Weekendavisen*, 2 October 1992.

[20] As was rightly pointed out during the discussion of this paper at the Durham conference, the critique of Danish society in Peter Høeg's novels is very much centred on the pressures towards uniformity in e.g. the educational system.

and democratic management can serve as a model to others. Britons and Nordics are quite experienced in this field, each in their own fashion. Many on either side of the North Sea have tended to regard their own countries not only as the centre of the earth, as most people would do, but as models that others would be well advised to copy. If there are sometimes problems at the personal or institutional levels between Brits and the Nordics, there may be this behind them. Brits who go to Scandinavia and try to save the natives from their own parochialism, mediocrity and pre-modern social democratic ideals have to be as tactful as Mellon if they do not want to be written off as patronising. Nordics who go to Britain to lecture the natives about their outmoded class obsessions and pathetic post-imperial pretensions will quickly be dismissed as smug and sanctimonious.

An indication of where the frontlines of this competition between social models may be moving was provided by a column in the Danish daily *Politiken* written by the Danish prime minister, Poul Nyrup Rasmussen.[21] The article was a staunch and unrepentant defence of the Nordic Social Democratic Model. There are, he wrote, two major philosophies around these days: the Liberal one and the Social Democratic one (No 'Third Way' here!). Nyrup sees it as the common task of Nordic Social Democrats to ensure that the Nordic model – which he identifies with, among other things, solidarity understood as common financing of a strong public sector via taxation, making sure that those who are well off pay the most – survives and is offered to neighbouring countries as well. I quote from the last section of the article:

> We have achieved much in the Nordic countries. We sometimes forget how spectacular some of the results of Nordic co-operation have been. The next phase ought to be an ambition to play a role in the wider world. In the neighbouring region around the Baltic as well as in Europe and globally. The Nordic model ought to leave its mark on the direction that Europe takes, and ought to give our part of the world new possibilities to influence global developments.

One might dismiss this kind of rhetoric as arrogant hot air for domestic use. At the same time it signals a certain confidence that it still makes sense to talk of a 'Nordic model'. The reference to the Baltic region is also noteworthy. No Danish political leader would have thought of including that ten years ago. But the idea of the Baltic as a laboratory where different of centrist social

---

[21] Poul Nyrup Rasmussen, 'Nordens chancer og pligter i EU'. *Politiken*, 12 February 1999.

models forms – by implication Anglo-American versus Nordic ones – can be tested is, of course, an interesting one and highly relevant for the theme of this volume.

Chapter 18

Culture and Society in Malmö and Newcastle since 1945

Natasha Vall

This paper examines the use of 'culture' as a tool for renewal and change in two northern European industrial cities. Malmö and Newcastle provide a fruitful site for this subject because the similarities in their respective histories are striking. They are both coastal cities located in peripheral regions within the boundaries of their nation states. Newcastle upon Tyne is England's most northerly city, whereas Malmö is located on the western tip of Sweden's southernmost region, Skåne. With about a quarter of a million inhabitants each, Malmö and Newcastle are small European cities. They have nevertheless both been significant international centres for heavy industry, and both have witnessed the economic traumas accompanying the contraction of their industrial base in the last twenty years. A list of similarities, however, does not constitute the basis of a fruitful historical narrative, unless it is related to specific evidence in each case. This chapter will also attempt to illuminate the relationship between the general and the specifics of each case.

The industrial background

Industrial contraction in Newcastle, which had been an intermittent reality since 1918, intensified after 1973. Between 1978 and 1987, there was a particularly high rate of manufacturing redundancies. In 1980 there were 189,000 jobs in Newcastle, providing 38 per cent of the city's male population with employment, of which 80 per cent were found in 28 manufacturing firms.[1] By the 1970s the city's principal shipbuilders had become entirely dependent on government orders for their traditional products. Following a cut in government subsidies in 1979, Newcastle's largest manufacturing employer, Vickers, announced 750 redundancies.[2] The decline in manufacturing was reflected in a sharp increase in unemployment, especially between 1979 and 1982 when the annual average unemployment rates rose from 8 to 18 per cent.[3] The process reflected the poor performance of British manufacturing industry throughout much of the twentieth century. Newcastle's shipbuilders were established as imperial trade expanded during the nineteenth century and exhibited a characteristic dependence on an often volatile market. Unemployment rates among shipbuilders in the early years of the century often exceeded contemporary levels. Shipbuilders in employment were nevertheless among the highest-paid in the country, reflecting a reliance on highly skilled labour that contributed to detrimental over-specialisation during the twentieth century. The legacy of this last development was evident in Newcastle until very recently. As late as 1976, 43 per cent of Newcastle's economically active males were classified as skilled manual workers, a figure that by no means reflected commensurate demand for such labour. This development has also been related to a lack of research and development in the largest British manufacturing companies, in contrast with Europe's successful shipbuilders in Germany and Sweden in the twentieth century. A tendency to eschew industrial modernisation can be related in turn to the classic British dissonance between industrial and finance capital, compounded by poor industrial relations.

Until the 1970s, Malmö's manufacturing sector appeared to contain all the ingredients that Newcastle's lacked. From the 1870s to the 1960s, Sweden's economic expansion was rapid: before 1960 its annual rate of growth was surpassed only by Japan's. Underpinning this expansion was a conspicuous adherence to 'Keynesian' policy, or rather an economic strategy that implied longstanding commitment to market regulation, a commitment which Swedish economic historians are keen to claim as derived, not from British liberalism, but

---

[1] Minutes of Evidence from the HC Employment Committee Session 1979-80: *The Work of the Department of Employment Group* (HMSO, 1980).

[2] Tyne and Wear Research and Intelligence Unit, *Economic Progress* (various reports).

[3] Newcastle City Council, *City Profiles 1991* (Newcastle, 1991).

from their own Stockholm School of Economics.[4] Between 1950 and 1970 Malmö entered a phase of exceptional expansion in which it surpassed the national average for proportion of workers employed in the manufacturing sector. Essential to this strength was the internationally renowned shipyard Kockums, which was the ninth largest in the world by 1950. British scholars of British manufacturing have conceded that Kockums adjusted to uncertain international demand through technical amelioration in a way uncharacteristic of British yards. They continued to expand during the 1960s and early 1970s, by which time employee accounts from the yard likened the process of constructing a vessel to assembly line production. Although Armstrong Vickers in Newcastle continued to sustain intermittent success prior to the 1970s, the incongruous combination in Newcastle of predominantly skilled labourers and a contracting industrial economy, provides a stark contrast to the experience of labour market regulation in Sweden.

Despite a century of adherence to Swedish *dirigisme*, Kockums shipyard suffered a decline after 1973, by which time much of the shipbuilding activity was heavily subsidised by the state. In 1985 the Social Democrats lost an election in Malmö for the first time in 66 years and during the early 1990s, Malmö's rate of unemployment rose from 2.4 per cent to an unprecedented 12 per cent. The case of Malmö and Newcastle, it seems, is an ideal example of the declining significance of national economic and political regulation in the unremitting circumstances of 'globalisation'. Clearly Keynesian stringency did not safeguard employment in the Swedish city after 1970. It could also be argued that both cities were particularly vulnerable to global economic shifts, due to the preponderance of larger units of production. The particular manifestation of this shared experience, nevertheless suggests that caution should be exercised before endorsing this thesis wholeheartedly.

An important but often overlooked feature of Sweden's economic history after 1945 exists in the part played by the public sector in macro-economic growth, particularly given that in comparison to Britain, Sweden industrialised late and de-industrialised early. Manufacturing industry was only partly responsible for the growth of Sweden's major cities. Indeed the proportion of the population employed in manufacture had declined significantly in most Swedish cities before 1973. Although Kockums was exceptionally progressive, much of Malmö's expansion was also due to service sector growth. During the 1960s the local authority, rather than the shipyard, was the city's largest employer and by 1970, public sector occupations were responsible for 40 per cent of the employed

---

[4]   See e.g. Lars Jonung (ed.), *The Stockholm School Revisited* (Cambridge, 1991).

population in Malmö. Approximately two-thirds of the new employment opportunities provided work for women, primarily in health, social services and education. In short, the rise of the tertiary sector prefigured the decline in manufacture in Malmö. This development also had an impact upon the particular ways in which the local authorities in the two cities used 'culture' as a tool for renewal in response to industrial decline.

Culture as a means of urban renewal

An emphasis on culture as a force against economic adversity is a common theme in many previously industrialised cities in western Europe. Since it opened in 1997, Frank Gehry's Guggenheim Museum in Bilbao has turned a run-down Spanish industrial town into one of Europe's premier tourist destinations. In Britain, Glasgow's programme of urban regeneration in 1990 won it the distinction of being nominated European City of Culture. This theme can also be discerned in Malmö and Newcastle. In 1990, the local Social Democrats identified culture as one of the strong sectors in Malmö, endowed with the potential to provide a new identity for the city,[5] while Newcastle employed cultural consultants to help the city capitalise on its artistic strengths. In a comparison of two industrial cities with large working class populations, examining 'culture' also has wider conceptual implications. The assumption has often been that the emphasis on the new 'cultural industries' is an added corollary of the impact of globalisation, signifying the declining significance of traditional working-class cultural pursuits. The comparison of Malmö and Newcastle nevertheless suggests that the rise of the cultural industries does not always represent an absolute discontinuity.

There exists a particularly strong tradition of research into Swedish associational life, or more specifically into the history of the Swedish 'folk' movements.[6] Much of this research has focused upon the period after 1870 during which associations, often affiliated to the Social Democratic Labour and Temperance movements, participated in the struggle for universal suffrage in Sweden. Declining membership of such associations has been associated with the growing functions of the Swedish welfare state since 1932 (the year in which the Social Democrats attained a position of power in national government which was not seriously challenged until the 1970s). In Malmö, the number of

---

[5] J. B. Påhlsson (SDP) Malmö Kommun *protokoll med bihang*, 25-26 November 1992 (Malmö, 1992), p. 183.

[6] S. Lundqvist, *Folkrörelserna i det Svenska samhället* (Uppsala, 1977).

voluntary associations performing charitable welfare services diminished significantly after 1932 and they had virtually ceased to exist by 1964. In 1954, however, the city provided a substantial grant to the newly established voluntary City Theatre Association. Ten years later, several new voluntary associations representing cultural organisations – broadly defined – applied for and received local authority sponsorship. These included the Labour Movement's Cultural History Association, Malmö's Association for Artists and the City Theatre Association. Clearly if Swedish associational life *per se* is to be viewed as the means by which Swedish citizens access, and are accessed by the state, then associations did not disappear after 1932, rather they assumed new characteristics. The growth of voluntary cultural associations in Malmö suggests that there are elements of functional continuity in the emergence of the city's cultural infrastructure, but that the municipality was now equipped to support cultural activity in the city, and anxious to do so. Furthermore, this also attests to the increasing demand for just such an infrastructure.

The British history of 'associational life' is quite distinct from that disclosed by Swedish scholarship. For Robert Gray, social reproduction through working-class associational life was as vital to the success of the British labour aristocracy as was economic and political representation.[7] Although the labour aristocracy thesis has been challenged, the new more diverse social history perspective substantiates themes which distinguish the British experience from the Swedish. Associational life in British scholarship is pivotal to working-class experience and organisation. It is primarily social and there does not exist an equivalent emphasis on the relationship with the state. Indeed, its very diversity suggests that, unlike Sweden, associational life remains organic in its organisation and growth, mirroring the organic development of industrialism. Paradoxically while it is amorphous, as confirmed by recent debates on the issue of 'community networks', it is also more class-based.[8] Newcastle shares the North East's tradition of sustaining a plethora of working class associations: the ubiquitous 'social club' has shown resilience even in the second half of the twentieth century. In 1986, the North East was recorded as having a higher concentration of social clubs than any other geographical area of Britain.[9] Compared with

---

[7] R. Gray, *The Aristocracy of Labour in Nineteenth Century Britain c. 1850-1914* (London, 1981), p. 40.

[8] See for instance R. Colls, 'What is 'Community' and how do we get it? A message for the member of Sedgefield', in *Northern Review* 1 (1995), pp 9-27.

[9] MORI, 'Public Attitudes Towards Clubs', Report submitted to the CIU in 1986.

Malmö, however, this tradition was not so readily appropriated by the developing infrastructure for official cultural activities after 1945.

On 17 May 1946, the Arts Council of Great Britain issued the *Report of the First North Regional Conference of the Arts Council.* The opening reception, held in Newcastle, was attended by some 180 people from throughout the Northern region.[10] The conference focussed upon the scope of activities a regional arts council could undertake. Central to the discussion, was the question of how to bring art to 'The Man in the Back Street':

> THE MAN IN THE BACK STREET came up for discussion throughout the conference. It was the fact that he had been open to the propaganda of the worst types of commercial entertainment manager. He had not much been affected by the revival in the arts and was not likely to take out the trouble to seek out new and comparatively expensive form of entertainment in some centre miles from his home. A brilliant metropolitan development in the arts would eventually have its effect on every corner of the country, but the immediate problem was to bring the arts to every man's doorstep at a price he could pay.[11]

The conference concluded rather ambivalently that whilst it was every man's right to enjoy his own choice, 'those who wanted a better type of art must induce the Man on the Back Street also to want something better'.[12] According to recent scholarship, the British Art Centre Movement, which established the regional arts councils after the Second World War, failed to generate interest in the arts at a mass level because the wartime audiences for the arts declined significantly after 1945. Rising affluence and an increase in consumer choice combined, it is suggested, to ensure that this choice was not to visit art galleries.[13] The attitude of the movement's prominent forefathers, such as John Maynard Keynes, is nevertheless of more interest to the comparison of Malmö and Newcastle. Keynes, it seems, was opposed in principle to participatory folk traditions in the arts. Indeed the tone of the excerpt from the Northern regional

---

[10] The Arts Council of Great Britain *Report of the first Northern Regional Conference* May 17th & 18th 1946 (Issued by the Arts Council of Great Britain, 1946).

[11] Ibid., p. 12.

[12] Ibid., p. 12.

[13] Richard Weight, 'Building a new British culture: the Arts Centre Movement, 1943-53', in Richard Weight and Abigail Beach (eds.), *The Right to Belong: Citizenship and National Identity in Britain, 1930-1960*, (London, 1998) p. 173.

arts council suggests that attitudes which ensured that 'the strenuous efforts not to appear patronising or didactic were sometimes little more than a patient waiting game, behind which lay a deep revulsion towards modern popular culture' were not restricted to individual reformers.[14] In Sweden, where there was a less pronounced liberal intellectual heritage, participatory traditions have flourished, and in the case of Malmö they contributed to the expansion of city's arts infrastructure after 1945.

The dual particularities of the British case which, on the one hand, perpetuated an elite tradition in culture and, on the other, adhered to the belief that participation was a matter for individual choice anyway, are central to understanding the special characteristics of Newcastle and Malmö. In 1963, the secretary of Northern Arts had acknowledged that the region's unions of trade and social clubs ought to be harnessed by strategies aimed at developing arts across the board. The 'social clubs' were nevertheless conspicuous by their absence from the Northern Arts authorised expenditure for that year.[15] Whilst it is not possible to establish whether this was a product either of popular disdain for the arts or of the apparent elitism in the organisation, the existence of both variables helps to explain the differing experiences of associational life in the two cities. It is reflected in the absence of established contact points for traditional working-class associations and the organisations responsible for official cultural provision in Newcastle after 1945. This in turn helps to explain why these developments remained essentially distinct in Newcastle and is also crucial to understanding the respective implications of the rise of the 'cultural industries' in the face of economic stagnation.

When Newcastle suffered high rates of unemployment, local enthusiasm for culture was motivated in part by the attribution of national economic recovery to the enterprise culture of de-politicised urban regeneration. It was this approach that subsequently characterised the property-led projects undertaken on the city's old industrial sites. In 1981, Newcastle Council inaugurated a rolling programme of regeneration of the Quayside with a view to stimulating business, social and recreational life in an 'historic' part of the city.[16] A government-financed agency, the Tyne and Wear Development Corporation, assumed responsibility for this task in 1987. The work of the Quayside Residents'

---

[14] Ibid., p. 177.

[15] North East Association for the Arts 1963/4 Annual Report (1964).

[16] Councillor Beecham, *Newcastle City Council Minutes 1980-81* 'Additional Partnership Allocation 1980-81', (1981) p. 899.

Association, which had protested against numerous applications for new bars and clubs by 1994, confirms the overwhelming bias towards leisure and recreational cultural facilities in the area. The redevelopment of the Quayside and similar projects have nevertheless come to be seen as the point of departure for the emergence of the 'place' entrepreneur whose objective was not 'profit from production, but rent from tapping human activity in place'.[17]

By the 1990s both Newcastle and Malmö had come to see 'culture' as a potentially cohesive force in economically turbulent times. The Social Democrats identified culture as one of the strong sectors in Malmö, endowed with the formidable potential of again providing an identity for the city.[18] In 1994, a study carried out by Arts Business Ltd for Newcastle City Council, Northern Arts, and the Newcastle Initiative advised the city to capitalise on its cultural strengths, which included Newcastle's status as capital of the Northern Region and its unrivalled chamber orchestra, but also its 'distinctive cultural identity'.[19] Recent scholarship has suggested that Newcastle reinvented its distinctive identity in the face of economic adversity by transferring regional particularity from production to consumption.[20] In this specifically local response, older patterns of associational life, especially drinking, are said to have prevailed. In 1994, the city's night life became the subject of sociological study, which confirmed that the old/new 'pride in their "toon" as it is affectionately known', was prevalent amongst Newcastle's youth and that 'their assessment of it as a place to go out largely reproduced this favourable attitude'.[21] The conclusion for the author was that in neglecting to harness these 'soft infrastructural resources' the local authority had discarded one of the vital components for the successful re-emergence of the post-industrial city. Based on the comparison with Malmö, the converse could be said to be a more accurate reflection of the city's contemporary cultural provision.

In 1990, Malmö spent proportionally more local authority fiscal resources on cultural provision than any other municipality in Skåne. Moreover it was second

---

[17] K. Shaw, 'The Development of a New Urban Corporation: the politics of urban regeneration in North East England', *Regional Studies* 27 (1993), pp. 251-286.

[18] Johan Bengt Pahlsson, SDP *Protokoll* 25-26 November 1992 p. 183.

[19] Arts Business Ltd., *Creative Capital* (London, 1994), p. 3.

[20] B. Lancaster, 'Newcastle – Capital of What?', in Robert Colls and Bill Lancaster (eds.), *Newcastle Upon Tyne: a Modern History* (Chichester, 2001). pp. 35-53.

[21] R. Hollands, *Friday Night Saturday Night. Youth Culture and Identification in the Post-industrial City* (Newcastle upon Tyne, 1995).

highest in the national expenditure amongst municipalities.[22] A large proportion of this spending subsidised the extension for the municipal art gallery and provided the sponsorship for the new private Rooseum gallery. The representatives from the Konsthall described Malmö as the Nordic region's new cultural centre, a claim that buoyant attendance figures helped substantiate. This image transformation for Sweden's most working-class city has been helped by the international success of its local curators: Sune Nordgren, formerly curator of Malmö's municipal art gallery, is now the director of Gateshead's Baltic Centre for Contemporary Art, whilst the former curator of Rooseum is currently head of London's Tate Modern. In Malmö investment in the combined development of Rooseum and the expansion of the Konsthall was also designed to facilitate collaboration with neighbouring cultural metropolises such as Copenhagen. As such, the Konsthall's remit encompassed the municipal cultural vision at this stage: reversing the city's industrial stigma could be achieved by emphasising its cultural significance, but also by looking outwards. In turn, this was linked to the city's other great project, which was gaining momentum by 1990, the construction of the Öresund fixed link with Denmark (completed in 2000).[23] It has been suggested that faced with an economic crisis, Malmö's municipality simply transferred the emphasis from large-scale industrial capitalism to large-scale culture, at the expense of a more vibrant cultural life at the 'associational level'.[24] Clearly, the participation in classic Swedish 'folk' associations diminished during the twentieth century, but alongside the growth of voluntary cultural associations after 1945 there emerged a framework for both large and small-scale cultural provision. It is this framework that has allowed the city to step sideways and ameliorate the changes implied by the loss of its manufacturing base.

Conclusion

In comparison with Newcastle, the emphasis on culture in the face of economic adversity in Malmö emerges as a carefully orchestrated plan, a product of infrastructural continuity on both a local and national level. In contrast to Malmö's enhanced municipal cultural expenditure following the onset of economic contraction, in Newcastle the local government reorganisation of the eighties impeded the city's ability to support the arts. After 1985, subsidies to the arts were removed along with support for manufacture. At the same time the

---

[22] Malmö Kommun *Protokoll* 25-26 Nov 1992 NR. 11, (Malmö, 1992) p. 186.

[23] Ibid.

[24] Ibid.

Northern Arts policy statement for the following year conceded that the subsidised arts in the region continued to be enjoyed only by the minority.[25] Seen comparatively, the impediments to providing a parallel platform for new cultural identity in Newcastle were both historic and exacerbated by contemporary economic circumstances. On the other hand, Malmö's continuities illustrate that the rise of the 'cultural industries', is not necessarily a corollary of the workings-out of global capitalism. The themes discussed in this paper nevertheless offer the potential of some interesting new turns following appointment of Sune Nordgren in 1998, as the Director of the Baltic, Centre for Art in Gateshead.

---

[25] Northern Arts Policy Statement 1986, *Northern Arts* 1961-86, (Newcastle upon Tyne, 1986).

Index

Crampe, Catherine, 15.
Cranfield, Beecher & Co., 147.
Crewe, Lord, 261-64.
Crewkerne, 147.
Cripps, Sir Stafford, 279.282,285.
Crommelin, Daniel, 163,167,
Cromwell, Oliver, 44,81,232.
Cronstadt (see Kronstadt).
Crop, J.A., 165.
Culloden, Battle of, 176.
Cunningham, John, 32.
Curzon, Lord, 254-255,257,
 262-264.
Cutler, Thomas, 73,
Cuxhaven, 218.

D

Daltera, Joseph, 142.
Dampier, Henry, 145.
Danzig (Gdańsk), xxiv,3-19,26-27,
 34,47-49,52-56,59,63-64,79,100,
 104,117,123,125-127,161,167,
 169,203,207-208,250,252,256,
 258.
Darwin, Richard, 104.
Davidson, Randall, 239-240,
 242-243.
Day, James, 142.
Defoe, Daniel, 117.
De Geer, Antoine, 140-141,146.
De Geer, Louis, 74.
De Moulin, Jacob, 80.
De Neuville, John, 163.
De Rodes, Johan, 81.
Delcassé, Théophile, 225.
Derby, Lord, 254.
Devizes, 147.
Dickson, Charles, 192.
Dickson, James & Co., 177-178,
 191.
Digges, Sir Dudley, 29,55.
Dirscham, 36.
Dogger Bank, 115-116,123,223.
Donne, William, 142.
Dover, 118.
Dowker, Thomas, 104.

Drammen, 123,173.
Drummond, Col. David, 39,41,46.
Dublin, 138.
Dudley, 155.
Düna River, 252.
Dünanberg, 203.
Dunkirk, 17-18.
Durham, 242.
Durie, Agnes, 36.
Durie, John, 22-23, 34-46.
Durie, Joshua, 35.
Durie, Robert, 35.
Durie, Simon, 35.
Dvina, Zapadnaja (see Düna River).
Dyke, William, 147.

E

East India Co., 74-75,144,175.
Eastland Co., 19,49,69,74,79,
 82-83,97,102,104,107,159.
Eden, Sir Anthony, 267,281-286,
 290.
Edge, Thomas, 56.
Edinburgh, 35,40,157,165,188,246.
Edward VII (King of England), 226.
Elbe River, 119,123,234.
Elbing, 26,30,34-36,38-40,49,79,
 104.
Elers, John, 104.
Elizabeth I (Queen of England), 49.
Elsinore, 11, 69,120,122-123.
Elton, Jacob, 142.
Ely, 4.
Erskine Family, 176.
Esbjerg, 226.
Esher, Lord, 233.

F

Fabricus, Dr., 40.
Falck, Zacharius, 95.
Feldmanis, Julius, 288.
Finch, William, 142.
Fincham, John, 59-60.
Fisher, Admiral Sir John, 219-223,
 225-236.
Fog, Bruun Juul, 240.